Finally, a doctor who gets it. Yeshua (Jesus) is the Healer—we are but His instruments. When we trust Him and His Word and pray, miracles happen. Thanks for sharing these inspiring stories that give God the glory.

—Rabbi David L. Barsky, D. Min.
Senior Rabbi, Congregation Beth Hillel
Pompano Beach, Florida

Dr. Speed has written a book of hope. Part physician, part priest, part prophet, and part parent. She helps us see what true wholeness is all about and puts God at the center of the enterprise, which is exactly where He should be. This is a unique effort, which will be of great benefit to all who read it.

—The Reverend Donald J. Curran, Jr.
Rector, Grace Episcopal Church
Ocala, Florida

This book *The Incurables* has blessed me in many ways. Author Teri Speed did an incredible job writing and informing the reader about unlocking healing of the whole person. She also has outstanding insights.

I have been a pastor for nearly sixty years. During that time, many came to Christ and many were healed. It was always a joy to see Christ change lives. However, there was always a disappointment when I prayed for the sick and they were not healed. After reading Dr. Speed's book, I have found new insight and courage. This book will bring hope and joy to all who digest its pages.

—Pastor Bert Allbritton
Founder, First Family Church
Dallas, Texas

Dr. Teri Speed is a rare person who has been willing to listen and let God take her beyond her medical training into healing of spirit, mind, and body. Only God can perform in this all-inclusive arena, for a man's knowledge is limited to his ability to comprehend even a small fragment of the complexity of life. Yet Teri has discovered that by listening to God—the Creator, the Author, and Finisher of our faith—we, too, can be used by Him to help bring others to wholeness. Even though, as she so emphatically admits, she may not understand exactly what is happening, the results are evident and give Him the praise and the glory.

Teri has hungered to be used by God at any cost or sacrifice, and thus she constantly grows in her faith in Him, knowing neither the consequences nor the outcomes, but simply listening and trusting. In this way, she has discovered the real key to doing God's will: not doing what we think He would have us do, but *listening to Him* to learn what He wants us to do in any situation. He speaks to her in a real way because she asks and listens in faith.

Teri is committed to proving my mother's adage: "Nothing beats a failure like a try." *The Incurables* demonstrates the reality of God's response to her kind of child-like belief.

—W. Elton Clemmons
Past President of
Men for Missions International

The Incurables

TERI SPEED, M.D.

Godspeed
Teri Speed
8-15-2008

CREATION HOUSE

The Incurables: Unlock Healing for Spirit, Mind, and Body
by Teri Speed, M.D.
Published by Creation House
A Strang Company
600 Rinehart Road
Lake Mary, Florida 32746
www.creationhouse.com

Cover design by Marvin Eans

Illustrations provided by Carla Speed McNeil

Library of Congress Control Number: 2007926961
International Standard Book Number: 978-1-59979-220-0

First Edition

07 08 09 10 11 — 987654321
Printed in the United States of America

Contents

Dedication

To Mother and Daddy, for your gentle, patient loving-kindness. All of your hard work in raising your "maverick" of a daughter must have paid off.

And to all who read these pages, I pray this book touches your spirit and leads you toward hearing our Lord each day in healing your spirit, mind, and body.

To

Wade Warren Speed

and

Douglas Carl Speed

Acknowledgments

TO MY PRAYER partner. You are my gift from God. Truly now I understand what it means to have a sister in Christ. Thank you.

A word of gratitude to the Reverend Donald J. Curran, Jr., Rector, Grace Episcopal Church in Ocala, Florida. Thank you for being you. Thank you for making God real and believable to all.

To the Very Reverend Paul M. Bailey, Rector, Grace Memorial Episcopal Church of Hammond, Louisiana. Thank you for all that you do to make Grace home.

My heartfelt gratitude to JB. You have taught me what it means to love—unconditionally.

Foreword

THE LAME WALK, the blind see, the brain-dead awaken to be restored with their families. The emotionally distraught are calmed, cancer is vanquished, and the chronic pain is no more. These are but a few of the things the Lord has allowed me to witness. I am drawn every day to the areas of medicine on which other doctors have given up.

When doctors say, "There is nothing more that can be done medically," my feathers get ruffled and I go to work. If God "healed them all" (Matt. 12:15, KJV), and "these things and greater shall I do" (John 14:12, KJV), then it stands to reason that everyone can be healed. In my mind this does not include the phrases, "only if it is curable," "only if we know how to cure it," or "only if we have the right drugs to do it."

I am an amateur on the Bible, but I'm pretty sure that my Bible says something to the effect of, "Heal the sick" (Luke 10:9). My Bible doesn't mention giving up, or pronouncing death over a person.

Have you ever heard a doctor tell a patient they only had three months to live? Give me a break. That doctor is giving a death sentence. More likely than not, the patient will die within the prescribed three months. My Bible says that the power of life and death is in the tongue. (See Proverbs 18:21.) Telling someone "You have three months to live" is using the power of your words very effectively to abandon someone to death.

Throughout the ages, man has sought to heal. There have

been witch doctors, tribal ceremonies, dentists, priests, rabbis, medical doctors, and many other healers. There have been faith healers and scientific healers. Yet still, some diseases remain "incurable." Have you ever asked yourself why? I ask that question each day.

I was the child who asked her mother "Why?" to everything in life. Some things just didn't make sense to me. Even now, decades later, some things still do not make sense. For example, why are there different places to go for healing? Some go to church. Some go to a surgeon. Some go to a psychiatrist. If the mind, body, and spirit all belong to one patient, why is the patient going three different places to see three different people for help?

What if there was one-stop shopping for your healing—the psychiatrist, doctor, and priest all working together toward healing *one* patient? It would be an improvement on the current situation where a patient must make appointments with three different people who more likely than not never communicate with each other. The superstores like Wal-Mart and Target have gotten the idea. They combined fast food, merchandise, eyeglasses, beauty, banking, portraits, pharmacy services, and a grocery into a one-stop-shopping destination.

Doctors, priests, and psychologists should think about this model. How wonderful would it be for you to walk into a consultation and have a priest (spirit), doctor (body), and psychologist (mind) all working together toward healing you, the patient? Sounds pretty wonderful to me!

The mind, body, and spirit are intricately interconnected. They do not work separately. They are fascinating in their ability to create.

If you are willing, allow me to take you on a short trip with your mind. It is a game, really. Are you willing? If so, let's go.

Let's take a trip with your imagination. You remember your *imagination*. It is that thing that you used as a child that created invisible playmates or made you believe that your stuffed animals were talking to you. Your imagination is an extraordinarily powerful tool. It is so powerful it can make you believe that you are enjoying this book. It can also have you thinking about pink elephants, or blue Cookie Monsters.

Imagine that you just walked into a small room where Bob is nervously awaiting your arrival. Bob has come to ask your opinion. You are an expert in your field, and Bob has taken his time to get to you.

Many questions are going through his head. "What will be said? What is the opinion? Will I be OK? Can I get help? Will I have something horrible happen to me?"

The two of you have never met and Bob really doesn't want to be here. As a matter of fact, if the truth be known, Bob would rather be *anywhere* else. As you close the door behind you and introduce yourself, you tell the nervous, jittery man, "Take off all of your clothes." As you watch Bob, you notice that he instantly obeys. Shifty eyes meet yours, and quickly look away. Bob concentrates on his shoes as if it were the first time his shoes have ever been removed. Bob bends over, unties the laces, and begins to sweat. You notice that he stopped speaking but occasionally lets out a grunt or a nervous giggle. The skin on his body has become damp. His clothes stick. He struggles to remove them quickly, but stumbles around fumbling over each button and zipper.

Why would anyone obey such seemingly bizarre commands? Why do some people command instant obedience? Can you imagine for a moment having this much influence over a complete stranger?

This is a glimpse into my life. As a surgeon I live this exact scene every time I meet a new patient. This is a humbling experience, for both surgeon and patient.

Through this pattern I began to have a slowly dawning awareness of the power and impact of my profession and my words. My career began to shift. Ever so slightly, it changed. Not much, mind you. It changed like a ship on the sea that made a midcourse change of a degree or two. The change certainly was not noticed by anyone except the "captain" (me). Ultimately, however, the ship reached a port hundreds or even thousands of miles away from the intended destination.

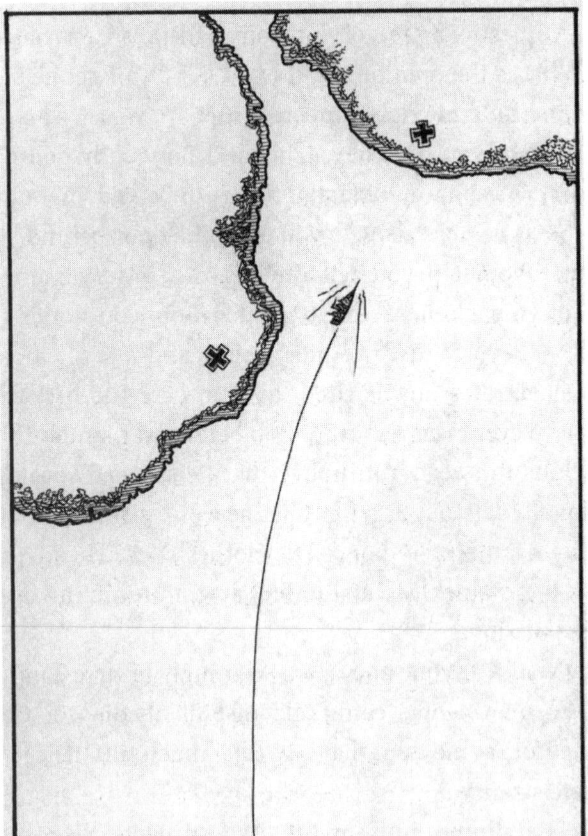

The Lord has a sense of humor. He used my innate curiosity to pull me into some deep waters where healing meant more than cutting people up and sewing them back together. I wondered, "Why do patients respond to me, and trust me? Am I such a wonderful orator? Certainly not, my chosen profession is medicine. OK, so what's going on here?"

My mind raced. My thoughts mixed into a jumble of what-ifs and where-fors. I began to ask questions that my colleagues could not answer. They were too busy to contemplate such nonsense. They were not interested in studying, unless it directly impacted their specialty.

Running from one surgery to the next one afternoon, I pressed my question further, "But this does directly impact your practice—and your personal life," but their attention was already lost.

None of us had been taught in medical school that patients would treat us as the final authority on a subject. We did not understand the implications or the responsibility when a patient said, "My doctor told me to do it," as if the doctor was a direct messenger from God.

Later that same day, a local physician asked, "Why would I want to watch every word that comes out of my mouth? I already have too much to do. You are telling me to monitor my words? You must be kidding! Patients understand what I mean when I talk to them." He walked away shaking his head as if to say, "Poor girl—she must have an overactive imagination."

But I wasn't joking. I witnessed the impact that we as physicians were having on people. I saw that by simply changing the way we talked, we could enhance or diminish a patient's prognosis. We could use this information to our success or our detriment. I turned to the Bible in the hospital chapel and was fascinated to find a Scripture verse openly and blatantly displayed in a purely secular world—and it was the moment my spiritual growth exploded to unimaginable heights:

> Death and life are in the power of the tongue.
>
> —PROVERBS 18:21

"If this Bible verse is true," I thought, "then how is this old saying explained?"

> Sticks and stones may break my bones, but words will never hurt me.

So, I had a dilemma: either words were powerless, or they had ultimate power—but which one?

As a child I ran crying to my mother almost every day for some perceived injustice, and she would calmly tell me, "If you wear your feelings on your sleeves, they will get knocked off. You have hot and cold running tears. Learn that people don't mean the things that they say. Don't take things so literally or seriously."

The next day would roll around, and again I would run to Mother and again she would attempt to calm my tumultuous emotions. I could not understand how or why words affected me so deeply. Other people seemed to go undaunted by the same words.

Over the years, I trained myself to become hardened to words. I attempted to build a wall around myself so that they would not "get to me." I developed some firmly held beliefs, such as "Words are nothing more than a means by which to convey a thought," or "There is no power associated with a word. It is just a word." Or is it?

Years later in my practice, I began to notice different

responses when I used specific words or phrases. Sometimes it was the inflection that made the difference. As the years passed, I modified my words and ideas. Patients responded favorably to some words and shied away from others. The power of words together with the strange phenomenon of "white coat hypnosis," along with my own personal spiritual growth, combined to make an already bold surgeon explore areas that were not fully exposed in school.

"White coat hypnosis" is when a patient, adult or child, sees the doctor walk into a room. The starched white coat is feared and the patient begins to stare blankly into space. Because of this phenomenon, most doctors enjoy family members coming into the examination room. The family member can then relay information after the doctor has departed. Doctors also ask patients to write out their questions and concerns prior to the appointment so that when they enter the dreaded room and forget everything, they have notes available to jog their memory.

White coat hypnosis has been humorous for me as a female surgeon. Most surgeons are male, therefore when I enter the room and introduce myself—"Hello, I'm Doctor Speed"—the patient looks at me and, expecting a male doctor and obviously having not heard my introduction, often says something like, "When is the doctor coming in?" Or, clearly surprised, "You're a woman!" as if I'm more or less likely to be competent as a surgeon because of my X chromosome.

The curiosity of words and their ability to impact lives began innocently enough but quickly grew into a driving passion. I used the same words with patients outside as well as inside the operating room. Often I recorded my voice to be listened to while the patient was under anesthesia. The patient would hear my voice in calm, clear tones giving suggestions while I was busy operating. The patient would be given audiotapes to listen to after surgery as well.

I started to venture into areas of healing outside of the operating room. Surprisingly enough, patients were healed, in some cases they were healed of supposedly "incurable diseases." Please do not misunderstand—I am a traditionally trained medical doctor. I believe in the power of medicine and doctors and surgery. They are all wonderful. But I was sailing into uncharted waters. Something began to happen and it was much bigger than me. Something greater was drawing me in. God knew what He was doing, but I sure didn't.

My heart broke every time a person told me of their *condition*, as if the condition had taken on a life of its own. What *do you do* with the incurable? Do you empathize with them? Send them home with no hope? Or do you work with them, listening to their horror story, but only wishing you could help? The bottom line is, do you give them a death sentence? Or hope?

I believe there is a mind, body, and spirit that work together to make this thing called an individual—and I do not know how they work. As a matter of fact, the older I get and the more I study, the more I realize how much I don't know. But what I do know is this: if you work with the mind, body, and spirit *together*, the patient will be healed of far more than a surgical issue. The patient can be healed of things that have been buried for a lifetime.

If you venture into the shadowy places in their life, the places where they have stored things the way one might store an old sweater in a closet, they can be lead to a spring cleaning of not only their body, but their mind and spirit as well. The Holy Spirit will help you find and clean all of the hidden corners of someone's life. God will use you if you give Him the latitude to do so.

My job as a physician is to allow my hands to be used by God to heal people, or so I thought. I discovered that He had much bigger plans for me. He planned to join me in talking with patients in the exam room (mind), the operating room (body), and in church (spirit). I gave the Holy Spirit an inch—and He took a mile.

Have you ever heard the story of the two men walking on the beach? As they walked, they talked and solved all of the world's problems. Under their feet, washed up on the damp sand, were thousands of starfish.

"I could never have imagined that there were this many starfish in the ocean, much less on the shore," one man exclaimed. The other man remained silent and looked out over the sand as if he had not noticed the starfish at all. He simply reached down, picked up a starfish, tossed it into the ocean, and continued walking. This man continued as he walked to repeat this—pick one up, throw it in the ocean.

Finally, when his companion could no longer stand it he blurted out, "Why do you do that? Why do you pick up one starfish and throw it into the ocean? Certainly you can see that there are thousands of them dying?"

Slowly, calmly, the man turned to his friend, holding one starfish out for his friend to see. "To this starfish, it means life." He then threw it into the water.[1]

Follow me on this wonderful discovery of hearing, healing, and help for both surgeon and patient. This is a story of people being brought into my life so the Lord could get my attention; the lame, the blind, and the pain-ridden. He allowed them to be healed in the process of dragging me through Holy Spirit boot camp.

I imagine most people are not as strong-willed as I am. Others may learn easier and without much fuss. But not me,

I am the stubborn scientist, the analyzer. If this stuff was real, the Lord was going to have to prove it to me, and He was going to have to do it loud and clear.

Several years ago my son was quite a discipline challenge. He had been through more than a small child should have. His small system was in overload most of the time. Therefore, anything added to this child would send him into places that no one wanted him to go. He would lash out at the nearest person or object. Since he was much larger than the other children, he could almost throw them across a classroom faster than anyone could see it coming.

As you might expect, I lived in the world's system at the time. Therefore, I first sought counsel from source other than God. There were doctors, psychiatrists, psychologists, and every other form of counsel a mother could think of to help her young son. I was so sincere in helping this child that I spent a fortune on the counsel of men (and some women).

As a last resort, I went to God. He told me what to do and I argued with Him (as usual). I told Him that the answer proposed was too simple. It would never work. Then I realized I was arguing with the King of the universe, repented, and agreed to try it God's way.

Of course no one was told of this new method. But faithfully, I followed my instructions. I was certain that I was wasting my time, but that it couldn't hurt, either.

Within one week, my son's teacher was delivering rave reviews of my son's progress. I was waiting for the children after school one day, expecting another report of my son drawing blood on one of his classmates. But what I got from his teacher was an earful: "You'll never believe what happened…He has matured so much...Something has changed, I don't know what it is...He is doing so well, I just had to tell you about the change in him."

In my prayer time that night I confessed, "Well, God, You got me, didn't You? I know what You did, how You allowed me to go all over the place seeking answers," I continued. "I know how You waited patiently on *me* to draw near to You, then You drew near to me. Yikes! That was it! The Holy Spirit was with me all along. But prophecy is subject to the prophet, according to 1 Corinthians 14:32. I had to be willing to listen and act in obedience to Your Word."

My son needed one thing and God was waiting for me to ask Him for the answer. And for the record, you can relax—if the Lord *was* going to send down a lightning bolt, He surely would have used it on me many times. His patience is immense, thankfully. Still, I'm confident that I tap-dance on His last nerve sometimes.

Foreword Discussion Questions

1. James 1:5–6 says ask God and He will answer you, if you *expect* an answer. Do you expect God to answer you? Do you wait long enough for Him to answer? Have you ever heard the voice of the Lord? Do you know the Lord's voice? Right now, ask the Lord to give you one word for yourself. Close your eyes, then ask. Keep them closed for just a few moments. A word will pop into you. Did you see it? Did you hear it? Did you feel it? Did you know it? However you received the word is how God talks to you. Pretty easy, right? Do it again. Ask the Lord to give you one word for _______. (Place someone's name here.) When the word comes to you in a moment, analyze again how the word came to you: seeing, feeling, hearing, or knowing. If you say, "I didn't get anything," do it again; you may not be familiar with receiving information this way, and your antennae may need tuning. There is no right answer. Go to a store, ask the Lord to give you a word for the clerk. Soon you will become familiar with the way the Lord speaks to you. My prayer partner "knows," my mother "hears," and I "see," so figure out which one you are. The more you practice the more comfortable you will become.

2. Imagine the color orange. Now that you have imagined orange, stop imagining orange. Whatever you do, don't imagine orange. Look around the room and look at anything that you like, but do not notice the color orange in the room. Did you do it? Describe what you did, what you saw and what your attention was focused on.

3. Describe how powerful your imagination is with great detail. Describe a time when you could imagine something wonderful, then it happened.

4. Remember a time when you used your words to heal someone. Describe the event. Remember a time when you used your words to harm. Describe the effect it had on the other person. Describe a time when words came from your mouth, and you wished that you could catch them and stuff them back into your head.

5. Sticks and stones may break my bones, but words will never harm me. Describe the meaning of this. Is it true or false? Describe a time when someone used this saying. How does this make you feel?

6. Describe your reaction and actions to a person in distress. Do you qualify your response based on the level of distress or their relation to you? Do you act first and ask questions later? Do you stand back and observe, looking for an opportunity to assist, or do you look the other way?

7. When was the last time you cleaned out your closet? Do it. Then come back to these questions. How many items were in there that you had forgotten about? How many items were no longer needed? How did you feel when you threw out the old and made space for the new? How many times did you take a trip down memory lane? Describe two of them.

8. The story of the starfish was told in the Foreword. What does it mean to you? What would you have done? Which character in the story best describes you?

9. Think of a time in your life when you listened to a friend's story and said, "I wish I could help." Did you mean it? If you learned some easy basic games that could help anyone in that moment, would you use them to lift the spirits of your loved one? Would you use them to help a stranger?

Chapter 1

The Lame Walk

KAREN WAS A beautiful woman. She was petite with blond, wavy hair and big penetratingly blue eyes. When we met, Karen was twenty-five-years-old with three gorgeous girls and a doting, dashing husband. Karen was a stay-at-home mom. She was the picture of the perfect wife with the perfect family.

Karen loved life, and loved her family. Karen's husband had a perpetual smile on his face. Have you ever met someone who was truly happy, and glowed from the inside? This was Karen's husband. Seeing the two of them made your heart warm. You would envy them if not for one thing.

Karen was crippled. She had to use permanent crutches to walk. The crutches were barbaric. The leather straps encircled Karen's arms tightly so she would not drop them. The leather tore into her skin. She had huge calluses where the crutches had rubbed. Karen walked, but with great effort. To take just a few steps was laborious. When on uneven ground Karen struggled to get her legs going in the same direction as her crutches. Everyone wanted to help Karen, but no one, including the doctors, could find relief.

Karen attended a charismatic church and had gone to the altar many times for prayer. She was a fighter. She was determined to find answers and help. She appeared to be soft-spoken and gentle, but you definitely got the impression that Karen was not waiting for the moment of healing to come. She was pursuing it as rapidly as she could.

Karen had never picked up her children. She had a sadness in her eyes when she watched the children play. Karen wanted to run and do things similar to the other young mothers. She sat on a bench watching as her children romped with friends, pushed each other in the swing, and climbed. Never knowing their mother any other way, the children would run to her for a kiss, or a pat on the head.

The children often coaxed her, "Come on mom, please?" They asked and could not understand. Friends were always in abundance, so Karen had help and companionship constantly. Always grateful and always cheerful, Karen hoped: "One day, I'll run again."

Karen seemed resolved to her lot in life. She never complained. As a matter of fact, others sought her out because of her ability to see the good in any situation. Karen loved people, children mostly. Whenever Karen had time, like when the children were napping, she sat at her kitchen table making treats for the Sunday school.

"This is my therapy," she would say, as she kept her hands busy. Karen always had something to give. She looked like the pied piper with children following her wherever she went.

The weakness in her legs had not affected other organs. She counted this as a blessing. She exercised daily to maintain her mobility.

In grammar school, Karen began losing strength and function in her legs. No one could find an answer. The "million dollar work-up" had been done to find a diagnosis, but to no avail. It seemed that this "thing" was creeping up her legs, slowly and surely. Like Guillain-Barré syndrome the weakness progressed. Guillain-Barré syndrome is a disorder in which the body's immune system attacks part of the peripheral nervous system. Unlike Guillain-Barré, Karen's condition had not started suddenly, and since diseases generally have well-defined courses, prognosis, treatment, and expectations, Guillain-Barré syndrome was the closest label that anyone could give Karen.

Karen underwent test after test. Doctors poked and prodded, drew blood, took x-rays, MRIs, and stuck needles in her back for spinal taps frequently. It seemed the harder the doctor's looked, the more hidden the etiology became. Frustrated, doctor's discharged her from their care, and referred her to yet another specialist.

When I met Karen she had been on crutches for fifteen years. She had not run since grammar school. She had not walked without assistance in so long that she had a hard time remembering it vividly. Her nerves were degenerating and the doctors had told her that she would be in a wheelchair soon with no hope of recovery.

"There is nothing more we can do for you," were the last words Karen heard from her neurologist. In fact, most of us would have given up, had we been in Karen's shoes—but not Karen. She read anything that she could get her hands on. She searched the literature, past and present, for clues to her weakness.

Karen came to me because she wanted to exhaust all possibilities. If there was a doctor around with any information, she wanted it. Karen taught herself medical terminology and spoke the foreign language of medicine quite well. She understood as much about the nervous system as she could.

She knew very little about my specialty (veins), but wanted any knowledge that was available. I quickly told her that I had nothing to offer, *medically*. But Karen didn't leave. Karen had picked up on and heard me qualify my answer. Karen just sat there staring at me. She looked right through my soul. She seemed to know something about me that even I didn't know.

"Is there anything else that I can do for you?" I asked nervously. Usually I am the one making other people nervous, so I was clearly out of my element.

"You can help me," was all she said. It was a statement, but it was also a question. My thoughts raced. "How could I help her? I am not a neurosurgeon, I am a venous surgeon. Why is she looking to me for help? I can't help her. Sure, we have developed a great rapport, but that won't make her walk. Why does she trust me? What does she want from me?"

Have you ever had the feeling that you knew something, and you were being drawn by some unseen force to do it, but you had no idea why, or how, or what was going on? That was the feeling in my body. My head began to swirl. I became light-headed, sort of like my brain shifted slightly.

"What?" I wasn't really directing my thoughts at anyone. I wasn't really asking anyone in particular, it was just a question. Then an answer came.

"Oh no, I'm dreaming! No, I'm not dreaming, I'm sitting in front of a patient. That can't really be the answer! My thoughts have run wild this time. Maybe I drank too much coffee this morning," I thought. In that moment, when my mind got quiet, I received an answer.

"OK, I'm hearing things. Not really hearing in my ears, but hearing something," I thought. My mind raced around the new information. Typically I'm an analytical thinker, so I began to process the new information. "Is there any possibility that this could be true? Could Karen be helped?" I argued, absolutely convinced that this was a mistake. My antennae had been tuned to the wrong frequency. My radio received someone else's instructions.

I continued thinking over the answer I had just heard, "Here is the problem. This woman came to me for my medical opinion, and I'm giving her a solution that's all in her head. I can't say that of course because she would reply 'I'm not crazy, I'm crippled.' How do I tell her the solution is in her mind? I'll tell her. No I won't!"

"I'll tell you what, I'll ignore you, and Karen will leave, and we can just forget this ever happened. OK?"

I continued the conversation taking place in my mind, "OK, OK, I'll give Karen the information and she can work it out however she sees fit. There is no reason to open my mouth and prove to her how ignorant I am, I'll just give it to her, and she can go away. Then I can yell at you out loud." On and on my mind raced.

"How about if I write it down, and she can give it to her priest, pastor, rabbi, or whatever? I am not going to do this. Now go! Get out of here! Now!" But the certainty of my knowledge was just there, as if someone had implanted a memory chip into my heart. On it was information about Karen's life, her past, her childhood, and her memories. All I had to do was use the information to help her.

"I'm not going to do it, I will not talk to her about this, and you can't make me," I pleaded, and begged, bargained, and silently screamed. But nothing worked. Whatever was inside of me, was urging me to continue.

I stared at her. And she stared back. Have you ever stared at someone? Just really stared? Time had no meaning. The two of us were lost in a time warp of some sort.

Finally, I resigned myself to be totally humiliated. You can never fail if you never put forth an effort, so here goes…one colossal failure coming up. Call in the clowns, because this is going to be ugly when she is finished laughing at me. And her husband—oh, brother! He will tell this story to everyone in church, and I'll be laughed at for years to come.

I whispered silently, "I'm willing to be the fool, so here goes...but just remember, You are going to be in big trouble. I will scream at You, if You mess this up. I have no idea how to start. I am not ready for this! Don't You have some priest or rabbi or someone who can interpret this stuff better than me? Surely someone who knows how to pray can handle this one. God, I'm just a doctor! Help!"

My mind reeled. Then, finally I was able to quiet the stampede of thoughts. The words began to flow from my mouth as if I knew what I was supposed to say. I knew the questions to ask, and what to do with the information that followed. I was being guided to help this woman by the King of the universe. I was trusting to do what I was being told. Karen, in turn, was trusting to do what she was being told by me. As the minutes passed, I became more comfortable with what I was "hearing" in my soul, and Karen became more comfortable with what she was hearing with her ears. We both knew that this was a divine appointment. We were both looking forward to seeing the fruit of our obedience.

When I say that I heard or saw something that God was telling me, it is kind of an intuition in the pit of my stomach. It is a knowing in the deepest part of my spirit. It is my heart talking to me.

I asked Karen some questions, to verify and cross-reference what I was being told. It all matched the wisdom I was given.

"If anything is inaccurate I am bailing out of this, do You hear me?" But no one answered. I think God took out His hearing-aides. He must have been tired of me yelling at Him. He didn't answer.

"Fine! Just peachy! Don't answer! Great! You lead me to the

edge of the cliff, tell me to jump, and when I do, You disappear. Thanks a bunch! What am I supposed to do now?"

Do you know the story of the mother eagle? I hope this is a true story, because it is how I came to understand what happened that day. The mother eagle pushes her baby out of the nest. The baby then flaps and flaps trying to get his flying to work. The mother eagle flies just under the baby, out of the view of the little bird. If the baby fails its first flight lesson, it will land safely on the mother's back. The mother eagle will then return the baby to the nest, and try again another day. When the baby flies, flight lessons are over.

With every timid question, Karen confidently verified the information. Somewhere along the path I knew that Karen would be healed; I knew that Karen would walk. I knew that she wanted it as bad as I did, and that we would not stop until we were finished. This was just a knowing, as if the largest part of me just knew what was happening, but my mind was screaming, "This is not possible! This woman cannot be healed this way!" My mind was the battleground but something had shifted. Some part of me was just listening to the still small voice that urged me to continue.

Obedience—just obey the urging, the still small voice. "Yea right, I'm going to obey some part of me that doesn't make sense. I am a doctor, things are done a certain way. Like a path, medicine is to be followed and not deviated from!" The scientific part of me was screaming at this newly awakened part of me.

An interesting thing happened as we talked. Karen became so relaxed that she would have allowed me to operate on her right there. She was receptive to any and all of my suggestions and comments. It was my job then to give her the right words and ideas. I had to give Karen the ideas of health and wellness, and normal functioning nerves and muscles.

We magnified Karen's feelings and emotions about her disease. We then compared those feelings with times in her life when she had felt this way before. Karen told me of painful events in her childhood. We healed those memories. I will talk about the actual process of healing a memory in a later chapter.

I believe the thing that makes me a good surgeon is that I'm too mean to give up. I'm too tenacious to walk away. If it has to be done, I'll get it done. Well, Karen and I got it done. We worked with her childhood memories, traumas, and guilt. We worked on unforgiveness and responsibility. We cried and laughed. We both felt as though something small had shifted. Although neither of us could adequately describe it, we sensed something and Karen stood up. Of course I had to help her. She was weak, but she stood. Her muscles had atrophied. Wobbly legs, like a newborn horse, were under her. She struggled to stand on them with a determination that this was the time to walk. Karen was on her way to recovery, not a wheelchair. Then she took the braces from her feet. She unstrapped the steel contraptions that held her feet in alignment with her legs.

My mind took over from where it had left off, "You have lost it this time. Karen is going to fall on her face, and you will have egg all over yours. Her husband is looking at you. You will embarrass yourself! Good show!"

Every buckle seemed to take an eternity to unbuckle, and watching her struggle with these things by herself was torture. I wanted to do it for her. I wanted to make it all right for her. Like the butterfly who must pull herself from the cocoon, Karen had to get herself from her braces. Her pitiful little feet were thin and frail looking from years of bondage.

Then it happened. She took a step, then another, then another, then she began to run. By this time we were both crying and laughing and screaming. Karen's husband, who up until then had been watching in silence, took off running after his wife and began cheering her on as she regained her strength. It was difficult to see through the tears. Karen described to me later what it felt like.

She said, "As I took that first step, I was confident that I was going to fall, but I heard you cheering so I took another step. I felt like some huge weight had been lifted from each foot with each step and chains were falling off of my feet and legs. My legs and feet became lighter and easier to move. I felt like I could run, and I knew that if I didn't keep going, I never would. So I ran."

Karen was healed that day of an "incurable" malady. The disease was consuming her, her life, and her family. She was willing to do whatever it took to get healed, and she did it. Karen picked up her infant daughter and cried. Then she picked up her toddlers and wept. Karen and her husband have never looked back.

Karen's doctors examined her several months later. They could no more explain her recovery than they could her illness. Karen called it a miracle; they called it remission.

The scientific part of me wanted answers and proof. The other part of me said, "Thanks."

Karen started a new job soon after. She began a new life. She began as a helper in the church day care. I attributed her improvement to her never-give-up attitude. She gave it to God. We met somewhere in the middle.

Occasionally I stopped by the window on my way to or from the sanctuary. I just wanted to look at her again. Occasionally her husband stopped me in the hall to say thanks. I was humbled every time, because I had helped Karen kicking and screaming. Of course her husband was no mind reader, so he could not have known the battle raging in my head.

For me, the miraculous had been witnessed. I had been granted the opportunity to see and to know that there was more to medicine than pills and potions, shots and surgery, scalpel and suture. I would never be the same. Surgery would never be the same. Medicine would never be the same. I had heard the voice of the Lord and obeyed. That last word was the tricky part.

We all have that urging to call our mother, but do you do it? Or do you wait for some other more convenient time? Do you turn down a new road to go to work, or do you stay where you are and get caught in a traffic jam? Do you get onto the airplane and pray that your antennae were picking up the wrong information, or do you reschedule your trip for another time?

Obey. Obey? Obey! Hmm. Something to think about.

"I really hope You aren't too mad at me for yelling at You," I prayed, looking into the sky. No clouds were overhead. "Thank goodness, no lightning bolts today. I'll try harder to simply obey without questioning next time, but You know me."

Chapter 1
Discussion Questions

1. Do you moan and groan about your life? In what areas?

2. Name five people who have a never-give-up attitude. What areas in your life could you develop this attitude? What dreams did you have as a child that you gave up on? Why did you give up? What dreams did you have that you followed through on? What was the difference in the two?

3. What do you do when you get a hunch? Do you argue? Rationalize? Dismiss the information? Obey? Do you obey instantly or later?

4. Consider that these hunches could be from God. If you *knew* that the King of the universe was talking to you, would you act differently? How?

5. Have you ever considered that you can have a two-way conversation with God? Have you ever asked Him a question, then sat quietly listening for an answer?

6. Define the word *prophesy.* Accord to *Strong's Concordance* (4394), prophecy is "the speaking forth of the mind and counsel of God. Prophecy is not necessarily, nor even primarily, foretelling. It is the declaration of that which cannot be known by natural means, it is the forth telling of the will of God, whether with reference to the past, the present, or the future. The purpose is to edify, to comfort, and to encourage the believers, while its effect upon unbelievers is to show that the secrets of a man's heart are known to God."[1]

7. Read 1 Corinthians 14. Describe the chapter in general. Write out every reference to prophesy contained in this chapter. What were your ideas about prophesy? After reading these passages, have your ideas about prophesy changed?

8. What about when people tell you no? Do you take no for an answer, or a challenge? Do you continue seeking answers?

1 Corinthians 14

Tongues and Prophecy

1 Let love be your highest goal! But you should also desire the special abilities the Spirit gives—especially the ability to prophesy. 2 For if you have the ability to speak in tongues, you will be talking only to God, since people won't be able to understand you. You will be speaking by the power of the Spirit, but it will all be mysterious. 3 But one who prophesies strengthens others, encourages them, and comforts them. 4 A person who speaks in tongues is strengthened personally, but one who speaks a word of prophecy strengthens the entire church. 5 I wish you could all speak in tongues, but even more I wish you could all prophesy. For prophecy is greater than speaking in tongues, unless someone interprets what you are saying so that the whole church will be strengthened. 6 Dear brothers and sisters, if I should come to you speaking in an unknown language, how would that help you? But if I bring you a revelation or some special knowledge or prophecy or teaching, that will be helpful. 7 Even lifeless instruments like the flute or the harp must play the notes clearly, or no one will recognize the melody. 8 And if the bugler doesn't sound a clear call, how will the soldiers know they are being called to battle? 9 It's the same for you. If you speak to people in words they don't understand, how will they know what you are saying? You might

as well be talking into empty space. 10 There are many different languages in the world, and every language has meaning. 11 But if I don't understand a language, I will be a foreigner to someone who speaks it, and the one who speaks it will be a foreigner to me. And the same is true for you. 12 Since you are so eager to have the special abilities the Spirit gives, seek those that will strengthen the whole church. 13 So anyone who speaks in tongues should pray also for the ability to interpret what has been said. 14 For if I pray in tongues, my spirit is praying, but I don't understand what I am saying. 15 Well then, what shall I do? I will pray in the spirit, and I will also pray in words I understand. I will sing in the spirit, and I will also sing in words I understand. 16 For if you praise God only in the spirit, how can those who don't understand you praise God along with you? How can they join you in giving thanks when they don't understand what you are saying? 17 You will be giving thanks very well, but it won't strengthen the people who hear you. 18 I thank God that I speak in tongues more than any of you. 19 But in a church meeting I would rather speak five understandable words to help others than ten thousand words in an unknown language. 20 Dear brothers and sisters, don't be childish in your understanding of these things. Be innocent as babies when it comes to evil, but be mature in understanding matters of this kind. 21 It is written in the Scriptures:

"I will speak to my own people through strange languages and through the lips of foreigners. But even then, they will not listen to me," says the LORD.

22 So you see that speaking in tongues is a sign, not for believers, but for unbelievers. Prophecy, however, is for the benefit of believers, not unbelievers. 23 Even so, if unbelievers or people who don't understand these things come into your church meeting and hear everyone speaking in an unknown language, they will think you are crazy. 24 But if all of you are prophesying, and unbelievers or people who don't understand these things

come into your meeting, they will be convicted of sin and judged by what you say.25 As they listen, their secret thoughts will be exposed, and they will fall to their knees and worship God, declaring, "God is truly here among you."

A Call to Orderly Worship

26 Well, my brothers and sisters, let's summarize. When you meet together, one will sing, another will teach, another will tell some special revelation God has given, one will speak in tongues, and another will interpret what is said. But everything that is done must strengthen all of you. 27 No more than two or three should speak in tongues. They must speak one at a time, and someone must interpret what they say. 28 But if no one is present who can interpret, they must be silent in your church meeting and speak in tongues to God privately. 29 Let two or three people prophesy, and let the others evaluate what is said. 30 But if someone is prophesying and another person receives a revelation from the Lord, the one who is speaking must stop. 31 In this way, all who prophesy will have a turn to speak, one after the other, so that everyone will learn and be encouraged. 32 Remember that people who prophesy are in control of their spirit and can take turns. 33 For God is not a God of disorder but of peace, as in all the meetings of God's holy people. 34 Women should be silent during the church meetings. It is not proper for them to speak. They should be submissive, just as the law says. 35 If they have any questions, they should ask their husbands at home, for it is improper for women to speak in church meetings. 36 Or do you think God's word originated with you Corinthians? Are you the only ones to whom it was given? 37 If you claim to be a prophet or think you are spiritual, you should recognize that what I am saying is a command from the Lord himself. 38 But if you do not recognize this, you yourself will not be recognized. 39 So, my dear brothers and sisters, be eager to prophesy, and don't forbid speaking in tongues. 40 But be sure that everything is done properly and in order.

9. Read Joel 2:28, "Then, after doing all those things, I will pour out my Spirit upon all people. Your sons and daughters will prophesy. Your old men will dream dreams, and your young men will see visions." Read Acts 2:17, "In the last days," God says, "I will pour out my Spirit upon all people. Your sons and daughters will prophesy. Your young men will see visions, and your old men will dream dreams." What do these verses mean to you?

10. Read Revelations 19:10. The essence of prophecy is to give a clear witness for Jesus. What does this mean to you? Do you want to give a clear witness for Jesus? Give an example in your life when you gave a clear witness for Jesus, without using the word *Jesus*. Is it possible to give a clear witness for something without using the words? Give an example.

Chapter 2

Learning to Listen the Hard Way

It was a glorious day to be on the water. The sun was shining, birds soared overhead, not a cloud in the sky, and a gentle breeze was blowing through the palm trees.

I sat on the front of a fifty-foot Carver, cruising down the Intercoastal Waterway near Daytona Beach. Anne had invited me to spend the day on the water, and thankfully I had consented. Never could I recall a more perfect setting, day, or company. All was right with the world. The others on the boat talked and laughed, and their voices were infectious.

Anne loved houses, decorating, and architecture. Whenever possible, she took the time to walk through houses for sale. Today was turning out to be no different.

We pulled up to a dock, and several of us grabbed ropes. The boat was docked, tied, and secure.

"Where are we going?" We all knew Anne, and she was going to take us on an adventure. Her house hunting was sure to be exciting.

"I bought this house," Anne laughed and smiled. "I couldn't resist it. I've always wanted a house on the Intercoastal, this one was reasonable, and I bought it." She acted like a giddy schoolgirl. "Come on, I can't wait to show it to you."

We all looked at each other with questioning glances, but who knew? Anne's house was magnificent. The lawn was manicured, the house in perfect condition, the dock newly painted. Who were we to question?

Anne urged us to go see the house.

Several people said, "Oh that's alright, we'll see it after the closing." Not me, I had to go. My curiosity was too much.

I had one of those feelings. You know the kind, one of those something-is-terribly-wrong kind of feelings. "But what could it be?" I thought. My eyes darted everywhere. "Is it the boat? Is it another boat? Is it the engine?" I wondered to myself. Instincts are rarely wrong, but this time there were too many choices. I could not put my finger on the problem.

"Come on, let's go!" Anne excitedly jumped from the boat. She rushed over to the realtor's sign and laughed, "Take a picture of me!"

"This feeling is getting stronger, but what is it, Lord?" I asked. Anne has always been known for her practical jokes. She can get into more trouble in less time than anyone else I know. Anne had run from the sign to the lush back lawn. She threw herself onto a lounge chair and exclaimed, "This is the life."

I reluctantly became the only sucker to leave the security of the boat. With Anne appearing to be comfortable at the house, "Surely she did agree to buy the house, otherwise she would not be so crass as to sit in someone else's chair. I don't see anything out of place," I argued with my mind, and ran to meet Anne.

We looked through the windows and skipped around the perfectly placed paths. To the right of the main house was a guest house. Two bedrooms, two baths, connected to the main house by a covered breezeway and an iron gate. The gate was a decorative girly looking thing.

Anne ran through the gate and around the front of the main

house. I walked. I was taking in all of the sights. I was enjoying the blooming azaleas. Three colors exploded from one bush, or so it appeared. Camellias were in full bloom, and the dogwoods created a white canopy overhead. Gorgeous! Simply gorgeous! I stood in one place and was surrounded by thousands of flowers. There was pink, purple, and white everywhere I looked.

Suddenly, Anne ran past me so fast I wasn't even certain I saw her. She slammed the iron gate behind her and ran for the boat. In the split second that I caught her out of the corner of my eye, she had disappeared.

"What's going on?" I yelled in her direction, but she was gone.

"Oh Anne, what are you doing now?" I said under my breath for no one in particular to hear. I was sure that she was playing one of her practical jokes, but I didn't hear her laughing.

A low deep growl appeared to my right. I heard it. I was frozen. My feet would not move. My head would not move. I was paralyzed by the deafening sound. "I will die today," I thought. My thoughts were racing. The sound of death. I had heard it. My eyes were the only thing that could move.

The fight or flight response had kicked in, but I was not about to fight this thing. He was the size of a lion, with teeth like an alligator. This ferocious beast was some sort of dog, but I could not identify the breed. I was on his turf, and he was not happy.

"Stand very still." I heard the words, but I wanted to run. The words were inside me, but I still wanted to run. I looked to the iron gate. Anne, my previously close friend, had slammed the gate leaving me to fend for myself with this angry, hungry beast. The only way back to the boat was through that gate. If I could get to the gate, I would never have enough time to open it, get through it, and close it again before being mauled.

"Stand still!" I heard it again, but where was it coming from?

The growling became louder and deeper. The dog's resolve was clearly to kill me. His eyes were trained on me like a scope on a rifle. He neither blinked nor moved. Every muscle was quivering. He crouched with teeth revealed so that I could see the entire set of destructive weapons intended for me.

"Very slowly, get on all fours."

"Have You lost Your mind?" I screamed in my head. "If I get on all fours, my hands will be the first to be destroyed, and I'll never operate again," I argued with the internal voice. "I will never be able to work again."

"All fours! Now! Slowly! Very Slowly!"

Sometimes I hate arguing, but it just comes naturally. This time, I was in no way interested in losing my hands. "If I make one false move, he will devour my hands. Think of something else. There has to be another way out."

"Now!"

With the grace of a ballerina, I lowered myself to the ground. Bending my knees first, slowly, ever so slowly, I went onto all fours. An eternity passed. "I'm not happy about this," my mind still screamed.

My fingertips touched the damp grass, then my hands lowered into position, blades of grass covering parts of my hands.

"Don't look away. Look him in the eyes."

His eyes were full of death. The blood vessels were bulging in anticipation of the kill. His eyelids were closing to focus on me. The intensity of his stare was cold. Never had I experienced anything like this.

"Don't blink."

Thank God I had practiced live mannequin modeling. One of my jobs in college was to stand in the display window of a department store and model clothes. The goal was to stand perfectly still and make people wonder if I was alive or wax.

"OK, but I'm not really enjoying this! What next?" I asked the voice. Out of the corner of my eye I could see my now former friends on the boat. They didn't move. "Couldn't they at least attempt to help me? Act like they like me? Come on, I thought they were my friends."

"Crouch down like him."

I bent closer to the dog, my elbows bent. We could feel each other's breath. I was not keen on smelling death. He was salivating thinking of his lunch.

"Take slow deep breaths."

"Yeah right, I'm going to breathe slow. Hyperventilate might be a more accurate description!" I attempted to slow my breathing. So did the beast.

The deeper my breaths became, the slower and deeper he breathed.

"Send him love."

"I am going to be eaten by this dog. Oh joy of joys, there is another dog, just under that bush, waiting for the signal to attack. Yeah! I'm really excited now! Two for the price of one! And You want me to send him love?"

I allowed my attention to change from death, to life. I allowed my focus to change while still not blinking. I began to feel love, not for the dog, but for my family. I began remembering times with my children when we laughed and hugged.

"Did he move? I thought I saw him relax. Maybe not." I allowed my thoughts to drift again. I imagined powerful times in my life where love was abundant.

His tense quivering muscles moved, but I didn't. He straightened his back and took on a more relaxed posture.

"Now what?" I asked loudly in silence.

"Wait, he will come to you."

"OK, I'm sure that I'm making this up. He is going to come

to me? Right!" I had no concept of this angry animal walking to me. I could however imagine him leaping, and ripping the flesh from my bones. I imagined his mouth around my neck, severing the blood vessels. Thankfully it would be a quick kill. I wouldn't suffer long.

The beast's hair had been standing straight up on his back. A line of demarcation ran the length of his spine. Slowly the hair began to lay down, but the weapons of destruction, his teeth, were still visible. The growling was still creating a taut fiddle string out of my every nerve.

He shifted his weight toward me. Our eyes remained locked. We were nose to nose. He shifted some more.

"Let him come to you."

"Oh God! Oh God! He's too close! I'm going to panic."

"Be still."

Have you ever been in a situation where time was in slow motion? This was certainly one of those times. I heard a voice. It was trying to help me. I was arguing with a voice, but no one was around. I had never heard a voice quite so clear or distinct before, but it seemed to know what to do.

The dog's eyes shifted away from mine. He looked at the ground and leaned more toward me. He touched my right arm with his nose and teeth. His growling slowed to a low rumble. His friend and partner in crime who had been crouching under the tree, turned and walked away. Some unspoken signal had been sent. He was off the hook.

The dog took a step in my direction. Full contact with my arm, teeth fully exposed, the dog was…nuzzling? No way. His teeth are still exposed. Then he relaxed his mouth, and allowed his weapons to hide behind his cheeks.

"Allow your arm to pet him. Slowly."

My bent arm was shaking from maintaining one position.

I sort of stroked his fur with my extended arm. He allowed his weight to press onto me.

"Slow."

"OK, OK, I'll do it slow." I began to sit back on my heels, allowing my arm, then hand, to touch his side. I stroked his fur again and he turned.

"Touch his head."

"No, that's the part that bites. One bite and I'll be unemployed forever!" But I gently slowly moved my hand to his head. He relaxed more and turned again allowing my hand to slide the length of his body and off his tail. He was walking away, toward the house to join his friend. He turned toward me as if to say good-bye, and rounded the corner.

"You can go now."

"No I can't, I can't get my knees to hold my weight." I began to stand and felt as though my legs would buckle. I reached the gate and used it for support. When I closed the gate behind me, I felt some relief.

Walking to the boat, and seeing the relief on my new ex-friends' faces brought the impact of the event fully into view.

"How did you do that? We were sure that you would be hurt. What did you do? Did you see the second dog? He was just waiting to join the feast! What happened?" They shot questions at me. I could not answer. The adrenaline stopped and I sat again on the front cushion of the boat. We were released from the pier, started the engines, and headed for home. We had enough excitement for one day. Obviously Anne had never been to the house before and clearly did not know that there were guard dogs around. This time her comedy almost turned out to be a horror flick.

That voice! It wasn't a voice really. It was a feeling. No, it was a…I just *knew* what to do.

"Thanks," I said silently.

That day was "a life-defining moment," as I tell my children. I knew that there was an intelligence greater that human. But until I personally experienced it, I had not really given much credence to it. I had not understood that the Lord would hold a two-way conversation with me. I thought you just talked to the air and called it prayer. And somehow, you were heard along with the millions of other prayers being sent "up" to heaven at the same time. The concept of every prayer being heard was a challenging one to contemplate.

James 1:5–6 had just played out in my life in such a way that I could not ignore it. I could no longer pray to some invisible God. I knew that He was present in a real and tangible way. I also knew that if I asked, He would answer. First Karen, now this. "Lord, why are You working overtime to get my attention?" He probably answered, but I was mentally on to the next subject.

You can "hear" just as well as I can. Everyone can. Read James 1:5–6 again. It says, ask and *expect* an answer. But how can you expect an answer if you've never heard His voice?

But you have heard this voice; I'm sure of it. Everyone has that "intuitive sense" that something is wrong, like I had while on the boat. I had not honed my skill at interpreting, but I knew something was wrong. Remember a time when you had a sense about something? The fun part is to work with it, but please do not go out and find a ferocious dog to start with. Actually, please don't ever go near one. It is terrifying.

I always start by saying a simple prayer, asking God for His wisdom, guidance, and protection. Next find a victim—I mean, an accomplice. This should ideally be someone you like and can play with. Ask them if they will play some games with you. By asking them to "play," you take all the stigma off of the "prayer." Whenever I talk about prayer, people get kinda weird, like prayer has to be performed a certain way, or it's wrong. So, since I wasn't raised in their church, I just ask them to play games with me. Everyone likes games.

Close your eyes, and say, "Give me a Bible verse for this person." One will pop into your head. Open your Bible (assuming you have one) and read it. Every time I've done this for myself or others, God has had interesting things to say. Don't get bogged down in formalities, just read. What did the verse mean to you? Keep it light, then move on.

Next, close your eyes again and say, "Lord, give me a song for this person." Just play, there is no right or wrong answer. Tell the other person which song you "heard" pop into your head. Ask them what it meant to them.

I was teaching a class called "Hearing the Voice of the Lord," and I asked everyone to pair up with a person that they had never met. We did the song request, and without exception the songs were significant to the recipients. It was amazing to see the faces of people receiving "words from the Lord," embedded in songs. One in particular was given to a man. The song was talking about a newborn baby. He was shocked. Only days before, he and his wife had learned that they were expecting their first child and no one knew except the couple. They wanted to keep it a "secret" for a while. God told on them.

It is not a requirement that you close your eyes. I only suggest it so that you do not have any distractions. I find that when I pray, I focus better without outside interference.

Ready for more exercises? If so, close your eyes and ask, "What does this person need to know right now?" When you get the answer, remember to always edify, comfort, or help. If you can't do one or all of those things with the information, don't give it. Simply ask again. "Please give me something else," and tell them what you received. Let everything you say be good and helpful so that your words will be an encouragement to those who hear them. (See Ephesians 4:29.)

Ready for another exercise? If so, say, "Give me one word that describes this person." Then when the word pops into your head, you are armed with a gold nugget. For example, if you heard the word *sad*, you could ask, "Have you been feeling a bit sad or down lately?" You already know that they have, but it is a great idea to get a confirmation.

"I got some bad news today," they respond. If you are comfortable praying out loud with this person, go for it. If you are not, then pray in silence. The King of the universe just gave you a nugget of gold—don't throw it away.

When I was very new at this whole intuition, hearing, listening thing, I heard about a teacher in Jacksonville. She was a pastor. I traveled there several days per week to study with her and her class. The class was three months in duration. I learned that God wants us to ask, and wants us to listen. The class was experiential. We did a lot of praying. The classes were held in the evening, and most of these three months I was tired because Jacksonville is a three-hour drive.

During that period, I routinely attended the Wednesday healing service at my church. The congregation was small and intimate. The service was quiet and reverent, just the way I liked it. One day after the service, I walked for the door as usual, but I heard my name. I turned to see the face of an acquaintance. Let's call her Casey.

"Will you please pray for me?" she asked. It wasn't a huge request, but she just stood there looking at me.

"Lord, I'm so new at this she will think I'm nuts. She doesn't know how I pray. You and I know that there are many different types of prayer, but she is asking *me*. What am I going to do?

She could have asked anyone else in this church, why did she ask me?" I'm always arguing and whining, especially when I don't want to do something. I had only been training for about a month, and was afraid that I would embarrass myself or worse yet, I would get it wrong and hurt her.

"Get me out of this, God," I thought, but He had turned His hearing aids off again. He wasn't budging.

"Sure I'll pray with you, but Casey you need to know that I usually ask God what He is interested in talking about before I begin to petition Him. Is that OK with you?" She sat there, a little confused, and a little uneasy. She said, "I don't know, I just felt like I was supposed to ask you to pray for me."

As I began, I thought, "OK, Lord, let's go. Don't let me mess this up. Please."

"Casey I believe that you are being given an opportunity to work with children at the church. You may be at a crossroads and need to choose which path to take. If you choose to begin ministry with the children, your inclination is to do everything alone. In working with these kids, you can have all of the help required or wanted, if you ask for it. If you don't ask, you will be overwhelmed with work.

"You are not required to take this opportunity, but if you do, it will be very fulfilling and gratifying. You will not second-guess your career change. You have come from a strict church environment with lots of rules and regulations. This children's opportunity will allow you to grow and expand. There will be lots of children laughing and playing with you. Was this anywhere close to answering your question?" I asked her.

She had tears welling in her eyes, and she said yes.

"Well then, let's pray for you and the children's ministry." We prayed in agreement that Casey's mind would be clear and focused during this time of decision-making. We prayed that she would make the best decision not only for her, but her marriage, and the church. We prayed that she would learn to ask for help before tasks felt overwhelming.

"I've never seen anyone pray like that," Casey thanked me, and we left the sanctuary. Not too long after we prayed, I heard that she accepted the children's ministry opportunity, quit her job, and was excelling in the position. Casey had enough energy to keep up with the children, and had enough ideas to stay one step ahead of them.

That was four years ago and Casey looks like she has always been the head of children's ministries. She has a perpetual smile on her face, and children are always around her.

That prayer helped both of us. It helped me step out of the comfort zone of the class, and put the information to the test. It helped Casey open her eyes to a different type of prayer.

Strong's Concordance puts it this way, "*prophetia* (prophecy) emanates from God, and is the telling of the will of God. It signifies the speaking forth of the mind and counsel of God."[1]

The prophetic chapter in 1 Corinthians 14:1 says, "Let love be your highest goal! But you should also desire the special abilities the Spirit gives—especially the ability to prophesy." I had asked God to teach me about intuition, and learning His ways. I had asked Him to lift me up to be able to teach others about Him. That first step can be very difficult to take. If only I could quit arguing with Him.

"Thanks, You did it again. I'll get it sooner or later. Please don't give up on me," I prayed as I left church that day.

There were clear skies and no clouds; "Oh, thank heavens, no lightning bolt today."

Please do not mistake my ramblings as gospel from a learned biblical scholar. I am a doctor. My attempts to help people are from that view and that basis. As I have said I am an amateur on the Bible. My focus is on helping the patient heal.

I am less knowledgeable about the spirit world. But that still small voice intrigues me. It talks to me in surgery and out. It is that voice that gives instructions and encouragement. It is also that voice that I argue with. I am not always obedient. I do the best I can to get through every day, learning as much as possible along the way. If the best I can do today is rest, then I count it a blessing. If on the other hand, I can help someone along the way…then that is great, too.

I am convinced that we all hear it; that still small voice that tells you to call your mother. Are you like me? Do you argue with it? Or are you obedient immediately? I tend to argue and question everyone and everything. So, through the years, I've done some pretty silly things. But here is the secret to listening:

Listen.

Here are the instructions again, just in case you didn't get them the first time:

Listen.

You can close the book now. That was it, the whole lesson—just, listen. James 1:19 says, "Be quick to listen, slow to speak." Sounds pretty easy right? Well for me nothing came easily. I had to kick and fight my way out of my parent's home. Some children just go away to college, their parents crying due to the suddenly empty nest. Not me. I could never do anything so effortlessly. I picked a fight with my father that resulted in us screaming at one another. Pretty smooth! I stormed out of the house, declaring that I would never talk to him again. Fortunately a parent's love is true, and he loved me through my rebellion. I am fortunate he didn't box my ears flat against my head.

One of my favorite places in the world is the surgical suites.

There is just something about it. In there I know what my mission is, and I go for it. It is so rewarding to get out of surgery with the complete confidence of the procedure. But this was also a place of nightmares. Some procedures did not turn out so well. There have been times when the patient had problems and the doctors and nurses did all that they could for the patient, only to meet defeat. It was there that I recognized the voice and heard it most clearly.

Imagine your worst nightmare when, all of the sudden, right in the middle, you have a flash of insight for how to react. You might likely respond, "OK. I'm listening." What you would be hearing is that still small voice, often called by many other names. (See 1 Kings 19:12, NKJV.) Some call it intuition. Some refer to it as the Lord Himself, while other times it is called the Holy Spirit. Sometimes it yells at me. Quite frankly I have never been much on semantics, but I can tell you that something greater than the surgeon is out there. Some people say that surgeons think that they are next to God. Every surgeon that I know personally thinks that he is the farthest thing from God. We hold peoples' lives in our hands every day. We strive for perfection in the surgical suites, but all too often we are proven to be mere mortals.

For example, one of my favorite patients was operated on. She had a very successful surgery. The procedure was a success in every way. She went home to recover, and called the next day frantic. Something was wrong. I immediately examined her, and saw no issues, no challenges; no physical problem was evident. The patient insisted that there was a problem. For weeks the patient returned to the office with a non-healing wound. I could not understand. I had done everything correctly. The procedure went like the textbooks. The operation was a success. The results of the surgery were great. So why wasn't the skin healing? Over the weeks that followed, I had the opportunity to spend hours with this patient. She told me of her life and her home. She helped me understand that there are three parts to healing. I, her surgeon, had addressed her physical body. Her mind and spirit had been neglected, and without those she simply would not heal. As I came to realize her mind, body, and spirit, this patient taught me volumes.

She taught me how to listen. She taught me to be quiet. She taught me to question, then to remain quiet long enough to hear the answer. Too often we ask questions, failing to wait for an answer. The Bible says ask, expecting an answer. (See James 1:5–6.) With this patient, I asked plenty of questions, but never once did I expect the Lord to answer me. Who was I to demand the attention of the King of the universe? Certainly He had better things to do than to answer the questions of one mere mortal.

But He did answer me. He could not get my attention any other way, so He got it through a patient. He taught me that I can cut and I can sew. I can repair and place things in their appointed order, but I cannot heal. I can physically repair the defect, but He heals. The patient and the great Healer together mend the skin, the organs, and the tissues that I cut through.

This patient demanded my ear. Only then did we find the cause of her non-healing wound. It was a simple thing, really. I had done my part in the operating room, or so I thought. But what she needed was someone to sit down, if only for a moment, hear her out, and help. Once I got it, I never again rushed through my thoughts with a patient.

My habit of sitting and talking with patients and families began because of her, that one patient who would not go away. Then something miraculous happened. I began to listen to the silence in the operating room in every surgery. Without fail,

I would hear something wonderful. It could just be a wonderful feeling of completion. It could be an urging to continue an exploratory surgery for a few more centimeters. As I began to listen, the information seemed to come more freely. Instead of a formal question and answer time with the Lord, I would just say, "Anything else?" and He was faithful to deliver.

Teaching people how to hear the voice of the Lord, that still small voice, is a fun thing to do. People tell me that they had no idea that those urgings were in fact the Lord. The Bible clearly says that He will be faithful to answer, if I ask, expecting Him to answer. (See James 1:5–6.)

So try it out. Ask a simple question like, "Give me a Bible verse to read today." When one pops into your mind, go read it. Then enjoy whatever is being told to you. It can be really fun, if you let it.

I'd like to tell you about yesterday. It began like any other day, making lunches in the kitchen for two growing adolescents, straightening the house, dressing, and generally being absorbed in mundane morning chores. My daughter was singing in her bedroom, my son was dragging huge garbage bags out to the street.

My cell phone went off. I reached for it and heard my prayer partner say, "We need to pray. This one can't wait." We both have children and the mornings are not a great time to listen actively to anyone, much less someone who needs specific prayer. Chores must be done, and the children packed off to school in a timely fashion. So, I listened with one ear, and got about half of the information, until she said, "Twenty-three week's gestation."

My mind began to race again, "What had she said? Who was pregnant? How old was the mother, and what had prompted this premature labor? Oh, rats, I wasn't listening fully, and had only pieces of the information. How can I pray when I don't know what to say?"

Once again I was told the names, and again, the children were talking to me so I was only listening with one ear. Oh, this was Frustration 101. "Ill get it, really I will, tell me the names one more time," I asked. After an exhausting moment of attempting to listen to three people at once, I was finally sure that I heard the mother's name, the aunt's name, my son's explanation of why he lost his shoes, and my daughter's explanation of why she could not empty the dishwasher before school.

I drove the children to school and allowed my head to fall back on the headrest. Suddenly that inner voice, the one that the Creator uses, allowed visions of the mother's delivery to come into full view. They were not at all what I had wanted to see, so I stopped listening and called my friend. I gave her the information that I had heard and seen. I told her that I was not really ready to listen to any more from up above, and actually I was timid about knowing more. So, I quit.

Hours later, the feeling of urgency to pray came over me again. I felt something was going on that I needed to know. So I relaxed and asked about mom and baby. Visions and feelings flowed through me so fast that I could not stop them this time. I saw the baby being born, breech, feet first. I could feel the tiny little creature beginning to move, then begin to cry and reach above its body. I saw that the baby was a boy. Other things came into the picture, but I will reserve those for a future writing. They are yet to occur.

We began to pray, we had agreed on the things to say. We prayed all day. Later that day, we got a report that the baby was indeed born, feet first. As the burden welled in us to pray, we had both continued for both mom and son. Some had the burden to pray for the baby, others had the burden to pray for mom.

You can use this as an example of how to listen and how to pray. When you listen, quiet yourself, your busy mind, your radio, and whatever else you have. For just a moment, allow your mind to be quiet. Don't daydream about cooking supper. Just stare at the floor or close your eyes. Drift for a few seconds, imagining a blank blackboard; whatever works for you.

Once you have the information that you asked for, ask how to pray. He will tell you. For example, if I had not asked what the Lord wanted me to pray for, and had been praying for the baby to be born alive, I would have been praying for something that was already going to happen. Was this due to the prayers of other people? I don't know. But I was told the baby would be alive, so the Lord did not want me to pray for that. I had only to *praise* Him for that fact, "Thank You God that the premature baby is alive!"

I was being led to pray specifically for the mother. I saw her fear. The Lord did not give us "a spirit of fear, but of power and of love and of a sound mind," according to 1 Timothy 1:7. So I prayed for mom all day, in the way that the Lord was leading me:

Lord, fear is not from You, so I come boldly to the throne of grace and in the name of Jesus, by the authority of our Father, and in the power of the Holy Spirit, I break the fear from my sister in Christ. I call on the peace that passes all understanding to fill her to overflowing. Father let every word that she hears be a comfort and a blessing to her. Surround her with such power and love and a sound mind, that all else falls away.

As the urge rose in me, I simply broke out in prayer. As I write these words, I haven't yet gotten another report on mom or child, so I will continue to pray until that time comes.

The Lord has a special soft spot for mothers. I believe that He wants us to be gentle with them as well. They have an incredible job, often it is too much for them to tolerate on their own. When a mother calls you for prayer, please hold it with delicacy and grace.

A friend (let's call her Shannon) called. Her nineteen-year-old daughter (let's call her Tina) was rebellious, drinking, staying out, and not coming home. Tina knew how to get into more trouble than she could get out of. Tina associated with druggies. She was mean-spirited with her mother, and had a job that couldn't pay the bills, much less the rent.

Tina, the poster child for rebellion, was missing. Tina had not called her mother in days. Tina knew that her mother would go into one of several orbiting patterns without daily contact, but still had not called. Everyone who knew or associated with Tina knew her story.

Shannon called me and asked me to pray. My first step was to ask the Lord about Tina. I saw Tina doing things that good little girls don't do. The Lord revealed many icky, nasty details of the last few days. How would I give that information to Shannon?

How many times do we hear the same things: give them "hard love," she has to learn her lessons sometime? Shannon did not call for a word from Teri. She did not ask for my advice. She called and asked for prayer, for a word from God.

So I had to stop thinking, and start asking God: "What do You want to happen here, God? Your child is hurting, this mother is frantic, and if You don't do something, tempers are going to get ugly," I prayed.

God gave a very gentle, encouraging word to Shannon. Did I give Shannon all the details the Lord had given me? Of course not. The Lord wanted me to know how important it was going to be, to handle this situation lightly, delicately, and gently. The Lord showed me that Tina was alive, and would phone her mother very soon.

Shannon received the word from the Lord, Tina was allowed to complete her mission of misery, and come to the realization (by herself, without mom's nagging help) that something had to change. Something drastic needed to happen in a short time.

"Praise God. You got 'em again," I prayed. "You encouraged Shannon. You soothed her anxiety-ridden heart. And with the conviction of the gentlest Father, You brought Tina to her knees in repentance."

Chapter 2
Discussion Questions

1. When you get a feeling of dread like something is not right, what do you do?

2. When have you had a gut feeling and quickly discovered that it was accurate? Describe the event.

3. If you had the urging to get on all fours in front of an angry, hungry beast what would you do? Obey? Or run for it?

4. When was the last time you were so frightened that you couldn't move?

5. Name ten "life defining moments." How did they change you?

6. When have you known that there was a greater power than you? Give detailed examples.

7. How often have you talked to air and called it prayer?

8. When you ask God a question, do you expect Him to answer? Do you quiet yourself and your mind long enough to hear? Do you expect Him to answer right after the prayer, or sometime in the future?

9. When you begin to pray, do you ask God what He wants to talk about first? Or do you do all of the talking?

Chapter 3

Healing of the Memories

LONG BEFORE I understood the Lord was pulling me in the direction of this type of healing, I met an Episcopalian priest named Father Al Durrance. Father Al, as I have come to know him, has been around the block. This man knows from firsthand experience how to integrate the mind, body and spirit. Father Al seeks the Lord for everything, listens intently, and obeys the Lord's callings. Father Al has been healed of "incurable" ailments, and has assisted others in the same. Father Al has been the kind of mentor to me that is hard to describe. I've been trained by some of the most learned surgeons in the world. I have been trained by some mean, brilliant men. But if you put all of these people together in a paper sack, and shook them up, you would not be able to compare to the wisdom that he enjoys.

Sitting next to Father Al is a powerful experience. He has a presence that is awesome. I can only compare it to one other individual on earth. General Norman Schwarzkopf. I had the fabulous experience of meeting the general and my life changed forever. I had never before been in the vicinity of a person that commanded such a presence when he entered a room. This man was learned, statuesque, handsome, brilliant, successful, humble, noble—and conspicuously quiet. I was speechless in the presence of the general. He was awe inspiring.

Father Al has the same God-given presence as General Schwarzkopf. Both Father Al and General Schwarzkopf were fully present when they engaged me. And I do mean engaged. When the general engaged me in conversation, I felt as though no one else was in the room. He not only looked me in the eye, his whole body, mind, and soul were there, too. You *know* when someone is just grunting at you, and when you have someone's undivided attention. Father Al, without exception, has always given me his undivided attention, whether surrounded by hundreds of people, or sitting alone in a room.

If you do not understand this experience, please experiment with it. The next time you are speaking with someone, look them dead in the eye; turn your body to them. Pay such close attention to their breathing that you anticipate their next breath. Listen so intently that you could complete their sentences. Be present, which means no daydreaming. This hopefully will help you understand the persona of these two great men.

In the preceding paragraph I said, "Pay close attention." If you are going to "pay" attention, it will cost you something right? You are "paying." The thing that you will use for currency is your time and energy. This time and energy will be well spent. You will receive great benefits. And those you encounter will remember.

For example, meeting and speaking with General Schwarzkopf changed my life forever. I learned how to listen and leave someone with the profound impact of being "heard." From the general's point of view, I would bet you a dollar that he could not remember me today. It was a short meeting, many years ago, and we talked for only a few minutes. This encounter, however, made such an impact on my life, that I mentally use it to judge my conversational skills yet today.

My father says, "You never get a second chance to make a first impression." The general sure made a first impression. In the briefest of moments he allowed me to truly understand a great and valuable lesson—how to listen. Whether I'm listening to the Lord, Father Al, one of my children, a patient, or someone on the street, I immediately recognize when I am listening and engaging in effective conversation, or if I am wasting my time.

The air around the general and Father Al is the same—*electric*. You feel as though the divine has touched the earth in this space. They have more wisdom in their little fingers than I will have in a lifetime.

Father Al has the patience of a saint. He has spent countless hours teaching me. One of the most valuable lessons that he ever shared, and one that I use often, is something he calls "healing of the memories." This is my understanding of what is happening:

Memories are stored. We do not know exactly where, but we do know that at least in part they are stored in the brain. There is evidence that memories are stored in every cell of the body. Let us make this easy to understand, so for now we will concentrate on the mind, more specifically the brain.

Since the body is a series of actions and reactions, we first need to explore some of the brain activities. To recall a memory, a particular part of the brain must be stimulated. This will trigger certain chemicals to be released in the brain. The chemicals chosen will be the same ones that were used initially when the event was first presented to your brain.

For example, remember your first kiss. In a nanosecond, you travel back in time to that moment. You recall the people. You recall the odors. You recall the place. You recall the feeling in your body. Maybe your body begins to tingle, just like it did all those years ago. You can feel the excitement, the anticipation, the nervousness, and the exhilaration of the moment. Then the moment when your lips actually touched! Oh, there are no words to describe that first kiss. Everyone has one, a feeling that is indescribable. Although words fail you at this moment, the feelings do not. You have recreated the moment so accurately you feel as though you were actually there again.

At the moment that you leaned over to be kissed, your lips so close that you could feel each other's breath, your brain was celebrating. Your brain was saying "yippee!" The anticipation was so intense that it was shooting off fireworks. There were a series of chemicals dumped into your brain at that moment to create that memory, cementing it forever.

Gaining access to that first kiss was not difficult. You traveled to that part of the brain containing the memory. Then you dumped in a certain set of chemicals. And instantly you are able to go back and relive that fabulous feeling.

Another analogy is your computer. When you type a document and save it onto your hard drive, it follows a certain path. You are able to retrieve this document any time if you follow the correct path. If you follow a different path, you will get a different document. So let us take this analogy one step further. The original document was saved. The computer does not care if it was saved yesterday or forty years ago. Following the same path will always get you back to the same document. But let us now modify or edit the original document. Is it possible to edit something on your hard drive? Of course it is. Anytime we want, we can access the original document. Then all we have to do is use the keyboard to change the wording on the original document.

Can we modify the document by pushing on the monitor? Of course not. Can we modify the document by talking to the modem? No again. We must follow the same path with which we originally created the document. At that point, we can edit and modify it to suit our present needs. So long as we follow the exact original path we can then monkey with it as much as we would like. When we access the memory, we can add words, insert clip art, photographs, or entirely new paragraphs.

This information is valuable. Let's say that you have a memory that is not as pleasant as your first kiss. Actually, not only is it unpleasant, but every time you allow yourself to remember it you begin to cry.

Different chemicals are released in my brain when I think of my favorite dog dying. Princess, that was my dog's name. Just the thought of looking at my precious pet lying on the side of the road, still attached to the leash I was holding, the sound of the car speeding off, and not even bothering to slow down, is enough to bring an entirely different set of chemicals to my brain. These are not at all like the other memories. My body doesn't feel the same, actually, it feels like a huge weight sitting in the middle of my chest. What happened to the butterflies, the excitement, and anticipation? They are gone, and replaced with sad, dark memories of digging a hole and placing my friend in it, because life had been forced out of its little body.

Now bring yourself out of that place so we can talk about how this ties into healing. It is not so easy to "snap out of it" is it? Sometimes we need to change our body position, or listen to upbeat music, or we could use what we know about memories. How can we use this?

If there is a certain set of chemicals produced when we feel sad, and different chemicals when we are happy, what would happen if we mixed them up? What would happen if we dumped just a little bit of "that first kiss" into "my dog is gone?" This is what we do when we heal a memory. We follow the same path as the original memory, then we rewrite the original document to say something slightly different.

Let's say that we remember "our family dog," and want this memory to have less emotional impact. We can edit it with new information, and accomplish our goal. Obviously we cannot bring Princess back from the dead, and we cannot pretend that Princess lived longer, but we can write into the memory. What if an angel of the Lord is standing with you in your memory? The angel does not allow Princess to suffer. The angel is visible to you and is comforting. It is able to talk to you; what does the angel say? Look closely at the angel and feel the warmth the angel gives off. Allow yourself to be surrounded by love. This angel is not only there for Princess, but is there to comfort you, too. Allow the angel to give you the comfort of the Lord. Allow this angel to go with you to the grave and hold your hand. When you are ready, allow the angel to take Princess to heaven.

After you have completed this assignment, and you have taken a break from these words, think back to the day your dog died. You will notice that the memory is still there, but the emotional impact is lessoned. This is a powerful exercise and anyone can be helped by it. You can do it yourself, or you can help a friend.

Now that we understand the process, we can apply it to some of the more difficult mental challenges. The ones formed when we were little. These memories are not rational like adult memories. Usually they are powerful, but make little sense to the adult mind. We can remember something, then say consciously, "Oh, that's ridiculous, I cannot have such a strong emotional reaction from that childhood memory."

Childhood memories create the glasses through which we look for a lifetime. Silly as they may seem when you are mining for them, do not underestimate the power that they hold. Once you decide that you are going to help someone, it is a great idea to have them choose a helper. Some like Christ to step into the picture. Others want a grandmother. Do not ever assume that you know who should step into a memory. In the previous example, I used an angel. Be careful in assigning helpers. You can get into deep waters without knowing how to get out. The person that I would choose may be far different than who you would choose. Seek the Lord and His wisdom in matters such as this.

The helper should be someone the child knows and trusts. Sometimes just interjecting the helper into the memory is enough to calm the child (the one in the memory). Once your helper steps into the memory, the memory changed and therefore you have changed the chemical responses to those memories.

Sometimes, the helper must talk with the child and tell them what will happen later in life. Occasionally, the child and the helper will take long walks on the beach. Whatever happens is OK so long as the child is healing, and the helper is helping.

I'll give you an example of how this works. Let's say Mary remembers a time when she was two years old. She has already told you that she trusts Jesus to be her helper. She was in a room where adults were screaming. She was afraid. She thought that she would be left alone. She thought the adults were mad at her. She thought the adults would be better off if she had never been born. Mary wept when she remembered this time in her life.

"Mary remain in this memory for just a little while. Is anyone with you Mary?"

"No, I'm alone. The big people are yelling." Mary's eyes are closed and she is reliving the memory.

"Mary ask Jesus to step into the picture, and tell me when you can see him." I say in a gentle voice.

"OK, He is in the picture." Mary's body appears to relax just a bit.

"Where is he Mary?"

"He is on my right." Mary seems to point as her body shifts to the right.

"What is he doing, Mary?"

"He is holding my hand." Mary is calming perceptively now.

"How do you feel when Jesus holds your hand?"

"I feel like I have a friend." Mary has stopped focusing on the adults, and has started focusing on herself and Jesus.

"Mary, look at the adults, what are they doing."

"They are still yelling, but it is Ok, they aren't yelling at me."

"Mary, Imagine that Jesus is talking to you, what is he saying?"

"He is telling me that my parents are not mad at me, they are just mad."

"Mary, you will grow up and have lots of love around. You will not be alone Mary. You will have a husband and two children that you adore. Continue holding the hand of Jesus. How does it make you feel to hold His hand."

"I feel secure. His hand is warm, and he is holding tight, while my parents fight. It feels like he won't let go."

"He won't let go Mary. Now when you are ready, allow your mind to bring you back to the present time. You can continue to hold Jesus' hand or you can let go, which ever is more comfortable."

"Now Mary I want you to keep your eyes open and think about being a small child, in the room when your parents were arguing. Tell me how you feel."

"I feel OK." You notice that Mary does not cry this time. "I don't feel so bad."

Have you seen any of those time travel movies? Someone goes back in time and tinkers with an event. The character then travels to the present time to find that things shifted and changed. Because the past changed, the future changed as well. This is a horribly loose example of what we will do, but maybe it will give you an idea of how this stuff works.

Maybe the infant child thought she would die. We would assure the little person that in fact she would live a long life, (obviously because you are reading this book). We would assure the little person that love is achievable, (and you love yourself enough to read this book). We would find the things in life that can help the child get through the event, traumatic as it was, with a different frame of reference. The child is not abandoned (remember we interjected someone into the memory that knows and loves the little person.) You can have the helper stay with the child, and not leave.

Are you beginning to get the process? When you assure the child of certain events that will happen in his life, you take away the hopelessness, and thus take away a tremendous amount of fear. God did not give us a spirit of fear, but of power, and love, and a sound mind.

By interjecting this helper into the toddler's memory, they are not alone, they are not afraid, they have love from the helper, and therefore they have the power to go forward in life with confidence.

Imagine what it would be like for a prisoner of war to *know* with all certainty, that on a given day, at a certain time, he would be rescued, and free. There would be a calm and a peace about him, because he would *know* that he would live, he would know that he would see his family again, he would not feel abandoned. His greatest fears would be gone. The fear of dying right then would be gone (obviously because he lived long enough to have a memory.) The only thing he would focus on would be the future. If the enemy pulled his fingernails off, he would look forward to tomorrow, because he would already have the knowledge of the time and date of his freedom. He would have seen the future and would have confidence in it. Remember that we are going *back* in time, so we already know the future.

This is what we do to your memories. We take that prisoner of war (the child), with feelings of hopeless despair, fear, and torment and we reframe the event so that the *memory* is filled with the feelings and knowledge of life, love, hope, salvation, refuge, warmth, security, and a future. With this information now in the memory, the prisoner relaxes. The prisoner is no longer in bondage to fear, but is free with hope and knowledge of a future. Of course this is all done with memories, and the result is a new person who views life with different colored glasses. The old hopeless responses are gone, and the new feelings remain. The old is gone, the new is here. The old man falls away; a new man is created. The old dark, dingy glasses are replaced with rose-colored glasses.

Behold a new creature that is not only possible, but is within your grasp. Touch your head. That is where the answer is. Point to your head. That is where the work is done. When the Lord changes the self-destructive beliefs and responses to productive, healthy ones, the mind and body are healed.

Chapter 3
Discussion Questions

1. When you listen, do you think of the next thing to say or do you hang on every word?

2. Listen, really listen to someone. It doesn't matter who. The voice on the radio, the TV, or your child. Engage them. If you catch yourself drifting just focus again. Face the person (or radio), lean forward, look them in the eye (or speaker.) Describe the feelings. What do you notice about yourself?

3. What does "pay close attention" mean to you? Describe what it will cost you.

4. Who has made the greatest impact on your life? What did you learn from them? How did it impact your life?

5. Remember your first kiss—really remember it. Then write about the feelings.

6. Choose a helper, someone who you trust with your life. Who do you trust completely?

7. Reread the section about Mary if necessary then heal a memory of your own. There is no right or wrong way to do this. Allow yourself to be guided by God on your healing.

Chapter 4

The Blind See

Mrs. Robertson came to the office for a medical consultation. She had horrible varicosities on her legs, and wanted them removed. The veins looked like huge snakes wrapping around her legs from her groin to her ankle. Mrs. Robertson's legs were painful. When she walked her legs hurt, but when she stood for periods of time, the pain was horrible. The pain had gotten so bad that she wore ace bandages around her legs, and most of her time spent at home was on the couch with her legs raised in the air. This was the only position that eased the discomfort. Her husband came to the office with her, to lend support.

I noticed the couple being helped into an exam room, as I exited another room. As the couple walked I noticed Mr. Robertson was walking with a cane, and Mrs. Robertson was holding him by the arm guiding him. He walked as though he needed more assistance than a newborn baby. I watched in amazement, at his inability to maneuver. The nurse and the wife, arduously assisted Mr. Robertson into the exam room and into a chair.

The nurse briefed me on the situation. "You'll like this next couple. The Mrs. needs surgery. The Mr. is here for moral support. But from the looks of things, he needs more than she does."

The appointment was for the wife, but my mind was whirling

at Warp Factor five about the husband. "What could have happened recently to result in this sudden and total blindness?" I wondered to myself. "It is obviously a new condition, because blind people have an uncanny ability to learn new behaviors. And had this happened years ago, he would have learned some skills."

It appeared that he had none. This man was fumbling and stumbling around everyone and everything, as though he was dumbstruck by his predicament.

I was preoccupied with the husband as I entered the room to find a pleasant couple. Mrs. Robertson greeted me and then Mr. Robertson held his hand out to the wall and said, "It is nice to meet you." His greeting was obviously for me, so I awkwardly took his hand. He realized that I was on the other side of the room and shifted in his seat, to face in my direction. This blindness was so new that he was having a hard time using his hearing to its full advantage.

The interview with the wife was uneventful and we discussed treatment options for her varicosities. When satisfied with the information for Mrs. Robertson, the couple thanked me and waited for me to leave the room. I asked Mrs. Robertson to get dressed, and stepped from the room.

I was awestruck by Mr. Robertson's total lack of sight. I was extraordinarily interested in his condition. After a minute or two, I knocked on the door.

"How would you feel about me examining Mr. Robertson. I realize that you did not come here for that." I asked standing halfway through the door.

"That would be fine." Mr. Robertson was happy for a doctor to take an interest in him. He perked up a little.

As I examined him I asked many questions. "How long has this been going on?"

"One year, it was this time last year when he first got sick," Mrs. Robertson answered for him. "He wouldn't go to the doctor, he's stubborn. He got a cold first, and he just laid on the couch. Then one morning I brought him his breakfast, and couldn't wake him up, so I called 911." She was visibly irritated with her husband. "If he had gone to the doctor when this first started, he wouldn't be in this way."

Mr. Robertson had had a sinus infection. He was stoic, and would not seek medical treatment at the time. The infection had eroded his bones and entered the optic nerve, causing sudden and complete blindness. By the time he entered the hospital, the infection had entered his bloodstream, and Mr. Robertson went to the intensive care unit (ICU). He fought for his life.

His doctors had done all that they could. They successfully saved his life, but could do nothing for his blindness. The infection had done significant damage in his brain.

They discharged him to the care of a team of rehabilitation experts. The doctors told him that he would never see again, and would have to be trained to read and write in braille.

Mr. Robertson had a cheery disposition, and seemed to be receptive to open communication.

"Ok Lord, You've got me hook, line, and sinker. What is it that You want to do with this one? He clearly would be willing to do anything, but this one is out of my league. Blind! Lord, he's blind!" I couldn't be quiet long enough for the Lord to tell me what to do. "This man has been blind for a year, and most of that time he was fighting for his life. He is simply happy to be alive and with his wife."

"So, what now?" My mind paused from its silent monologue. In a flash I saw his childhood. And in that moment I knew that Mr. Robertson would see again.

"Mr. Robertson, are you interested in regaining your sight?" He nearly jumped from his chair.

"Yes, yes, but how? The other doctors told me that they had done everything. Is there a new treatment or surgery?"

"No, Mr. Robertson, there isn't." And I watched him sink back into his chair dejected.

"Mr. Robertson there are some games that we can play. If you play with me, I believe that we can successfully get at least part of your sight back. No guarantees, but I truly believe it."

"Ok Lord, I did my part, here's Your chance to do Yours. I just told a blind man that he will see again. I can't back out, can I? Maybe if I just run from the room, they won't notice, and I could disappear."

"Here we go, God."

"Mr. Robertson would you be willing to change some things in your life to get well?" I waited only a second for his response.

"I would change anything to see again." He seemed anxious to help the process along.

"Your wife said that you have trouble asking for help. Is this an area that you would be willing to change?

Mr. Robertson was a proud man, and never asked anyone for anything, especially not help. This was what had gotten him into trouble with his illness in the first place. He refused to go to the doctor to ask for help—an antibiotic, perhaps—so he had suffered the ultimate distress, near death and blindness.

I explained as best I could the process of mind, body and spirit as I understood it. Mr. Robertson was not real receptive to the spirit part. God to him, was the Person who punished him, so he had some stretching to do.

Willing to do what I suggested, Mr. Robertson and I started

digging into his feelings, his darkness, his dependence, and all of the other feelings associated with this new blindness.

We allowed his mind to take us on trips into his past where he felt these same feelings and we "healed the memories of a small boy abandoned, and neglected."

"Mr. Robertson are you willing to forgive those people?" I asked, feeling certain, that he would.

"Yes," and he cried.

He forgave the grown-ups that should have protected him. He talked to them through his small child understandings. He invited an Uncle into his memories. His uncle was able to be interjected into the memories and allow him to feel safe, connected, and loved.

We explored, and cried, laughed, and worked. Finally, we achieved the miracle. Mr. Robertson began to see some lights. He could make out the difference between light and dark. The more we worked, the more he was able to see.

We worked until we were both exhausted. We both felt as though we had just run a marathon. Mrs. Robertson sat there the entire time, quietly crying. The tears ran down her cheeks, but she dared not move for fear that it would disturb us.

If anyone tells you that what doctor's do with patients is easy, let him sit with me for just one day. That myth will be dispelled quickly. There are those who said that Mr. Robertson's eyes would have healed on their own. The neurologist and the neurosurgeon on the case would differ with you. Personally I don't know and don't care —this man was blind as a bat when he walked into my office, and could see when he left. What happened in between, only God knows, but I sure liked the result.

Mr. Robertson left that day without his cane. I heard from them many times over the years, as they sent postcards from various places telling me about their adventures. They always end their cards with a note that they are praying for me.

Mr. Robertson had many times in his life that reinforced what was in his "core" beliefs. He had a childhood filled with darkness, despair, and hopelessness. He had made a vow at some point in his young life that he would never again ask for help. He would be alone, and self-sufficient. He would live as an island. Mr. Robertson craved security, warmth, affection, and nurturing, but he was drawn like a moth to the things that he grew up with.

You want to know what the Lord showed me? I'm not going to tell you, because you may interpret it differently than I did. But I will tell you that I was certain that if Mr. Robertson and I could get to the real issue, we would get his sight back. You see, the Lord showed me that this was not about blindness, it was about living in isolation. The blindness was simply an extension of his beliefs. He was blind to anyone who could possibly assist him.

Sure, he had blamed God for his blindness. But Mr. Robertson knew that it was his own fault. He had to reach out to God for this healing, and he did.

Mr. Robertson was healed that day of several issues. He had more work to do, and was always faithful to ask for help. Mr. Robertson found a counselor to help him with day-to-day issues. He no longer had the stubborn nature that forced him to refuse other's assistance.

Mr. Robertson was healed, not only of his recent blindness, but of his lifelong struggle of self destruction.

Chapter 4
Discussion Questions

1. What in your life can you change? Are you stubborn? Anxious? Self-Centered?

2. How is this trait harming you?

3. How does it make you feel? Describe your feelings in detail.

4. If you eliminated it from you life, how would your life improve?

5. Close your eyes and travel back in time to the first time you ever felt the same *feelings*, as described in question #3. How old were you? Where were you? Allow your helper to step into the memory. Where is he? What is he doing? How do you feel with your helper with you? What does your helper say to you? Then open your eyes.

6. Remember again, your answer to the first question. Analyze your feelings now. How have your feelings changed.

Chapter 5

Psychological vs. Physical

During medical school we were trained that eighty percent of patients go to the doctor because of a psychological issue. Wow, 80 percent! That is a lot. Therefore most of the patients seen in a given day need a counselor, not a physician. If we look at it another way, one hundred percent of the people that come into the doctor's office have three things to consider: Mind, body and spirit. Eighty percent of them could potentially be helped and healed with mind therapy, memory therapy, "core" therapy, or counseling whichever you would like to call it. They could be helped maximally if intercepted early in the process.

I have a hard time believing the remaining twenty percent of the patients are purely physical with no need of counseling or prayer.

Where does the spiritual attention come in? Have we forgotten that without a spirit there is no body, nor mind? Without a spirit there is death, and the doctor's job is done. The grave-yards would be full. It would stand to reason then that we give attention to this area. Oh well, the good news is that some of us are catching on.

The eighty percenters start with a psychological issue. They don't know that they are thinking themselves sick, but they are. As a man thinketh, so he is. (See Proverbs 23:7, KJV.)

It is usually at this point that he goes to the doctor and asks for a pill, potion, or relief. The doctor obliges and everyone is happy; everyone except the mind and the spirit of the patient. Only one-third of the patient was cared for.

The patient returns to the doctor with the same or similar complaint. The doctor treats the body again. Only this time, the doctor suggests that the patient go to a counselor. The patient replies, "You think this is all in my head? I'm not crazy I'm sick. I need a pill not a shrink."

The doctor helped the body with a symptom, but not with the problem (the one in the mind). Did anyone address the etiology of the disease? No. The response from the patient about counseling was so negative, the doctor will be more cautious in future interactions with patients.

Had the patient been receptive to counseling two thirds of the individual could have been helped. Potentially the originating challenge could have been discovered, and dealt with. But if not, the patient could become a chronic patient.

Doctors have passions just like the rest of humanity. But, when it comes to chronic illnesses, most doctors shudder at the idea of a patient remaining in his illness for long periods of time.

Chronic means ongoing or longstanding. The word *chronic* makes most doctors cringe with the certain knowledge that the patient is going to be placed into a situation of no return. The patient will be returning frequently or will be better, then worse, then better, then worse.

Patients with chronic illnesses are desperate, hopeless, sometimes incurable. Mostly they are resolved to having "their" disease for the rest of their lives. Doctors have given them an assortment of pills, potions, surgeries, and therapies. Some doctors have said, "it is in your head", and some doctors have discharged the patient with out a single word.

As a doctor, my idea of helping someone is this. The patient comes to the office. I assess the situation. If it is within my area of expertise, I offer the options based on my experience and knowledge. If it is not within my field, I refer the patient to someone who can potentially help. Then we as a team determine the best treatment plan and implement it. The patient gets well, or at least significantly better. The patient is discharged with a successful resolution to his ailments, and complaints.

When a patient presents with a chronic complaint, and they have seen every doctor in town, I wonder the same thing that every other doctor wonders, "Is it all in the patient's head?" "Do I have anything to offer this patient that other doctors didn't have, or were unable to give?" The answer is yes! Remember, 80 percent of patients need a psychiatrist! It *is* in their head. The advantage that I bring is my understanding of the mind. The professors in medical school taught us about the eighty percenters, but didn't teach us how to get them well. You see, patients are seeking help. They are crying out to be healed. They don't know how to do it, so they come to us for help. The problem is that most doctors are so weary from seeing sick people all day, they become tired of losing the battle of the ill. They feel like they are on a never-ending treadmill of sickness. The young spunky medical student has become a tired physician feeling like a tidal wave of illness has descended upon him.

Chronic illness has captured my heart, because of its very nature.

Let me tell you a short story. I was board certified and was a successful practicing physician. Patients came and went, just like in my training. My superiors had taught me well, and rarely did I experience any trepidation in doing a differential diagnosis on a patient. There was a nagging problem with a certain segment of patients though. Too often to ignore, patients would come in for an issue, and would also ask me to look at their legs. They had painful legs. The patient would describe going to doctor after doctor, only to be told to live with it. The patient would expose a leg to display a grotesque array of gnarled veins wrapping around their leg like a serpent. The veins often were so huge that the patient would wear ace wraps to keep the veins from bulging too horribly. The patients would show me ulcers in various states of infection, oozing, and carved out lesions on their ankle.

But the story was always the same. "The doctors have done all that they can do. The doctors have told me to live with it."

So, I decided to find out more. If we could send men to the moon, then certainly someone on this planet could treat this disease. So my search began. Slowly but successfully, I found the experts in the phlebology (vein) world. I asked them to teach me, and they did. I traveled to wonderful and varied parts of the world to train with these surgeons. I had the fabulous fortune of operating with them and being trained by the best.

Dr. John Bergan, of The University of California at La Jolla, was one of these mentors. Dr. Bergan had such compassion for the patients, it was palpable. Dr. Bergan would gently and easily help the patients that everyone else had given up on.

Dr. Bergan had reason to be short-tempered. He trained vascular surgery fellows, surgery residents, students, as well as take care of an ever-growing patient base. I never once saw him lose his temper.

Once in the operating room, a nurse had fumble fingers, and just could not do anything correctly. She seemed intimidated by the presence of so many high-powered surgeons in the operating theatre, but her job was to hand Dr. Bergan instruments. After many fumbled attempts to retrieve lost scalpels and forceps, Dr. Bergan gently spoke to her and stopped the surgery for a few seconds. His calm demeanor and soft words were all that the nervous Nellie nurse needed to resume her duties and help him in his pursuit of a successful surgery.

Dr. Bergan believed that the most important person in the world was the one in front of him, at that moment. I learned a great deal more than surgery from him. He was always a gentleman, and a gentle man.

Operating with surgeons is treacherous, when surgeons get upset, they are likely to scream, throw things or be just down right unpredictable. But Dr. Bergan was the consummate steady state. His persistent pursuit of therapies for the vein patients was admirable. And I was blessed with the opportunity to learn from this master.

I returned to my practice in Florida armed with the knowledge of some great surgeons. I had learned my lessons well and soon became the last stop for varicose vein patients. Instead of sending them away empty handed, I could offer treatments and therapies that worked. One chronic illness became manageable, and treatable. Many legs were saved and many lives were changed.

This quest for treatment of the chronic phlebology patient spilled over into my medical practice as a whole. Other chronic illnesses gained my attention, and I began to look for common threads.

I remembered the eighty percenters. Could this classification of "chronic" somehow be an indicator? Could it be that a great majority of these patients had started with a simple manageable mental challenge, and had grown into a life altering "chronic" condition?

Consider the placebo, a medicine which has no inherent pertinent pharmacologic activity, but is effective only by virtue of the factor of suggestion. Let us look at a practical, everyday use of a placebo. A child scraped his knee and runs to his mother. His mother says, "Let's kiss it and make it better." The child stops crying as soon as the kiss is administered. This is a suggestion and an action, which was effectively administered to the child. The child got better, not because there was a pharmacological agent in mom's kiss, but because the child "believed" that the kiss would make it better.

In the surgical world I told my patients that if they walked one hour per day, they would have a painfree surgery. They were required to start walking prior to surgery, then continue after. I also told them "in all my years of operating on people, no one has ever used more than three pain pills." I would then follow this with, "I am prescribing thirty pills for you just in case you are the first patient to need them. I know that there is a possibility of you needing pain killers, and I will give them to you in case you are the first, but I don't want you to be the first, do you?"

Anyone out there who routinely creates pain in individuals can use this same technique. It works every time. The mind of the patient has been convinced of the painfree surgery. And I've never created a drug dependence. My patients just don't do it. Long before they have surgery, they talk to other patients in the waiting room, and are reassured that their surgery will be pain free. My patients speak eloquently about how I treat them, operate on them, and deliver to them a pleasant experience. This is as opposed to "traditional surgery," where the patient is recovering for six weeks and pain-ridden for most of it.

The surgery I perform is no different than other physicians. I simply convince the patient of a different post-operative course. Am I tricking them? Yes, absolutely I am! I understand the power of words, and the ability of words to give life or death. I use my words to help the patient have a pleasant experience, while achieving their goal. Is post-operative pain a requirement? No, it is not. Pain is an indicator that something is wrong in the body. Once the mind has received that information, there is no further need for pain.

Pain clinics are sprouting up. They treat patients with drugs, shots, surgeries, and more. The doctors have their hands full. When a person is referred to a pain clinic, it is usually the last stop.

"We have nothing more to offer you." These are the commonly used words from frustrated physicians, trying desperately to help.

Patients and physicians develop a strong bond. The patient has a sense of security with "their" doctor. When a patient is referred to a different physician, the patient feels alone. Fear enters the picture and the patient must attempt to form a new bond with the new physician. If the new physician does not meet the expectations of the patient, often there is a feeling of abandonment and isolation.

If a physician refers the patient to a psychiatrist or counselor, the patient feels like the original doctor is writing them off as crazy. This could not be further from the truth.

Many books have been published regarding the association of diseases and their originating psychological issue. Having this knowledge ingrained in physicians would be wonderful. It would facilitate the process of treating the symptom and the cause—the body and the mind. Then two-thirds of the individual would be healed.

I think most patients would prefer words of healing from "their" doctor. Think about this. This means that I as a physician must use my words wisely, and persuasively to achieve the desired result. I do not believe that a patient must live in pain after surgery, therefore, I convince them that "mom will kiss it, and it will not hurt anymore." I use grown up language of course, but this is the link to that inner part of the child that I can get hold of.

The links between the mind and the illness have been studied. Books have been written about them. So why then do we continue to treat only the body, leaving two-thirds of the individual out of the equation?

I will give you some of the common ones that purely by my observations seem to repeat themselves on a regular cycle. This is not an exhaustive list, and is not written to supercede medical care. Quite the contrary, I believe that this information should be used in conjunction with your doctor.

The process of putting this list together was experiential. Sometimes, I "heard" from that still small voice, and sometimes I stumbled on information from the patient.

I read about priests teaching "prayers" for healing. Then psychiatrists and psychologists began talking about healing "from the inside out." I am sorry to say that we physicians, the ones that treat the body—the "outside"—are the last to catch on. Don't take my word for it, go memory mining for yourself:

> Diabetes—self hatred, and a lack of balance in their life. Diabetics often look at themselves with a scornful eye. They do not like themselves.
>
> Depression—repressed anger. If you ask a depressed person to describe their feelings, they frequently will say, "My feelings don't matter." Something obviously is repressed. Continue to dig and you will find the anger. But be careful with this one, because the anger may be directed at you.
>
> Back Pain—fear is the most common element here. The fear may be of family issues, financial issues, or

> career are among consistent examples. Often the fear is worse than actually confronting the issue.
>
> Dementia—these patients have experienced more pain in their life than they can handle. They escape into a place where they are comfortable and happy. These people can usually come back to the present and stay for a while.

There are probably as many aches and pains, diseases and syndromes as there are personal issues. When a person says, "my legs are hurting," the first thing I do is ask God. The second thing that I do is ask the patient. If these two things don't match up, I keep digging.

Sometimes the patient refuses to tell you about their issue. Like Virginia, you will read about soon. She had cancer, and we could not find an obvious issue. I kept hearing conflicting information from my spirit and from her. In this case I always trust my spirit. Patients can lie, so ask, "How many drinks do you have per day?" If the patient says four, you can bet your bottom dollar that lab tests would come back indicating double that amount. Their liver will tell the truth, even if they won't.

I believe that patients don't want to lie, they want you (the helper or physician) to think well of them. For example, treating someone for a heart attack. Ask a heart attack victim to describe his pain, and you are likely to get, "My chest feels like an elephant is sitting on it and crushing it. This one is not too hard to figure out, right. They are dealing with a broken heart. Now it is your job to go memory mining and find the memory, heal it and help this person. If their spouse is sitting in the room, they are not likely to tell you of their first love and how "crushed" they were. They are not going to tell you that they never recovered from the trauma of seeing their best friend date the love of their life. And forty years later, most people would say something like, "Oh it was nothing, it was a long time ago." These words are a guaranteed trip down memory lane.

Other times the patient has stuffed the memory so far back into the closets of their life that they really don't have a conscious memory of it. Then the digging gets really fun. You hear the whisper from your spirit and must trust that information.

Is the heart attack a twenty percenter or an eighty percenter? At the point of the heart attack he is both. He needs help from every angle. If the heart is damaged too much, too much pain has passed through that heart, the heart will stop forever. But if you can get to him before that, you have great things in store.

Let me tell you a story. Every year, my sister and I go home. We bring all four children and move in with our parents for a month. It is a wonderful time of laughter and playing. Work is the farthest thing from my mind.

Biking and swimming and singing. These are the things that we enjoy.

In the middle of this period, last year, my assistant called me and told me, "Dr. Speed, I'm sorry to bother you, but I just got a call that you want to know about." She knows me better than I know myself.

"A woman forty-eight-years-old just called. She is having open-heart surgery in two weeks, and she is scared. She wants to know if you will work with her. She wants to know if there is anything you can do. She is really scared."

My dilemma was simple really. I was six hundred miles from my office. There was no way that I could meet her and get her ready for surgery two weeks later unless I cut my only vacation off right then—and I treasure my vacations.

"Call her and ask if she would be willing to work with me

over the phone. If the answer is yes, then I'll do it. If she says no, please give her a referral to a local counselor."

"Hey Doc, she said the phone is fine. Here is her number."

I called her and we talked for an hour. I told her the process as I understood it. I told her that we would not be able to meet in person, but did not tell her why. I asked her to get a headset for her phone, so that she could lie back without holding the phone. And when she had that all hooked up, we would start. She called within twenty-four hours with her homework done.

"Lie back and let's get comfortable with each other." I asked her questions and she became relaxed. I gave her suggestions and some she could accept and some she couldn't. We identified many areas that needed exploration. For the first day, we simply did some relaxation exercises. She seemed pleased to continue, so we talked every day.

During the phone sessions, I lead her down paths to her youth. She sometimes went effortlessly, sometimes she resisted. Since we were dealing with a severely weakened heart, I wasn't anxious to stress her too much.

She recalled being alone, stuck behind a door for several hours as a toddler. She was terrified. She was certain that she would never see her mother again. Imagine the feelings. The only thing that she could hear, were voices that sounded very far away. So we went to that small child, and had her interject someone into the memory. Once the extra person was in the picture, we had them talk to the small child and tell her all of the good things that were going to happen in her life. The terrified little girl was calmed. When we finished for that day, she felt as though she could go through with her surgery. As you may have surmised, the patient was very afraid of enclosed spaces. The thought of someone putting a mask on her and holding her head down, while she breathed gas was too much for her. She could not bear the thought of it. She considered canceling the surgery. After we found and healed this memory, she was instantly relieved of the fear. She also discovered that she could close doors in her house, and not get fearful.

We worked every day for about an hour. We only had two weeks to prepare her for surgery, and neither of us wanted to leave anything to chance. If a patient is ready to go through surgery, it is an easy matter. If the patient is nervous or scared the surgery is never quite as easy.

Sometimes we talked and laughed, sometimes we had so many memories to deal with, we just dove right into them. But then we got the breakthrough that we were looking for. She called and said that she had been calm all day. She knew that she was ready, and she wanted to have the surgery. No trepidation, no fear. She felt excitement that she would be able to travel again, and play golf. She and her husband could run with the dogs. She was ready. She confessed that day, "I was really afraid of dying, and I'm not now." The feeling of death was gone, and she was ready to begin the path to recovery.

Now you may be asking, why wasn't she healed completely? Why wasn't her heart healed? Why did she need open-heart surgery? I don't know. These are God's issues. I did what I could. I asked Him what he wanted of me and I was obedient. He did the rest.

She went through a flawless surgery. I returned to Florida the day after surgery, and walked into her hospital room. She was up and around. She looked great. And she healed quickly.

We don't always know what healing means. I want it to mean 100 percent healthy in mind, body, and spirit, but sometimes the Lord has other plans. Sometimes, I need to operate to help a patient, sometimes I don't.

Chapter 5
Discussion Questions

1. What are you suffering with? Allergies, depression, chronic fatigue, increased weight, acid reflux? What is it that you want to change? (Choose something different than from previous chapters.)

2. Are you willing to have "counseling" to get rid of it?

3. Would you tell me that you need a pill, not a shrink?

4. Do you have a "chronic" condition?

5. Would you consider that 80 percent of your problem started "In your head?"

6. Describe your *feelings* regarding your chronic issue. Write in great detail about your feelings.

7. Describe a recent memory that hurt very bad. Write in detail about it. Then heal the memory. (Remember your Helper.)

8. Recall and describe a childhood memory that scared the socks off of you. Heal the memory. (Remember your Helper.)

Chapter 6

Fibromyalgia No More

HAVE I LOST my mind, why am I drawn to take care of the people that no other doctor wants. Believe me my name is not Mother Teresa. I have no desire to go to Calcutta and live amongst the poorest of the poor. So why is the Lord placing this burden in my heart for the hopeless.

"You are sent to *this* place." This is all I've heard from my spirit. Is the Lord telling me that I am to work with the people of my community? I have no idea. Usually when you are sent, you *go* somewhere. The only place that I am going is crazy, waiting on the next person who has some incurable illness that I can get my hands on. Why doesn't the Lord just hook up the Bat phone and allow me access to the Throne room. Then He can tell me what He wants me to do, and I will do my best to obey. But this urging to help the helpless is really getting interesting.

"I'm a surgeon Lord, can't You use me to cut people up? Maybe I can do some mission work with a team of surgeons, and we can work for You in a needy area, and I can do what I do best, operate on people?"

Do you argue with the Lord? I must be a hard study for Him. He trained me to be the best surgeon that I can be, then uses me to do other things. Wow. The Lord sure has a sense of humor. He keeps pushing me into this healing thing, and

I keep operating on people. The more I am open to Him, the more patients show up on my doorstep with other "incurable" illnesses. I yell and scream at Him, and fortunately He hasn't sent a lightning bolt down for me yet. He must be most patient, because my earthly Father would not allow me to argue nearly so much. My daddy would probably just tell me, "Hush and get to work, and quit your whining."

It was a day like any other. Patients came and went, consultations and surgeries, treatments and injections. Nothing special had happened this day, including meeting Barbara. She came in for an evaluation of her varicosities. She needed surgery to remove the bulging tortuous snakes running the length of her legs. The leg issue was routine for me, and we scheduled her for surgery. There was something about Barbara though, she had a strong belief in the Lord, and didn't mind sharing it. She let me know at every opportunity that she was a God-fearing woman, and did her best to lead a Godly life. Barbara held her beliefs in high esteem and was uncompromising.

I am pretty quiet around people when I initially meet them. My daddy used to say, "be quiet and let people wonder how smart you are, or open you mouth and prove to them how ignorant you are." "Be quiet and learn. You cannot learn by talking." Although I've never asked Daddy where he got the phrase, the Bible puts it this way,

> When there are many words, transgression is unavoidable, But he who restrains his lips is wise.
>
> —Proverbs 10:19

> A truly wise person uses few words; a person with understanding is even-tempered. Even fools are

> thought to be wise when they keep silent; when they keep their mouths shut, they seem intelligent.
>
> —Proverbs 17:27–28

Initially, I remain relatively in a receptive mode around strangers, so that I can learn. People often get the impression that I am shy...not! But I am not about to open my mouth and prove my ignorance. Daddy taught me well as a youngster. Then as I began studying Proverbs, the Bible confirmed my father's teachings. I tell my parents that it is their fault that I am the way I am. It is fun to tease them, and watch my mother's reactions. But in my adult life, finding actual Bible verses to back up my parents' teachings has been profound.

Barbara had prayed with some high-powered people over the years and had been involved with more miracles than I could imagine. She was a wealth of information.

"Oh no, I'm getting that nagging feeling again." She had a chronic illness that had not been healed. Uh oh, here I go again. "Lord, no! This woman is capable of doing anything she wants in prayer. I am *not* opening my mouth. Not now, not with her, no, no, no!" If there had been a mind reader around he would have heard me *screaming* at the Lord.

She had fibromyalgia. She suffered greatly. She had a physician who was trying to "manage" her fibromyalgia with drugs and advice. Barbara was tired, you could see it in her eyes. She didn't believe she would ever have relief of her chronic pain. She was hurting, and attempting to live with it.

The more Barbara and I talked, the bolder I became. Finally I asked her, "Do you want to get rid of this fibromyalgia?"

Shocked, she said "Well...well, yes, of course I do, but there is no cure. There is no way to get rid of it." This was a conditioned response from years of going to doctors. She knew the words, and believed them to be true.

"What if there is a way? Would you be interested?" I quickly asked, and quietly hoping that she would say no, so I didn't have to prove myself out to be a charlatan. Barbara said, "I am always open to prayer." So we began.

Barbara was more than willing to participate in the process. She was open and eager to rid herself of the thing called fibromyalgia. Barbara told me of her life, family, and childhood. She laughed when she recounted memories of long ago. You know the process of healing of the memories, so I won't go through it here. We healed many things in her memories and got rid of the fibromyalgia that day. Barbara was in a state of disbelief, shock, and amazement. She was so accustomed to having recurrent bouts that she put off the celebration.

By the time we took Barbara to surgery for her varicosities, her fibromyalgia had been gone for months, and she had enjoyed the results of being pain free. Barbara had tried everything to rid herself of that malady. She was tired of trying, and was tired of the medications prescribed for it. She went through the surgery with flying colors, and to this day, three years hence has had no recurrence.

Since taking care of Barbara and her fibromyalgia, I've treated many people with this "incurable" issue. It has become one of the fun ones, because "It" responds so well to these healing techniques. These techniques are nothing new of course. Throughout time, men have always healed the mind, and the body followed. They have also done it the other way around, they have hurt the mind and the body followed. We are an interconnected mind, body, and spirit. You cannot do one without the other being affected.

Let us heal the body, begin to exercise, eat right and get proper amounts of sleep. The body begins to heal and strengthen, so guess what happens to the mind. You got it. The mind follows.

The mind is rooting for the body saying, "Wow, you started taking better care of yourself, and I feel better, too."

I have left out the spiritual part, for the sake of convenience because you get the point. Feed one and the others benefit. Harm one and the others are harmed. Beat a child physically and his emotional and spiritual life suffers. Praise a child and his body and spirit fly.

Chapter 6
Discussion Questions

1. Has the Lord ever pushed you to learn new skills? What were they? How has He used these new skills?

2. Do you hesitantly learn new skills or do you embrace the opportunity knowing that God will use them to His Glory?

3. When you meet someone new, how do you act? Are you receptive, receiving, quiet or talkative?

4. Have you been prayed for and not healed? Have you "believed" for something and it did not come to pass? Have you considered that maybe God is waiting until you find another avenue to receive your blessing?

5. To receive from the Lord, are you willing to change the way that you are thinking? Are you willing to change some habits? Are you willing to do what it takes to push through and conquer this change?

Chapter 7

Fighter Pilots

ARE YOU BORED yet? Have you tired of hearing about the helpless and the hopeless? My life seems to be filled with them. The Lord has placed something inside of me that comes with the territory. It is that thing that makes me stop at car accidents. I am the one running toward the injured.

One of my most memorable car crashes—let me set the record straight, I am not in them, and I have not caused them. I often arrive at the scene soon after the crash to take care of the injured—was a bad one, people were seriously injured. There was blood everywhere. I am well versed at handling blood, it is my job, I do it for a living. But this time, things were ugly. I mean really ugly, if you catch my drift. I found a woman, who had passed her need for a doctor. She needed the medical examiner.

I took a moment and a breath to compose myself, when I heard a whimpering that seemed to be coming from a pile of metal rubble. It was very faint, like it was either far away or very weak. The car looked like a piece of aluminum foil wrapped around several trees. I ran to the crumpled metal and could not find anything that looked like a door or handle. I climbed on top of the car and a hole was there, where the sunroof should have been. I went in head first, faster than I thought possible. Inside a cocoon of metal, as if the car had just folded around it, was an infant in a car seat. He was just whimpering. I was able to get the belts opened and the child extricated from the metal.

Miraculously, the child was alive, without a scratch. I couldn't say the same for me. While diving through the metal to find the baby, I had been scraped and cut. I looked more like a victim than a rescue worker.

I had on previously white pants. You know the kind. Your favorite pants, the ones you wear and feel good in? Instead of white jeans, I looked like I had just walked through a Jackson Pollack studio. Splashes of blood were everywhere. Grass stains and ripped fabric made up the rest of the outfit.

A paramedic arrived. He was clean, young, and shocked at the sight before him. He had gloves in hand and attempted to hand them to me saying something intelligent like, "Would you like to put these on?" I'm always on my best behavior (don't believe this last statement) and I thanked him for his thoughtfulness and kindness and said, "It seems to be a bit late for those."

I can't help it. I have this belief that there are only two kinds of people in the world: the fighter pilots and the rest of the world. Some of us run to the accident, the rest of the planet runs away. Some of us run to the fire; the rest just stand there and watch the house burn, wondering when someone will come to help. Some of us fly planes, everyone else rides. Some of us search for survivors, while some wait to put on rubber gloves so we won't get our hands dirty.

Some of us are just hard-wired this way. I can't stop, just as others can't start. It is the way the Lord programmed us. The person who is nauseated at the sight of a drop of blood will not be able to walk up to a car that has flipped seven times and tolerate the scene that awaits. I will never be able to sit and watch without running to help.

The Lord knows these things about you, and me. He also

knows that He has a hard time getting my attention sometimes. So, He keeps me on my toes, by testing me occasionally. Sort of like a fire drill to see if I will listen quickly, or if I will argue first. Well you can imagine what my response is most of the time. And this particular evening, He was really struggling with me.

Usually my testing ground is in broad daylight, on roads in the city. I get the urging, or feeling to go down a certain road. If I do it correctly, I am rewarded with green lights and no traffic. If I ignore Him, I get traffic jams, and I hit every light on this side of the Mississippi river. This can be very frustrating, especially if I have my own agenda. I love to learn, but why does He want to teach me when I have something else to do? Can't He wait until I get my chores done?

These urgings come too often to ignore, and If I pass my training sessions often enough, I'm greeted with a new set of rules. Fortunately, I am usually able to catch on, ultimately.

Just when I think I know what the Lord is calling me to do, He changes the menu, and I have to choose again. I was comfortable with the feeling of turning down certain roads, and then He changed the feelings.

I really have a hard time with moving targets, so He uses them to keep me on my toes. The Lord seems to be insisting that I continue to grow and "hear" more subtle things. I can imagine him laughing, "Ok it's time to change things up again. Everybody watch, and see how she handles this one!"

I really don't want to be a hard study for the Lord. I want to understand whatever He is trying to teach me, and move on. My frustration level rises when I can't figure things out. Although I attempt to acknowledge when I "hear" things, often I confuse it with my own insecurities.

It was about nine o'clock on a moonless night. Several of us had gone to an auction. We were all tired and ready to go home. We jumped into the car. It was so dark out that even the most comfortable people would have been extra cautious. I was driving. My infant daughter was in the back seat with her Godmother. The men were comfortable as passengers. This in itself was strange, because I am rarely the driver. On the drive home, we went down a dark lonely stretch of Highway 301 between Wildwood and Webster, Florida. Nothing is on this road except a couple of pig farms. The road is so narrow, that even during the day, it will give you the willies when you meet another vehicle on the road. There is no shoulder, only a huge ditch. If your tires fall off of the black top, you are going in the ditch.

"Stop the car!" I heard it in my spirit. I looked around. Nothing out of the ordinary. No car crashes, no cars, no people.

"I must have made it up. This road is creeping me out," I thought as I drove toward home. I don't like that stretch of 301 in the daytime so driving at night was not high on my priority list. Everyone had funny experiences at the Webster Critter Auction, so the car was full of laughter.

"Oh no, the baby needs to be changed, stop the car!" Voices from the back seat were laughing and rolling down the windows. Obviously a smell had emerged from the car seat that was not pleasant.

"I'll stop in Wildwood, as soon as we can get off of the road." I continued driving on that spooky dark road. I had a strong feeling that said, "Stop the Car!" And as usual I argued with it.

"I can't stop, if I do, there is no shoulder only a ditch, and we can't stop in the middle of the road. Someone would hit us before they even saw us." A feeling of dread had filled my body, and I slowed the car to a near crawl. Not one car had passed us, neither had one car come from the opposite direction. "Surely if I stop I would be in the middle of the road, I would not have time to alert an oncoming driver. Even my headlights seemed too dim, and not illuminating the road. Maybe there is a fog that is causing this feeling. There are *no* cars on this road." This was odd, since we had recently left the Critter auction, we anticipated at least some other people to be traveling home.

Once the odor had been ushered out of the window, we resumed our laughter about the people and animals at the Critter auction.

"Stop the Car!" Now it was yelling at me. This was no urging, this was down right loud.

I slowed the car more. Then my daughter began to scream, like only an infant can. Nothing consoled her. Not her bottle, not a pacifier, nothing. She was screaming like we had buckled her skin into the seatbelt and pinched it.

This time I stopped and pulled over as far as I could. As luck would have it, there was a piece of a concrete drive, and I pulled onto it. I hopped out of the car, looked around still sensing terror, but trying to remain calm. I spoke to my infant who immediately stopped crying. We all looked at each other and shrugged. "Oh, well, some things just don't make sense." I closed the back door to the car. As I was reaching for the handle to my door, a car came out of nowhere from behind us. I had not seen his lights coming, nor had I seen him getting close. I was simply startled and surprised by the sudden appearance of a large Buick passing so close to me, I hugged the car. It felt like the car had glided past within inches. Surely it was more than that, but I don't remember him changing lanes to avoid me. Well anyway, he passed, I watched his tail lights disappear quickly into the darkness. The road again resumed its isolated existence.

I was so rattled by the proximity of the car that I cautiously, and slowly got back into the car, then onto the road. The feeling of dread was intense now. "Well, it must be because of that other car." I tried to console myself.

Everyone else in the car was calling me Grandma Moses because I was driving so slowly. "Oh, alright, I'll pick it up." I wanted to believe the worse was over, and I could relax.

"Stop the Car!" I heard it again.

"Who said that?" I asked as I saw something in the ditch to my right going in the opposite direction. A large object flew over my car, and another hit the undercarriage of the car. I slammed on the brakes just behind the Buick that had passed us minutes before.

Everyone, except the baby and her Godmother got out of the car. We all ran to the man, "What is it? What's wrong?"

The man was clearly in shock, he had hit something, and could not tell us what. "There were two," was all he could say.

"Hopefully it was a deer," I thought. But the man didn't look like he had hit a deer. This was much worse. The men grabbed flashlights, and started combing the ditches.

I walked down the road, looking for what I had hit. A large can of beans had hit the underside of the car, and had burst. Further down the road, I found another can, that was intact. It had bounced farther.

"Oh, God, please tell me this didn't happen!" My thoughts were screaming, hoping that the groceries did not belong to a person but maybe they had been blown out of a truck.

"It's a bicycle, or what is left of one." I could not see who was in the ditch, but between my car and his, to our right were the mangled remains of a bike. It looked like a pretzel twisted on itself. I could not believe that it had been a usable tool just minutes before.

"Teri, we need you over here!" I dreaded those words. I ran

as fast as possible down into the ditch. What I found was what mother's nightmares are all about. This is the reason mother's break out into cold sweats when the phone rings in the dark of the night.

A truck appeared and parked behind my car. Several men emerged. They lived at the next farm. A young boy had ridden his bike in the ditch to get them. "So that is what I caught out of the corner of my eye. It was him peddling his bicycle furiously." I was comforted that he was alive. He was shaking violently and not talking though. His eyes darted around like he expected someone to pop up at any moment.

As the story unfolded, two teenage boys had ridden their bikes to the store in Wildwood, several miles away, to pick up a few things. They were on their way home, riding their bikes down the middle of the road. They were playing chicken. Since no cars had gone down the road in a very long time the boys were cocky and loud. Out of nowhere a car appeared and hit one of the boys, barely missing the other. The man driving the car had stopped as soon as he hit the boy. The other boy rode down the ditch to the closest farm to get help.

We helped the driver sit down and attempted to calm him. Unfortunately, he had seen the boy on impact, and could not handle the site. His system went into shock, and he was making no sense. Rescue workers arrived and helped him into an ambulance.

As I stood there, the enormity of what had happened sank into my soul. I had heard the command. "Stop the car." I was not obedient, so my daughter filled her diaper. I still did not stop, so she screamed in such a way that I could not and would not ignore her. Who had pinched her hard enough to make her scream like that? Finally I stopped the car. Had I continued to be disobedient, I would have been the one in shock. I would have hit that teenage boy. Whenever I am getting a bit too big for my britches, and feel like I am catching on, the Lord replays the visual recording of that night, and what I found in the ditch after they yelled, "Teri we need you over here!"

I am reminded that God is always here to help us, and to give us information to guide us on our way, and protect us on our path. He doesn't do it once or twice. He continues to give it, even when we are stubborn and don't listen. The way that you "hear" is your bat phone with God. Everyone receives differently.

Think of it this way. I have an old television at my house. It has rabbit ears on top of it that are used for the antennae. I must adjust them frequently to get the best reception. At your house, you have High Definition television. You receive signal differently than I do. We both receive if we turn our respective televisions on. If we don't turn them on, we get silence.

I had finally come to the realization that I was one of the fighter pilots, and it was OK with me. While others prayed prayers of petition, I had a different calling. It was OK to be different. Or was it? I had asked God to use me. I had asked God to help me know Him better. But I had this strange idea that prayers and talking to God were supposed to be some silent, kneeling, reverent thing. It was supposed to happen on my knees in church. It seemed that God loved to catch me off guard and see if I could tell if it was Him.

Speaking of prayer, one day I was in the sanctuary of the church. My mind was not at all focused on the sermon. For some strange reason, I could only focus on leaving the church. "Well certainly this is not God urging me to leave the church. God just would not do that."

"Get up and go outside." The feeling would not leave me.

The priest was talking, and the congregation was listening.

I had to go to the ladies room. "Oh I can wait." I thought as the priest droned on. Every second was agony, I had to go to the ladies room. I wasn't listening to the sermon anyway, because my body was screaming at me. "I'll just wait until he's finished, then I'll make a mad dash to the door." I tried and tried to sit still and focus my attention on the words coming from the front of the church.

Mind over matter. Certainly I can sit here long enough to be polite to the priest. But my body became more uncomfortable. I scolded myself for drinking coffee prior to the church service. Nothing worked. Finally, I leapt from my seat and bolted for the door. In my hurry, I'm sure that I made quite a scene. The door flew open and I ran down the corridor.

"Doc, Hey Doc. I need you. Please do you have just a minute? Doc, I just need to talk to you for a second." Has anyone ever said those words to you? You know that you are in for a lengthy discussion, and it is going to be one that you are not interested in. It is not going to be just a second, or a minute, or even a few minutes. It is going to be a long conversation. Oh Bother. I looked at the sanctuary. I looked at the ladies room. I felt trapped in time. I couldn't just walk off. I saw the desperation in her eyes, and heard the panic in her voice. I was frozen to the spot and drawn to her aid.

"Please excuse me for a moment, I must excuse myself, but I'll be right back." I tried to go, but she persisted. She began to follow me. "OK", I thought, "she can follow me, then we can talk".

Once inside, she began to cry quietly, and talk. My body was screaming. But then as I looked at her, all notions of myself disappeared, and her words began to sink into my soul.

She told me of her ordeal with the pain doctors. "I've been operated on to cut some nerves. After they cut the nerves, the doctors said that the pain would go away. It got worse. I can't bear it. The doctor put in a morphine pump, and it worked fine for a while. So long as the morphine pump was in my body, I could push the button, and I would feel fine. But then the pump fell out, and the doctors will not replace it. The doctors said that I am too dependent on the medication. The doctors don't want to give me any more drugs, they say I'm taking too much, but I can't tolerate the pain."

Agnes had been working when a forklift operator dropped a huge piece of equipment on her. She was pinned beneath the equipment for hours, while they removed the debris and equipment from her. Her leg was crushed, and in that moment, she had been sure of her transition to heaven. It was not to be though, and she survived. She ultimately was left with a nerve that fired at will. Reflex Sympathetic Dystrophy is a horrible disease that affects a nerve and the overlying skin. The nerve is injured and it fires constantly. Even removing the nerve from the body, doesn't cure the problem. The overlying skin goes through a series of processes where is becomes swollen, then atrophies. The pain of the overlying skin can be worse than the nerve. Agnes was desperate. She had heard the stories, she had heard the verdicts, but she was having a hard time believing that the rest of her life was going to be spent in such torture.

Agnes saw me in the hall and asked for help. A divine connection? You decide. She had previously been a patient of mine and knew that I was a surgeon, not a pain specialist. She saw me in the hall and yelled at me. She demanded my attention, when normally she is a mild mannered soft-spoken woman.

I do not leave the sanctuary during sermons. I just don't do it. I was however compelled by my body to get out of there at that exact moment. Had I seen her after the service, I would have had my children with me and we would not have had the freedom to talk openly.

Agnes's condition had frustrated her doctors beyond their capabilities, and she needed help. She looked at me with that look. I knew that she would be my next victim. So I took one of those resignation breaths, and went to work. I got her to relax, as much as possible and we began to talk.

You know the drill. Ask God. He will tell you where to start, and if He doesn't (or you don't listen) start anyway, He will catch up and tell you where to go.

"This feeling that you have inside your body, when was the first time that you felt it? Had you ever felt a similar feeling before the accident? Imagine that you can go back and remember a time like that. It may have been as a young adult, or as a child. Now just imagine that you can remember the first time that you ever felt that way." Agnes easily and effortlessly trusted me enough to follow my instructions and she remembered many things in her childhood that had felt hopeless, helpless, and betrayed. We spent some time traveling around in the pond of memories healing the earliest ones that could have caused these feelings. She was open and willing to try anything.

Agnes used a white light to join her in the accident. She was able to rewrite the memory with the certainty of living, healing, and laughing. She was able through the white light, to assure herself that she would live another day, to see her husband.

Sure she had been injured, but not every injured person develops Reflex Sympathetic Dystrophy. Something was causing it, and I was going to find it, Lord willing. I was going to go in and cut it out, like I cut out body parts that malfunction. I was after a memory that had created a toehold for this pain. She began to experience a calmness and some relief. She allowed the white light to go into her childhood, and heal.

"I don't want to quit, it feels good," Agnes told me. It had been a long time since she had been pain free. Relief was enough to motivate her. Slowly but surely, we knew we had made progress when she looked up and said, "I don't hurt."

Agnes and I quit for the day, as people started leaving the sanctuary. She was not completely relieved of her pain, so I gave her a tape to listen to at night. For Agnes, relief was good enough.

Agnes followed through with her homework assignments. I gave her a recording of my voice to guide her through some relaxation exercises. She called a few days later, "My husband saw such an improvement in me, he started listening to the tape. He loves it."

They began a new chapter in their life. They were touched in ways that they could never have imagined.

I've heard it said that God would never interrupt himself. He would never get me out of church to help someone; that would constitute interrupting himself. I don't limit myself to such things. If I left the church, and helped one of His that was hurting, then I'm ok with that. I have asked Him to use me when He needs me. I have not put any limits on when or where. It would appear that He hasn't either.

The difficult takes some focused effort. The impossible takes just a little longer.

Chapter 7
Discussion Questions

1. Do you run to the fire, or away? Do you run to the accident or away?

2. Are you a fighter pilot? Do you help first and ask questions later?

3. Do you argue with God or obey His still small voice?

4. Do you follow your own agenda and keep your God time separate, or do you listen to His still small voice all day?

5. Do you recognize His voice, or do you sometimes confuse it with your own thoughts?

6. Do you rationalize "those urges" away?

7. When you get the feeling that danger is around what do you do? Do you obey that still small voice and get out of the environment, or do you say "There's nothing to fear here?"

8. When was the last time you said, "I knew that would happen?" What did you learn from that experience? Will you be more obedient next time?

Chapter 8

Brain Dead Wake-up

I BECAME MORE COMFORTABLE with my new understandings and questions. I was finally catching on to the fact that God was using my natural curiosity to develop the skill of asking. You see, when a patient has a chronic problem, the first question that I ask is why? I ask God, and I ask the patient. God usually answers first, because it is a reflex of mine to immediately question everything.

If a patient says, "I have arthritis," immediately I think, "Why?" As a child I drove my mother nuts with this question, now I'm bothering God with it. Fortunately, He has taught me to "hear" Him. I believe that He uses my natural "fighter pilot" mentality to show me how to develop the skill of listening. As I'm running in to help some poor unsuspecting soul, I ask and expect an answer. He has taught me to go boldly to the throne of grace, and He answers, usually before I get myself into too much trouble.

Just when you get comfortable with something, the Lord in His infinite sense of humor will kick you right out of your comfort zone. So, this was the day that my dear friend, and prayer partner called. She had been called to pray for Elizabeth. Elizabeth was a woman who had undergone surgery for brain cancer. Approximately half of her brain was removed, and Elizabeth never regained consciousness. She was on life support and the family was attempting to make the decision to "pull the plug."

The way we understood the story, Elizabeth had a hard life. Her husband had died, and her relationships with her family had been other than glorious. She had decided to go through the surgery because the surgeons thought that by removing a small amount of the tumor, she would improve for a while, and would allow a better quality of life. By debulking the tumor, chemotherapy, or radiation would be more effective.

During the surgery, it was discovered that after debulking a portion of the tumor, the bleeding could not be stopped, and more brain matter had to be removed. The tumor had invaded more extensively than previously thought. The surgeons were forced to remove much more of the brain tissue than they had intended.

Until this time, I had worked with everyone in person, one-on-one. This was my comfort zone. I knew the results. I met the patient, asked God for input, I talked a certain way, and the patient responded, then results were not far away; pretty simple when you get a few under your belt. But as I said before, the Lord was ready to stretch my friend and me. We talked at length about what to do. This patient was in some other state, far away. So going to the hospital to speak to her was out of the question. What do you do when the right things are not in place? You either think outside of the box, or you give up. Not us—we were going in.

Remember when I said there are only two kinds of people in the world—those who run to help and those that run away? Remember my belief that there are fighter pilots, and then there is everyone else? Well, plenty of fighter pilots get shot down; some never make it home. Some are heroes; some are buried in their burning wreckage.

All right, here is how it went. Brainstorming 101. Often when I am thinking of my mother, she calls. Often when my friends think of me, I call them. I get a "gut feeling" that the oven is on, then walk into the kitchen to find that my children have placed cookies into the oven, forgotten them and run outside to play. The cookies are just right , and ready to be removed from the oven.

There are times when I get the feeling that I just want to go to the store, down a different road, and in front of me is a horrific car accident. I am able to get to the people as soon as the car settles to a stop. If this is all possible, then it is also possible that we can do these things by intention. If it is true that there is no time or space in the spirit, then who cares if I am physically with the patient or not? She will know what I am doing with my friend, to help heal her—we hope.

With these thoughts in mind, my friend and I decided that the only thing we had to loose was, nothing. If we did nothing, the lady died. If we did something, and the lady died, at least we tried and failed. Success can only follow an attempt. If we never tried, we never would succeed. We were willing to go down in flames, with the possibility that we could help. We believed that this woman was brought into our lives for a reason. We had to take advantage of it, and do the best that we could.

If we did something and the lady was helped in some way, we would know that there was a new avenue of healing for us to participate in. So we committed to doing all of the "normal" things that we had done for others, only with the caveat that Elizabeth was not physically present and we would have the intention that Elizabeth would receive whatever she needed from us.

Did I mention that both my prayer partner and myself are physicians. If a member of the local medical society had been sitting in listening to this conversation, I'm sure that he would have raised an eyebrow, or ordered a straight jacket for both of us.

I asked God what He wanted, and I'm pretty sure that He said something. I'm also positive, that I didn't understand him. I wanted Him to say that she would live a long life, but he kept showing me things that I could not interpret. So we decided on a particular prayer.

We did this every day. Together, we decided to pray the prayer of faith, in agreement, and talk the way we do with patients in our presence. We prayed for her as if she were right in front of us. We spoke to her body and told it to mend itself. We called on angels to protect her from any negative thing. We called on God to heal her in every way that she needed. Then the phone call came. The family was going to remove Elizabeth from life support. They had decided to pull the plug. Elizabeth had not improved. She had not worsened. She just stayed the same. The doctors had expected her to worsen and deteriorate every day. But she had just stayed the same.

Had something happened? Had our efforts and prayers and intentions helped or just kept her alive for a few more days? We didn't know but we were not going to give up without a fight. No one knew what we were doing anyway. No one could ridicule us for trying, because no one knew (except the Lord). But we continued, harder than before. We spoke several times a day and decided on certain words and prayers. We had our heart and soul into it.

We were certain that if they pulled the plug, she would have no chance of survival.

We felt as if we had failed. We felt dejected and miserable. How could we have been so stupid as to think that we could in some way affect a person thousands of miles away, who doesn't even have the ability to decide if they want to be healed. Maybe

Elizabeth wanted to die, and we were going against her will. We had thousands of questions and no answers. No matter who we spoke with, they could not answer our questions. Why had we taken such a vested interest in a woman that we had never met? Why were we drawn to this woman in such a profound way and spent hours attempting to help her? Still we didn't give up, until the phone call. They were pulling the plug. We were finished. It was over.

For over a week, I licked my wounds and tried to console my spirit. I had been called to try something new, and it had failed. I knew this going into the venture. Why couldn't I get over it? Just work on myself with the words that I knew would be helpful, and I should feel better, but I didn't. I felt miserable and the more I thought of Elizabeth, the more I thought of Elizabeth. I was positive that I would never hear about her nor her condition again. I would never know what happened. Just when the thoughts of Elizabeth had begun to wane, my dear friend called me. "You'll never believe what happened!" She was screaming into the phone and I could not understand a word that she was saying. "Elizabeth woke up! She woke up! Elizabeth woke up and the doctors don't understand what happened. The doctors said that it was a miracle. They said it was impossible for her to wake up, she didn't have enough brain matter to wake up, but she did. They sent her home!" My friend screamed into one end of the phone while I screamed into the other. When the reality of the situation finally sunk into my thick head, I just collapsed into my chair. "Had Elizabeth really awakened? Had she really been discharged from the hospital? Had she really been able to care for herself enough to go home? But they said that she would be a vegetable if she ever woke up. She is not! She is alive. She is at home with her family!" "She was discharged home from the ICU!"

Now all bets were off. I was overwhelmed with emotion. The roller-coaster ride that my emotions had taken over the past week had taken its toll on me. I was exhausted. What had happened, what had worked, had we been helpful? Had there really been no distance in the spirit. Had her spirit wanted to live? There were more questions than answers again. But for some reason, Elizabeth was home.

You are probably ready for this story to end, but not quite yet. Elizabeth went home, and was reconciled with her family. As we learned later, there were many things that had happened in her life that needed to be healed. Elizabeth had been estranged from her sister. The girls had many tumultuous times throughout Elizabeth's life, and when Elizabeth's husband became sick and died, the sisters grew further apart.

Elizabeth loved her sister very much and wanted to convey those thoughts. Elizabeth also had children. The relationships had not been good. Through the return home, Elizabeth was given the opportunity to mend those bridges and give to her children the things that mattered most, Love.

She had a wonderful time and we had a report of her enjoying herself.

Then not long thereafter the shocking phone call. Elizabeth had died. My friend and I were in shock, again. We had stopped working and praying too soon. How could we have done this? We had failed miserably and could not console each other. All I could do was cry. I felt as though nothing had helped, and the heaps and piles of emotional baggage that I had accumulated over the years had just been piled on top of my head. I wept. I wept for Elizabeth. I wept for me. I wept for the family. I wept for my friend. I just let it all out.

When I finished feeling sorry for myself, and calmed my mind, the revelations came. Elizabeth had been healed once and for all. She had been hanging on to life, so that she could go home and heal her relationships. She had done the things that she wanted to do, and needed to do. She was then free to go home to her Maker. Elizabeth was given the greatest gift that my friend and I could have given another. We gave her the extra help she needed to boost her along the way, to be healed on earth, then healed in heaven. A peace came over me and finally I was able to lie quietly, and my soul was again at rest.

Chapter 8
Discussion Questions

1. Have you ever prayed for someone who wasn't physically present? How does this work? Are prayers answered if you are far away?

2. Do you pray in faith, or do you pray with doubt? Do you ask God what to do or do you just dive right into prayers of petition?

3. With a distance prayer, do you pray for what you want to happen, or do you ask God what He wants? Do you pray for long life, or do you pray for complete healing?

4. How do you feel when your prayers aren't answered?

5. Quiet your mind and think about one person who needs prayer. With this person in mind, ask God, "What do You want me to pray for this person?" You will get an answer, and when you do, pray.

6. If a doctor said, "She will never wake up," could you still pray in faith?

Chapter 9

Healing Comes In All Forms

MY BUSY SCHEDULE had thinned to almost nil for the day. I looked at the list of patients that had previously scheduled appointments. For some strange reason, the phone was ringing incessantly, but every call was a cancellation for that day. Only one patient remained. Her appointment was early in the morning. My thoughts filled with baking the day away with some chocolate chip cookies. Or maybe I would make a delicious gumbo for the evening. My thoughts were traveling through the cookbooks.

The phone rang again. I expected the last patient to cancel. And she did.

But not in the way I had expected. She was crying so hard, the sound of muffled moans was coming through the receiver.

"Betty, are you OK?" I asked quietly. After a long pregnant pause and many sniffles, she said "No, Jennifer is dead." Jennifer was her sixteen–year-old daughter. Jennifer and her boyfriend were traveling down the interstate and lost control of their vehicle. The vehicle flipped many times and both children were lost in an instant. Neither of them made it past the crash site.

Betty could hardly speak. She kept saying, "She's gone. I can't believe she's really gone." And like all grieving people Betty talked of the things that she should have done.

Betty wept and talked for a while. She must have looked at a clock, because she suddenly said, "I'm so sorry that I've kept you, you must have many patients to see, I'll let you go now."

Without a hesitation I said, "Betty, would you like for me to come to the funeral home?" She said yes, then thought again. She didn't want to disturb my "busy" day.

How weird is this? Every patient cancelled except one. And that patient needs a house call. Never mind that this house call is to a funeral home. I arrived to greet Betty and her husband. Betty hung on to my hand as if I would disappear should she let go. I was in awe about my schedule, but at least I could be with Betty at this time.

Betty asked me to go see Jennifer. Jennifer was having an autopsy performed on her and believe me, that was no place for family. The autopsy room is actually off limits to everyone, family or not, and for good reason, too. Without going into details, let just say that no one wants to go there, and no one should be allowed there.

I have either performed or been involved with too many autopsies to count. I went to Jennifer at Betty's request. Then returned to Betty.

Betty just sat in her chair, motionless, waiting to wake up from her nightmare. Seconds stretched into hours. People came and went. Some cried, some stood in shock. Still Betty clung to my hand. As if she needed something from me. Betty's husband Tom apologized for my inability to leave the room. "Tom, let me tell you a story…" I told him about the morning, the cancellations, the last patient on the books, and the phone call from Betty.

"Tom, I think for some reason I'm supposed to be here," I said.

"I don't believe in coincidences. Someone upstairs wants me here. So, when Betty no longer needs me, I'll leave." He seemed comforted by these words, and the story. He was comforted in knowing that I had not left a waiting room full of patients.

I sat with Betty forever. A day can last an eternity. If you don't believe me, try it for yourself. Watch the clock for something special to happen. It will take an eternity to force that clock to move each second. Still confused about Betty taking comfort in me, I began to ask questions.

"Ask, and expect an answer," or something to that effect. (See James 1:5–6.) So, I began to ask. The questions flowed through my head and the answers came just as effortlessly. I was meant to be here with Betty today.

Betty and I had a professional relationship, doctor/patient. Betty trusted me. I had operated on her, and had seen her in the office many times since the surgery. Betty was a petite woman. Soft spoken and reserved, she never wanted to appear abrupt. She was the kind of person who could mingle in any crowd. Betty had a perpetual smile on her face and an upbeat personality. Her hair was always in place, her body always fit, and her nails done to perfection. Betty had two daughters, both in their teens. Betty and Tom had married young. High school sweethearts from the beginning, they married immediately after college and set up house in the same small town in which they had been raised.

Everyone envied them, until today.

Jennifer and her boyfriend had been together for three years. From the moment they met, they were inseparable. Jennifer and her beau were following in Betty's footsteps, in love and happy in high school. Jennifer and her boyfriend were expected to go to college, marry, and have children. Both families agreed. Both families enjoyed spending time with each other.

So what would this family benefit from my presence? When

the answer came, I did the usual thing. I started arguing with God.

"NO!"

"NO!"

"I'm not going to do it!"

"I am here for moral support only. I am not their priest! I am Betty's doctor! Give me a break!" The arguing was in my head and in my heart, the rebellion continued in silence. If only I could gracefully removed myself from this funeral home, then maybe I could leave with some shred of dignity. "NO! I am not their spiritual mentor. Goodness, I need some help here myself. I will not tell them what you are saying!"

My arguing continued until I was exhausted. God won again. He had outlasted me. "What do you want of me?" Then the answers came in pictures. I kept seeing a young girl with long golden curly hair jumping from one cloud to the next. As the child jumped, her hair sparkled and danced with her. There were beautiful clouds and a crystal blue sky. Everything was sparkling. "God they are grieving, this is not the time for this, please give me something that I can say to them to relieve them a bit."

Again he gave me this image in my heart.

"Betty, are you a religious person?" I quietly asked.

"Yes, I go to church." She said through her tears.

"I mean, Betty…Tom…do you believe that the Lord speaks to us…sort of like sends messages through people?" I stumbled over my words. Stammered and choked was more like it.

Finally I just blurted out, "Betty and Tom, I keep seeing an image in my heart. I am going to tell you what it is. Pray about it. Please!"

In my head I said, "I committed myself now Lord, if I make a fool of myself, You and I are both on the line."

Betty and her husband had never heard anyone speak so frankly about the Lord before. They had followed their intuitions before, but they believed that the Lord quit speaking after He wrote the Bible. Oh, was I in trouble. "These people will think I fell off of my rocker and hit my head."

I opened my mouth and began: "The image is of a young teenage girl. She is skipping and jumping from one cloud to the next. She is happy and well. She is so beautiful that it is hard to describe how she glows. When she jumps she squeals a little, as if the small sound will help her jump with glee to the next cloud. Her hair glistens and sparkles. Her face is translucent. She does not look directly at me, but she seems to be hanging around long enough for me to get the picture accurate."

My breathing had stopped. My words had fallen on ears that could not hear. "God , these people are grieving the loss of their precious daughter, and I'm talking about some vision. They are going to throw me out of this room, and with good reason. I am so mad at you, when I get out of this place, I am going to scream out loud instead of in my head!"

Betty had gone from crying silently, streams of tears flowing constantly, to weeping and wailing. She screamed when I quit talking. She threw her face into her hands. Her husband stood suddenly and threw his body around hers. Betty and Tom looked like one of those Greek statues in the museum, not moving, just making sounds from somewhere in the bowels of their bodies; intertwined and moaning, crying and holding each other, as if not an inch could come between them.

My time had come. It was time to crawl to the door, with my tail between my legs. I was embarrassed, confused, and humiliated. I had stepped out on a limb and the limb broke. There was no rectifying what I had done. I had to get out of that place and fast.

As I rose from my seat, Betty sensed my movement, and murmured. "Please! Wait!"

Betty attempted to compose herself. She wasn't very successful. Tom sat next to her, but still no light could be seen between them. Betty said, "This morning, as my older daughter and I were driving to the funeral home, we were talking. Kim, my older daughter started talking about Jennifer. Kim began to paint a word picture. Kim said that she imagined Jennifer in heaven already. Jennifer was always happy on earth, so she was surely enjoying Heaven. Jennifer was probably jumping from one cloud to the next, squealing between each cloud."

The impact took a few moments. What had Betty just said? Had she described my vision, or had I described hers?

"Don't you see, don't you see? It is a confirmation that Jennifer is in heaven, she is OK, and she is happy. Oh, thank you for sharing your vision. Tom and I were so scared that we had not prepared Jennifer for death. Maybe she had not gotten to heaven. But now we know! Jennifer is OK. She is jumping from cloud to cloud," Betty continued. " We are not the best Christians, we don't go to church as much as we should. We thought this was God's way of punishing us. Jennifer's death was a punishment for our not raising our girls well enough. But now we know that we are not being punished. Jennifer is not being punished. She is OK, she is happy."

There was no way that I could have known how they were tormenting themselves. Tom and Betty had more fear than imaginable. This moment touched them in ways that a mortal could not have. God had touched them.

Instead of jumping for the door, now I collapsed into the chair. So this was the point of the entire day. God wanted to heal a part of Betty and Tom. God knew that I would argue, but He also knew that I would obey. Maybe reluctantly, but

I did my best. Betty thanked me repeatedly. Tom looked at me and smiled with his eyes. He said thank you, without making a sound. He nodded his approval to me, then quickly returned his focus to Betty.

Betty let go of my hand, released me in effect, and was wrapped in the arms of her childhood sweetheart. They cried tears of joy, and grief. They talked to each other comforting each other with the vision given to them twice in one day. They laughed and cried at the same time.

Quietly, and without notice I stood and left the room. This time, no one summoned me. My job was done. The Lord spoke through me in a time of need. He could not get Betty's attention any other way. Betty was too sad to hear Him for herself, so He rescheduled my entire day. He sent me to Betty. And she heard Him. Once outside, I cried. My heart began to ache. My knees buckled. My legs would not carry me, so my truck became the bench. The impact of what just happened overwhelmed me. Only a few blocks from my children's school, I drove like a drunken sailor toward them. When they came towards me, I hugged them and cried. "Momma, what's wrong?" They wondered at their mother's emotional embrace.

"I am so happy to see you and hug you," is all I said. Tears spilled over my cheeks like a faucet that had been turned on and left to run. There was no slowing the tears for now. "Hot and cold running tears," as my mother would say.

I am reminded of a story from many years ago. Healing does in fact come in all forms, and this one incorporated many. Our family had decided to go to a place called "The Bitter End." We had a fabulous time, relaxing and playing on the gorgeous white sand beach. We each had separate bungalows, with hammocks on the porch. I loved napping the day away, feeling the ocean breezes gently rock the hammock back and forth.

A catamaran had scheduled a tour. It would take us to the Baths, a series of rock cutouts formed by the currents and waves. Huge tunnels and lakes were beneath the rocks, and we could play for hours there.

The whole family decided to go on the tour, and we climbed on board. The front of the cat was my favorite place, so I went there with my daughter. We laughed and played as the sea spray made huge blasts from the side of the boat. We jumped on the front swing. It was a glorious day.

We reached the Baths, and were greeted by many other boats with the same idea for the day. Sail boats were docked everywhere. We took a small dingy to shore, and the warm sun called to me. I decided to take a nap under a palm tree, while everyone else went exploring in the caves.

I had dressed in a white linen sun dress, because I knew that I was not going to swim, I was just along for the ride. Actually, I had not planned to go to the baths at all that day, but at the last moment jumped on the boat as it was leaving. I did not have on a bathing suit, but it was OK. I had been to the baths many times before, and would just make it a lazy day on the ocean. Who could ask for anything more?

Our group went off to explore and I took my mother's credit card, and a hundred dollar bill, to hold for her. Oh how wonderful a lazy afternoon is in the tropics!

Through my relaxing, I thought I heard someone scream, very far off, but a scream nonetheless. I sat up to witness dozens of people running down the shore. By now you can guess what I did; I got up and ran, too. Something or someone was in the water.

"She's dead! She's dead! She's too heavy, we can't get her."

A middle-aged woman had gone into the surf to snorkel with her husband, and had died. Her husband was frantic, but could not do anything. He was about one-third her size. We all jumped into the water, and got her as close to the sand as we could. The surf was very rough, and tripped us and threw us back into the deep waters. Finally we devised a plan to get several men under her, and several on the sides of her, and "ride" a wave onto shore. Then maybe we could attempt to help her. Attempting to perform CPR (cardiopulmonary resuscitation) in the ocean would be virtually impossible, what with the waves crashing over your head.

It worked. We had her partially on the sand. It wasn't enough to keep the waves completely off of her torso, but at least we could start CPR. A large man stood in front of the waves and acted like a wall to break the major force of the waves crashing into us.

"I'll take the chest if someone will take the mouth!" I yelled to no one in particular. Another woman said, "OK! I've got the head." Between breaths and chest compressions we understood that we were both surgeons, both on the same catamaran, and both had our children exploring the Baths. She was no bigger than me, so there was no way of moving this woman to higher ground. We had to do whatever we were going to be able to do right there.

I don't want to give too many visual effects, but have you ever seen a medusa? This woman was not just dead—she was *really* dead. The face was blue, and every blood vessel was popping out from the skin. There was no telling how long she had been without oxygen, but for some reason, neither of us would stop the CPR. We kept asking each other, "Call the code?" Neither was ready to give up. Why in the world didn't we call this code?

We were both accustomed to performing and calling codes, it was not as if we were interns. But still we continued on.

We were physically exhausted from performing chest compressions and were not convinced that she was receiving adequate airflow, so we decided to reposition. When we did, I saw a flash of a vision, sort of like I just knew that we had to start over, and give her a "thump." This is when you stand up and hit the mid chest area of the patient as hard as you can, in the attempt to "shock" the heart back into its normal sinus rhythm.

So, I stood up, grasped my hands together, and swung as hard as I could with my whole body down onto hers. I've never before or since hit anyone so hard. I thought surely I had broken my hand, and a few of her ribs. She did not respond immediately, but she looked as if she were trying to breath by herself. We assisted for a moment, then she began gagging and spitting. She not only had a pulse, but a breath. I fell back into the surf, there was no more energy in me. The sight of her breathing was overwhelming. In all my years of performing CPR, I had never seen any quite this dramatic. How long had she been in the water? How long had she been without oxygen? How much brain damage would she have from this? The water was cold. I really can't tell you what the temperature was, but it was cold. Maybe it had helped her by keeping her body temperature down.

Neither of us knew or cared. Our job was done. We looked up to see hundreds of faces, staring and cheering, as the poor woman threw up all over us. We didn't care, she was alive. My formerly white linen dress was the color of surf and sand, as transparent as tissue paper. Oh well, I hadn't noticed.

"I can't find the hundred dollar bill, nor my mother's credit card." I was talking to no one in particular. Two men pulled their snorkel gear onto their heads and dove under the huge boulders that we were sitting close to. Within a few minutes they had retrieved them both.

Our patient sat up. She looked around for her husband. When she saw him, she asked, "Why are all of these people staring at me?" Several men had brought a small boat around one of the boulders, to load her up and take her to the next island to the hospital. It took six young strong men to get her into the boat.

She was admitted to the hospital for observation, and she did fine. We checked on her several times during our stay, and she recovered well, with no obvious deficiencies.

I've thought back on that day many times. What are the chances of two doctors being on a boat, both clearly "fighter pilots?" When I "heard" to do the cardiac thump again, I was certain that she was beyond saving. Why hadn't we called the code? Why did we coax each other on to continue the CPR. Had we both "heard" continue.

This was one of those times where listening was clearly the right thing to do. In my mind, she was beyond saving, but God knew better. He had more plans for her.

What would you do if you were in this situation? Would you look at the physical world or would you continue to ask the Lord questions. Next is an example of my never give up attitude. Sometimes I go down in flames, but I go down fighting till the Bitter End.

Example of a Clear Witness for Jesus—Revelation 19:10

A group of fifty people went to a prison in Miami. This was called the Prison Invasion. Surely, we must have looked like we were invading the place. The inmates all wear blue. The most boring, dull color that the eyes have ever beheld. Then, in walked fifty people in yellow, red, purple, and colors that, to the outside world seem normal.

We were there for one reason. To pray for these inmates. We were divided into groups of two or three, and sent into the common grounds to help as many as possible in the few hours of that day.

Our group was praying for a young woman in extraordinary pain. She was bent over and obviously not having a lot of fun. Our team (excluding me) prayed for her. I tend to separate myself and watch , so this is what I was doing (as usual). I watched this woman go from a huge pile of pain, to a crying sobbing mess.

The team had prayed for her. She did not get healed, and the team said, "bless you" and they moved on to the next person. Of course, there I am, still watching. This woman's body slumped over to an impossible position.

A person could read her thoughts, because they were being broadcast throughout her body. "Wonderful, just peachy, I had one last chance to get healed, and nothing happened. They walked off. I will live with this pain forever. The doctors can't find a cause. They won't give me pain medicine. I will be like this forever. In the prison of my pain, in the prison of Miami. I guess God just didn't want to heal *me*."

So, I asked God what He was going to do about it. God told me, and I went and prayed. The pain went away. The woman stood up and began to weep. Her pain was gone. Her strength was returned. She was able to walk. She knew God healed her.

This, as wonderful as it sounds is not the point of the story. Sorry. Two young girls had been watching me all day long, (watching others get prayed for.) Don't you know when someone is watching you, and every time you look at them, they turn their head? Well, this time, they didn't look away. They had forgotten to be shy, and had gotten caught in the act. They had witnessed the woman in pain. They knew her. They had seen her receive prayer with no results when several prayed. Then, they watched me, (once again stand back and watch, ask the Lord, and finish the work that others had started.) With this clear witness for Jesus, I had nothing to do. Jesus had already done the work in their hearts for me.

I turned to the young girls and said, "What? What do you want?" "Why are you following me around?" One girl said that she wanted what I had. The other said that she wanted to get what I got. Within a few minutes, one girl had healed the other. Both received from the Lord. Their blessings were supernatural. No amount of glorious sermonizing could have done more for those two. In all my days I could never have talked enough to convince two young beautiful girls in prison that they needed Jesus. So, The Lord knows that I ask first, pray second. He knew that He wanted them to see different styles of prayer. So He set up the entire scene, right down to my sarcastic question, "What? What do you want?"

"Thanks God. You did it again."

Chapter 9
Discussion Questions

1. What would you do if you received Betty's call? Would you have cancelled the last appointment, and gone home, rejoicing in the free day? Would you have gone to the funeral home?

2. Would you have been bold enough to tell Betty about the vision, or would you have left without telling her?

3. What would you have done if your prayer group had prayer for someone, and the person did not receive their blessing? Would you have walked away? Would you have said, bless you? Would you have asked God what He wanted?

4. If two young girls had been following you around, without making eye contact, what would you say when you finally looked one of them in the eyes? Would you have made first contact?

5. What would you have done if these same two girls had said, "I want what you have," and the other said, "I want to do what you do?" Would you have told them that it takes years to learn to pray like that, or would you trust God to handle their heart, while you teach them to stand on God's Word?

6. Would you go to a prison to minister to the people there, or would you save that for others to do?

Chapter 10

Rose-colored Glasses Are the Best

LET US EXAMINE how the impossible healing with Karen was accomplished. I will share with you my theory of the mind and how these things are done. It will become very clear and not so much hocus-pocus once you understand what you are dealing with (at least from my perspective.)

There is a mind, body, and spirit. In medicine, doctors tend to focus only on the body, and its actions and reactions, forgetting about the other components of the whole person.

There is the spirit, that part of the person that gives life to the body. It is the part of the person that is the hardest to get our hands or thoughts around. Essentially because there is little that we understand about it. We seek to learn through religion, spirituality, or by whatever means the individual feels comfortable. The spirit is connected to the King of the universe, the Lord. His guidance is the thing that compels me to continue on.

Then there is the mind, the thinking, processing part. It tells the heart to beat, the hand to get off of the hot stove, and the foot to step. It has the ability to be educated or injured. There are many aspects to this thing called the mind.

Try as you may to separate the parts of the individual you cannot. Once the spirit is separated from the other two, death occurs. Separate the mind, and a vegetative state occurs. Separate the body, and the spirit and mind have no place to function.

We are an interconnected triune of mind, body and spirit. How then can we ignore one to concentrate on the other? How is it that the medical profession has concentrated so much on specialization that it has divided the fields of psychiatry (mind) and internal medicine (body).

How wonderful would it be to *un-specialize* medicine, and have the priest, the psychiatrist, and the internist work as a *team* on every patient!

Our society is programmed to go to the doctor and get a pill or a surgery. It is a stretch to consider that two thirds of the individual is neglected in this interaction. So often I hear, "It is nice to have a surgeon that prays." Any surgeon worth his salt prays. Because all surgeons know that we are nothing more than glorified seamstresses. We can cut and we can sew, but we cannot heal. Only the creator of the Universe, the one who created the body in the first place can knit together the threads of human tissue. We are trained technicians who know how to cut and sew body parts. It is then the patient and his own healing that determine the outcome. We doctors have been given incredible influence over the healing process. The Lord allows us the power and influence to help people in ways that others are not allowed, but ultimately it is the patient and the Lord who determine the result. We then must watch and assist when able.

When the child is forming in the mother's womb, it has a body and a spirit, while the mind is akin to a blank canvas. It has no experiences to draw from, and no frame of reference. The mind is like a sponge ready to absorb anything and everything that comes its way. The world is new and exciting, full of surprises and new experiences.

Imagine that a child comes into this world learning the English language. This is the only experience that the child is exposed to for all of his formative years. At the age of ten, the child meets a German speaking person. The child cannot understand German, and is confused. But hard as he may try, he cannot, because he has no reference with which to compare. The original stimuli, English, is the standard by which the rest of the child's life is measured.

Imagine for a moment that the English training is the core of the child's life, as a circle around the child's head. This core has created a truth about who the child is. Now, imagine a protective coating around this core. So that whenever an outside stimulus does not agree with "I'm English" it bounces off of the protective coating.

The child is unable to receive German information. The German may be telling the child such vital information that within seconds the child will live or die based on his acceptance or rejection of the information. The child is unable (not unwilling but unable) to accept the information at any level, so he is oblivious to the perils that await him.

Is this becoming clearer? The original input into our brain, into our mind, the very things that we were exposed to as children, are the framework, or the core around which we form our lives.

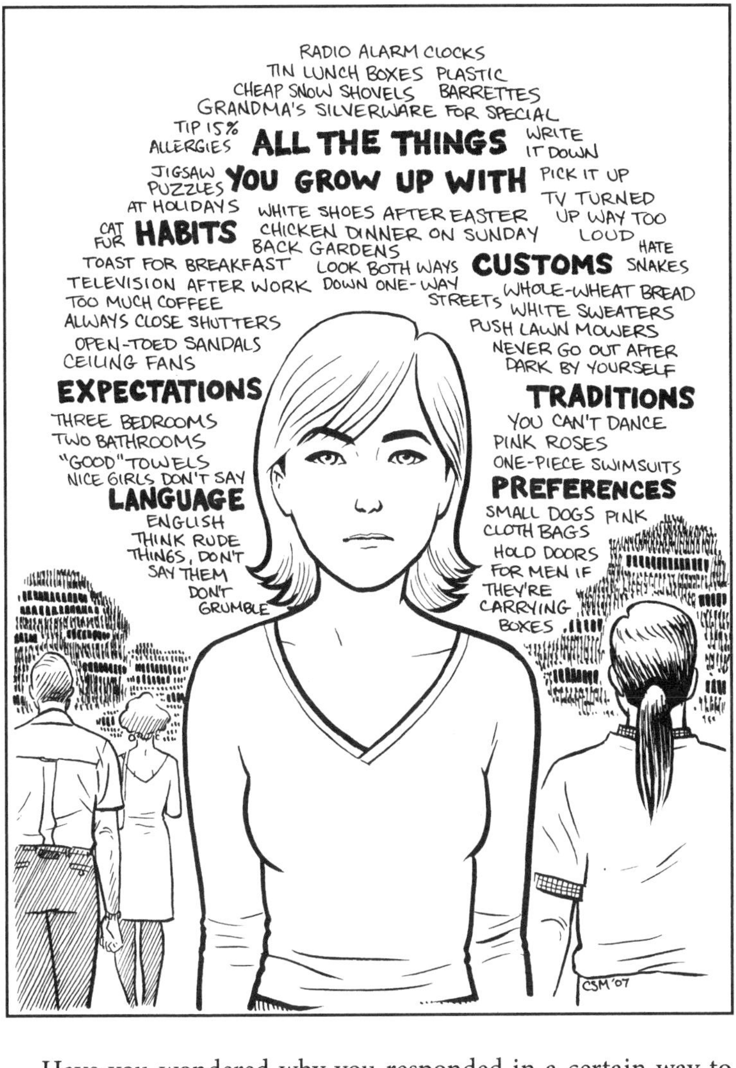

Have you wondered why you responded in a certain way to a word, and the person standing right next to you responded in a totally different way? You were responding and reacting based upon your original experiences. Throughout your life those things that support and give a feeling of security to that original stimulus, will be allowed to enter your inner core easily, and reinforce the belief of who you are. Others will not.

Let us take a model from the psychiatric world. If a child is born of an alcoholic, there is a great chance that the child will be an alcoholic. Genetic predisposition and the exposure to the chronic behaviors of the alcoholic will be the child's example of "normal." Normal to this child would be quite different from the behaviors of a child raised in a house of quiet contemplation.

Today's society blames our parents for all of our misgivings. Is there truth in this? With this model of our mind, it is in fact our parents, or those who raised us, who gave us our original stimuli. These are the standards by which we live the rest of our lives.

Here is another example of original stimuli. A child is brought into the world with a family who nurtures, cuddles, and provides ultimate security and love. This child "is secure, loved, and nurtured." This is the basis through which this child views the world and everything not in agreement will fall away from this, just like the German words were rejected from the English child. Every large or small amount of information that is introduced to this child in agreement with *security* will be reinforced, allowed to enter the core and will support the original system. Over this child's life, this will be the filter (the rose colored glasses) through which the child sees life.

Let's talk about Suzy. She is a precious person. No matter what happens to her, she always has a smile on her face and is optimistic and happy. Let me tell you the end of the story first, and you tell me about her parents. Can you figure out what kind of childhood she had?

Suzy married the love of her life Bob, and they had a fairy-tale wedding. They were happy. Suzy's husband Bob was in the military, so they moved frequently. Suzy gave birth to three beautiful children. They were her focus and joy. Suzy and Bob had achieved all that they had dreamed of. Who could ask for more?

One day, the fairy tale came to a crashing end. Bob had begun drinking and using drugs, to relax. Nothing that Suzy said could convince him to stop. To Bob, Suzy was nagging, and it irritated him. One day he snapped. He was not pleased, and put his fist into Suzy's face. He broke her cheekbone, and bruised her horribly. Bob verbally abused her, along with the physical abuse.

Over time, Bob's abuse came at more frequent intervals. Suzy could expect Bob to do something to her or the children every day.

Suzy focused all of her attention on sheltering the children from the temper tantrums of their father. But the abuse became worse, and Bob soon exacted his rage on a regular basis. Bob would hold Suzy by the throat, up in the air, until she passed out. Then he would drop her to the ground. He would laugh as she fell into a crumbled heap onto the floor. The children were granted the opportunity of seeing this scene regularly.

Outsiders did not know about the violence in the house. Suzy had marks on her body that betrayed her secrets. She would lie to her parents and friends about them. Suzy went to the emergency room many times with injuries sustained at the hands of prince charming.

"I fell down the steps," she would say to the emergency personnel. Knowing that she was not telling the truth, she looked at the floor.

Then one day, Suzy packed up the children, and left. She divorced Bob and started over. Suzy told me these stories, sometimes crying, and sometimes laughing, but always, she would say things like, "I'm going to be fine" "I'm OK because my children are protected, and we are healthy."

Suzy found things to be positive about. She had an uncanny ability to focus on the good in any situation. Suzy had a smile on her face that was infectious. You knew that it was not a smile of pain, but one of joy and laughter, and gratitude. Suzy could look disaster in the face and find something good in it.

"How can a woman, who has been so abused, and tortured for years, find good in a horrible situation? Why didn't Suzy crumble into a heap of hopeless despair and cry about the fate handed to her?" I wondered.

Suzy had parents that nurtured her. They were the kind of people that hugged each other, and did not raise their voices to each other. Suzy's father was a gentle man. He was able to accomplish his desires with the softest voice. He commanded attention by his presence, was as steady as a rock, always dependable, always reliable, and always available with open arms. Suzy's mom was an incredible woman. Nothing rattled her. She was quick to laugh, and slow to anger. She was always hugging and laughing, talking and supporting her children. Her life was content, and it showed.

Suzy had as her "core," goodness, love, protection, calm, consistent, and nurturing etc. She rejected hostility, anger and fighting. She did not recognize or understand German or anger, Spanish or hostility, abuse or neglect. Suzy saw these things, but rejected them.

Today, Suzy is married to different man. This man reflects who she is, strong, quiet, steady, stable, nurturing, loving, and supporting.

Let's talk about Sam for a moment. Sam was raised in a family of arguing, hostility and hatred. Sam thought people had to fight to exist. Sam wanted acceptance from his father but never got it. Sam's mother was aloof and sad. She sat for hours in solitude, not responding to the cries from her children. Sam's father regularly came home drunk and hit the children. It was not uncommon for Sam's father to throw lamps or ashtrays across the room. Sam lived with fear, and anxiety.

Like everyone in life, Sam had a need to find security, love, safety, and acceptance. Sam certainly could not get these at home, so he began to look elsewhere. Sam saw kids on his block, laughing and together. Sam went to the group and wanted to fit in. The other kids were smoking and told Sam that if he wanted to be part of the club, he had to smoke. So, Sam lit up. Through the coughing, choking and horrible taste, Sam began.

"Sam, you got it man! Go on, it gets easier with time." His peers cheered him on, as he inhaled and gagged.

"I belong here, they like me. Listen to the cheers."

Sam became part of a group. They stole cars, and cursed at each other. They beat, shot, stabbed and laughed at other children, and the injured. This group bonded and although they were a bunch of misfits, they were misfits together. This feeling of belonging was filling a basic need for Sam. Anger and hostility were reinforced daily.

Fast-forward to Sam's adult life. Sam is married with two infant children. He smokes and watches his infants coughing on the smoke. His wife dislikes the smell, and has asked him to quit. Sam wants to quit and knows intellectually that smoking is bad for his health and the health of his family. Sam decides that he will never smoke again, and puts the cigarettes down. Soon, feelings begin to creep into Sam: feelings of abandonment; feelings of rejection; feelings of hostility. Sam feels left out.

"I have everything that a man could want? I want to quit smoking, why do I feel bad?" he would ask. Sam's answer is in his childhood.

When I asked Sam about his feelings, he said, "Like an old

friend is being taken away," and "feelings of peer pressure." Sam's peers are pressuring him to quit smoking, but only twenty years ago, his peers were pressuring him to *start* smoking.

How do we help Sam? Is there anything that we can do? Good question. The answer is yes. When the mind is healed, then the body will follow. As the mind thinks, so he becomes. (See Proverbs 23:7.) This is the basis by which lives will be transformed, and healed—spirit, mind, and body.

Understanding now that the inner "core" belief of a person forms the filter of his thinking, it is not a stretch to see then that a person views the world through his own set of glasses. Rose colored or dark, the first glasses are the main filter for a person's life. These must be changed for Sam to rid himself of the difficult feelings.

Sam thought that he had overcome his child hood. Sam found a wife that loved and nurtured him, a successful career, and children that fulfilled every other need. Sam had a nagging feeling in him though and couldn't quit smoking. He was frustrated, and felt that smoking was controlling his life. Smoking wasn't controlling his life, his childhood glasses were. Smoking is the symptom of a deeper issue. Smoking is the thing you can see, it is the outer reflection of the inner struggle.

Sam failed to stop smoking many times, and so developed a habit of failure. This habit of failure reinforced the inner belief that Sam "is not good enough." This failure was accepted and reinforced and cemented into reality.

"I really am a failure." Sam acknowledges.

Anyone looking into Sam's life would call him a success. Despite his wife's encouragement, Sam felt more and more dejected.

Sam is actually feeding his own destruction. Sam knows that the more he tries, the more he fails. The more he fails, the more he is sure to fail. Sam's beliefs are actually beginning to destroy the very thing that he had worked so hard to create: a life filled with love and happiness with his wife and children. "Something" was sucking Sam into a black hole.

I've heard it said that acknowledging the past will heal it. Sorry, all of the acknowledging in the world did not change Sam's core beliefs about himself. Sam knew who he had been, and didn't want to go back there again. But he felt powerless.

Sam is who he is and that is all there is to it. Or is it? Is there a way to reframe Sam's inner core, and give him the things that he needs, and wants?

Now hold onto your hat, because this next part may challenge you a bit. Don't throw anything at me, just try this on. Imagine that you need a coat. You walk into a store and there are hundreds of coats. Some are neutral, some are brightly colored, some are short, some are long. You go in and enjoy trying all of them on. You find one that fits perfectly and purchase it. This is the coat that you take home.

Try on this information like trying on coats. Just try it on for size. If you like it, take it home and use it for yourself. Share it with those that you love. If you don't like it, just discard the ideas, and throw the information away.

This is how I do it:

In the middle of a friend telling me a heart-wrenching story, I ask them if I can help just a little. I've never had anyone say no. Then in that moment when they are sobbing and weeping, have them remember a good time, one that makes them laugh. Obviously if I am a friend, I can say, "Hey remember when I dropped an entire carton of eggs in the middle of the kitchen floor. The egg went everywhere. It took forever to get that cleaned up." If they start laughing, I have them go back to the miserable story that they started. As soon as they are in the throws of describing the horrible feelings, I have them remember the eggs all over the floor again. By repeating this once or twice, it is difficult for anyone to fully feel the misery of a few moments ago. They can't do it because you have mixed a little funny into a lot of sadness. The sad memory is forever changed ever so slightly by a chemical. From now on, the memory will remain, and the emotional impact will be lessened.

If you are not a friend, but a helper it would be a good idea to ask them about a particularly good time, so you can use it as your happy place. Then go for it. If you can't get a happy memory from the other person, ask the Lord, He will gladly supply one. (See James 1:5–6.) People get very caught up in their own misery. They do not know that an option is as close as their own brain. When a person is miserable, and venting it on you, change the subject. That's right, change the subject. They will think that you don't care, you are not listening, and a variety of other things. But do it anyway. Say something like, "Tell me about a time when you laughed so hard, you wet in your pants." Whoever you are talking to will be absolutely convinced that you have lost your mind. Remember though that we are digging for gold, not trying to win a congeniality contest. You have to dig through a lot of mud and rock before you get the gold. The gold this time is a memory that has enough of an impact, to dilute some of this misery. Your goal is not to empathize, but to bring some light to a dark situation. Keep focused, especially when their eyes start crossing and they say something like, "What difference does that make?" Your answer should be "It means the world to you." That should sufficiently confuse them to allow you to continue.

If you want to help this person, stay focused on the goal. The goal is to dilute the misery with happy thoughts. As soon at you get one piece of happy information, cling to it and use it. For now, we will use the laughter and the wet pants.

Have your victim go back to their misery. Have them feel it as intensely as before, coach them if you need to. Tell them to fill their body with the sadness they were experiencing just a few moments before. As soon as you are sure that the person is feeling it totally, say something silly like, "Oh my goodness, I was just thinking about you wetting your pants, and I can't get that vision out of my head," and laugh when you say this.

Your victim's eyes will probably cross, and they may look a bit dazed. If they do, then you have achieved your goal. You have just struck gold. You have mixed a little funny with a lot of sad, and the brain feels different.

Next, you have them remember the sad event, you will notice that your victim is having a hard time getting as deep into their sorrow as before. This is because the chemical in the brain has shifted slightly. You have rewritten the hard drive. Instead of leaving the document the way you found it, you modified it. They maintain the memory, but the emotional impact is far less.

Summary of the Steps I Use

1. Identify a happy time, one that always makes you laugh.

2. Identify the problem, the one you have sad or bad feelings with.

3. Have the victim remember the problem

4. Change your focus

5. Have your victim remember the funny

6. Change focus
7. Remember the sad
8. Change focus
9. Remember the funny
10. Change focus
11. Now remember the sad and tell me how you feel.

If the emotional impact is not significantly reduced, simply repeat the process until it is. At some point the person will feel silly and will burst out laughing. This is sure to get a change of emotional impact.

The next example is as if I were sitting in front of a patient:

I talk in a soft quiet tone, "Remember a time when you were sad, so sad that you cried. Feel the sadness that you felt. Remember who you were with. Were you inside, outside, with someone or alone? What was the event? Feel in your body the sensations that you felt that day. This is not much fun. You feel icky. You remember the events as if they were yesterday. You feel the heaviness pressing down on you that could crush you."

"Now look at the clock. What time is it?" (This is simply to get them to change your focus)

"Now, remember laughing with friends. Did you do it? Instantly you can go to a place in your memory banks and a flash of laughter with friends. You may hear the laughter, you may imagine that you can see them laughing, or you may imagine that you can smell the aroma of the room. Go ahead, spend just a few moments imagining yourself doing a belly laugh. You remember, the one where you laughed harder than you thought you could, and your stomach started to hurt."

"Now look at your arm. How many freckles do you have?" (This part is simply to get you to change your focus again)

"Now breathe deeply. Now breath deeply again and hold the breath for just a second or two, then exhale."

"Analyze how you feel now."

"As soon as you are ready, remember the sad time again. Does it feel the same or just a bit better?" If the answer is the same, repeat the process. If they can remember the sad event without as much intensity, then you have realized the effect that we are looking for.

Our bodies retain memories, and thus the chemical reactions to those memories. Whenever a memory is recalled chemicals are released into the brain. These are the same chemicals that were released during the original event.

With this in mind, it is possible to reframe memories and create different chemical responses to specific memories, thus different feelings and different reactions to those memories.

I maintain that this is not only possible, but has been done for millennia. We as a medical profession have turned a deaf ear to things our forefathers took for granted. Our predecessors did not have the kind of miracle working drugs that we have today. They had only the power of their profession, and the ability to convince a patient of an outcome. The suggestions used helped the patient get well. I believe it is time to reintegrate the mind, body, and spirit healing. Then our calling to heal can be more fulfilling and the patients can have what they came for.

Feelings are strange things. They seem to come from nowhere, but they are linked to events that entered your mind long ago. These feelings may not be consciously linked to a memory, but with some effort, and coaching, you can retrieve the memories that are holding you down. Like any exercise this technique will get easier with time. It is just an exercise, not hocus-pocus.

Although I've not talked about the spiritual part of this technique, I would like to tell you about Myrtle and how the Lord used me to help her, and used her to get my attention, again.

A patient of mine, let's call her "Myrtle," I must change the names of the patients to protect their privacy, but the stories are powerful. So, Myrtle came in for a consultation. She had some leg pain, and wanted a medical opinion about treating the symptoms. We talked for about ten minutes.

"Your leg pain can be treated easily with vitamins." And I wrote the information on a pad for her. I was sitting on a stool, next to the exam table and therefore was looking up to her. She sat very still, like she was afraid of something.

"Are you OK?" I asked as I looked back at my pad. No answer came from above. I looked up to see her eyes wet with the beginnings of tears.

"What?" "Did I say something, if so I am so sorry!" I attempted to stand quickly, but got tangled in the stool. My lab coat has a really annoying habit of getting caught under the exam stool wheel. When I attempt to stand up, it jerks me back down to the floor. It is virtually impossible to look serious or professional when your lab coat yanks you back to your previous location. Or worse yet, to the floor. Who designs exam stools anyway? I believe someone intentionally designs wheels that will grab your coat and laugh as you are falling?

I really don't try to be a clown with lab stools, but they have it in for me. Without fail, if I sit on a four-legged stool, it bucks me off, and I land on my backside in the middle of the exam room. How is it that four legged stools can have enough gumption to intentionally throw a grown woman across the floor?

If the stool has five legs, it eats my lab coat hem. I'm not kidding. I've purchased new lab coats, in an attempt to keep one without a tear. You know, like your dressy clothes. You keep them for special occasions. But, as soon as I buy a new one, the stool searches it out and eats it. I know that lab stools have it in for me, so I never use them in surgery. My comedy routines are too dramatic, so I limit them to the exam rooms. Once I even started wearing short lab coats, to fool the stools. But still it jumped right up there and ate it, too.

The only solution I have ever found is to eliminate lab coats from my attire. The problem with this is the perpetual problem of patients thinking that I am the nurse. Without my formal starched white lab coat, which clearly says, "Dr. Speed," I am called the nurse. I don't have a problem with nurses. Actually I have a soft spot for them. You see, I went to nursing school—for an entire day—but I was a complete failure. Those people who call themselves nursing instructors are the meanest women on the planet. So, I promptly flunked out of nursing school—actually I quit—and enrolled in medical school.

At least when you are abused and screamed at by a man, he moves on with his life. When a woman gets mad with you, she will scratch your eyes out for years. So medical school was the lesser of two evils. I found it easier because men will tell you what they think of you straight away. They will embarrass you and humiliate you publicly. Then when you have learned your lesson they will join you for a good laugh.

Myrtle saw my clown act with the stool. I landed on my backside attempting to extract my lab coat from the wheel. Finally I just ripped it, my usual process of relieving myself from a stool. It works really well, but lab coats don't last long around me.

In the middle of her sobbing, she was laughing. Tears were flowing out of her eyes, and she was laughing and crying all at the same time.

"What is wrong, why are you crying?" I attempted to look like a serious professional doctor, smoothing the wrinkles and dirt from my coat.

"My husband. I was thinking of my husband." Then the tears really turned on. She was sitting erect, weeping.

"Then why do you cry?" I asked attempting to get to the specific memory.

"My husband died six years ago, and I cry every time I think of him." She had been in this predicament for way too long.

"Do you want to cry when you think of him?" I asked, because I did not want to take it away if she wanted it to stay.

"My husband was the funniest man, he could make me laugh at any time. When I saw your coat getting wrapped under the wheel, I just knew what was coming. I started crying, because that is something that he would have done. He would have done it on purpose, though." She relayed stories of their meeting, getting married, and then his death. When she got to that point I was convinced that I had taken her too far down this path. My mind scolded me, "You should have stopped while you were behind. She is so far gone, you will never be able to help this one. Stop asking her questions, you are just digging a bigger hole."

Myrtle was a gentle, quiet woman, and did not enjoy public displays of emotion, so she confined herself to her own home most of the time.

"Boy am I in over my head. Lord, how am I going to redeem myself? She thinks I'm a clown, not a serious health care professional." The Lord soothed my nerves and reassured me that His ways are not my ways, and that this woman was here to see me. Not just anyone, she needed what I had to give. "But really Lord, did she need the stool routine?"

"Ok Lord but I'm not real sure of myself this time. You could realistically be on your own with this one." I kept telling the Lord He didn't need me.

Then a calm came over me and my embarrassment ebbed.

"Would you like to think about your husband without crying? You have so many wonderful memories, it seems to me that you should enjoy them. You can, you know?" As my words ended, so did her interest.

"I've tried everything. Nothing helps, I've been to counselors. I've been to church. I've done everything," she said with resignation.

I thought, "Oh, so this is why she came to see me, Lord. You send me the hard nuts to crack. Thanks a bunch. Could we have started this thing without me landing on the floor? You know this woman thinks I'm about as serious as...well thanks a lot!"

Myrtle began to straighten her clothes, in preparation to leave.

"Myrtle, I know that you probably think I am a clown already, but would you allow me to prove it to you? You told me that you don't want to cry when you think of your husband. I can help you, if you will play a few games with me. How about it? I can't possibly embarrass myself more than I already have. All you have to lose is a few minutes and a few tears."

Myrtle seemed willing to try. She had no confidence in me, and quite frankly, I was wondering about me, too.

So I had her remember the most wonderful time in her entire marriage. She began to smile. Her body changed perceptively. At the same time, I noticed that she naturally touched a certain spot on her leg. Every time she thought of happy things, she always touched that same spot. "OK, let's use that spot, Lord." He was directing me to different techniques.

"OK, Myrtle, close your eyes and remember when you found

out that your husband passed." That created a flood of tears. "Myrtle, open your eyes, quickly sing row, row, row your boat." She already thought I was a clown, so this was confirming her suspicions. But she sang. She laughed out loud at herself as she sang really off key. Her arm fell again on the same spot.

"OK, Myrtle, remember again, when you found out about your husband passing." She did, and instantly she had a change of her body. "Myrtle, count backwards from twenty-five."

Her eyes crossed, and she smiled, and she counted backwards from twenty-eight. "Thanks Lord, it is working. We are getting it!"

"Myrtle, think of your husband." Her arm rested on that same spot. "Think hard about him. How do you feel?"

Myrtle had accomplished the impossible. She was able to tell me stories about her husband, and the clowning around that he did, without crying. I had her tell me more stories. She did so without crying. We diluted the pain with the laughter. We used her own memories and actions to her advantage.

I had no way of knowing that her husband played tricks on her, and acted like a clown. But someone else did. The King knew what she needed.

Remember the spot on her leg that she always touched when she laughed, and for some reason didn't touch when she cried? It acted like a trigger or an anchor. We used it to help her. Without placing too much emphasis on it, I told her to put her arm there, whenever she thought of her husband and she instantly began to smile.

"Pay attention." This is one of those times, when I reaped the rewards of paying attention. It cost me my undivided attention. The reward was a simple thing like touching her leg when she laughed. She did it every time. We used it to further ensure that laughter would come when we needed it.

Familiarity is that thing that draws you like a magnet. We have talked about an English-speaking child looking to another English-speaking person for confirmation. This child cannot understand the German language, even if the German speaker is trying to save the child's life.

Imagine that you speak English and you enter a bar in West Berlin. It is during the occupation, so many languages are spoken in this dark, dingy, musty place. The lights are low and the music is so loud that your ears are ringing.

Behind you, you recognize the language coming from a man who is drunk and unruly. He is hanging onto the bar, slurring his words, and verbally abusing the patrons and the bar tender.

Look to your right. You see a group of Russians. They are blond haired, handsome, soft-spoken, sitting quietly in a group, laughing and talking. They are enjoying the time spent with friends. Each of them in turn talks, and the others listen intently. One is more beautiful than the other in his posture, behavior, and mannerisms.

Look to your left. There, standing in a small open inviting group, you see a handful of Italians. The Italians are waving their hands and talking as quickly with their hands as they are with their mouths. They are all smiles. The food that they are enjoying is filling the room with fabulous aromas. Each Italian is laughing, talking, playing, and encouraging his friends. They are scientists. They have just successfully launched a project that will bring Berlin into the twentieth century. They are excited about the success that they have achieved; they are all taking at once.

Now imagine that straight in front of you stands the most gorgeous human that you have ever seen. This person is everything that you have ever wanted in a physical mate: stature, weight, build, height. And, oh, they are successful in business. This person is the kindest person that has ever walked the planet. The perfect combination of physical characteristics and mental fortitude is available in this one body. This person speaks Mandarin.

West Berlin during the occupation was a great place to visit, and a rotten place to live. Bombs were always being detonated on the other side of the wall, and intimidation tactics were in play. Everyone had their guard up at all times. The tension was high and the people were plentiful. The only relief from the intensity of the day was the evening trips to the saloon for a relaxing evening respite.

Where are you going to sit in this bar? You speak only one language, English. The Italians look inviting and fun, but you don't speak Italian, and could never join in the conversation. The Russians are just as inviting, and are wonderfully similar to you in poise and manner, but you speak no Russian and would not know how to ask for their favor to sit with them.

Standing in front of you is your dreamboat; the person that you have looked for all of your life. But you will not know about it because, you don't speak Mandarin and will never know that this person fills all of your requirements in a mate.

Where is your comfort zone? The English man, however drunk or unruly he may be. You can understand every foul word that tumbles from his mouth. Unfortunately, you are familiar with him. You move away from him in an attempt to distance yourself, and not be associated with such a horrid display of human degradation. But, more often than not, you hear him and understand his words, and since you do not have to think about what he is saying, you have the opportunity to recognize his actions and look at him.

You focus on his behavior, because he is the familiar one in the bar. You wish that you could strike up a conversation with anyone else in the bar, but no one speaks English, except the unruly one. Unfortunately, you get the whole package. Either you learn another language, or sit alone by yourself; of course you could join in conversation with him. Yuck.

Then the unthinkable happens. The English man needs assistance, and since no one else speaks English, you are recruited to help. You lend a hand with the mental understanding that you will only do what is necessary to assist the drunk as far as is essential, then you will remove yourself from the scene.

The English drunk has fallen and injured himself. He has no identification. You feel some sense of duty to help. So instead of just taking a minute of your time, you look up to realize that you have just spent the entirety of your relaxation time involving yourself with this drunken horrid person. And all because of the familiarity with his chosen language.

Notice for a moment if you will, that there were others in need of assistance that evening. The Italian, the gorgeous one in the entry hall, needed directions. Had you been familiar with his language, or his directions, you could have spent the evening with this gentle person.

Notice the Russian who was sitting alone at the table in the corner. He would have loved company for the evening, because his family had just sent word that he was a new father, and he was reveling in the new life waiting for him. He would have shared stories and laughed, and filled you with dreams of his home, had you been familiar with Russian.

But you were only familiar with English. So you got a good dose of the English man. It was not pleasant, and your shoes are full of his vomit. You smell like you have just come in from a three-day drunk, when in fact you did not consume a drop of alcohol.

Familiarity is the thing that you have seen and experienced. Familiarity is the thing that draws you backwards instead of forward. Had you walked forward in the bar, you would have run head long into the perfect mate of your life. But you were pulled back into the pit of familiarity. You were pulled back into the things that had gotten you where you were. Familiarity is the standard by which you compare everything in your life.

As I have said before, you come into this world as a blank slate. Your mind is like a sponge ready and willing to take up and absorb anything and everything that comes its way. As stimuli come into your world, you see them and accept them as your standard, because that is the first exposure. You are now beginning to record things into your mind. By the age of five, you have developed your core beliefs. You are wonderfully and perfectly made. You are a combination of all that has come into your life for these past years. English was one of the things that were compounded every day.

Not a day nor many moments went by when English words were not directed to you. So, English became the standard by which everything else was measured. Thus when the English man was the only familiar thing around, you gravitated to it. It was destructive, it was abusive, and it was foul. Yet it was where you went. You recognized it and you gravitated to it.

This is how our brains work. We are comparing every input and every thing in our lives to the core that is in us. Wouldn't it be wonderful to pull that core from our brain, and our mind, and analyze it? Then we could decide if it was what we wanted. Sort of like the memory chip in the computer. We could just take it out and replace it with another memory chip. Or reprogram it instantly to do our bidding.

Unfortunately, there is no way to pull the whole entire brain out and look at it. However, we can analyze a portion of it at a time. Look around your life. Those things that are in your core are reflected in your outer world. The things that are deep down are the magnets that draw you through life.

If you speak English, you surround yourself with English speaking people, because you know this language. If you are a runner, you participate in this activity every day, and have something in common with others that run. Maybe you love to cook. When you smell food, and taste it, you are drawn into a daydreaming state where you imagine the ingredients the chef used to create the food.

Whatever you are familiar with will draw you like a magnet, like a moth to the light bulb. So let us take this idea and see what use it could be to our lives.

Imagine that you are a single man. You think that you are an OK kind of guy. You have always thought that you would marry, have a family, and settle down. But for some reason, you keep meeting the same kind of woman. And every time you break up with one woman, you find yourself in a relationship with the same kind of woman again. It seems to be a never ending cycle. You've talked about it, you've fussed about it, and now you are considering being single forever. All of the women that you date are wild, crazy, footloose, and fancy free.

For some strange reason, the same woman keeps appearing in your life, each time with a new name, but essentially the same personality traits, and actions. What will you do?

You could try to stay single. But this will not last long, because it is not your deep desire. You could fret over your inability to find the right person. You could moan about there not being any "Good Ones" left. Or you could look inward and find the magnet that is attracting these women.

Like the English person, you are seeking only those people

that you understand. When you are confronted with German, Russian, or some other dissimilar thing, you have no known experience with; you are not attracted to it. And you simply move away. More often that not, you never even gave conscious consideration to many women that came through your life.

So what is it about you that is familiar with these wild women? Take a deep breath, and relax. *Feel the feelings* that you experience when you are attracted to the wild side. Then when you really fill your body with these feelings, ask yourself a question. When was the first time I felt this *feeling*? Notice, you are not associating people or events, you are associating feelings.

You may experience a sense of freedom, or excitement. You may have a sense of conquest about your new catch. Your feelings are really the key to this. Allow yourself to travel back in time through your memory banks, to find the first time that you felt the same feelings.

You will imagine a time in your young life that had similar feelings, or that created these feelings. Your *English* feelings. Once you identify the original feelings, you can do something about changing them.

Remember the healing of the memories that I described previously. Now you can reprogram your brain to what you want, not what is familiar.

Let's say that you want to attract women who are the motherly, nurturing type. Once you've identified the feelings you get with wild women, then you can change them. For example, maybe you were a sickly child and always looking out of the window while the neighborhood children played and laughed. You felt alone in your quiet home. Your brothers and sisters were out throwing the ball in the lawn and having fun. You couldn't join them because of your malady. So day after day, you watched, and day after day you longed to join them. Fast-forward to the adult you. You associate quiet, soft-spoken women with illness and solitude, and wild crazy women with health, fun, and camaraderie.

Yeah! Right! An adult knows the difference between these. But remember, we are looking for the things a young child thinks; the emotions and responses of a young child. This youngster associates wild crazy loud and boisterous with health and vitality and fun. This youngster was craving friends to play with, and longed to be part of a fun group. This youngster feels alone and neglected at home, in the solitude and quiet of home.

Can you see how this child would grow up and be drawn to "going-out"? This adult-child still yearns for the friendship and laughter of being "out." Being out, going out, laughing, jumping, you get the point. So, as you move through life, this is your "English" core. You are drawn to people who fill this need. Simply deciding to settle down has not changed your inner core. It is still there. It still draws English-speaking people to it.

To change these things, it is important to find this initial event; in this instance, the ill child looking out of the window. How can such a simple event in the life of a small child make such a profound impact on the adult? Well remember throughout the growing years, this has been compounded and reinforced multitudes of times. Over and over, you are drawn to the people who are going ou*t* to have fun. You subconsciously are drawn to them. You like this need being met, so you go more.

Then you decide that you want to settle down. Your core has not changed. The "real" you is still there. You meet a wonderful girl that would make a fabulous mother and wife, and you never give her a second look. She bores you. She is the type of person who enjoys a cold day, a warm fire, a good book, and your company. You run like a scared puppy, because she evokes feelings of quiet. What is quiet associated with? Inside, isolated, alone, neglected, left out; and on it goes.

What if you replayed the memory of looking out of the window as a small child? Then allowed someone, anyone you love and trust to appear in your memory. (Father Al always invites Jesus, and I allow the person to choose who they want. If you use this technique, it will be yours, so do it however you like.) This trusted person tells you that you will soon be well. You will have all of your friends in your home. You will know that the illness will not separate you forever from your friends; you will be with them in two days. You are filled with the confidence of recovery. You imagine that you jump from the couch, get your clothes on, and your friends all pour into your home to visit. They are eating cookies, and milk, and everyone is laughing.

So now revisit this memory. How does it feel to bring up the memory of the boy at the window? Not so bad, as a matter of fact it doesn't have much of a feeling at all. It is just a memory, nothing more. The emotional reaction attached to the memory is not there. It is neither good nor bad, it is just there.

Now the next time you "go out" on the town analyze your feelings when you meet a wild woman. How do you feel? You will notice that it is what it is; instead of a yearning to fill an emptiness, it is just a chance meeting. You want to find a nurturing woman, and now you notice people that you never noticed before.

Let's Make a Cake

When you remember, a certain set of chemicals is released in your brain. Then every time you remember the same thing you release the same chemicals. Soon, you associate these same chemicals (feelings) with this memory.

Imagine that you had an illness as a child and you found

yourself at the window. Feelings of loneliness, isolation, neglect, and despair were experienced. Even though the illness was short lived, you continue throughout your life to have a profound memory of it. Sort of like it happened yesterday. As soon as you remember the window, being inside looking out, seeing your friends play, the emotional chemicals of loneliness are released into your brain.

This same feeling (emotional chemicals) is reinforced every time you are presented with a similar view. This same feeling (brain chemical release) is experienced whenever you think of others having more fun than you. So your memory chemicals of loneliness are set at an early age.

The adult has many experiences that reinforce this feeling (the one that releases the same chemical in the brain as loneliness). The adult yearns for the fun feeling, and so is drawn there to counteract the loneliness feeling.

Feelings of fun, excitement, and joy evoke a *different* set of chemicals in the brain. Whole specialties of medicine are devoted to researching the chemicals released in the brain under different circumstances.

So let us keep this basic.

Imagine that you are baking a cake. The batter is white. You mix and mix and mix, but for some reason the batter never changes color. You want another color, you mix and think about another color, but it never changes. You try to believe another color, but still nothing happens.

What would happen if you dropped one drop of red food coloring in the cake batter. Try it some time. You'll be amazed. The batter turns pink.

Sort of like when you place a red wash cloth in a washing machine. If anything white is put into that same water, it turns pink. We have all done that one before. Pink under shorts! How could something so small, make everything in the washer pink?

It is like this with the brain. You can have a whole head full of "white" stuff, and by putting in a small amount of "red" the entire brain can become pink. The white stuff may be feelings of isolation, neglect, boredom, and despair. By adding one drop of red, which in this case is feelings of fun, togetherness, and joy, the memory (the chemical) is changed.

Don't get me wrong, I am not trying to brainwash you into believing you were well when you were in fact sick; just take some of the emotional impact out of that memory. The memory will remain intact, but the emotional response evoked from the original memory will be lessened or negated. I hope this makes sense. You will recall the memory; you will *feel* different about it.

But back to the emotional chemicals. Here is my version of how this stuff works. This will sound very elementary, but here goes. You are a chef, and when you remember loneliness, you make a batch of loneliness in your brain. Then when you remember fun you make a totally different mixture in your brain. If you could take one drop of that fun mixture, and put it into the loneliness chemical, you could turn it pink. It doesn't take much red to turn a cake pink. It doesn't take much red to turn an entire load of laundry pink. And it doesn't take much fun to change loneliness into a neutral emotion.

Remember the time in front of the window. Remember it is full glory. Feel the intensity of the emotions as well as you can, and allow yourself to really go there. Your brain is sending certain chemicals out to make this happen. Now remember a fun time a really fun time when you had one of those deep belly laughs. Remember it in full glory. Remember it so much that you imagine that you are there. And enjoy the feeling.

Now, just allow yourself to drift back to the window. How does it feel now? Better? The same? Not quite so bad? Now remember that fun time again and really allow yourself to feel it again.

Each time you mix the loneliness with some of the fun, you will turn the loneliness a bit more pink, and the emotional impact of that event will lessen. This is a very simple explanation of what happens.

Chapter 10
Discussion Questions

1. What is your earliest memory? Who was with you? How old were you? Close your eyes and drift back in time to your earliest memory. How does it feel?

2. Look around yourself right now, in the life that you currently have and describe your core. Example: you speak English, slow to anger, very sociable, happy, and quiet.

3. Describe the glasses that you look through. Are they "rose colored," in that you always see the positive side of things? Or do you look for and see obstacles and negativity—"dark colored glasses"? Now be honest with yourself, no one is looking.

4. What are you familiar with? Opulence or meager? Hamburgers or caviar? Diet soda or a martini? Silk or blue jeans? Write thirty (30) things that you are familiar with.

5. Pick one familiar item, for example: hamburger. Next, think of something totally opposite of a hamburger, let's say sushi. Now go out and eat it. Remember, when you do this exercise, pick something that you are not familiar with.

6. Write a description of the experience. Include you feelings before, during and after the event.

7. Next, go and eat the hamburger. Write a description of the experience, including feelings of before, during, and after.

8. Compare your notes. Compare the feelings. Compare the ideas of the two. Compare the adjectives written about the two.

Chapter 11

No More Pain

MARTHA WAS ONE of the most incredibly chronic, hopeless patients that I had ever met. She was a patient that all the other doctors in town had discharged. They told her never to return. Martha had undergone fifteen surgeries by the time I met her.

My partner said to me, "You go in, see her, and discharge her from the practice. I never want to see her again. She doesn't want to get better, and I don't know what is wrong with her. She must be crazy. Send her away. She has no *physical* illness." Unfortunately I was the doctor on-call and was now in charge of her care.

I took a deep breath, and picked up her four-volume chart. The nurse knew Martha well. The nurse looked at me pathetically and walked away. I was leaning against the outside of the exam room door, reviewing Martha's records. The chart was heavy, and awkward. It contained surgical and lab reports, correspondence to and from physicians, and exam notes.

Martha had fallen ill three years earlier. Martha underwent surgery after surgery for pain. Martha didn't have many organs left in her body cavity. From reading the chart, it appeared as though they had all been removed. (OK this is a joke, but there were several missing completely and several missing in part.) Martha's abdomen looked more like a road map than a stomach.

The chief complaint was *intractable pain*. Oh goody! Now I was really excited. "I am a surgeon, I give pain, I create pain regularly, and this woman wants me to assess her for chronic intractable pain. Doesn't she know that there are pain control doctors in the city that specialize in this?" On and on my mind whirled while I reviewed the many ailments and co-morbidities. Yikes, I wondered how many adhesions she had. One organ was certainly sticking to another after all of those surgeries. The scar tissue inside her abdomen must be more prevalent than normal tissue.

I took a deep breath, slapped a smile on my face, called the nurse, and entered the room of despair. Martha, although my age, looked thirty years older. She was slumped over on the exam table moaning and clutching her abdomen. Martha's husband was in the room, cowering in the corner. He looked like someone who had just returned from Vietnam, and was in the throws of post traumatic stress disorder. He was certain to have a flashback at any moment and we would all be in trouble.

I attempted to focus on Martha. I motioned to the nurse to keep an eye on the husband for fear that he would hit the deck. Then we would have two patients instead of one. The nurse escorted the husband into a chair, and I took another breath. Breathing is a good thing, try it some time. When you don't know what else to do, breathe. It can give you a second to clear your head, and start over.

I said hello and introduced myself. Having already read the chart, I was very familiar with what was going on physically, but I wanted the information out of the horse's mouth.

"How can I help you?" I was certain that there was nothing that I could do except listen, but I thought it best to ask anyway.

Martha grunted and asked for pain medication. She cried uncontrollably and clutched her abdomen. She assumed the fetal position, and was drenched with perspiration.

"Martha, lie flat on the bed, I need to examine you." I said in a low voice. As she attempted to move, she screamed. This was no ordinary scream, this was one of those primal screams that animals do when being eaten. It was blood curdling. It was a scream that ran up my spine so fast, every hair on my body stood straight out preparing me to die. That split second in time when my adrenaline was pumping so fast, the lion in the jungle would never have been able to catch me.

She would in no way allow me to touch her. Everything hurt. She screamed when I touched any part of her body, including her toes. "Oh brother," I thought, "this is going to be loads of fun for both of us."

With some quiet coaxing, Martha allowed me to do some parts of the exam. I'm not going to tell you that I did a perfect exam, because I didn't. But I was comfortable that Martha did not need emergency exploratory surgery. Every sign and symptom was present. Everything that I touched elicited a significant response. Nowhere in my medical training, had I seen an acute abdomen like this. Maybe the pain pills had worked to soothe her, but all I could do was stand there and wonder what had gotten this previously beautiful specimen of a woman into this horrid, pain-ridden predicament.

I thought, "OK, now, either I am going to walk from the room and tell her that there is nothing that I have to offer her medically, or I am going to stand here and look stupid." So, I sat down. The longer I sat, the calmer she became. Martha was accustomed to physicians remaining in the room for two minutes or less, then prescribing or referring. No one wanted to stay with her for too long, for fear they would be trapped.

I could find no pathology, nor any physical illness causing her pain. Every organ that could have been the etiology of such pain was removed. So I sat there longer and just stared at her. The nurse left.

Martha realized that I wasn't leaving, and she relaxed more. Not much mind you, just an imperceptible amount; enough to stop squirming on the uncomfortably hard exam table. Seconds became hours, as I just allowed myself to sit next to her. In reality I didn't know what else to do. Nothing had prepared me for the sight in front of me. My heart was breaking, for the husband, the children, the family, for Martha, and for her situation. Certainly we could do something for her.

"But what," I asked the Lord? "There has to be something. What has caused this? What is she thinking?"

"Martha, do you want to die?" I whispered.

She answered in a mumble, "Yes, I'm tired of hurting like this. I don't want to live like this." She looked at me through the corner of her eyes. She was honest, but was afraid that I wouldn't like her answer.

She wept, and I said nothing. I sat quietly, and her husband slumped in his chair. Obviously he had been part of this for too long, he was numb to the whole situation. He looked like he was in some phase of shock, sitting like a mummy in a tomb.

I allowed her to cry softly, and bitterly, and loudly, and quietly. I just sat there, staring at her. My heart and my compassion reached out to her, but my hands remained in my lap. "Surely the Lord knows everything and He knows how this woman is hurting, so I'll let Him use me to just send her whatever she needs right now." My thoughts, and my mind became quiet. I allowed my spirit to stop questioning, and wait.

I said, "Martha what if there was a way to heal you, would

you be interested?' Martha stared at me. She was mad. Then she was furious. How dare I imply that she wanted to be ill!

"What do you think?" She thundered so loudly that everyone in the clinic heard her. The nurse rushed into the examination room to my aid.

Softly I continued, as if Martha's anger had not been felt, "Martha, there may be a way to get rid of your pain, if you are willing to play some games with me."

"Are you stupid or just crazy, lady, I've been in pain for so long I don't remember how to play, I just want to stop hurting." Martha bellowed.

I took another deep breath, my heart pounding so loudly, that I was sure it would pop right out of my chest. I had heard the Lord speak, that still small voice came to me, during my silent observance of Martha, or so I thought.

I had nothing to loose. If I had heard correctly, Martha would be healed and never need another one of us doctors. If I was wrong, Martha would still be in pain and she would leave the office thinking that she had just met the craziest doctor on planet earth.

I was willing to take the risk, but was Martha? She just screamed at me, and the Lord kept telling me to wait (I hoped). Have you ever waited on the Lord? He takes a really long time to do stuff. I get impatient waiting on the Lord, especially when a crazy frantic hysterical woman is screaming at me, and the nurse is trying with all of her might to remove me from the room so I don't get hurt. Oh, and by the way, here is my greatest advice, never pray for patience. The Lord will grant this prayer immediately and will place events and people and obstacles into your life that will help you to develop patience right then and there. A word to the wise.

Martha finally calmed a bit. Do you have children? I do.

Whenever a child is screaming, how do you get their attention? Do you scream or do you lower your voice to a whisper? I whisper, and it changes the tone of the event immediately. Children will rise to the occasion, no matter what the occasion is. If you scream, they scream louder. If you whisper they notice and look at you and begin to whisper. Being a mother has taught me more than I would like to admit. So this is what I did with Martha, quietly and calmly, I told Martha to sit in front of me. She obeyed and quit screaming. Her crying became soft and she had tears falling from her cheeks without the convulsions of her body and mouth. I told her that I would help her get healed before she left the room, and she just sat there in disbelief staring at me.

I asked her to close her eyes, and use her imagination. I asked her to imagine a time in her life as an adult or child when she had no pain. A time when all was right with the world. I told her the type of place that I wanted her to go. Maybe inside, maybe outside, maybe sunny, maybe not. But it was a time when happiness reigned, and joyous laughter surrounded her. A time before now. A time when smiles leapt onto everyone's face. The memories held happy thoughts. She described her "happy place" to me. She was able to do this with ease, and we began her healing. Remember that it is the "core" beliefs that are formed as a child that color the way Martha will look at everything in her life. So, we must get Martha to a place where she trusts me enough to relax and explore times past. Times forgotten that formed the core of the child Martha. Times that could have created a destructive spirit and were killing the adult Martha, without conscious knowledge of it.

Martha had been raised in an abusive home, her father had sexually abused her and she felt guilty and filthy. Nothing that she could do would wash this filth away. Guess where she developed her diseases. If you can't guess, it was in her female organs. Martha told her mother about the abuse, but her mother could not or would not accept the information. Martha felt as though she was at fault for her father's actions. She was furious with him for his behavior. Martha hated her mother for not protecting her. Martha and I found a time in her young life that had been filled with love, and happiness and acceptance. This time was one that she could draw from and use as a basis to heal the things that had wounded her.

Martha remembered being in her mother's womb and being safe and secure and cared for. Remember that the "core" is the place that is like a sponge. When you get back to the core and the original inputs, you can help the patient to compound *those* healed feelings and reinforce the good so much that the rest of her life is colored through good glasses, not bad and guilty ones. So we began. We talked of her security, we talked of her love, we talked of her feelings of provision, and for an eternity we compounded these "core" feelings found in the womb. It was the only place to get them, because the infant and child Martha had been terribly abused. Remember that the "core" is formed from conception to approximately age five, so Martha was in for five more years of bad "core" belief input. We had to gather as much good stuff from the womb as possible and rebuild her core to a strong one so that the oncoming events in her life could bounce off of her and not overwhelm it with negativity. This was no small feat, because we knew of traumatic events that were to come in the life of this small child. So, on and on we went with the compounding, reinforcing and loving of this not yet born child. Soon, a change came over Martha's face and she began to show signs of relaxing. Martha was able to say positive things about herself freely, and a gentleness formed on her face, where only pain and terror had previously been. We healed memories, felt acceptance, protection, and safety of her environment, until it seemed that Martha could imagine going through the birth process and going into the harsh future of her childhood.

Martha was able to remember her infancy and childhood now through new core beliefs, and understand things about her father and mother that she could not have fathomed before. Instead of viewing herself as guilty, she understood that her father had an illness, and her mother was filled with fear. She was able to forgive her father for his actions, and allow herself to see that she was not to blame. She began to see her life through new glasses, and all of her life took on a new and wonderful color. She saw lessons in her life, instead of guilt and pain.

Martha's body became so relaxed that she asked if she could lie down. When she did, she looked like a weight had been lifted from her, and she lay perfectly flat on the uncomfortable table. She had tears flowing from her eyes, so I asked her, "Tell me about the tears?"

After several moments, she took a deep breath and sighed. She said in a whisper, "I don't hurt." As if she were trying to keep it a secret. If her words were heard, maybe the pain would find her again and it would jump on her like before. The pain had had a life of its own, and now she was looking around the room as if to see where it had gone. She was afraid to move, certain that when she did, she would again experience the excruciating crushing horror of her past three years.

"Martha, the Lord wishes all to be healed." "It is OK for you to get well." My words fell to the ground like rocks. "Martha, let's get you off of the examination table." She looked at me with terror, but obeyed my words. Her fear of the pain returning was overwhelming. "Martha, I am going to ask you to do some things, and I just want you to trust me. This time Martha you are on your own. Now roll over, and sit up." Martha quietly and reluctantly obeyed. She slowly moved her deformed, scar-ridden body. She realized that there was no discomfort, nor pain. She sat in front of me in disbelief. Her face turned from fear to wonder.

"Martha, get up. You need to do this on your own. I am not going to help you. You are on your own now." She sheepishly looked at her husband who was still sitting in the chair, but had begun to take an interest in the goings on. He saw his wife move in ways he hadn't seen in years. He just watched in silence. Martha looked at him for help, but he didn't move. Martha moved one leg and didn't scream in pain. "Oh thank you God," I thought. Then she moved the other. She stood up and felt her body.

Martha pushed on her stomach, and felt nothing. She took a step, and felt no pain. She was weak from years of surgeries and no exercise, but she began to move. She sat down and stood up. Slowly she realized that her pain was completely gone. Martha's face transformed to one of beauty. She had a gentleness in her face that told the rest of the story.

Martha and her husband hugged, something that they had not done in far too long. Martha's pain had prevented it. Now they stood in a long embrace, looking into each other's eyes, and giving the love to each other that each so desperately wanted.

I quietly departed the room, and resumed the hectic pace of a surgeon, taking out sutures, staples, and reviewing others' lives. I told the nurse to leave them in the room as long as necessary, and not to disturb them. As I passed the examination room over and over again, the door closed and no sounds emerging, I wondered at the conversation between husband and wife; the reunion of lovers that had been lost while still together.

Several months passes before Martha reappeared. She

phoned me to say, “Hey Doc, I want you to know some things. I am working again. I love my job. My husband and I are happier than we’ve ever been. I rode my horse the day after I saw you, and my horse was happy too. I’ve been riding more and more and I have my life back. There are things that are so wonderful, I don’t have time to tell you all of them.” Martha talked for thirty minutes, relaying the changes that her life had taken. It was as though she had had the most wonderful life, filled with love and laughter, and learning, and optimism.

“You are the only one who didn’t give up on me,” she continued. “Thank You. And my husband thanks you. He is standing right here, and he says thanks, too.”

Thank you seems like a horribly inadequate phrase at times like these. Martha was unable to convey the gratitude that she felt, but was trying desperately to. Martha’s life was now one of productivity, health, vitality and vibrancy.

“Yeah God, for giving us mortals the means to learn from You to heal our fellow man. You said to heal the sick. Thank You for healing Martha and allowing her to have the life that You wanted for her,” I prayed.

Chapter 11
Discussion Questions

1. Imagine a time in your life when all was right with the world. Really go there in your imagination and see the sights, smell the aroma, hear the sounds. What were you wearing? Describe your feelings when you brought this to mind.

2. Do you have a "condition" that has taken on a life of its own? Do you claim it by saying "My pain" or "My problem?" Do you give it a personality by saying "My fibromyalgia acted up today," as if it were an unruly adolescent?

3. Are you willing to take its identity away from it? What would you gain by getting rid of this "thing"? Have you used your "condition" to get out of activities?

4. Close your eyes, pray a prayer of protection, then ask God, "What do You want me to know right now?" Write down the answer. Be as descriptive as possible.

5. Pray as directed by God.

Chapter 12

Cancer Is Vanquished

SOMETIMES PEOPLE COME into our lives that change us forever. With physicians, every patient fills that description. Every patient stretches us to read more, study more, and be better at what we do. People come into our lives for a reason, a season, or a lifetime. Virginia came into my life for a reason. Up until I met Virginia, I had the mistaken impression, like most everyone, that cancer was a death sentence. Like most people, the word cancer evokes a certain physiological response that is not pleasant. It makes me think about life and death, drugs and radiation, pain and suffering.

Cancer also evokes memories of cures and healings. But the first response is always the same for me—Oh no, cancer!

Think of your response to the word *cancer*—the big "C". Just saying it makes me cringe. Every hair on my body stands on end and there is a feeling of terror that rushes through my veins. I can feel is palpably, like a rush of heat through my body. Does your body do this? Do you feel something like a death wave flow through you when you hear that word? We have all had acquaintances that have had cancer. We have all heard of someone that was told they have cancer. We have all been acquainted with the medications, radiation, surgery, and all too often the fight for a life.

Just the mention of cancer evokes responses that we do not

understand. Let's say that you have heard of cancer, but it has not touched your life. Your response may be different from a person who has already battled and won the war on cancer. Your response may be fear, and the next person may have a response of "Ok here we go again." Your response will be based on your experiences with cancer.

If your wife lost the battle with cancer, your response will be one of death and loss. If your son was told that he had three months to live, fifteen years ago, your response will be one of "let's go…we will fight and win." So, no matter who you are, you have some type of response to this dreaded thing. My response is based on losing the most important man in my life.

My grandfather was the only man that I have ever known to have loved me just because I was me. He was one of those people in my life that was so special to me that I can hardly think of him yet today without tears coming into my eyes. My grandfather was perfect. He had only two grandchildren, a girl and a boy. Being the only granddaughter, I was the apple of his eye. He had had no daughters, so to have a granddaughter was the icing on the cake. There are people who would probably tell you that my grandfather was fallible and human, but to my young mind he was perfect.

Tampaw was my grandfather's name. In my brother's attempt to say Grampa, he said Tampaw and the name stuck. So, by the time I arrived on the scene, two years later, Tampaw was his name. Tampaw was the most wonderful example of a man that I could have imagined. He treated me as if I was more important than anyone else in the world. Throughout my young life, if I wanted to talk to anyone, Tampaw was the person. We could talk about anything. Tampaw spent hours listening to my childish ramblings, and acted interested. Not just interested, but he looked me in the eye and hung on my every word.

I felt as though someone heard every word that I said, because when I talked, he listened with his whole body and mind and he heard me. To this day I can recall our conversations and the wisdom that he imparted into me as a youngster.

My poor parents dealt with a rebellious teenager, who wanted nothing more than to run away from home and live with her grandparents. Probably in retrospect they should have sent me there to live, and I could have been disciplined by my grandparents. But it was not to be, my parents took the brunt of my growing and learning and allowed my grandparents to be the rescuers and heroes. My parents deserve a metal of honor for having put up with me for so long without hanging me with duct tape from the highest tree. Of course as a child of thirteen, fourteen, fifteen, I knew everything. It is a funny, ironic thing, though. The older I get, the less intelligent I get, and the more I realize that I don't know. But I digress.

Living in south Louisiana it was hot and humid most of the year, but that never deterred my Tampaw and me. He would always have my favorite fruit at the house awaiting my arrival. I would gorge myself on fresh cherries, then we would run together into the living room. We would sneak into the hallway and set the air conditioner on fifty-five or sixty degrees Fahrenheit. If Gram caught us, she would act very upset at our frivolous games, and pretend she were scolding us. We would laugh and run into the living room.

Looking back at these things now, it is certain that my grandmother not only knew what we were doing, but actively participated in it. She never changed the thermostat or was angry. She always just shook her head and walked back to her previous activities. Funny thing, she always allowed us to have hours of time together, just appearing long enough to deliver popcorn or fruit.

Tampaw and I would light Gram's candles (you know the ones saved for special occasions) and giggle like we were getting away with some covert activity. Gram kept certain things, "special things" for company. We were not allowed in the "living room," especially not kids. Kids belonged outside, not on white carpet and fancy furniture. Tampaw would secretly tell me he hated to go into the living room because he would always spill something and Gram would get mad. But somehow, Tampaw and I were allowed to use the living room for these "secret" times.

Next we would light a fire. It had to be a roaring fire, the kind Northerners make to keep warm. Now, get this picture correct: southern Louisiana, ninety-eight degrees in the shade, and my grandfather and I have cooled the inside of the house to fifty-five degrees and lit a bonfire in the fireplace in the formal living room. The neighbors must have thought we had gone insane, but we never concerned ourselves with those matters. Tampaw and I would sit in front of that blaze for hours, trying to keep warm in the cool air. Every so often we would rotate to get a different body part warm. Our talks and time together were the things that bonded us. It was also the thing that made our parting so intense.

Tampaw called me one day to tell me that he couldn't come to get me. He wasn't feeling well. This was a huge blow because my grandfather had never told me "No" before. He didn't give me money or other tangible items, he gave of himself. So I was panicked. I knew something was terribly wrong.

In those days people could drive at fifteen-years-old, and I had recently acquired my drivers license. Mother heard the panic in my voice and allowed me to take the family car to see my grandfather. He looked pale and weak, but kept a smile plastered to his face as he told me that he had to go to a doctor. Within a day, Tampaw was hospitalized and people were whispering around me. No one dared tell me what was going on. Finally, Mother sat me down and said, "Tampaw has lung cancer." The total devastation and denial, all at the same time, overwhelmed me. I went to Tampaw and wept. We cried, we grieved, and my young heart split in half. No words could explain to a fifteen-year-old child why her grandfather was being ripped away from her. Day after day, my mother told me that I could drive to the hospital after school. How I longed to skip school and go wherever Tampaw was.

Then it happened. I walked in to Tampaw's room and he wasn't there. I was overjoyed; finally they had healed him and helped him, and sent him home. I stood in the doorway of that cold sterile hospital room and saw no cards, no flowers, no loving grandfather with open arms. I jumped up and ran to the nurses station. I was so excited I could hardly talk. "When did Tampaw go home?'

"Who?" the nurse asked quizzically.

"Tampaw!" I screamed. "He is well, he went home, when did he go home, how did Gram get all of his things without me?" The nurse continued to look at me questioningly. "Edgar Thomas! When did you discharge him, Did Gram come and get him?"

The nurses looked at each other in total dismay, who was this excited child and who was she yelling about? Finally a nurse appeared that I recognized. I ran up to her, firing questions faster than I could think them. Her only words were "He expired." Then she turned and walked away. The echoing of her shoes remained as a sign that she had continued walking. My shocked, surprised, bewildered eyes turned to the other two nurses. "What does expired mean?' I asked choking back the emotion that was welling inside my throat.

One nurse looked at her lap, the other walked away quickly.

"How can this be? Where did they take my grandfather? Where is he?" The nurse just sat there staring through me as if I was some invisible screaming ghost. She looked like she couldn't talk and couldn't move, all at the same time—and I collapsed.

Hospital floors are not designed to touch or to be touched with any part of your anatomy except the bottom of your shoes. They are as cold and as uninviting as those horrid nurses. Every cell in my body wept. I wanted to scream out loud but all my body could do was whimper, and moan. My mouth was quiet but my mind screamed so loud that the angels on the other side of the planet must have heard me. My whole existence had just collapsed around me. Somehow, through the fog, I realized that I was alone and no one cared. I had only a cold cement floor and a sterile hospital for company.

My mother had tried to catch me before I left for the hospital, but had missed me coming and going. My grandmother, too, had made attempts to intercept me prior to my arrival at the hospital, but to no avail.

No one stopped and spoke with the young girl on the floor. No one noticed her despair. No one stopped their appointed rounds long enough to notice that a young life had just forever been altered by two words. Still today I cannot tell you how I drove from that hospital to Gram's house, but I remember parking Mother's car, walking up the drive, and opening the door. I stood there waiting to hear Tampaw's voice, his low deep voice, excitedly inviting me to see what treats awaited me in the fridge. All I heard was silence. I couldn't walk, or talk. I couldn't move.

Mother walked up to me and held me. She didn't have to talk. She just held me. There were so many people at Tampaw's house, but the house was silent. I heard nothing, no voices, no sounds. I tried hard to find Tampaw, I walked from one room to the next in delirium, looking for him.

"Where are you? Are you hiding? I'll look at the thermostat, and if it says fifty-five degrees, then I'll know he's here." But the thermostat said seventy. There was no fruit waiting in the fridge. As a matter of fact, there was no treat for me at all. No fire had been lit, no candles were burning; Gram's special candles were standing coldly, awaiting the guests that would never come. Just my Gram, sitting in a corner of the kitchen, holding her arms out to me.

Her face filled with a compassion and a knowing about me. She understood what I couldn't. She had seen years come and go. She had seen joy and sorrow. She just held me. I sat at her feet with my head in her lap. Her tears dropped warmly onto my cheeks and I felt the weight of the world descend upon my shoulders. We sat for hours as people paraded by to talk. I'm sure she spoke to some, I'm sure someone tried to make small talk, but I never heard a voice, just a deep silence, a lonely sound that sucked all of the energy , vitality and life from my soul.

It has been thirty years since my Grandfather went home to see the Lord, and still, when I hear the word *cancer*, I remember my first exposure to it. I have used my own methods to heal these memories, but it will never change a child's loss of her grandfather in her formative years. The impact of this event shaded many events to come in my life.

Having given you a glimpse into my life, and a taste of my reaction to a particular word—*cancer*—you can see how I can have empathy for your reactions to a word.

Virginia had some reactions that I would like to tell you about.

Virginia was a friend of a patient. This particular patient

knew that I would pray with anyone for any reason. She knew that I would do whatever I could to ease the suffering of anyone. The patient had occasion to be the recipient of many of my techniques of healing of the memories, and such. This patient called me and told me about Virginia. I told the patient to bring Virginia to the office, and I would do what I could. No promises, no expectations, no nothing until I met the woman. I attempted to convey the importance of the woman making her own impressions and opinions of me. And, I would ask the Lord about Virginia.

Well, you may expect that the patient told Virginia that I was about two steps away from divinity itself, and I could do anything. Virginia came into my office expecting a miracle or a lightning bolt to fall from the sky. She looked at me like I was Elisha and her name was Naaman. She was expecting some wonderful words from my mouth to fall upon her stricken body, and it would all be over. She would be healed. I had to disappoint her. I am not Elisha and Naaman didn't get a great show of miraculous power either.

Virginia was frail, she was excited and she was shaking like a cold scared puppy who had just been removed from the warm bath water.

So, we began to discuss the process of healing. I told her how I work. "Virginia, we are going to first talk about you and your life and your expectations. Next we are going to do some simple healing exercises, then, we will get into some more advanced healing modalities. If at any time, you become uncomfortable with me or what we are doing, just let me know and we will stop."

Virginia, was ready to run from the office screaming, as Naaman was ready to go home without his miracle. Naaman's helper encouraged him to do whatever was necessary, even though it wasn't glamorous. Virginia looked at her husband and her friend, my former patient. They both encouraged her to sit down, relax, and give me a chance. Virginia, wide eyed, like a deer caught in the headlights of oncoming traffic, reluctantly sat down. Virginia sat on the edge of her chair, ready to leap up and run at any moment.

Have you ever tried to do your job with a nervous Nellie? Virginia was going to make me work for this one. Oh my. Virginia didn't hear one word that I said. She looked at her friend every few seconds and her eyes darted back and forth.

Virginia, as the story unfolded had a picture perfect life. Her parents loved her, her childhood was peaceful, except for a few bumps and bruises from local bullies. Virginia had been nurtured and loved. Virginia had it all, a wonderful husband who loved her and catered to her every want. She had several children who had grown into successful adults. Virginia was the picture of perfection, or so it seemed. My mind was whirling, "How can a person with so much good stuff be dying of terminal cancer, and so far it has been refractory to treatment? What am I missing? OK Lord, You are on Your own here, because I'm not getting anywhere with this woman. I'm about to think that cancer is not treatable. All the other incurables are treatable with these methods, but cancer is too much. If You want to help her through me, You had better start talking, because I can't find anything in her past memories to heal," I thought.

I gave up. I sat back, not telling her about my failure, and I asked her if she wanted a cup of coffee. Her friend went outside and her husband went to the car. Virginia and I laughed and talked about our children. We laughed at the stages that children go through and the interesting things that children do. The more we talked about our children, the more something kept nagging at me.

My mind raced again, "How many children did Virginia say that she had? Why is it that she only talks of two children. 'Something' keeps telling me she had three births? Maybe I misunderstood." My mind was working on overdrive. Over and over I tried to get back to the number of children, covertly of course. I began to ask detailed questions about the children. I told of my daughter, and asked about hers. I talked about my son and asked about hers. Still, Virginia would not talk about any other children. "What was going on? Why did I feel that there was another child?" Finally I just blurted out, "Have you had harsh words with anyone?"

Virginia said, "No." End of story. I could not elicit any harsh feelings, words, or actions toward anyone in her life. Now I'm skeptical. Come on, no one?

I don't know about you, but never a day goes by when I don't think something harsh. Maybe I stub my toe. Maybe someone drives in a crazy way. Maybe my children get into a fight. But I have harsh thoughts, and all too often harsh words. But Virginia had none. I don't believe her. And I asked her these questions, "Are you willing to do whatever it takes to be healed? Do you want to be healed?"

"Yes!" Virginia answered emphatically. She told me that she wanted to live a long life with her husband. She wanted to meet her yet unborn grandchildren. She wanted to grow old gracefully with her wonderful husband.

"Then tell me who you have been saying or thinking harsh things about." I looked into her eyes. An eternity passed. She just sat there. I told her, "Your cancer is not an accident. Your cancer is in your throat for a reason. I want to know why. If you want me to help you, then you help me. Who do you speak harshly about? The reason your cancer is in your throat is because—that is where words come from." You have been holding something back and it is eating you alive. Something that you don't want to talk about or even remember. Something that is so painful, that you would rather hold it in than allow it to come out." I slowly began to describe the effect of words on her life, and how they had the power to heal her, or kill her. The power of life and death is in the words.

I softly and quietly told her of the profound effect on her life, that the good words had, and the destructive words were having. She began to look at her lap. She then began to cry silently, with tears rolling off of her cheeks and making a puddle in her lap. She did not move, and I noticed that all of the tears were landing in the same place. She then began to weep harder. Surely she was remembering something that had hurt her. She now was remembering things that we could heal.

Virginia told me of her parents. Apparently there was a time when her parents had talked of abortion. They resolved to keep her and allow her to live, have a birth, and thus a wonderful life. But Virginia talked of the underlying feelings of insecurity, of knowing that there was a time in her past when the possibility arose of her being murdered. Of course she was in her mother's womb when these things were going on, but isn't it true that the mother and child are in the same surroundings at one time? Whatever her mother was feeling at the time, was conveyed to the unborn child. The unborn Virginia knew that her mother and father were having difficulties. She knew that she would be a burden to them in some way. She knew that by coming into the world, she would create hardship in the family, and if she didn't exist then the family would be better.

Remember the "Core." The core is formed by stimulus input from conception to five years old. She had this experience in utero, in her mother's womb. Then the rest of the "core," her young life, was filled with wonderful loving, happy memories.

But this event had been recorded into the core of Virginia. It was small and it had not been compounded like the good stuff, but it was still there. So, what created a compounding effect to have Virginia start destroying herself from the inside out? There must have been more in this life, because from working with patients for many years, I have seen that it is not just one event, but the compounding and reinforcing of negative events that causes disease.

Virginia was reluctant to talk about anything negative. She had been taught that a negative person was a bad thing. Virginia was a good person, therefore, she had to convey to the world that she was good, even though her thoughts were filled with painful memories. Virginia could not admit that she had these negative thoughts, because it would betray a negativity about her.

Virginia slowly began to trust me. She slowly began to shift her eyes this way and that. Virginia was remembering times in her marriage and in her motherhood that were not perfect. She began to admit that she was not perfect, and she had some negative thoughts and words. As she did, we slowly approached each one with caution and allowed Virginia to heal them at her own pace.

Then we came upon a memory that was too painful to tolerate. Virginia's son (remember the one that Virginia would not mention previously) was a total disappointment. Virginia and her husband had been hurt so badly by this child, that the couple could no longer consider him an offspring. They had lived through some horrible abuse at the hands of this child, and were no longer willing to tolerate the son's behavior. In attempting to heal themselves from obvious abuse and actions, Virginia and her husband had chosen to ignore the events, and place them in a "closet." The couple chose to place that section of their life behind them.

Virginia's decision to walk away from a situation is understandable, and most of us would say or probably do the same thing. Virginia had been physically, verbally, and psychologically abused by her own child. She couldn't take any more and decided to do something about it. She shut off those memories and emotions. She decided to no longer allow that particular pain to enter her life.

So, what exactly is the problem with this? Well, Virginia already had a negative event of rejection and feelings of unworthiness in her core. The longer the new events took place, the more rooted and firm they became. The compounding of these events and feelings became so overpowering, that they began to trigger self-destructive behaviors in Virginia. Although she consciously made this decision, she had already allowed so much to be reinforced in her mind and memories, that she was just putting a band-aid over the problem.

Consciously deciding to walk away from abuse was the right decision. But, the painful memories were destroying her.

Imagine for a moment that you have had an accident, and during that event, a splinter was lodged under your skin. At the moment of the accident, you felt bad, horrible maybe, and you learned to avoid similar situations. There is a problem though. You learned to avoid future similar events, but you never removed the splinter. The foreign body, or splinter was left there, and sooner or later your body will try to remove it. The splinter may become infected, or it may become encapsulated with scar tissue. It may begin to move around, or it may trigger a negative reaction in your body, that sets off an autoimmune response that tells your body to produce bad things. The splinter doesn't belong in your body, and it should not be there.

In the surgical world, we remove the foreign body, drain the abscess or infection from the area, remove the scar tissue, then clean the wound with fresh water. The wound is closed, and allowed to heal. Only after the foreign invader is removed and eliminated, is the body allowed to heal and regain its normal functioning, and stability.

So, Virginia had avoided future events. This was a great decision. But the foreign body was still in her body. The memories of the horrible events had been allowed to stay inside of her, and fester. The longer they festered the more they destroyed her. She was literally killing herself. This was called cancer. Throat cancer. She didn't want to die, she wanted to live. She was willing to get the foreign body out, and clean the wound, to eliminate this thing from her life. Virginia had heard the word Cancer and had given up. To Virginia it was a death sentence. She looked to her doctors for answers, and when they had done all that they could do, she panicked.

Virginia had taken all of the drugs, done the surgery, and had the radiation. Still her cancer grew. Her terror grew. She was more afraid of the word than she was of death itself. She was more terrified of what the cancer would do to hurt her than she was of going to meet the Lord.

As fear gripped Virginia she became a walking time bomb. She became depressed and nothing helped her. There was no joy nor happiness in her life. Even her husband could not make her smile. She focused all of her energies on her cancer, and had no idea how to focus on healing.

"Virginia, are you willing to forgive your child?" was all I asked, and I set off a chain reaction that nuclear physicists would have been proud of. I will not attempt to convey the explosion that followed. This stoic woman, the one who had nothing bad to say about anyone, all of a sudden had plenty to say, and none of it was niceties or pleasantries. She expounded on every vile and horrid thing that this child had done, and the fact that this child did not need to be forgiven. "As a matter of fact, he should go to hell, where he belongs."

When the tide began to ebb, I interjected, "Virginia, your memories and your feelings and emotions are killing you, not your child. If you really want to live and be healed, then we have to find a way to help you, regardless of your child's whereabouts or actions. We must work with you and your emotions. Are you willing, to be willing to forgive him?" I asked in a quiet voice so that she would know that I was saying something very important.

"Virginia, all I'm asking you to do is what you already agreed to. You asked me to help you live. I am willing to help you, but what that means, is that you do part and I do part. All I want from you is the possibility that you would be willing to be willing to forgive your son. Be willing to learn from this situation, and we can continue on." I spoke slowly, then more slowly. I repeated myself intentionally so that the words would sink into her. I didn't really want her to answer too quickly, but wanted the words to reach into her soul, so that she could begin the healing process on her own.

"OK," was all she said. She uttered the words so quietly, that I was not sure that I had heard anything. I looked at her for more, but there was none. She had agreed, but she could not utter another word.

"Virginia, you are going to be fine. You are going to heal. You will get rid of this thing that is eating you. Since you want to feel better, and you are willing to cut open and scrape out the nasty stuff, you will be fine." And the work really began. We had found the problem. We had finally found the injury and the pain.

"Virginia, think about the last time that you saw your son." She sort of shrunk back into her chair. She was obviously reliving it in living color. "Virginia, tell me about it, who is with you?"

"No one."

"Virginia, how do you feel?" Since she was so reluctant to speak I had to dig feelings and events from her, "in your memory, where is your son standing, what is he doing?"

"He is looking at me, like he wants to hit me again, his eyes look more like demons that human, I'm scared." Her body was recoiling from the memory. "Virginia, ask God to step into your memory, and tell me when He is there."

"He is there."

"Where is He standing, and what is He doing?

"He is standing between us."

"Virginia, look at God, then tell me everything that you notice."

"He is very white, sort of a gold white. He is facing away from me, looking at my son. He is not real happy with Gregory. I am hiding behind God; Gregory can't see me anymore. God is so big that I am completely behind Him."

"How do you feel?"

"Like Gregory needs to straighten up, or God will be more angry than He already is." Virginia's voice stopped shaking, and her body was beginning to relax. "I am not so afraid anymore, God won't let Gregory hit me again. I kind of feel sorry for Gregory, like he doesn't know what he is doing."

"What is Gregory doing now?"

"He just turned and walked away, God is still standing between us."

"Virginia, can you forgive Gregory and allow him to leave you, your memories, and your life? Can you allow him to keep walking, like he is now?"

"Yes."

"Virginia, if you are comfortable with God staying, then it's OK, and say whatever you want to say to Gregory." Virginia talked about how hurt she felt, and that she had made a decision, she was not going to allow Gregory to reappear in her life. She told Gregory that she was sorry but she had endured all that she could. She told Gregory that she forgave him, and would pray that he would be healed.

As soon as Virginia was finished with Gregory, we did the same with mom and dad. Virginia cleaned her memory closet. She allowed the old dirty worn memories to be discarded or cleaned. She no longer had to worry about opening the closet door. Now she could easily talk about her son, without years of emotions exploding out. She had a fresh new look at her life. She was not happy that her son had chosen a dark path, but she was comfortable with allowing him to go. Her body relaxed, and her eyes told the story. The eyes are the windows to the soul, and her soul was free. Free from hiding the secret, free from covering up old hurts, and free to explore the future.

She knew the process, and could now continue to heal herself, without my help. She stood up, and hugged me. It was not the hug of a nervous jittery person afraid of her own shadow. No, it was a full body hug that said, "Thank you." The kind that told me that the next time I heard from Virginia, she would be a different person.

Two weeks later I got the report that Virginia had been to the doctor. The doctor had performed a pet scan to look at the cancer. It had not only gotten smaller, it was gone. Nothing showed on the test. No other therapy had helped in all of the years of treatments, but now the cancer was gone in two weeks.

Not a trace remained. The doctor called it a miracle. He did not understand, and Virginia told him how God had healed her.

Virginia was smiling and laughing and playing with her husband. She was enjoying her friends. She felt better than she had in years. Virginia had her life back, and her future. The cancer was not the problem. The cancer was just leaves on the tree. It was the symptom, not the cause. The roots of pain and despair were addressed and healed. The roots of destruction had been healed, and replaced with roots of life and joy.

Virginia was able to learn from her experiences with her son, instead of turning them on herself. She was now able to see that expressing her feelings was an acceptable alternative. She was able to see others in a new light, and was able to appreciate more people. She had a new vitality to her step.

When you listen, if you *really* listen, concentrate and focus, you will hear much more than words. You will hear a still small voice telling the rest of the story. Using Virginia as our example, every time she said *children* I heard and felt that there were more than two. No voice spoke into a loud speaker (unfortunately). I'm still asking for that direct red line phone, but in lieu of that the Lord filled in the blanks of Virginia's descriptions. He allowed me to feel the vacant empty spaces that Virginia had created when she made the difficult decision. A hole was left in her spirit, and God wanted to be invited in to fill it. Virginia was too overwhelmed with her struggle with cancer to see that she was suffering a greater loss; the one of a mother for her son. You see, it was as though her son had died, only worse, because she knew that she had to choose to bury him, forgive him, and release him to God's grace.

Chapter 12
Discussion Questions

1. Who came into your life for a reason, then disappeared from your life? What was the reason? What did you learn from this?

2. Who came into your life for a season? What was the season? What did you learn?

3. Who came into your life for a lifetime? What do you continue to learn?

4. What reaction do you have to the word cancer? Where did you first experience it? How have you changed since then?

5. Are you stuffing memories into a closet in you mind? What memories have you done this with? How would you feel if you could just clean them out of your mental closet?

6. When was the last time you did a spring-cleaning of your mind?

Chapter 13

Putting It All Together

WHETHER YOU ARE attempting to improve yourself, help console a friend, or heal a patient, there are many tools that can be used. The Lord "healed them all" and has commissioned us to do these things and better. So, heal the sick. Leave them a bit better than the way you found them. Don't envy someone else's ability to use their intuition, gut feelings, or still small voice. God is trying to get through to you and He will keep trying. Look at me. If He can get through my thick head, He can surely get through yours.

When I was first studying the Bible, I thought praying had to be some momentous act. As if praying could only be done on my knees, in a quiet place, with lots of reverence about it. As God was pulling me closer, I realized that God really has a sense of humor. He knows my insecurities, so He would use them often, to break them. I always had and still have the option to say no to Him, but if I begin to argue, guess who wins—Him. He will always get in the last word with me.

Everyone has the innate gut feelings. This is the toehold that God has in you. Choose to develop it and God will take advantage, jump right on board, and teach you. If you choose not to develop it, I believe that He is OK with that too. But He will never leave you or forsake you. He will always be there. As a mother coaxes a toddler to take his first step, the Holy Spirit will show you the way to develop this skill. And I use the word skill with intention. I believe that it is a skill to be exercised, sort of like riding a bike.

You tried and practiced, and one day you had it. You could ride a bike. Throughout your life, you don't lose the knowledge or the skill of riding a bike. You have it. This is just like that still small voice. You have one, everyone does. Are you going to develop the skill of riding a bike to the point of winning like Lance Armstrong? Or are you going to ride around the neighborhood for fun? Will you perform in tricks and stunts in Cirque-du-Soleil or will you ride down the beach?

God has given you the ability to hear. It is up to you to use it, practice with it, and have fun. Ask and God will answer, like He did in Wal-Mart one time. I had taken my daughter to purchase school supplies. That time of year when the entire world has descended into Wal-Mart. Everyone was anxious, some were angry, and the whole store was in chaos. Parents were attempting to purchase supplies for their children. Employees were attempting to keep the shelves stocked. But as soon as they organized one isle, the next shelf was in chaos.

As my daughter and I approached the checkout stand, we noticed that the girl behind the register had been crying. No one seemed interested in this young girl's distress. As a matter of fact, it seemed just the opposite. As people collected their items, they were rude. No one had the time or patience to stop long enough to talk with a child in need. They had their own problems. They didn't need to add more.

Of course my daughter saw what was coming. She is a very sensitive child. She has been around me long enough to know that I would have a hard time walking away from this clerk without attempting to help.

My daughter said "Hi" and the clerk just barely looked up.

Her face was red from crying, and her eyes were still moist. My daughter said, "How would you feel if I prayed for you?" The clerk responded with a shrug of the shoulder as if to say "whatever." The clerk said OK, but obviously still pouring misery into her own brain. My daughter quickly, quietly listened for any instructions from the Lord. After she was sure that she heard correctly, she addressed the clerk and said, "You have the most beautiful hair and nails. You must have spent a tremendous amount of time on them. I just wanted you to know that," Within seconds, we could see that the second helping had been dumped into her brain. Just one drop of red coloring, the coloring coming from the emotional chemical of happiness, had been dumped in. In just a moment, it had changed the color of distress to a better one. As my daughter and I walked away from the clerk, and collected our bags to leave the store, the clerk said thanks and we could see from her posture that she meant it.

It only takes a moment to mix a new chemical in your brain or in the brain of someone else. The chemicals are all there ready to be poured like the ingredients of a cake stand waiting to be mixed. They lie there like red food coloring waiting to be poured into cake batter. They are waiting to be thrown into the wash, to turn your shorts pink.

Look up James 1:5–6, "If you need wisdom—if you want to know what God wants you to do—ask him, and he will gladly tell you. He will not resent your asking. But when you ask him, be sure that you really expect him to answer." I use the New Living Translation. When I started studying the Bible it seemed that the foreign language of medicine and surgery was all that my brain could handle. King James was difficult at best. When this Bible was presented to me, I rejoiced because I was able to "get it" quickly. Then as I began teaching others to read and study the Bible, it seemed like a readable version. So this is the one that I use the most.

The Lord will tell you what needs to be done to heal your memories, your body, and your spirit. Suffice it to say that listening to the Lord is really a good start. We all pray, and we all talk *to* God. But, who stops long enough to *listen* to Him? Do you? God will tell you how to do the things you want to do.

We have explored how I learned to listen, and obey the Lord. Now it is time for you. Gentle words bring life and health. (See Proverbs 15:4.) The words I heard that day with the dog definitely brought health and life. Had I run, I could not have made it far. Had I fought, I would have lost. The gentle firm words welling up in me saved my life and my hands. They had been given for counsel, and comfort.

If words have enough power to give life and health, they certainly have enough power to give hurt, and pain. Sharp words are swords, and bitter words are as arrows. (See Psalm 64:3.)

So why do we teach our children, "Stick and stones may break my bones, but words will never hurt me?" The Bible directly contradicts this. Proverbs 18:8 clearly states that words cut deeply, down to the innermost parts of a person. It would appear that words are more than a simple form of communication. They are weapons and tools as Proverbs 12:18 says, in the mouth of the wise they bring healing.

> A gentle answer deflects anger, but harsh words make tempers flare.
>
> —Proverbs 15:1

> Kind words are like honey—sweet to the soul and healthy for the body.
>
> —Proverbs 16:24

> Your tongue cuts like a sharp razor.
>
> —PSALM 52:2

> Worry weighs a person down; an encouraging word cheers a person up.
>
> —PROVERBS 12:25

So, the Bible disproves the old "Stick and Stones" saying. Throughout the Bible, we are instructed to analyze our words prior to allowing them out of our mouth. If the words are destructive, we should weed them from our mind and heart. If the words are constructive, then they are fit for company, and may be released from our mouth.

> And so I tell you, keep on asking, and you will receive what you ask for. Keep on seeking, and you will find. Keep on knocking, and the door will be opened to you. For everyone who asks, receives. Everyone who seeks, finds. And to everyone who knocks, the door will be opened.
>
> —LUKE 11:9–10

Example: Business Men's Conference

I was invited, with a team of others, to prophecy over men's businesses. We were asked to pray for thirty minutes. These men had come to get an accurate word from the Lord. They were not interested in generalities. They were not interested in "God Loves You." They wanted to make business decisions based on God's revealed word.

Ok, now the pressure was on. I had to get an accurate word. Then, deliver it in such a way that it magnified my Father. I must make sure that the words delivered, were His heart in the situation. Oh yea, and here was the best part. The prophecy needed to answer the question in the man's mind. (We asked the Lord the answer before we asked the man the question.) Have you heard the story of Joseph?

The Lord said that this particular man's business was about the fail. The Lord made this really clear to me. This man was headed off of a cliff of disaster, and soon! Yikes!

How would you deliver this word from the Lord? Here is how I did it.

I went back to the Lord, and asked more questions. Once I had the answers, I began to give this man the word of the Lord.

This is what I said, "The Lord wants you to know that opportunities are being presented to you for a new business venture. This new business is one that you would not normally entertain, and might otherwise overlook. This new business will provide everything that you are currently looking for: your needs, your financial requirements will be abundantly met, security will be evident, and stability will be a wonderful part of this.

Now about your current venture, the Lord has been telling you about the future of that business. It's future is not bright, which is why this new one is so appealing. If you continue with the present business, you may encounter financial difficulties, and challenges. (I actually saw him falling off of a cliff, yikes.)

After the prayer and prophecy was over. The man told us that just before he had entered the room, a friend had excitedly and enthusiastically invited him to join in a new business. The man had not even given his friend the time of day, and had not given his full attention, because the opportunity was not interesting to him. He had overlooked the opportunity. (Thank you God you did it again!)

His current business was in financial disaster, and without a miracle, the business was headed for ruin. He had held onto the business, hoping and praying for a positive turn. He had placed himself and his family in financial peril due to this business. He was considering borrowing money to help. (Remember the cliff?)

Because of the accuracy of the confirming words, the man decided to look closely at the new opportunity.

"Yeah, God! You really are pretty alright!"

Chapter 13
Discussion Questions

1. You are walking into a store when you see someone in distress. What do you do?

2. Your friend calls and tells you a heart-wrenching story. What do you do?

3. Your child has just started crying and relaying a story from school. What do you do?

4. You ask the Lord for some information about a person, and He gives you some dramatic information. What do you do?

5. You hear the sadness in your friend's voice. What do you do?

I trust that the answer to every question above is "Ask God," and if you cannot think of how to give an uplifting word, then keep them quietly in your head, and then pray for that person.

Chapter 14

A Summary: Hearing the Voice of the Lord

God still personally communicates with us today:

> So I say, let the Holy Spirit guide your lives.
>
> —Galatians 5:16

> When you are directed by the Spirit
>
> —Galatians 5:18

> Since we are living by the Spirit, let us follow the Spirit's leading in every part of our lives.
>
> —Galatians 5:25

> For he is our God. We are the people he watches over, the flock under his care. If only you would listen to his voice today! The Lord says, "Don't harden your hearts."
>
> —Psalm 95:7–8

> That is why the Holy Spirit says, "Today when you hear his voice, don't harden your hearts."
>
> —Hebrews 3:7–8

> So God set another time for entering his rest, and that time is today. God announced this through David

much later in the words already quoted: "Today when you hear his voice, don't harden your hearts."

—Hebrews 4:7

If you need wisdom—if you want to know what God wants you to do—ask him, and he will gladly tell you. He will not resent your asking.

—James 1:5

But when you ask him, be sure that you really expect him to answer.

—James 1:6

After he has gathered his own flock, he walks ahead of them, and they follow him because they know his voice.

—John 10:4

My sheep listen to my voice; I know them, and they follow me.

—John 10:27

When the Spirit of truth comes, he will guide you into all truth. He will not speak on his own but will tell you what he has heard. He will tell you about the future.

—John 16:13

So let us come boldly to the throne of our gracious God. There we will receive his mercy, and we will find grace to help us when we need it most.

—Hebrews 4:16

For the essence of prophecy is to give a clear witness for Jesus.

—Revelation 19:10

God in the Smallest Details

The following is a transcript of the actual e-mails between myself and a Jewish, believer friend as we sought the Lord's help in finding a home for a puppy. In it, we can see God is even interested in abused puppies and using us to help them. God tells us to pray about everything, at all times. Enjoy!

From Bobbie:

> Today please pray that an abused dog I found at the synagogue Friday night will find a good home. When we got there, he was cowering in the entranceway. His metal collar was so tight that the skin on his neck was rubbed off and the imprint from the chain was on his flesh. Someone from my congregation ran home and got a huge metal cutter and I held him down while he cut it off. The skin had grown into the links and it fell to the ground with pieces of skin. I was hysterical, crying my eyes out. (Sorry to be so graphic, but you're a doctor.) Anyway, I took him home for the night and kept him in the garage and Sat. a.m., I took him to my vet who treated the neck, told me he was four months old, in good health except for malnutrition and the neck wounds, and was mostly black lab. He agreed to keep him for a few days while we tried to find a home for him. Bottom line—the person who took him home on Monday just brought him back to vet's office because her dog wouldn't accept him. Vet just called and told me to come and get him and I can't because my subdivision allows only two dogs per household not to mention the fact that David (husband), though a dog lover, doesn't want another one. (Moses was a rescue dog and he's a handful.) This might sound trivial to you, but I truly believe that the Lord sends me all these strays because He cares about them.

("Consider the sparrows...") I've brought home a lot of stray people in my time as well...many who got saved and that was part of His plan, too.

From Teri:

I'm always looking for ways to hear God's voice.

So I asked Him whom you should talk to about the dog.

This is really interesting, please let me know if any of this is correct.

But here is what I heard. Someone in your life who just had a baby, or is due to deliver soon, also does cleaning. I'm not sure what they clean because I saw a bunch of straw...I also saw an ironing board.

I believe this person also has a small child because I saw a booster chair that you would use to feed a baby at the table.

Do you know anyone like this, or do I need to go back to the well?

It is fun to ask God questions about such things, but not knowing if there is someone in your life like this, it is hard to judge.

Let me know.

From Bobbie:

Rosie is a Brazilian lady who cleans my house and has a two-year-old, but she is on vacation in Brazil and won't be back for another week. Today one of her friends is at my house substituting for her and when David gets home I will have him ask and get back to you. The straw may represent a farm. What kind of farm do you have (tee hee)?

From Bobbie:

I just called Juan, Rosie's husband, and he said he talks to her every night and he will ask her if she wants him...we'll know tomorrow, but I know that Rosie goes nuts with dog hair because she is always complaining about mine. We'll see.

From Bobbie:

Oh my G-d—Oh my G-d—Oh my G-d—Oh my G-d—I'm trying to pick myself up off the floor. Juan JUST CALLED ME BACK AND SAID THAT HIS PARTNER WANTS THE DOG! (Juan is a painter.) IF HIS WIFE SAYS OKAY HE WILL TAKE HIM TONIGHT!

From Teri:

God even attends to the little details of our lives. Yeah God! Thank You Father that You even care about sending this puppy to Bobbie, so it could go to the home of Your choosing. Obviously it is important enough to have me, a fledgling prophet, practice hearing Your voice enough to tell me things I could never know. Thank You Father that you have led us to a place in the spirit that we know that we can ask You anything, even about where You want puppies to live. Thank You, God. I love You. Let us know God if this is the perfect home for the puppy, and if not, we will come back to You for more wisdom. Let us always seek Your will first, and not our own understanding. I love You, Lord.

From Bobbie:

David is on the way to Glen's to pickup the dog (and pay the bill) and Juan will pick up the dog tonight at my house. Of course, Rosie doesn't know yet; Juan said he will tell her he has a "surprise" for her when she gets home. (Oy vey.) I suggested a nice pair of earrings to go along with the "surprise"—real ones, of course. Thanks for all your prayers. I thank G-d for you! You are such a blessing to me! I'll call you and we'll get together…I can't wait to see you! Maybe you can come down for some of the Jewish Holidays…you know, the ones the Lord commanded us to keep "in all perpetuity." You know, those Feasts of the G-d of Israel—the ones He never did away with—the ones the church ignores—(Oh well, I'm getting off track.) Now we have to pray that Rosie loves Jeremiah, (that's what I named the puppy.) Or else it's back to the drawing board…Thank You, Lord! Thank You for Your prophetess! Thank You for putting us together! Love, Bobbie

From Bobbie:

Juan didn't finish at work until late so the puppy spent the night with us (in the laundry room), but will be picking him up at 5 p.m. so we will see what happens when Rosie gets back. If it doesn't work out, I have my coordinator at work sending out e-mails like crazy to find a back-up. *I only know that the Lord wanted you to get a confirmation that you heard correctly because I never, ever expected a reaction like I got from Juan.* Be blessed today, my sister. We will talk soon. G-d is good, all the time.

From Bobbie:

Hello my sister—Just a quick note to let you know that Juan picked up the puppy Thursday night and gave him to his partner and we haven't heard a word, thank G-d. No news is good news. The statue of limitations on puppy-return is about to run out.

Keep prophesying...keep trusting...keep doing...and keep expecting results..."For I know the plans I have for you, plans for your welfare and not for calamity; plans to give you a future and a hope" (NASB). Jer. 29:11 is for you today. Love, Bobbie.

Chapter 14
Discussion Questions

1. Close your eyes, ask the Lord for one word for a person. After you receive it, treat it like a gold nugget. Do not throw it away. Pray for that person with this word in mind.

2. Ask, "Lord what do You want me to know about this person?" When the answer comes, pray for or with this person as directed.

3. Ask, "Lord how much do You love this person?" Deliver this to the person. I must tell a story. The Rector of our church asked this question once while he was counseling a young woman. The Lord told him, "She is the apple of my eye." When the Rector delivered this word to her, he had no way of knowing (God did) that she had been told this very phrase by her own father. It held special meaning to her, so she received it with great warmth, and truly from the heart of God.

4. Ask for a song.

5. Ask for a Bible verse.

6. Ask for a word of knowledge.

7. What is going on in this person's life right now? Be careful to always edify, comfort, and help.

8. What does God want to do about a certain situation? Remember my praying for the premature baby? He wanted me to pray for the mom's fear, although my mind had told me to pray for the baby.

9. Choose a helper, then heal a memory.

10. Heal another memory. You remember how to do this. After you choose a helper, ask the helper to step into the memory. Where is the helper, what are they doing, what are they saying, and how are they changing the memory? Does your helper say anything to you? How are your feelings different with the helper in the memory? Allow the helper to stay as long as needed. (Maybe forever.)

11. Change your focus. Analyze the memory. Go back to it, and see how the memory feels. If it is not significantly better, and the emotions are not improved, do it again.

Afterword

The Girl Before the Doctor

I GREW UP IN a small South Louisiana town. Outsiders knew Hammond, my hometown, only because two main interstates intersected there: I–10 and I–55. If you blinked, you had passed the city limit signs.

People in Hammond smiled and took a fabulous interest in the lives and families of their loved ones. Talkative busy bodies knew me and told my parents *everything* I did. I was afraid to get into too much trouble. Dad would find out prior to my return, and man-oh-man would I get in trouble.

Hammond was an ethnic mix of various sorts. The majority of the town was Italian. The Italians were short, stocky, loud, and very sociable. I was tall, green-eyed, and contemplative. (Not all of the time, though. Sometimes I was loud.) They looked up at me like I was from another planet. I grew up thinking I was the Jolly Green Giant. They made fun of me and laughed, "How's the weather up there?"

Being tall in a town of short people made me think outside of the box. Children are cruel, no matter where you live. At thirteen, I was nearly six feet tall.

Grace Memorial Church was home. I was comfortable there. It was and is today a small Episcopal church with just a few hundred members. The people of this church have always been my extended family. Even today, I go "home" to Grace. My generation has now raised children and grandchildren.

For some reason there was always an extraordinary interest in children at Grace. The youth group was frequently together and going somewhere or doing something. We would travel, sing, cook, and do most anything together. Our youth leaders got us into projects, probably trying to keep us out of mischief. The days of youth groups, choirs, mission trips, and summer camps were playful days.

We never went without. Mother and Daddy were wonderful providers. They worked long and hard to mold us into good people. Daddy taught us how to appreciate the outdoors, bringing in our own food, and cooking it. He made sure that we went into the woods and saw the great sights of nature. He frequently took us to visit his hometown of Chatawa, Mississippi.

Grandma Speed, Daddy's mother, had sixteen children including two sets of twins and the rest were individual births. Each of them had several children. I was surrounded by so much family I thought the entire state of Mississippi was related to me. (And many of them are.)

Grandma was always in the kitchen, and as an adult I realize why. She had no choice. If she stopped cooking, someone went hungry. Her house was small, but it never mattered. We didn't notice those things. We just loved being there. I'm still not sure how she kept up with all of the grandchildren, but every Christmas each of us young-uns had a present under her tree. My brother and I hid and read every present until we found the ones with our names on them. She never forgot us.

Grandma cooked mostly with a frying pan and lard. It was the best tasting food on the planet. She cooked fried fish, hush puppies, chicken and dumplings, cornbread, mustard greens, and fried chicken. Oh, just thinking about her kitchen makes me revisit childhood. The smells that drifted across the fields down to the barn were enough to get us running for the house. Grandma always looked the other way when we reached for a sample.

"Get outta this kitchen," she would yell, "'fore I take a switch to yeh."

We screamed and ran for the door, knowing the only reason we left with food in our hands was that she was playing a game with us. We loved going to Grandma's house.

In a pasture close to Grandma Speed's house was the hay barn. It was so tall to my little kid eyes, I was sure it touched the sky. My uncles cut the hay, bailed it, and stacked it in the barn. It was a favorite play area of mine. If you looked real hard between the bails, you found places just big enough to crawl into. Openings and tunnels were obvious to an adventurous child.

As I crawled through the narrow passages, huge caverns would open up under the mountainous stack, and I played there. Totally surrounded by hay, like an igloo, I spent hours tunneling and exploring. That is until Uncle John came looking for me. If he found me in the hay, I was sure to get it on my backside. I would lie perfectly still and try not to breathe, but my breathing echoed so loudly I was sure he would find me and reach in and snatch me from my cocoon.

More often than not, Uncle John pretended that he didn't know where I was, and go back to the house, yelling, "I can't find her. She's not in the hay." But later on, he sat next to me at the table gently pulling hay from my hair never asking about its origin.

We loved the swimming hole in Chatawa. That was the place where I felt safe. I walked for hours through the woods under the canopy of wisteria, and lay under it. I never understood how wisteria got that high up into pine trees, then bloomed, and cascaded down into beautiful flowing falls of flowers. When I looked up, all that was visible was the brilliant purple of the flowers, and the streaming rays of sunshine flowing like water through the holes.

The ground was covered with the purple petals that had fallen. Petals formed a blanket on top of the pine needles. This beautiful inviting carpet was mesmerizing, sort of like new fallen snow, coating the forest floor with shimmering hues of purple.

I stretched out on the mattress of wisteria petals and pine needles and entered a fantasyland. Tinker bell would fly around the pine trees and the fairies would join her. As an adult I know that the fairies were lightning bugs, but as a child they were real fairies. They loved to dance and fly playfully all through the woods. They would beg you to follow them farther and farther. As the fairies flew, new adventures awaited. The hills were inviting and the animals were plentiful.

The river at the swimming hole was a magical place. It was filled with every life form imaginable. We caught catfish for our supper, and we watched our uncle catch water moccasins with his bare hands. I never associated danger with this river, though. It was a place to enjoy and play. There were cutouts on the river's edge. I imagined and dreamed of the people that made these caves. The caves were so alluring that I went as often as possible. Sometimes the river would rise and the caves would get washed out, but occasionally the rushing water would leave behind treasures. Other people must have liked the caves, because remnants of fire rings were often found, evidence of nights spent on the river.

There are so many memories of this river that they are an integral part of my growing up. My cousins, uncles, and aunts would camp on the sandbar in the middle of the river. Actually it was a rock-covered high point, and it was the most uncomfortable sleeping imaginable. Mosquitoes the size of birds, toads that sounded like they could haul the young ones away, and unidentified biting creatures were plentiful, but we had fun. We put all of our provisions on our shoulders and walked down the river. I say *we* because the adults walked, and the children swam up river as best we could. We could not touch bottom, so we were generally pulled by one of the adults through the strongest currents, then let loose to swim in the calmer waters.

Mother and Daddy worked long hours and gave us everything they had. Of course we didn't appreciate it then. All we knew was that other kids had more than we did, and we wanted it. I always had clothes and food and shoes, but I was embarrassed that my mother made my clothes. I wanted "store-bought" clothes like the other children. As an adult, I think back to the countless hours my mother spent on the sewing machine, making just the right outfit for me, and I cringe at my ungrateful nature of those years.

My mother was, and is, not only a seamstress, but one of those gifted, creative souls who makes heirloom quality items from just an idea. Now, being a surgeon, I appreciate her hours patiently teaching a daughter who was not interested. Because now, you see, I also am a seamstress. I cut and sew for a living. Because of my mother's tutelage, I am able to "see" the end result long before I ever make the first incision into a patient's body. I am able to cut and sew for hours if necessary without ever becoming fatigued. Her patience and gentleness guided me into my chosen field.

Her patience was, and remains, much greater than mine. Mother would watch, then she examined my work.

"Oh no, not again!" I lamented. If I had a stitch out of place, she would quietly hand me the ripper and say, "Do it again."

I hated ripping. To me it seemed that whatever sewing was there was good enough, and it could stay.

Mother would say, "*You* know it's not right, and that's all that matters. Rip it out." Again and again, I sewed the same seam. I truly believed the fabric would fall apart from the repeated abuse. Sooner or later I would get it correct and she would allow me to move on to the next seam. She is a perfectionist in her projects and it shows. Everything she touches turns to gold.

As an adult I treasure the moments we spend together. I still marvel at her ability to see something in her mind, and then assemble the pieces into masterworks. She does this with clothes or curtains, bedspreads or pillows.

Even her culinary skills are fabulous. She spent hours cooking and no one ever missed a meal. Mother was always a fabulous cook and all of her children became interested in the culinary arts. Of course we didn't help as much as we should have, but as adults, we all have become skilled at creating tasty meals.

Carla forgive me—I must tell this story

As children none of us were particularly adept at preparing meals. Carla, my sister, was less than disinterested. She is eight years my junior. By the time she was old enough to fend for herself, our older brother and I were off finding trouble.

Carla had absolutely no interest in the kitchen. She opened cans of SpaghettiOs and ate directly from the can. Pouring the contents into a bowl would have necessitated cleaning said bowl, so the can was adequate.

She grew up, moved away, and got married. Often I wondered, sometimes out loud, how she and her husband survived on SpaghettiOs. For some reason she never found my concern all that amusing—but, I really did worry about them. She was always the "blast cooker." If she wanted something cooked or heated, there was only one setting—high. She burned everything—even water.

To my absolute shock and wonder, she secretly became a gourmet chef. I have no idea what happened, how, or when. Maybe they were starving to death, or beginning to take on the resemblance of SpaghettiOs. Maybe she learned out of necessity. I had heard rumblings about food from her husband from time to time. But I could not imagine that she was really cooking.

One summer recently we were all home for the annual vacation at Nana and PawPaw's house. Carla and I each had two children, so the house was filled with laughter and toys.

One day I was stirring a roux in Mother's kitchen. This can be a laborious task if you dislike cooking, but Mother and I were chatting and stirring, chopping and stirring, peeling tomatoes and stirring some more.

The roux is the basis of Louisiana cuisine, consisting of oil and flour in a seasoned, cast-iron pot, and cooked until it browns. Although it sounds simple enough there is an art to making it well. I am not a gourmet cook, nor have I ever attempted to be. I can whip up a batch of gumbo or jambalaya for dinner, but I'm not exactly Paul Prudhomme or that Emeril guy.

Mother stepped out of the kitchen at just the wrong moment. The moment of truth had arrived, and I was commissioned to finish the roux. Mother went to tend one of the children. I was on my own.

"Oh, peachy!" I thought. At some point in the process, I got nervous. An excellent roux and a burned disaster are only about thirty seconds apart. I had crossed that line more times than I could count, burned the roux, and thrown the smoking pot out the back door. So my natural tendency was to stop the browning process a bit early. To burn it would mean starting over, and that was too similar to ripping seams for me. My roux therefore was always light. This was no exception. I picked up a pitcher of water to pour into the pot to stop the roux.

"What are you doing?" my sister yelled directly into my ear. "Give me that. You don't know how to make a roux." She snatched the wooden spatula from my hand and rescued the roux from my feeble, inept attempt.

Clearly in shock, I relinquished my duties and watched her expertly and calmly finish the roux. It smelled divine. It was perfect. She had completed the roux to a dark, rich, wonderful brown. She did not appear to be on the verge of a burnt mess. She quickly and confidently created the desired result.

"How did she do that?" I asked out loud, unable to keep my words inside my mouth. I picked my jaw up from the floor. The shock of my sister cooking and expertly making a roux was, well...let's just say I licked my wounded ego and left the kitchen.

"When did she learn to cook?" I asked Mother. "A roux?" I continued. "There is no way *my* sister is teaching me to make a roux. How did this happen?" Mother just laughed, obviously knowing about Carla's skill.

Somewhere, some time after she married she had taught herself. She had endured years of teasing and harassment by our brother and myself. She had become the best cook in the family. She treated us to a delicious meal—but I still remembered the child blast cooker, the one who could burn water.

Mother and Daddy live so close to the railroad tracks the house shakes when the trains go by. There are three sets of tracks in our backyard, and if more than one train blows down the track, you just need to put your life on hold for a couple of minutes. The noise is deafening; you cannot hear yourself think.

The "City of New Orleans" was a passenger train that traveled the tracks twice a day. I watched, wondered, and wished. Someday, I would go on that train, and follow my dreams.

The tracks were a playground for me. The long endless steel went somewhere, and I wanted to know where. I put pennies on the track, and then would run under the bridge when the train went by. The tremendous thundering of the train would frighten me to the very bottom of my being. I was afraid that the train would see me and jump off of the track and get me—for some reason, it always stayed on the tracks and kept going. I loved watching the trains and marveled at the mass, the movement, and often the inability to stop. Trains have a funny way about them. They don't deviate. People do crazy things around railroad crossings, but trains just stay on course. They start slowly, and stop slowly. It had something to do with the momentum and the great size of the machine, but they plow through whatever is in their way.

Today, I live near another set of tracks. In the quiet of the evening, the distant rumble can be heard long before the train arrives. It echoes down the long, straight stretch of track. Occasionally the conductor will blow the whistle, but usually just the thundering of the cars is heard. The sound makes me relax, all these years later. A warm comfort enfolds me, like the bed of my childhood.

Spring Grove was the name of the plantation where my great-grandparents lived. Oh, how I loved going there. One hundred-year-old oaks lined the long drive from the road to the house. It was the most beautiful place on earth. It was like Tara in *Gone with the Wind*. The house was huge and stairwells brought you to secret places for children to play. Or should I say, for me to play.

The attic was filled with treasures. My Great-Gram kept everything, and I loved going upstairs to dig through the dusty old attic. The stairs made strange squeaking sounds like a haunted house. The boards were old and I could never make it up the stairs without everyone knowing where I was. On each step, you could place your weight just so, on the edge of the boards, and if you did it perfectly, you could make one step without making a sound. I'd sneak up, hopefully unnoticed, in anticipation of my next discovery. "Maybe I'll find buried treasure, or jewelry this time," I thought. I got excited just thinking about what awaited me. Eventually I'd give up on being quiet and just bolt up the remaining stairs. If I heard footsteps on the stairs I would hide—as if the entire house didn't already know where I was and what I was doing.

Old dresses and hats from long ago were folded and stored in cedar chests. Great-Gram took delight in my dressing up and having fashion shows for her. The hats had feathers and sequins. The gowns were magnificently made, with bows and flowing trains. The elegance of yesteryear was preserved perfectly for a young girl to discover. Great-Gram never fussed with me when I made a mess. She seemed to take joy in watching me rummage through her treasures. Actually she encouraged me to see what else I could find.

One wooden crate in particular held my interest on every visit. In it lived every piece of correspondence that Great-Gram and Grandpop ever touched. Letters from their son during the war, love letters between Great-Gram and Grandpop, letters from their son to his future bride, and letters to and from their parents. I sat in that box and read about my Gram, their eldest daughter. I learned about my great-grandparents' lives through these eloquently written letters. I drifted to times past, and a slower, gentler life.

To my young mind my grandmother (Gram) had been old forever. "How could they be talking of my Gram riding horses, and sneaking out of windows to meet her boyfriend at the river?" It was hard imagining Gram doing anything that young people did. I read about her meeting my grandfather. I read about her being "courted" by many of the young men in town. It was fun to sit in that dirty, worn crate and dream of another time with young people and their lives. I dreamt of living on the plantation and watching with bated breath as the horse and carriage arrived to carry Gram to the local dance. Her suitors must have been most handsome and desirable, because she finally chose my grandfather, who was just perfect. If he was the best in that whole group, Gram sure must have had fun courting.

"Gram is older than dirt," I thought. "If Gram were young once, a million years ago, then Great-Gram must be a dinosaur." My Grandpop was much older than Great-Gram. The town gossip was still known to describe "how he took a child bride." Funny thing was, she didn't look like a child to me. She had more wrinkles than a Shar-Pei puppy.

One day when I was about five-years-old, Great-Gram pulled me to her for a hug. She whispered in my ear, "Go into the attic and choose something. You may have anything up there that you can find. But don't tell anyone." It was our secret.

So off I went on my covert mission. In retrospect, I realize that Great-Gram just wanted to get rid of me for an hour or so. But in my mind I was on a top-secret, vital mission. I quietly left the room without fanfare. That was tough because I loved making a grand entrance and exit. I tried very carefully to go up the stairs without being discovered, placing my foot on each step carefully so as not to make a sound. If I missed a step someone would discover my quest. It must have taken thirty minutes to get up those stairs. But I did it; no squeaks, no haunted sounds. I made it. Can you imagine the laughter from the adults sitting under the stairwell in the formal living room watching and listening to a child sneak up a set of noisy stairs?

I knew where I was going. In the middle of the attic, just to the left of the stairwell, sat a special cedar chest. I opened it every time I entered the attic. This chest smelled horrible, like a mothball factory. The clothes and blankets in this chest were impregnated with that distinct smell. Most would find the combination of cedar and mothballs rancid, but I have always associated it with that special old, worn trunk. It was the treasure chest that held the ball gowns, the special shoes, and Great-Gram's handmade quilts and crocheted afghans. I inspected every garment, quilt, and throw. I marveled at the stitches, because most were made without the aid of a sewing machine. Every stitch was evenly placed, and the threads matched the garments perfectly. Mother would have been pleased had she inspected them.

"I can have anything I want! I can have this," I said with a lighthearted flare, as I observed my reflection in the full-length mirror. I danced around and twirled, imagining myself wearing each gown. The antique mirror was just like the one in *Sleeping Beauty*. If you looked and then moved, people would appear and disappear. As an adult I know this piece of glass was hand-blown and thus distorted images in the reflection. As a child, I loved to gaze at the way my body changed as I paraded in front of it. Sometimes I was fat, sometimes skinny, sometimes tall, and sometimes short.

Each ball gown was lovelier than the last. I dug each and every item from its crypt imagining that it belonged to me. Then one caught my eye. It was the most magnificent blanket I had ever seen. I attempted to pick it up, but it was huge. It was too big for me. It had been crocheted, and it had to be mine.

"Great-Gram will not allow me to have this. It is too pretty.

Certainly she wants to keep this one," I thought with resignation. But instead of going on to other things in the chest, I just sat there and examined every loop and every thread. Whoever made it put buckets of love into it. The afghan appeared to have little balls crocheted into it that from a few feet away appeared to be lace. I was sure that I could not have it, so I decided to play and pretend it was mine. I imagined that it covered my bed and daydreamed of its maker.

Finally I emerged from the attic somber-faced. Violet, Great-Gram's cook, friend, and housekeeper saw the look on my face and ushered me into the kitchen.

Violet was the most wonderful person. She tried to teach me to cook. She had a stool in the corner of the kitchen where I sat. I wasn't tall enough to reach the counter without the stool, so I claimed it as *my* stool. She handed me a knife, taught me to use it, and as we worked, we talked. Violet was easy to talk to. Once we finished preparing the food, she put her knife down, looked me in the eye, and said, "OK missy, you have told me about everything in the world, except why you are so downtrodden. Tell Violet what is going on."

"Oh, I found something in the attic that I want," I started, "and Great-Gram will not allow me to have it. She told me I can have whatever I want," I sniffed, and bowed my head.

"If your great-grandmother told you something, do you think that she lied?" Violet's words were so quiet you had to listen real hard to hear them. She bent over and looked up into my sad eyes.

"No, I don't believe that," I answered. "She would never lie, but what I want is so special and she doesn't know it is in the cedar chest. I just found it in the way-bottom of the chest," I said. "Violet, it is the most gorgeous thing I've ever seen. I love it. Do you know who made it?"

"Let's go together, and see this thing," she said. She took my small hand and up the stairs we went. I always felt safe and loved when I was with Violet. For some reason, the stairs did not squeak this time. As a matter of fact we sort of floated up the stairs, with her lifting and swinging me around and up and down each stair. Violet knew just how to cheer me up, and she had done it in an instant.

"Here it is," Violet said, triggering my next reaction. I regained my sad look just as quickly as Violet had cheered me up. Violet took one look at the crocheted afghan and found a place to sit down.

She told me about our families, hers and mine; stories that I had never heard. She told me about how her grandparents and my great-grandparents worked and played; how close everyone was, and how the generations of our families had intertwined. She told me about learning to read and write using a candle. She told me about my Great-Great-Gram, the person who had made the afghan. She had spent many hours on the porch in the cool evening breeze, talking and crocheting. There was no television or electricity, so people sat on the porch until dark. Candles were saved for emergencies. Our families had been together for many generations.

We lost track of time and before we knew it we heard shouts from downstairs.

"Where is Violet? Where is Teri?" they hollered. "Violet! Teeeerr-rrriii!"

So down the stairs we ran, laughing and riding down the banister. Well, really I'm the one who rode down the banister. Violet held my hand so I wouldn't fall and crack my noggin. Just before I reached the last step, Violet whispered in my ear, "Go tell your Great-Gram what you found. I know her. She will not go back on her word. If she told you that you can have it, it is your job to tell her what you want." And with that she disappeared around the corner.

"Violet, oh Violet, do it for me, please?" I pleaded with her, but Violet was already gone.

"What are you girls whispering about?" Great-Gram asked, and motioned for me to come to her.

"Uh, well, uh, I, uh, found, uh, I was in, uh, the attic..." It took forever to get out just a few words and I was stammering and stuttering, frightened to request the coveted afghan. Violet poked her head out and quietly waved her hands in encouragement. Her lips were silently saying "Go on, tell her what you found."

"Great-Gram, Violet found something," I said, hoping to blame it on Violet. Violet was now jumping up and down and waving her arms trying to say no and pointing to me, but I was too scared. I couldn't say any more.

"Violet, do you have any idea what this child is trying to say, or why she is so distressed?" Great-Gram was always quiet, and her gentleness was palpable now.

"No," was all Violet said and disappeared again.

"Teri, I don't bite. At least, not hard. What do you want to say to me?" Great-Gram smoothed my hair. I loved the way she caressed my hair. It felt like a dream, and I began to relax.

"Your mother made a crocheted afghan and I want it, but I'm sure that you will say no, so I can't find anything else that I want to have, so I left it there, and Violet won't help me say anything to you, because..." My words came flooding from my mouth so fast she must have mistaken me for a magpie. She continued to caress my hair, until finally I stopped babbling.

"Violet, I know you are standing behind that door," Great-Gram said. Slowly Violet's smile emerged from the hall. She had been listening to every word. Great-Gram nodded to Violet as if they had some secret code and handshake, or maybe they had lived and worked together for so long they just finished each other's sentences. Nevertheless, Violet took my hand and back up the stairs we went.

Violet picked up the afghan and handed me half of it. We carried it down the stairs. We made quite a production of hauling it, with lots of laughing and grunting as if we would be crushed by its weight. Violet's husband and my grandfather were standing on the porch just in time to hear the commotion. They offered to help. I yelled yes, but Violet waved them away. She and I got that huge thing out of the house and into the back of my grandfather's car. Then we ran as fast as we could back to the kitchen to get a cold glass of iced-tea.

That beautiful afghan is still mine. Looking at it now, I can still taste the sweet tea in Violet's kitchen, hear the conversations held over cut-up vegetables, and feel the love of that wonderful plantation life. I'm all grown up now, with children of my own, and I enjoy watching my children bond with their grandparents making memories that will be cherished forever.

A local college was of special interest to me. We lived one block away. People came from all parts of the world to study there. People were excited and fascinated with life. They were happy to be there. The university was the source of many dreams because I wanted great things like the people of that place. As a child, I walked through the huge, sprawling, shadow-covered paths under the oak trees and lay beneath the umbrella of branches. I listened to the students hurriedly changing classes, laughing about their adventures. I fell asleep many a day under those wonderful trees, dreaming of the days when I would be old enough to go to college.

College came, but by then I had discovered a larger horizon—Louisiana State University. That was my dream. So, off I went to Baton Rouge and well, you probably guessed it—I sat under many an oak tree, watching the sun drift through the leaves of the umbrella-covered branches of those grand oaks. The years passed quickly and I graduated from that great university. My dreaming didn't stop there, though. I had my sights set on medicine. And so, this small-town girl with dreams of tomorrow and far off places at the end of that endless train track entered a field of strict rules, formulae, and precision. Yet somehow, the dreams never vanished. I still search for tomorrow, and better ways, and more healing. Still my dreams continue. When I'm told that something can't be done, I take it as a challenge, not an answer.

This is the way I see it: we sent men to the moon, and there were many who said we never would. Flying to space is so commonplace now that it barely makes the news anymore. There are ways to heal that we are only just discovering. There are other ways of healing that are as old as civilization itself. Healings occur—I see them often, because of my profession—but sometimes they happen out of context, and those are the cases that really get my attention.

Afterword Discussion Questions

1. Describe your hometown. Name ten things that you disliked about your hometown. Name ten things that you enjoyed about your hometown. Describe each one and the effect that it had on you.

2. Describe the home of your youth. If you moved, describe each one. Name ten things you liked about your home. Name ten things you disliked about your home. How did these affect you and help to create who you are?

3. How many people lived with you? Describe in detail how they affected your life.

4. Describe your parents, and the people that had a significant influence on you as a small child. Do this with at least five more people:

   A. Name,

   B. Characteristics of that person,

   C. Describe in detail the positive and negative attributes of this person, and the effect that each had on your life.

5. Write out ten specific memories (good and bad) of your childhood.

6. Describe your childhood favorite place to go.

7. Describe your childhood favorite person. What were their characteristics? Why were they your favorite?

8. Name someone you trust *completely*, whether dead or alive.

9. Where do you go to daydream? As a child where did you go to daydream?

10. What activities did you enjoy as a child?

11. Name the people from your childhood that you need to forgive. Are you willing to forgive them?

12. Using the techniques you have learned, heal, forgive, and change those things discovered in your childhood. Remember to use your helper.

Notes

Chapter 1

1. Web site: http://www.parablesite.com/, accessed May 3, 2007.

Chapter 3

1. *Strong's Concordance* (Peabody, MA: Hendrickson Publishers, 2007).

Chapter 4

1. *Strong's Concordance* (Peabody, MA: Hendrickson Publishers, 2007).

Chapter 16

1. *Strong's Concordance* (Peabody, MA: Hendrickson Publishers, 2007).

About the Author

Teri Speed, M.D. was born and raised in south Louisiana. She attended Louisiana State University Medical School in New Orleans. After residency, she earned her Board Certification and furthered her training in Phlebology, the study and treatment of vein disease. She was voted "Best in the Field" and was the last stop for patients with severe vein disease, ulcers, and inflammation. Her passion was helping those vein patients who had been discharged by other frustrated doctors. Patients from all over the world flew in to enjoy the results of her extended knowledge and surgical talents.

Since the beginning of her practice, Dr. Speed has been drawn to look for ways to help the helpless and the hopeless. Currently retired from her surgical practice, Dr. Speed now spends her time devoted to the hopeless in a new way—she integrates the healing of the body with the mind and spirit through techniques developed during her tenure as a surgeon. The frustration of chronic diseases and patients non-responsiveness to therapy led Dr. Speed to look deeper into other types of healing. She was dragged through *Holy Spirit boot camp* to discover that patients heal faster and more completely when all three aspects of the person are addressed: the spirit, the mind, and the body. She teaches simple techniques of healing that anyone can use.

For Wade

WADE WARREN SPEED was God's gift to my hometown, Hammond, Louisiana. He owned and operated several businesses, as well as performing so much charity work that I'm sure I do not know of it all. He provided the scholarship money for one student per year to go to Southeastern Louisiana University School of Business. He organized the men and boys of the church to cook for the community several times each year. He worked approximately four years on forming a foundation for the church, which would collect money, invest it, then provide this investment for the church to be able to survive in perpetuity.

On a Sunday morning in early December 2005, Wade woke up early looking forward to the wonderful day that lay ahead. He was excited and childlike about the gift that he would give the church. Like Christmas morning for a five-year-old child, Wade leapt from the bed and ran to the kitchen. He didn't bother with the dishes after breakfast because they could wait. He couldn't. He poured a huge cup of steaming, hot coffee into a "go-cup" and headed down the dark gravel road that left his property. He bounced and laughed as the coffee tried its best to jump out of the cup.

Have you ever tried to ride the bumps of your car, holding a cup of hot liquid high in your hand so it won't spill? If you hold it just right, and allow the gravity and bumps to move your arm as a shock absorber, the coffee will remain in it's appointed container.

Once on the blacktop Wade relaxed and looked at his shirt for evidence of coffee spots. "None! Yeah!" he thought out loud as he turned onto the highway. Once at church, he poked fun with a young girl who would serve with him during the church service that day. He loved to tease, and this morning would be no exception. She laughed, ran, and giggled as she loved their playfulness. They had served together many times before and were comfortable with each other, like sister and big brother.

After church, Wade donned a chef hat and went to the church kitchen to prepare breakfast for anyone who was hungry. Always the servant, he prepared a wonderfully tasty breakfast for all.

A general church meeting was held after breakfast, and everyone showed up. A special presentation was to be heard, so the building was packed with eager minds. Wade, standing tall and statuesque, rose from his seat and delivered a most eloquent speech. A foundation had been formed so that money would never be an issue for the church. Grace Church would survive long after we would be gone, because Wade had created this storehouse for God to bless:

> The LORD will command the blessing on you in your storehouses and in all to which you set your hand, and He will bless you in the land which the LORD your God is giving you.
>
> —DEUTERONOMY 28:8, NKJV

> Honor the LORD with your wealth and with the best part of everything you produce. Then he will fill your barns with grain, and your vats will overflow with good wine.
>
> —PROVERBS 3:9–10

> My child, don't lose sight of good planning and insight. Hang on to them, for they fill you with life and bring you honor and respect.
>
> —PROVERBS 3:21–22, NLT

Our parents were bleary-eyed as they listened to their eldest son speak with such ease and grace. No words could have described the fullness of their hearts that morning. Wade had honored them and the whole community by his selfless devotion. Wade had built a "storehouse" for the church, with which the Lord could bless. Wade had honored God with the best part of everything his land produced, and he kept good planning and insight foremost in front of him.

Wade, beaming from the busy morning's activities, decided to treat himself. "I've had such a wonderful morning, I will top it off by going up and punching holes in a few clouds!" Wade arrived at the airport and pulled his single engine airplane from its protective hanger. Opening the hangar door, and pulling his baby from the hanger, allowed the sun to highlight its wings, which filled his heart to overflowing. "It's a good day; this is the day the Lord has made."

He flew that day with a smile in his heart. He enjoyed everything about it. The sky was clear, the clouds were few, and the airplane hummed as he looked over God's Creation.

No one, except God, knew that Wade would go home that day. In the cool of the evening the fog rolled in. Wade was only one mile from the end of the runway when the fog rolled over his plane. In an instant he realized that he had vertigo, and was going to land short of the runway. He saw a heavily populated area below him. In that instant, he knew that if he landed, he would take the lives of many innocent people with him. If he had taken the present course, he could, in all likelihood, have lived through the unexpected landing. He changed the course of his plane and chose to hit a piece of ground next to the community below him. In doing so, he knew that there was little chance of his own survival, because he would lose control of the aircraft; the lift would be gone, but at least there would be only one life lost. The people on the ground would be safe. He pulled back hard, the plane climbed at a steep angle and passed safely over the neighborhood. Wade leveled out and pushed his plane over into a dive in the hope of regaining enough speed to restore control. The plane landed nose down in a field next to the neighborhood.

Because of Wade, this book is published. Because of Wade, the church has a financial foundation. Because of Wade, bright young people will have the opportunity to be educated. Because of Wade, many people discovered what it meant to be a true friend. Because of Wade, I learned what love means.

A portion of the sale of each book will go to the things that were birthed by this wonderful man who I am proud to say was my big brother.

ELECTRICITY

By the same author

NONFICTION

Trollope
Rebecca West: A Life
Vita: The Life of V. Sackville-West
Edith Sitwell: A Unicorn Among Lions
Elizabeth Bowen: Portrait of a Writer
A Suppressed Cry
Hertfordshire

FICTION

The Grown-Ups

ELECTRICITY

A Novel

Victoria Glendinning

Picador USA
New York

For information, address Picador USA, 175 Fifth Avenue, New York, N.Y. 10010.

Library of Congress Cataloging-in-Publication Data

Glendinning, Victoria.
Electricity / by Victoria Glendinning.
p. cm.
ISBN 0-312-15117-9
1. Young women—England—History—19th century—Fiction.
I. Title.
[PR6057.L43E4 1997]
823'.914—dc20 96-34540
CIP

First published in the United States of America by Little, Brown and Company

First Picador USA Edition: March 1996

10 9 8 7 6 5 4 3 2 1

For Roy and Aisling

First Notebook

Chapter One

When Godwin gave me the beautiful manuscript books to write in, I told him that I feared I should never dare to use them.

'Write about yourself, begin with something you remember and continue from there,' he said, and strode out of the room in his riding boots, leaving the books on my bed.

I wrote nothing then. It was not the right time. But if not now, when? It is my own story after all.

Sunday afternoon, waiting for the stranger. I was eighteen.

I sat on the left of the fireplace. My father sat on the right, his back to the brown door. My father's name was Alfred Mortimer, and I suppose he would then have been about forty-seven.

It was an autumn of terrible gales and high tides engulfing the coasts. That was over. The world was waiting. The day was fading, discolouring the muslin curtains that covered the window, dimming the already dim reddish-brown velvet drapes and the leaf-patterned wallpaper. The plant on the mahogany table was a black silhouette and the brass urn in which it stood was losing the last of its gleam.

I could no longer see to work. I let my *petit point* subside on to my knee, the needle spiking a purple woollen rose. My father could no longer see to read the newspaper. He let it fall as he always did in a crumpled mess, rasping the silence.

'Little pet, come and sit on my knee. Make an old man happy.'

'I'd rather not, Father.'

'You used to love me, once.'

'I do love you, Father.'

We stared into the coals. The fire, though it was burning low, grew brighter as dusk congested the parlour. My eye was caught by a thread, lit up in the fire's glow, dangling from a bobble on the braid of the red velvet runner overhanging the fireplace. When I was little I used to play a game that the bobbles were my child friends. I had counted them and given them names, alphabetically: Ada, Beryl, Cora, Dora, Eleanor, Frances . . . I was forbidden to touch them for fear I should pull down the runner along with the jar of spills and the two Venetian glass vases and the statuette of Garibaldi and the framed photograph of my parents done at Bridport on their honeymoon.

Sometimes, alone in the parlour, when I was small, I had stretched up on tiptoes and tapped one of the bobbles with my forefinger to make it swing. An act of defiance.

Out of habit I still counted the bobbles. The one with the dangling thread was Eleanor, the fifth from the end on the side nearest to me.

I smoothed the puckered canvas of the needlework, folded it, and put it in my workbox on the small table on my right. I smoothed the brown wool of my Sunday dress over my knees. Soon I would have to go upstairs. It was the bad time of the month, for me. I glanced at my father, wondering if he knew, if he could tell. One should not write about such things, nobody does.

Father had closed his eyes. I stared at his whiskers, more gingery than ever in the glint from the fire, at the heavy ridges of flesh on his cheeks, the blunt creasing of his stiff Sunday suit across his stomach and thighs. I had never liked sitting on his knee because of the scratchy material of his clothes, the biscuity smell of his whiskers, the tobacco and curry on his breath. We ate a lot of curry at Dunn Street. How often had I seen my mother and Jane in the kitchen, standing over a piece of grey meat on an enamel plate and resolving, in low voices, that the only thing to do with it was to curry it.

Still less, when I was very little, had I liked the game that Father liked best – setting me between his spread knees while he drew me towards him, pressing my head against his waistcoat and watch-chain, letting me go, pulling me against him again, with loud cries of 'Oh' and 'Ah' and 'Ho Ho' and 'Who is Father's little darling?'

Father's trousers smelled nasty and under the trousers was Father.

I prayed as I looked at Father that he had not fallen asleep. When he slept, slack-bodied, breathing so heavily, out of control and seemingly at the mercy of something, I experienced the strangest sensations. I flickered inside myself – as if in fear, but it was not quite fear. I never wanted to watch him sleeping but I never could refrain from doing so.

He was not sleeping. He stirred, opened his eyes.

'What time is this young chap coming, then?'

'About half past five, Mother said. His train gets into the Euston station at five o'clock.'

'What's his name again?'

'Mr Fisher. Mr Peter Fisher.'

We sat on. In the kitchen Mother was giving instructions to the girl. We heard Mother's thin high voice, Jane's mutter. The two cats, Jet and Amber, black and marmalade-coloured, slithered round the half-open door of the parlour and prowled about.

Generally we ate the evening meal at six o'clock at the kitchen table, waited on in a casual fashion by Jane. Today, to welcome Mr Fisher, we ate in the parlour at the smarter hour of half past seven.

Mr Peter Fisher. The young man whom I saw across the table, beyond the candle-flames, had wild black hair framing an oval face as white as his collar. His mouth, under a moustache that made me think of revolutionaries, was thin and long. It was a hard mouth, but attractive. Behind spectacles his eyes swam greenish, enlarged. He took the spectacles off when Jane placed his dinner-plate before him, folded the wire earpieces carefully over the lenses, and laid them beside his place. When he spoke he smiled, his long mouth turning up at the corners.

'I am myopic,' he said. 'Short-sighted. But in close-up, for details, I see wonderfully sharply.'

I took in his black coat, slopping off his slender shoulders. The coat was short and buttoned-up, like a reefer but made of thicker, rougher material, and he wore a down-turned collar on his shirt. He looked like a working man and yet he did not. I had never heard such broad vowels in a north-country voice before and to me he sounded almost foreign. Peter Fisher, bending his neck towards his plate, began to dissect mutton. I looked at his big knuckles, and at the knobbly joints of his long fingers. His hands seemed too much for his wrists to bear.

In the course of the meal my parents asked questions to which they already knew the answers from my Aunt Susannah, Mother's elder sister. She had married a Bradford mill-owner, Uncle Samuel Huff, and risen in the world. Peter Fisher's father had worked for Huff & Co. as a clerk. Peter Fisher was now twenty-one. Since his father died five years ago the Huffs – in particular Mrs Susannah Huff – had kept an eye on the boy, who was delicate and clever, and encouraged him in his passion for scientific study.

There was a letter from Peter Fisher still propped on the kitchen dresser, read and reread over the past weeks by my parents and, surreptitiously, by me:

Dear Mrs Mortimer,

My mother has been given to understand by Mrs Huff that you would be willing to accept me as a lodger in your house, if terms can be agreed. I believe that Mrs Huff has written to you about my reasons for wishing to transfer to London. I have been offered the opportunity of employment in the electrical engineering workshop of Mr de Ferranti. As my studies and practical experience in Charlton and in Newcastle, under Col. R. E. B. Crampton, have made me strongly desire to make my career in the exploitation of electrical energy, which I believe to hold the key to the nature of the universe, I am very anxious to accept the offer.

The workshop is in the attic storey of 57 Hatton Garden. I should be away from the house until evening all day except for Sundays, and would require my breakfast and dinner. I believe that I am neat and clean in my habits, and that Mrs Huff can vouch for my good character if she has not already done so.

I am a little concerned about how I shall get my clothes washed. At home my mother sees to everything. She suggests that for a further small consideration the matter might be satisfactorily arranged. I await your reply. . . .

The letter was well timed. As Aunt Susannah well knew, my father had just lost his position. He was unemployed. He had been book-keeper at Ingleby's soap factory, and was let go when some discrepancies were found in the accounts. I only understood this later, from Aunt Susannah. No blame was cast on my father, but it was felt by all parties that a change should be made in order to avoid any unpleasantness. It was the beginning of the depression, and Ingleby was laying off a great many hands in any case. Our whole neighbourhood was feeling the pinch, and times were hard at 49 Dunn Street.

They would have been much harder, and Jane would have been let go, had it not been for Mother's annuity from a small family trust. Father administered and controlled this money, treating it as his own. I believe he sincerely forgot that it was not his own.

The one commodity in which we were rich was soap. Mr Ingleby, to demonstrate his philanthropy and commitment to social improvement, allowed his employees to help themselves every quarter-day to as much of the product as they could carry home. It was understood that to hire a conveyance for the purpose would be a gross abuse. The garden shed at Dunn Street was stacked high with cardboard boxes of the strong-smelling oblong yellow bars, each one an 'Ingleby's Ingot of Hygiene', as the wrappings said. Mr Fisher's laundry would pose no problem.

Nevertheless, the 'further small consideration' was agreed. Jane the daily maid, who read, like me but with some difficulty, any letters that were left around, knew that the extra work would devolve on to her while the extra money would not. Jane had come to work for us when she was thirteen – still a child, although I, who was a year older, behaved more childishly then than she. But I had taught her to read and write. Her spelling remained primitive. Her reading was better, but it would have taken her many stolen half-hours to decipher Peter Fisher's letter. Now, as she stood by Mr Fisher's chair and pushed under his bony nose the dish of potatoes for a second helping, which he accepted, Jane's manner was not gracious. Mother cast her a pleading look.

Peter Fisher did not notice. Whenever he looked up he was confronted, through the candle-flames, by me. I had taken trouble with my hair. I put it up, but in such a way that it seemed as if it might at any moment tumble down. Because it had recently been washed, single threads and strands stood away from the rest. I had been greatly pleased by the golden halo effect I saw reflected by the light of two candles in my bedroom mirror.

I did not know anything about Mr Fisher's speciality at that time, and neither did my parents. So when, gazing at me, he began to speak of filaments and static electricity, he might as well have been speaking Chinese.

Mother noticed however how the new lodger looked at her daughter, and so did Father. He pinched his lips together, and moved his backside about in his chair, making it creak. I just smiled. I was inexperienced, full of unused energies, and young gentlemen did not come to our house every day of the week. That is the only way I can explain my behaviour, if it needs explaining.

'Tell us about your work, then, young fellow,' said my father. 'Tell us about this electrical lark.'

'Did you perhaps visit the electrical exhibition at the Crystal Palace last year, Mr Mortimer? Are you familiar with the principal of arc lighting?' asked Peter Fisher. 'Do you understand something about carbon rods and the alternating current flowing between them?' He addressed my father but he looked at me.

'I shouldn't want electricity anywhere near me, I'm sure,' said Mother. 'My father wasn't having it when they wanted to hang wires for the telegraph over our farm. They sent a gentleman down from the Post Office to explain it was quite safe, but my father was against it all along. The electrical fluid they have in those wires would leak all over his fields and into the house. Very dangerous.'

Mr Fisher's weariness showed in his face. This was perhaps a conversation he had had before. But he was a polite person.

'You are perfectly right, Mrs Mortimer. There is always some leakage. There can be danger, in certain circumstances. Electricity, when it is accumulated in large quantities, is capable of producing the most violent and destructive effects. Such as thunder and lightning. But that is not the case with telegraph wires.'

'My father said nothing would grow under those wires, and the animals would get sick. He didn't want the electricity.'

'It's the magnetic fluid, isn't it?' said my father, making a bid for authority. 'It's well known. People with the power cure diseases that way. Animal magnetism. It's well known. Unseen forces. Mesmerism and all that. It's well known.'

Mother was glad of his support while sensing that whatever it was that he had said contradicted, as usual, whatever it was that she had said. She blundered off on another tack:

'All these inventions, so quickly. Telegraphy, telephony, tele-everything. There's nothing left to invent, that's for sure. We are all perfectly content with gas lighting. I'm very fond of oil-lamps myself, they are perfectly safe if you don't buy the rubbishy ones in the street markets and if you bring up children to blow across them, not straight down on them, when you put them out. There's no call for electrical lighting. The very idea gives me nightmares. It's playing with fire. It's why we've been having all these storms and the wrong kind of sunsets.'

'I believe the remarkable sunsets are due to volcanic dust from the eruption on the island of Mauritius,' said Mr Fisher.

'I assure you that we are being sent signs and portents. We're not meant to meddle with what we don't understand. God will punish us. You'll see.'

'Now, Mother,' said my father, happier now that she had made a fool of herself and, in addition, humiliated the young know-all. He glanced at my mother with gratified distaste. I think Father was interested in ladies but that he did not really like them. I know he hated, in our small house, coming across any evidence of female laundry and of the plugs and rags that Jane boiled up in the copper. I know that he hated the pads and stuffings that disguised the inadequacies of my mother's figure. Sometimes he said outrageous things to her when he thought I could not overhear:

'There is always either too much or too little of a woman, in the matter of bosoms and hairs. Either way it is repulsive. And Charlotte' (that was me) 'is becoming just like the rest of you.'

What my father Alfred Mortimer liked was little girls. Charlotte, his little pet . . . But I would not come and sit on his knee any more.

'Electricity,' said Mr Fisher suddenly, 'may be a separate material entity, a fluid as people call it, or it may be something that is present all of the time, an ingredient of all matter, of absolutely everything that is in the universe. That is what I believe, but it has yet to be determined. Only the effects of electricity are observable. No one has ever actually seen an electric charge.'

There seemed no appropriate response. We all thought our own thoughts as we tried to digest both what he had said and the sour plum tart bought in from the pastrycook's. Jane was not up to desserts. Sometimes she would cook apples to a green-grey pulp, which Mother called 'pury'.

'These are Annie Elizabeths,' she would say then, coaxingly, to my father. 'You know you always like Annie Elizabeths.'

I thought that she meant the apples came from someone called Annie Elizabeth. Once, I asked who she was.

'Just a kind of apple,' said Mother in her fading-away voice. I imagined Annie Elizabeth as an apple-woman, or a woman-apple. I was little, then.

There were plum-stones in the tart. They killed all conversation. Mother, Mr Fisher and I edged the stones out between our lips and on to our spoons as delicately as we could. Father spat his out directly on to his plate.

The silence was broken by frightful noises – curdled howls and yowls, coming from the kitchen.

'The cats!' gasped Mother, clutching her napkin to her front. 'What can be wrong? Where's that girl?'

Father went on eating and raised an eyebrow, to register both the inconvenience of the eruption and reproach to those responsible for its continuance. I got up and made for the door. Peter Fisher rose too, jolting the table as he did so, and followed after.

There was no one in the kitchen, which was lit only by a lamp on the table turned down low, and the glow of the coals between the bars of the range. I saw through the scullery that the back door was open to the dark. Jane had gone out to the privy. Amber and Jet, emitting those unearthly sounds, were hunched on the kitchen floor, their flattened faces staring towards a dim corner, their backs turned to what made me suddenly shriek. All over the kitchen wall behind the cats a tall shadow danced and leaped, a misshapen not-human giant with wild, angular limbs.

Peter Fisher turned up the lamp on the table. He followed the cats' gaze and we saw something small jumping and jumping jumping in the corner between the range and the dresser.

'It's a frog. It's just a frog.'

'Oh, poor frog! We must save it.'

I pushed past him and bent to pick up the frog in my cupped hands. My fear that the cats would kill it overcame my horror of its scaly softness and its spasms. I rushed with the frog to the back door, deposited it outside and slammed the door shut. Amber and Jet abandoned their poses and, tails high, stalked in and out under the legs of the kitchen table, forgetting.

Without intending to, I touched Peter's hand as I pressed past him to reach the frog. The connection changed the world for me. For both of us. We did not forget. Over the following weeks we proceeded to fall romantically in love, in order to make our hunger for one another acceptable both to ourselves and to our mothers.

I realise that I have not yet written here my mother's name. I think I only learned it myself long after I could read, and saw 'Rose Henshaw, Howden Farm' inscribed on the flyleaf of *David Copperfield*. I asked her who Rose Henshaw was.

'I am Rose Henshaw,' she said. 'Or rather, I was. When I married your father I became Rose Mortimer.'

I was impressed, vaguely understanding that another life lay buried with the name Rose Henshaw. I have a memory, which is the memory of Mother's memory, of little Rose swinging on an old apple tree which leaned so far to one side that it had to be propped by a great branch, forked like the ones that hold up washing lines; and of bonfires lit in the orchard, in the cold midnights of a northern spring, to save the apple blossom from late frosts. Rose watched the fires, and the incandescent blossom, from her bedroom window.

But I had no impulse to ask more about that lost girl or about Howden Farm. Mother was Mother. Before Aunt Susannah came to stay with us I never heard anyone call her Rose. Father called her 'Mother' as I did. On his lips the name carried a weak charge of irony verging on insult, as she was not a motherly figure and in any case had only achieved the condition of maternity once, with me. Jane called her 'mum', in a mumbled kind of way, which was nothing to do with motherliness but was Jane's rendition of 'madam'.

Poor Mother, poor Rose Henshaw. In the honeymoon photograph on the chimneypiece there is brightness in her face and grace in her figure. Her thinness then was slenderness, her smile was hopeful. Once on the high street in Camden Town I saw a little puppy trotting along cheerfully on the pavement beside all the people, stopping to sniff something, setting off again, full of curiosity and confidence. The puppy did not yet know that it was lost. I hurried away because I could not bear to witness the moment when the puppy-dog should realise that it was not beside its master, and that the forests of trousers and skirts around it all smelled of strangers. It would not know where it was, or the way home. All that carefree jauntiness must collapse into doubt, and then shivering fear.

Mother's only hold over my father was her feminine dependence upon him, and even that was pretence. The bit of money after all was hers; and she was far less silly than she allowed herself to seem. It was part of her character with him that she was terrified of spiders. If she came across one in their bedroom she would call downstairs to him in panic:

'Oh, Alfred, a spider, a spider, please come quickly and take it away, oh, Alfred, come up, please, it is dreadful, a real monster!'

With a lifted eyebrow and an air of indulgence he heaved himself out of his chair and tramped upstairs. From the parlour, I heard his boots on the floorboards above, and his grumbling reassurance, and Mother's fluting plaintiveness: 'Don't kill it, don't kill it, I can't bear it, just get rid of it, out of the window, I declare it is the biggest one I ever saw, oh, Alfred . . .'

This often-repeated ritual forced my father to pay attention to her, if only by paying attention to the spider. He was not displeased, he never failed to play his manly part. I was in the scullery one day when there was a truly gigantic spider, more than an inch across, with thick black legs, squatting beside the enamel washing-up bowl in the sink. I am not disturbed by spiders, but even I should have thought that one was worth comment. I prepared to spring into action on Mother's behalf.

She saw the spider. She stood at the sink with the kettle in her hand. She set down the kettle, picked up the spider by one of its legs, looked at it for a moment as it struggled, then crushed it on the tiled floor with the flat of her shoe and took up the kettle again to fill it – and all this without pausing in her talk with Jane about the leakiness of the cellar and the consequent dampness of the coal.

I think I always knew I would marry Peter Fisher, right from that first evening with the frog. But when in the weeks that followed I allowed myself to daydream, I also determined that I would not play-act like my mother. I would not pretend with Peter Fisher, not about anything, ever. I would tell the truth. Life, however, makes ascertaining the truth impossible, let alone telling it.

Meanwhile the conversations round the dining-table, and for long after we had finished eating and the dishes had been cleared away, grew no more amicable. Mention of Sebastian de Ferranti, whom Peter admired greatly, always caused trouble.

'Ferranti is the coming man. A genius. And he's only my age.'

'Ferranti,' said my father, savouring the name. 'Another whippersnapper like yourself, is he? Fine old English name, Ferranti. . . . Greasy foreigner, is he?'

'He comes from Liverpool,' said Peter. 'His grandfather was a famous musician.'

'*Musical*, is he, your Ferranti? A very *musical* young man. I see. I know the sort. Should be horsewhipped.'

'Not musical in the sense that you mean, sir,' said Peter, turning scarlet. 'On the contrary, he is walking out with the daughter of his legal adviser, a Miss Gertrude Ince.'

This seemed a complete *non sequitur* to me. Months later, Peter explained. I had not known that some men loved other men – though I can perfectly well understand how they might. The problem with Peter and my father was that neither of them would give up. Peter persisted in explaining the general excellence of Mr de Ferranti, as if he thought that my father would concede the point.

'His uncle is a university professor.'

'At Oxford, I presume?'

'On the Continent. I am not sure where.'

'What did I tell you? Greasy foreigners, the whole lot of them. And speaking of grease, and of dirt, what can you tell me about the manufacture of *soap*? Well?'

'I believe soap can be made out of any fatty substance,' replied Peter carefully. 'Animal fat, or vegetable oil, mixed with potash. Acid with alkali. My mother makes her own. She uses wood-ash, and tallow residue which she fetches from the candle factory.'

Father banged his palms down on the table. 'Ha! I happen to know, young man, that Ingleby's soap is manufactured from tallow, resin and soda. Furthermore, it is so thoroughly refined that it contains seventy per cent water and is still as hard as a rock! That's what I call science.'

'It's certainly what I call profitable,' said Peter.

Father persisted in asking questions about electricity. Peter Fisher, in love with his subject, rose to the bait every time, not knowing or not caring that Father was needling him.

Electricity, he told us, his eyes very bright, gives a pure and perfect light.

'Wax, tallow, benzole, gas, paraffin – they all pollute the air and rob it of oxygen. The soot from gas spoils everything. It tarnishes gilt. It darkens paintings. It rusts metal, and rots leather. The sulphur in gas fumes gives people headaches and kills plants.'

This silenced my father for a moment. My mother had a permanent headache, and the ferns we planted in the brass pot on the dining table always died after a few months and had to be replaced. My father, with a loyal glance at the gas brackets and their fizzing blue fishtails of flame, fought back.

'It's those cats that kill the plants. I should prefer not to specify how, with ladies present. Besides, the gas flames warm the room. Gas lighting may be considered a boon in that respect, in the winter.'

'You may be interested to learn, sir,' said Peter Fisher, 'that the three gaslights which are burning in here have exactly the same deleterious effect on the air that we are breathing, as would the combined inhalations and exhalations of no less than fifteen grown men.'

But my father was not interested in learning anything. He could not get it into his head that power stations were not actually manufacturing electricity. I must admit that I had difficulty with this too.

'The whole universe is probably one almighty power station,' said Peter Fisher – more patiently, for my sake. 'We speak of the current, or flow, of electricity, but that is a metaphor.'

'Well then,' said my father, 'if you electricians take as much of this metaphorical stuff out of the air as it seems you intend to, you will upset the balance of nature. It stands to reason. You are endangering life upon earth. Everything will run down. It will mean the end of civilisation, a return to barbarism.'

'Electricity is not consumed like gas or oil. It does its work and then – well, I suppose you could say it goes on its way, passes on.'

Mother was looking more than usually puzzled. I knew that this was because she was not sure what a metaphor was. I told her in a quiet voice that a metaphor was describing something in terms of something else.

'Why should anyone want to do that?' she asked me.

Peter Fisher was listening. I wished my old teacher Miss Paulina were there to answer for me. I did my best, poorly.

'Either because you cannot find any other way to express what you mean, or in order to make a poetic or colourful effect. Like when you say God is love, or the cats are the very devil.'

Mother turned to Peter Fisher:

'In what way is the flow of electricity a metaphor? What is it really, if it is not a fluid?'

He breathed deeply. 'Electricity,' he said, 'is a medium of communication between two objects.'

'Or two people?' I asked.

He looked at me. 'In certain circumstances.'

'In that case,' said my father, 'perhaps I should harness the unseen forces of electricity to communicate to my pert daughter that it is past her bedtime.'

I rose obediently. As I passed behind his chair he swivelled and caught hold of my arm.

'Give us a goodnight kiss, then. Make an old man happy.'

Chapter Two

Peter Fisher went back north to his mother for Christmas. During the few days that he was away I thought about him all the time, my thoughts spinning away into empty space since I did not know what he was feeling, and nothing had yet been said.

We began to become acquainted properly on Sundays as 1883 ended and 1884 began. Mr Fisher – as we still all addressed him – accompanied the three of us Mortimers to church, with everything washable about us as shining clean as Ingleby's Ingots of Hygiene could make it.

Peter Fisher was not normally a church-attender. He had lost his faith in the Christian God, he informed me. He told me that even his mother did not know. She was a strict Bible-believing evangelical and she wanted her son to be a preacher. She had taught him that he had a special destiny. I myself was a little shocked by his atheism, but I thought that it was honest of him to tell me. He was the first avowed non-believer that I had met.

In the hallway at 49 Dunn Street beside the hat stand there was an engraving by E. Gambart of 'The Light of the World'. I only know the engraver was E. Gambart because it said so in tiny printing at the bottom, at child's-eye level. It is a picture of Jesus Christ standing at a door in a garden in the night with his right hand on the latch and a lantern in his other hand. He has a halo and a crown of thorns. I think my mother had cut it from a magazine or an annual and had it framed. It is a very famous picture by Mr William Holman Hunt, and it was in the Royal Academy exhibition a long time ago, before I was born.

Peter always stood and looked at it with me. He did not comment and I was glad that he did not, because I feared that he would say something scathing. It was not the religiousness of the picture that I liked. But I had been looking at it all my life, and I always loved that lantern, dangling low from His left hand, with holes in the dome of it making a pattern of bright spots. I used to wish we had a lantern like that, to make patterns of light on the ceiling.

Peter came to church with us because he did not want to upset my parents. Also, the walk home from St Jude's was the one opportunity in the week that he and I had to talk without interruption. On all other days he was out of the house by seven o'clock in the morning to walk to his work, and did not return before six and sometimes later.

We attended St Jude's Church, which was a mile and a half away from Dunn Street, in preference to St Luke's on the corner. My parents disliked the Puseyite tendencies of St Luke's, even though it was modern and warm, being equipped with cast-iron hot-water radiators so impressive and ornate that they substituted for the tombs and monuments which dignify more ancient churches. The heated atmosphere of St Luke's was heavy with flowers and incense. The vicar intoned the services in a special voice, thick with a sort of tremulous joyfulness. When a statuette of the Virgin Mary appeared in one of the side chapels, my parents abandoned St Luke's and its sweet-voiced vicar utterly.

I was very sorry. Hanging on the pillar nearest the pew where we always sat in St Luke's was a wooden board. At the top of the board, in black copperplate writing, were the words: 'A Table of Kindred and Affinity, Wherein whosoever are Related are Forbidden by the Church of England to Marry Together.' Underneath were two columns of smaller writing. The left-hand column was headed: 'A Man may not marry his:'

and then all the categories of people whom he may not marry. The list on the other side was of all the people whom a woman may not marry.

I always used to read these lists during the service when I was a child, and very puzzled and fascinated I was too. I love lists. List-making is my only natural talent. A man may not marry his mother, daughter, father's mother, mother's mother, son's daughter . . . on and on. The very idea of these notional non-marriages made my brain reel.

One of the forbidden categories was mysterious to me: 'deceased wife's sister'. I was unfamiliar with the word 'deceased' and read it as 'diseased'. A man may not marry his diseased wife's sister. Once when Mother was poorly – she was frequently poorly when I was little – and Father and I were returning from church together, hand in hand, I asked him if Mother was diseased. Because, I said, if she was, he must not marry Aunt Susannah. His reaction frightened me. He pulled away his hand. He looked down at me as though I were a little monster. He was, for once, lost for words.

When the muddle had been sorted out he made a joke of it, telling the story at home in front of other people and mortifying Mother and me horribly for our different reasons.

I suppose that I am remembering this now because just a few months before Peter Fisher came to lodge with us I had read in the newspaper about the debates on the Deceased Wife's Sister's Bill in the House of Lords. Because of my childish mistake, and my interest in the Table of Kindred and Affinity – which was, one could say, the first sensational literature to come my way – I read the reports with interest. I remember that a bishop expressed his conviction that the poor did not regard the existing law as a hardship. I do not now suppose the rich did either. Widowers at the top and bottom of society, if one may judge from reports in other parts of the newspapers, simply cohabit with the sisters of their former wives if it is convenient. Only for people in the middle, where rules are important, is there sometimes scandal or secret shame. In any case, the Bill was thrown out at the third reading, the Lord Chancellor having opined that to change the law would lead to the breaking up of one of the most sacred and intimate relations of social life.

I wonder still of which sacred and intimate relation he was really thinking. For if a man might marry his wife's sister, after her death, he might feel free to cast his eye longingly upon that sister while his wife lived, thus committing adultery in his heart.

If I was sorry when I had to abandon my study of the Table of Kindred and Affinity and all the purple pomps at St Luke's, the vicar was even sorrier. He came to call on us, and sat for an uncomfortable half-hour with Mother and me in the parlour. I was younger then, so said nothing at all. Since Father was not at home, Mother was able to hold him solely responsible for our defection.

'Mr Mortimer cannot abide – practices,' she said apologetically.

The vicar moaned on about truth, beauty, and the Universal Catholic Church. It did him no good.

'We have always been just ordinary Church of England, you see,' said Mother.

A routine was established by which I walked with my father, and Mr Fisher with my mother, on the way to St Jude's. Mother I think was as undecided about our lodger as she was about most things, but it must have been obvious that Father avoided him as if he were a bad animal. He said impolite things about Mr Fisher when the three of us Mortimers were alone.

'I can't stand that outlandish voice droning on about electricity, and in my own house. The fellow is a monomaniac.'

My mother tolerated remarks like that from Father, whereas when I made critical comments about other people she would always say:

'Charlotte, you go too far!'

I think she said that to me more frequently than anything else, when I lived at home. 'Charlotte, this time you have gone too far!'

So we two walked together on the way back, lagging behind and taking different routes through the streets to make the journey last longer. Our best conversations only began when we lost sight of the stumpy figures of my parents round a corner in front of us. It was Peter who set the agenda for our conversations. It was as if he needed to learn how much and how little I knew, and he needed me to know the ideas that illuminated life for him.

As a matter of fact I knew a good deal. Until the previous summer I had been attending the Misses Sweetnams' school in Goodge Street, on the upper floors of a house overlooking the street market. The noise and smells of the market made the ordered quiet of the schoolhouse seem even more special. The teachers' name gave my father the opportunity for one of his jokes: 'Haven't they sweetened 'em enough yet, then, all those girls?' he would say with sickening regularity.

I had taken drawing (at which I was good), the piano (no good at all, and I never touched the parlour piano at home), a little French and Italian, English history and literature, and some mathematics. I had acted in plays; I was, I still am, an excellent mimic.

I did best in history and literature, because they were taught by Miss Paulina Sweetnam, the younger of the two owners of the school. When I thought, as I often did, that I did not want to become like my mother, the image of Miss Paulina always came into my mind. I suppose she must have been in her late thirties during my four years at the school. She was slim and erect, with very neat dark hair and a gloriously short, straight nose. My own nose is not long, but it is what Miss Paulina called aquiline. Sometimes she wore a white collar and a dark tie, like a man, but she was not mannish. Her hands were small and delicate; remembering now what Aunt Susannah told me about assessing people by their thumbs, it irks me that I cannot remember what hers were like. I suspect that they were small and delicate like her fingers, which would explain why she was schoolteaching and not standing on public platforms lecturing about the Rights of Women.

It was not just that Miss Paulina was a good teacher. I liked her and she liked me, and she put it into my head that there was nothing I could not do if I wanted to. She often quoted Christ's words from the Gospel of St Matthew, 'Ask, and it shall be given you; seek, and ye shall find; knock, and it shall be opened unto you.' She said most female maladies grew out of thwarted aspirations and unused abilities. She wanted me to take the entrance examination for one of the university colleges for women. She said that I was capable of it, and although as a woman one could not of course graduate and obtain a degree, the education and the experience could transform my life.

I pretended for her sake to take this possibility seriously, but I did not. Universities did not exist for my parents, most certainly not for females. They probably did not even know that women's colleges existed. I never even broached the subject with either of them. I did not want to go to one of the women's colleges anyway, the idea appalled me. In any case, it was around that time that Father lost his position at Ingleby's, and it was made very clear that there was no more money for educating me; even if I had not been due to leave the Misses Sweetnams' school that summer anyway, I could not have stayed on. Miss Paulina said I could try for a scholarship. But she knew the battle was lost.

If Peter Fisher had not come, I should probably have found a position in a shop, measuring out ribbons and putting buttons in paper bags. I had been educated in Goodge Street for something better, but neither I nor my parents had access to anything better. Yet I knew that something would happen. I used to say to myself when I was a schoolgirl that I was waiting for my real life to begin. When Peter Fisher came, I thought: 'Now my life has begun.'

But I feel a terrible regret when I think about Miss Paulina. What would she say if she could see me now? Would she weep or cheer? It is impossible to imagine her in this place, the way it is – Miss Paulina in her neat clothes, with her little hat on her shining hair, with her clean pale gloves and her hopes for me. I do not want to think about her any more.

Her gift to me was a wider vocabulary than my parents' and a belief that I could have and could do anything that I wanted. Ask, and it shall be given you. I only had to ask. And she made me into a reader. Father called me 'the Termite' because in my last two years at school I worked my way through the four volumes of Lord Macaulay's History of England, all the plays of Shakespeare, the novels of Jane Austen and – because they were, by some freak of chance, in the house in Dunn Street – the poems of William Blake. There were also three or four of Charles Dickens's novels, and some of Trollope's, and a lot of Mrs Oliphant's, with whose bolder heroines I identified myself.

So I was not a total ignoramus. But the things I knew were not the same as the things Peter Fisher knew. He was quite impressed by me because his own hard-won education was not literary. I was unable to keep my resolution never to pretend about anything with him. He assumed I followed all his explanations and arguments, though I did not. I could not. But I pretended to, all the while attempting to hold on, not to the specifics which so absorbed him and defeated me, but to some large idea upon which the detail depended. My responses and questions were about abstract principles, or drew parallels from everyday life. However naive they were, they caught his attention.

Nor was I wholly honest about myself. I only showed him the bits of my heart and mind that I knew by instinct he would like, just as I wore the clothes that I had noticed he admired, and arranged my hair in the way that I thought he would prefer. I presented a Charlotte Mortimer whom he could love, because I wanted him to love me. Women cannot help doing this. The trouble comes, I have found, when they are quite satisfied that they are loved. They then brutally thrust upon the lover's attention the hidden dark side of the moon, which emerges all the blacker and angrier after its concealment. This too women cannot help doing. Honesty is the best policy, as I first determined. But we are so afraid of being unlovable. Really being in love is squalid, it is like going fishing. But I did not think so at the time, nor the other time either. I felt as if I were sincere and single-minded – and therefore, surely, that is what I was.

On a dank Sunday in February, both of us chilled by the clamminess of the church, we nevertheless idled on our way home, walking slower and slower. We were of the one mind that the rector's sermons had a depressing rather than an inspirational effect.

'I believe it is his intention to bring us down, for our own good,' said I. 'How I do hate that phrase, "this vale of tears".'

'What is your own religious position, Miss Mortimer?'

As we walked, I was turning between my gloved fingers a holly leaf torn from a garden hedge in passing.

'It is not something I have ever been forced to think about. But since you ask . . . I do not think I have any views, in the way that my parents do, about rituals and practices and so forth, and travelling on Sundays, and whether or not the post should be delivered on Sundays. People get angry about that kind of thing. I cannot believe that God cares one way or another, if He is God.'

'But who is God, what is God? For you, Miss Mortimer?'

Since in order to talk one must have a topic, and since life at 49 Dunn Street did not furnish much material, metaphysics became our topic. Peter's metaphysics were tied up with the new work he was doing with Mr de Ferranti – installing electrical lighting, involving apparently 'a thousand-lamp dynamo', in a big hotel in Holborn – and with the theories in the technical books and old copies of *The Electrician* that he read at night in the back bedroom at Dunn Street.

Sunday after Sunday he told me his thoughts, never looking directly at me for more than a second since people walking side by side must look straight ahead or bump into lampposts. He courted me with his science. We made love with our voices only.

'Think of the language of the liturgy,' he told me. 'God is almighty, all-powerful, invisible. God is power, is creation and destruction, is energy, is the divine spark, is the prime mover, is the Light of the World. To be without God is to be in outer darkness. Lighten our darkness, we beseech Thee, O Lord. God is electricity. Electricity is God.'

'But that is a metaphor,' I said. 'You might as well say, God is water. Perhaps all religions and all sciences and systems are metaphors for something that we cannot know. So we choose the one that makes sense to us.'

'You are right. Plato said that God was a geometer. Isaac Newton imagined a clockwork universe. The metaphors are ways of getting nearer truths that we can know if we apply our brains. If human brains can encompass geometry, mathematics, and so on, then God if He is anything is a geometer and a mathematician and everything else besides. At the very least. Because He made the brains too. But our insulation in self makes us imagine an identity for Him. What if he isn't a He but the Thing itself? The unseen force. Not a musician, but music. Not the all-powerful, but the power. Think of the advances and inventions even since you and I were born. It's only the beginning.'

'But what if, as Mother says, we are not meant to know? Or even if clever people can invent new things, we might not be able to control them. If I were put in charge of one of your generators or accumulators, for example, I could do terrible damage.'

'But you could learn. I could teach you everything I know, in a matter of months.'

'Better that I should stick with drawing, church on Sunday and the poems of Alfred Tennyson, only I suppose now we must learn to call him Lord Tennyson. I do not think poets should be lords. Anyway, what you could teach me might not be enough. If once I were set going, Mr Fisher, I would not be able to stop. I might go further even than you. I might go too far.'

I spoke lightly but what I said startled and excited him. I had become something that he terribly wanted to have. As for me, I knew that he was something that I not only wanted but had to have.

He was not a good prospect as a husband. I saw that quite clearly. He was neither handsome enough nor impressive enough for anyone else to understand quite why I wanted him so much in spite of his lack of prospects. I did not understand it myself. It really was a matter of 'unseen forces', and the inevitable. I was like Titania falling in love with Bottom because he was wearing the ass's head, in *A Midsummer Night's Dream*.

It is possible that I should have become obsessed with whatever male lodger had come to 49 Dunn Street. Yet Peter Fisher had a quality like no one else. If you have been raised as he was to believe that you have a special destiny, it must be impossible to think of yourself as just an ordinary person, even if you do lose your faith. I wanted to have a special destiny too.

In my world, where nobody (except Miss Paulina) cared very much about anything, his obsession with his science was in itself magnetic. His passion for me partook of exactly the same intensity, and so seemed like an infidelity to his vocation. This excited me, as a woman might be excited who has attracted a young monk.

He might have given up his religion, but he had found a new one. His saints were Michael Faraday, who discovered electromagnetic induction; James Clerk Maxwell, whom I'm not quite sure about but I know he did some famous equations; and William Siemens, who died very soon after Peter came to lodge with us, so naturally I heard a very great deal about him. He had a lot to do with the telegraph cables under the sea, and with electrical generators, and he had plans to make London a 'smokeless city' – some hope – by piping gas from central furnaces into every house. He couldn't try it because Parliament said that if it were something that could make a profit, someone would have done it already.

Another of Peter's saints was David Hughes, who had just invented the microphone, which is something that enables you to hear what people are saying a long way away. I like the sound of David Hughes because he is an improviser. His first microphone was made with nails, sealing wax, and a tin money-box. The battery consisted of three glass tumblers in a cigar-box. Well, there was more to it than that. Mother was appalled when she heard, over tea, about the microphone. She said that bad people would be able to eavesdrop and discover everyone's secrets. Peter told her that was exactly what the Duke of Argyll had said in the House of Lords, which gratified her. In time, Peter said, the microphone would make it possible to hear all over London the speeches made in Parliament. Mother said she could not for the life of her see why anyone would want to.

There seemed to be no topic of the day, especially if it had to do with progress, which did not start up an argument at our table. The Channel Tunnel, which was also being debated in Parliament, was another one. Peter Fisher was enthusiastic about the idea of an unbroken railroad link with the Continent. Father took the view that the tremendous cost would outweigh any advantages, and that the Fenians would blow it up in any case as soon as it was completed. He had a point. That February there was a bomb in the cloakroom at Victoria Station which shattered the glass roof and set the gas pipes on fire, and two more found before they exploded in portmanteaux at Charing Cross and Paddington.

But Peter was a true believer in progress. Love was the rival religion. Both Peter and I believed in that. But it was not just Peter Fisher, this stringy, wordy, ardent young man, that I wanted. I wanted something else that could be reached through and beyond him. He was my metaphor.

Meanwhile winter became spring and I changed my thick, dark Sunday wrappings for lighter colours and stuffs, feeling prettier by the moment. The sun made my hair even fairer, and I took to wearing it long and loose under a hat. Mother wanted me to wear bonnets. She thought hats were fast and bohemian. Peter Fisher and I were very happy, we glittered in the stuffy little house and we glittered in the dirty town sunlight.

Those are the best times, the times of anticipation when the thrilling, longed-for thing has not yet happened but will quite certainly happen soon, nothing in the world can stop it happening. There is a stillness in the centre of the excitement, the stillness of water in the very last second before it slides over a precipice and turns into a wild, roaring waterfall. I had the same silky, silvery sensation later, in the days of my convalescence at Morrow Park, waiting for Godwin to look in on me before he went out to ride. Waiting for what had to happen.

On our walks back from St Jude's that spring, Peter Fisher would take my arm, once my parents were safely out of sight. Then one Sunday, as he was telling me as usual about electricity, he took my left hand. (Always, I walked on his right.)

He suddenly said: 'Please, take off your glove.' He pulled off his own at the same time. Our hands flew together and the contact, never renewed since the incident with the frog, was shocking. Drowning in sensation we walked on unsteadily, both breathing strangely, bare hand winding round bare hand, fingers binding and unbinding. As we grew accustomed to such nakedness the shock diminished a little, only to be reactivated when fingers felt for a new pressure. He began to speak again, but I interrupted:

'Just hold my hand quietly,' I said, 'as if we were children.

Otherwise I may fall down. Or die. Then go on telling me about science.'

He disciplined his hand and gave a kind of groan.

'Entropy,' he said, 'have I ever mentioned entropy? Entropy is unavailable or wasted energy. Scientists believe that the whole universe may be running down because of entropy, in that all matter and all energy in the whole universe will end up in a state of inert uniformity, with nothing able to give energy or to take energy from anything else.'

'Or from anyone else? No heroes or villains any more? No dramas, no love affairs?'

'You personalise everything, Miss Mortimer. Entropy is almost beautiful, like the ultimate note in music. The energy is not lost, it is still there. Entropy is a perfect distribution of all energy, a perfect equilibrium, an equalising.'

'It sounds very peaceful. And very democratic. Is not perfect distribution, and the equalising of society, what the Radicals call for?'

'Entropy is peaceful and democratic in the way that death is peaceful and democratic. Entropy means the ultimate death of the universe or, in microcosm, of any closed system.'

I was attracted and repelled by that phrase: a closed system. Death, I thought, death in life; and I thought of growing older, growing old, in Dunn Street.

The idea did occur to me, even then, that marriage might be yet another closed system.

'There is much technical terminology,' Peter went on doggedly, 'with which you must become familiar. You remember I told you about friction. The body which has been rubbed is called "the excited body", and when the body is sufficiently excited and touched – even your hand – there is a crackle, and a spark passes through both bodies. That's the electric spark.'

Unlike many girls of my age and condition, I knew the facts of life, thanks to Miss Paulina. I felt myself becoming red in the face. I stopped walking and pulled my hand from his.

'Oh!' he exclaimed, blushing too. 'I don't mean bodies in the sense that you think. It's the word the books use for – for just any physical substance, a clumping of matter.'

It was a critical moment. Either I must laugh or I must act as though I were offended. I laughed and, facing him and looking deep into his eyes at close range for the first time, I said:

'It's about us though, isn't it? Bodies are bodies.'

He kissed me. I knew, with satisfaction on the one hand and a sinking of the heart on the other, that yes, we would be married. One door opens, a thousand doors close. But behind the one door there may be other doors. Nothing remains the same, nothing is for ever.

His face buried in my neck, he said my name for the first time: 'Charlotte.' I said his name: 'Peter. My Peter.' I had wanted to ask him whether I myself, as a mere clumping of matter in an envelope of skin, were a closed system. It no longer seemed the right question. I was wide open to Peter, and to everything on earth. We looked and looked at one another as if we could never stop, and the sun came out.

'It has just been discovered by Professor McKendrick,' he said, 'that when a ray of light falls on the retina of the eye, an electric current is set up.'

'I can well believe it.'

'I have no money,' he said, 'but may I speak to your father about us?'

Sedately, gloved, and walking a foot apart, we turned into Dunn Street.

There was no opportunity that day for Peter to speak to my father. There was a telegraph boy outside 49 Dunn Street when we came up. The telegram was for Mother. Samuel Huff, her sister Susannah's husband, had died of apoplexy. I suppose there was a big funeral in Bradford. I cannot remember, I know there was a lot of fuss in our house.

Uncle Samuel had a nephew, Bullingdon Huff. The family spoke of Bullingdon with awe. I did not like the sound of him. He had been educated at Oxford, and he was a doctor – a mad-doctor. He treated patients in a private asylum in Essex called Diplock Hall. Bullingdon inherited Uncle Samuel's mill, which he immediately sold off to Mitchell Bros., the biggest firm of mohair and worsted spinners in Bradford. This upset my aunt; but she, as the widow, was left a hefty income.

Bullingdon had married a Lady Araminta Something, whom he called Minty. My parents tightened their lips at the mere mention of Lady Araminta. She was one of the few topics on which they agreed.

'Say what you like about old Samuel Huff,' said my mother, 'but he had lovely manners.'

'Samuel Huff was a ruffian,' said my father.

'Beautiful, beautiful manners,' continued my mother dreamily. 'He knew how to treat a lady.'

'Samuel Huff counted precious few ladies among the women of his acquaintance.'

'Lady Araminta is a lady, the stuck-up thing. She must be. It stands to reason.'

'Lady Araminta goes so very far in that direction that she cannot any longer be considered a woman. Which proves my point.'

How was it that my father always contrived to be right, even when he was wrong?

The chief consequence of Uncle Samuel's death for our family was that a few weeks after the funeral Aunt Susannah, not knowing how to deploy herself in her widowhood, found tenants for her house in Bradford and came to us at 49 Dunn Street for a visit of unspecified duration.

Chapter Three

So now there were five of us at table. After Peter's first week we had returned to eating in the kitchen. This was a small, dim, damp room with flaking whitewash, the irregularities of the plaster marked by coal-dust. When Jane was instructed to wipe the jagged lines of dirt away, she only achieved vague areas of greyer grime. The window overlooked the yellow brick wall of number 51 and the alley, or gulley, that separated the two houses. There was no room to seat five round the table in the kitchen, so now the evening meal – which I have learned to refer to as dinner, although at 49 Dunn Street it was called tea – must always be set in the parlour.

The first evening of Aunt Susannah's visit, Mother poked me hard in the back with her finger as we went in to eat, whispering:

'At the very least you might manage to say something to your poor aunt about her great loss.'

This instruction left me too at a great loss. As we sat down, I murmured to my aunt:

'I am so sorry about Uncle Samuel. You must feel very sad.'

Aunt Susannah removed her napkin from its ring and unfurled it. She spread it over her considerable lap. We all had napkin rings at Dunn Street. Mother's and Father's were of some yellowish substance, bone or ivory I suppose. Mine was wooden, as was Peter's. Aunt Susannah's was real silver, with rope-patterned borders and her initials, 'S.H.', engraved on it in curly capitals. Her napkin ring was one of the many personal items she had brought with her from Bradford.

Immediately, Jane came in with the soup. It was Jane's standard soup, the one Mother called good nourishing vegetable *potage*. Jane made it by boiling up chopped onions and carrots in water in the tall black pot and adding large chunks of turnip, parsnip and potato with the addition of a great deal of salt and pepper. She added to this brew as the days passed, tipping into the pot any leftover vegetables from our meals. The cats were meant to have the meat scraps. Sometimes I saw Jane scraping our dirty plates straight into the black pot before she clattered them into the scullery sink. If she boiled a new batch of soup for a long time, it appeared as a pale brown vegetal mush right from the first day. If she was in a hurry or if the fire was slack, the soup turned out watery with gollops of parboiled vegetables in it. That was how it was on Aunt Susannah's first evening.

Now I come to think of it, Jane did not really cook at all in the sense of 'cuisine'. She did not combine ingredients to make a dish that could be given a name. How could she? She was young and poor and no one had taught her. She took raw food and, by boiling, broiling, baking or frying, made it not raw. Different kinds of not-raw stuff were served up in different dishes. That is all there was to it.

My solicitous advance to my aunt hung in the air along with the peppery, washing-day odour of Jane's soup. My aunt took a spoonful and then smiled at me. She had artificial teeth which were not rightly centred. The two big front teeth were off to the left, and an eyetooth was almost in the middle. I seemed to be looking at her sideways and full-face at the same time.

'Your uncle was unwell for a long time, Charlotte. He was sticking it out for as long as he could. Hanging on, he was, because he could not tolerate the idea of his wife being at liberty to come and go, getting on with life without him. A decent man, a good man according to his lights, was Samuel Huff, but a dog in the manger. He had to go in the end.'

I did not know what to say or where to look. Peter, not being family, was legitimately able to go on eating his soup as if nothing were happening. He was not, in any case, sensitive to atmosphere. Mother made whimpering sounds. Father looked across at Aunt Susannah, extremely intrigued. She pointed her soup spoon at him.

'Those women who devote themselves as people say to the sick are not holy saints, Mr Mortimer. Don't you think they are, not for one moment. They are devoting themselves to nothing but their own satisfaction. They wear themselves out trying to prevent some poor soul from going to his just reward at the proper time, because without him they are nothing. I had no further need for anything that Samuel Huff could give to me and so I could let him go. . . . I am speaking of intangibles, need I say.'

She did need to say, since I'm sure the rest of us were all, at that moment, thinking of Samuel Huff's money, which Aunt Susannah must surely be very glad to have.

Aunt Susannah should have been an ugly and even an offensive woman, but she was so full of life, which meant in practice full of herself, that it was quite irrelevant whether or not she was good-looking, or even agreeable. Vitality attracts. She had coarse sandy blonde hair piled up under her cap, and such low-growing and bushy eyebrows that she appeared to have hairy eyes. She had a big body – 'all bust and bum' as she described it to me upstairs – which she elaborately upholstered in shiny black-beetle materials – the very deepest black, in mourning for Uncle Samuel. Every fold and ruche was edged with stiff black braid. The braid itself was trimmed with jet beads. More jet encrusted her long yellow ear lobes.

She looked like a coal mountain. If you wanted to be very impolite, you could say that she looked like a slag heap. She was about twice the size and had twice the personality of her younger sister, my meagre mother. It was very hard to believe that they were sisters at all. Maybe Granny Henshaw led a double life, though I doubt it.

The Henshaws came from the north, and the way Aunt Susannah pronounced her words was similar to the way Peter spoke, but with an overlay of refinement. My mother had lived in London so long that the ancestral colour was all but bleached from her voice.

I have modelled my own diction on Miss Paulina's. I am never sure to what extent I have been successful in this. My father talked like the other people around us in north London.

Aunt Susannah's arrival gave my father a new interest in life. 'Not so much Henshaw as cocksure' was his judgement. Aunt Susannah amused him. She behaved and spoke with an individual blend of coarseness and gentility which precisely suited him. A coarseness in him leapt out to meet the same quality in her, both of them knowing that he would remain 'Mr Mortimer' and she 'Mrs Huff' and that they were safe with one another. They became conspirators.

The genteel coarseness they shared manifested itself on that first evening. I did not like it. It was always very obvious in Dunn Street when any of us, Father in particular, went out to the privy. He would get up from his chair without a word, and with elaborate casualness tramp off down the passage, through the kitchen and scullery, and out of the back door – with a peculiarly cautious tread, as of someone trudging through snow, which he never employed on any other errand, not even when trudging through snow. On his return he walked faster, lighter-footed, and banged doors. Sometimes there would be a delay as he paused for a long time in the kitchen, to chat to Jane I always supposed. He was an irascible man but always indulgent to Jane. Her smallness and thinness would appeal to him, oh poor Jane. . . . Then he would whistle on his way along the passage, and drop back into his chair with an affable grunt. Nothing could announce his purpose or advertise its fulfilment more eloquently; but he never made any comment and neither of course did we.

Once Aunt Susannah came, however, he would say with what I fear might be called a leer, as he did on her first evening:

'I think I shall just step outside and smell a rose.'

And Aunt Susannah loved it, and smirked, and looked archly at Peter with a boys-will-be-boys expression.

Really, Aunt Susannah was in heaven in our house. She

patronised Mother and flirted with Father and flirted with Peter too, who was looking in his weird way completely beautiful because of love – his white skin purer than ever, his great eyes greener and brighter, his black hair wilder and more alive. I could not keep my eyes off him. Nor, I noticed, could Aunt Susannah. She made much of the fact that she had known him since he was a little boy, and made this long acquaintance an excuse for taking all kinds of liberties. With vicarious pleasure she fostered our romance. When he took off his glasses and laid them beside his plate, she said:

'When a gentleman who wears spectacles removes those spectacles in a lady's presence, it is a sure sign that he is interested in her. Much more than interested – though he may not yet know it himself. Remember I told you that, Charlotte. The great question is – which of us three ladies has caught his fancy?'

She flashed her big hairy eyes and her gleaming eyetooth round the table. I was horribly embarrassed. Peter, who was without guile, was not. Gravely he looked at my aunt.

'No, Mrs Huff. What you say may be true, but I remove my glasses to eat because I see my food better without them. It is a question of focal range.'

Once, I came into the parlour with the evening tea and witnessed a scene which still makes me laugh when I think about it. Aunt Susannah was a toucher. She liked to lay her hands on her interlocutor, particularly if her interlocutor were male. If seated, her mittened hand would tap Peter's knee as she made her point; standing, she would touch his shoulder or remove an imaginary hair from his coat. When I came in she was standing in front of the fire, raising the back fullness of her skirt more than just a little in order to warm her legs. Since they were too courteous to sit while she stood, Peter stood on one side of her, Father on the other.

At the culmination of whatever story she was telling, and she was always telling stories, she inclined herself sideways towards Father, tilting her head as if about to lay it on his shoulder. Almost, she was leaning on him, archly, knowing he must respond by throwing a ready arm around her shoulders to support her. I imagine her idea was that any onlooker (preferably

Mother) would remember only his impetuously outflung arm; and also, that she had a deprecating smile in readiness for when she should extricate herself from his flattering but inappropriate embrace.

Unfortunately Father edged away, just a tiny fraction. Aunt Susannah's graceful inclination, unsupported, became a lurch. She lost her balance, and must have toppled over on to the hearthrug had she not thrown out a hand and caught hold of the armchair.

Yet this is the woman who was the third greatest influence of my life before my marriage, after Miss Paulina Sweetnam and Peter. Aunt Susannah was sure of herself, and held her opinions with vehemence. In comparison with my mother she was like a brightly coloured picture set against a black and white engraving.

After Aunt Susannah came, there was nowhere in the house for my poor mother to be. I wish now that I had supported her more. Some horrible part of me allied itself with those who proved their strength by diminishing hers. Perhaps Mother connived with this. One of the things that Aunt Susannah said to me was, 'People always get what they want, in the end, and you might be surprised at what some people want.'

I should describe the plan of our house more fully. We were attached at one side to number 47. Our staircase went up the party wall on the right, just beyond the hat stand and 'The Light of the World'. The first door on the left was the parlour, with its window facing the front, on to the street. At the back was the kitchen, and beyond that the scullery, with the sink and the mangle. In between the kitchen and the parlour was a small room which we called the morning room, and which was officially Mother's domain, though I had done my school exercises in there and still used it when I wanted to read quietly. There was not much furniture in the morning room – a worn blue plush settee, Mother's work-table and her Singer sewing machine, a glass-fronted bookcase containing all the books we had in the house, and a couple of upright chairs. There was no space for anything else.

Upstairs, my parents slept in the front room over the parlour.

The middle bedroom was mine – or was until Aunt Susannah came. Peter had the small back bedroom, a colourless cell in which the only splash of brightness was the jade-green jug and basin on the washstand. The back bedroom was unpleasantly noisy because of the gurgling of the water tank that fed the sink beneath.

Aunt Susannah was contributing handsomely to the family budget, much more than Peter, and she intended to have her money's worth. Without saying a word she took over the morning room as her private sitting room. She spread an Indian shawl over the settee, placed a fearsome photograph of the late Mr Huff on the mantel shelf, and laid a square of Brussels carpet over the linoleum on the floor. Jane was required to light the fire in there every afternoon, which was unprecedented. Mother always said that the room was quite warm enough, benefiting from the nightly parlour fire on the one side and the warmth of the kitchen on the other.

Aunt Susannah liked to talk. It was more than that. To be talking was her natural state. All she needed was another human presence, and speech poured from her like water from a pipe. She never hesitated, or considered what she wanted to say. There was a direct link between her mind and her mouth, with no intervening bends or obstacles. 'I'll just give the fire a stir,' she said before stirring the fire. To think was to speak, for her. Not to be talking caused congestion. You could sense the pressure building up.

When there was nobody available to talk with her, Aunt Susannah sat on the settee in the morning room with the door open and did her knitting. She knitted when she talked too, and she knitted in the way that she talked – automatically and, when alone in the morning room, furiously, because of the unease that silence bred in her. She wore black lace mittens and there was something fascinating and disgusting about the little swellings of flesh puffing up through the tight spider-web of the lace as her fingers flickered around the yarn and the needles clicked.

It was never stated in so many words that Mother was no longer to use the morning room, and sometimes she flitted in and out, or hovered in the open doorway, as if staking a claim which would lapse were it not regularly reasserted. The truth was, it had well and truly lapsed. When Mother stood on the threshold, uncertain, Aunt Susannah would say in an irritated voice:

'Well, our Rose, are you coming in or going out? Make up your mind.'

The ice-cold marital bedroom was Mother's only refuge from her sister. She went up to bed earlier and earlier, sometimes even before we had had our evening tea. Father generally followed her quite soon. Mother got the benefit, or took the consequences, of the stimulation provided by Aunt Susannah. The thud, thud, thud of the marital bedhead against the wall that adjoined the middle bedroom was more frequent after her arrival. Before, I had heard it chiefly on those nights that followed one of Mother's spider panics.

I cannot say at which point in my girlhood I knew what my parents were doing when I heard that thud, thud, thud. I simply registered that I was hearing it. If nothing is said, even to yourself, nothing is happening.

It was Aunt Susannah who initiated the ritual of cups of tea in the parlour at about ten o'clock in the evening, before we all retired. Jane, having washed up and stoked the kitchen range for the night, had slipped off home well before then, so the tea-making fell to Peter and me. We were delighted, since this gave us an opportunity to be alone together. We made sure the kettle took a long time to boil on the fire, already banked down for the night by Jane with a bucketful of slack, by putting an unnecessary amount of water in it.

During those half-hours in the dim kitchen, with the black beetles just beginning their nightly invasion from the dark corners, we lived – in microcosm, as Peter would say – through everything that was right and everything that was wrong about our future marriage. With our arms around each other's waists, we gazed at the red coals at the base of the fire and at the black, curly-spouted kettle on the hotplate. I enjoyed our silences, but Peter liked to tell me things.

'What happens when the kettle boils?'

'We make the tea.'

'No. What is this phenomenon, a boiling kettle?'

Already I was rebelling. Peter made everything ordinary that happened into a lesson. For him, it was the breath of life and he wanted us to go through life on a shared breath. So I did my best.

'The fire makes the water hot, and hotter. And hotter.'

'Why does it?'

'It just does.'

'That is opaque information. If you were to understand what water is, what fire is, and what air is, you would give a better answer.'

'It would be a different answer. Why would it be better?' Each frivolous response elicited more information and more questions. There was only one way I knew to put a stop to this sort of thing. When we kissed, and our hands flickered over one another through and between and under our clothes, we moved into a different universe, and one where I had more power than he. I do not think I can write even here about what we did with one another, nor about my sensations. It is probably the same for everybody.

I took to keeping a hairbrush in the dresser drawer so that I could tidy myself, afterwards, checking my appearance in the cracked mirror on the kitchen well. When we emerged with the cups and saucers, the teapot, milk jug and sugar bowl, carrying one tray each, I would be all liquid within and pink without, and my voice was husky. Peter looked whiter than ever, and shaky. He was clumsy with the cups. I kept my eyes cast down, but Aunt Susannah would never let anything go by:

'The little darlings,' she said, laying down her knitting and sighing.

It is true to say that Aunt Susannah's sentimental public approval of our attachment made life much easier for Peter and me. Neither of my parents, now that we had such a powerful ally, made any objections to our engagement. Looking back I can see that the whole atmosphere in the house was heightened. I never thought of this before, and it is an appalling thought – but remembering the way my father used to stare at me when I brought in the tray, I have no doubt that I as well as Aunt Susannah and probably Jane, contributed to the frequency of the thudding of the bed in the front bedroom.

Aunt Susannah was not so sentimental in private, as I had plenty of opportunity to discover.

A bed could have been placed in the morning room for her. I can understand that my mother might have sheered away from that plan. It would have made the usurpation official. In any case Aunt Susannah made a pronouncement:

'I like to go upstairs to my bed. Up the wooden hill to Bedfordshire, as our dad used to say.'

I knew when I saw Peter and Father struggling with her huge travelling trunk up the stairs and into my room that my fate was sealed. She would share my room with me. And so she did. For quite a long time that trunk was not unpacked; my aunt made do with the articles from her smaller luggage. I had a superstition that so long as the trunk was not opened the new sleeping arrangements were not definitive. I arranged one of my aunt's shawls over it, to disguise it as an ottoman. It was to no avail. The day I saw her in our room with the trunk open, and piles of garments mounting up on her bed, I knew all was lost.

My aunt took possession of my bed, which was large, with heavy posts but no curtains. The small iron folding bed, intended for child visitors who never came, was brought out from the cupboard under the stairs and placed crosswise at the end of the real bed, for me. The room was further cluttered by a new chest of drawers – mahogany, with big knobs – for Aunt Susannah to keep her things in. On the top of it she put a mirror on a stand, and around it she arranged photographs, half-full bottles of her Parma Violet scent, and an array of pills, powders and medicines. From the right-hand pinnacle of her mirror hung a little bag into which she stuffed twists of her hair cleaned from her brush and comb; and from the left-hand pinnacle, a royal blue velvet pincushion in the shape of a heart. I liked that blue heart. It looked fat and cheerful.

On my own little chest there was just my 'jewel box' – a wooden casket about eight inches long and five inches wide, with a shiny yellow varnish and a picture of Osborne House printed in black on the lid. The inside was padded and lined with magenta satin. It had been a farewell present from Miss Paulina when I left school. I had no jewels to keep in it, apart from a string of mock pearls, my blue glass beads, and a silver ring set with a turquoise.

Aunt Susannah had a large quantity of capes, pelisses, shawls, wraps, tippets and so on, which she stowed away in the middle drawer, all jumbled up. Her eyesight was not so good, and her chest was in the darkest corner of the room. All these confusing garments were black. I used to watch her from my iron cot as she rummaged among them, bent over, blocking with her body what light there was from the window in the early mornings or from the candle late at night. She recognised each item by feel, kneading with her mittened hands the soft dark mass of wool and velvet, fur and feather, as if it were a litter of black kittens that only she could tell apart. Muttering phrases of appreciation, doubt, disgust, she turned and turned the heap, fingering textures and trimmings, pulling out a corner now and again just to check, until with an exclamation – 'Aha!' – she found the one she was looking for. They all looked much the same to me.

Over Aunt Susannah's corsets and underpinnings, which she kept in the top drawer, I prefer to draw a veil. Mercifully, so did she. She had a large square of pink silk which she spread at night on her chair over the clothes which she had just removed. She assured me that this practice, which was as new and as bizarre to me as any High Church practice at St Luke's, was quite usual among real ladies – so that the sight of their intimate garments might be kept from the prying eyes of servants, or from any gentleman who might call while she was taking her coffee in bed in the morning.

In the context of Dunn Street this was fantastical. Also, I wondered where she had learned it. Perhaps from a ladies' magazine? Sometimes I wonder whether Aunt Susannah had not herself been in service before she married Samuel Huff, though I never would have dared to ask her.

There was not room for a second washstand, so we had to share. The china basin and cold-water jug on my washstand did not match. The jug had a pattern of inky-blue ivy leaves, but its basin had got broken and been replaced by a plain yellow one that I did not like. Jane brought up two cans of hot water instead of one every morning, and my aunt and I took turns to wash ourselves in the yellow basin. I always went first. I was aware of her beady eyes upon me, assessing me from behind, as I bared parts of my body and soaped myself.

'Grand pair of legs you've got there, our Charlotte. What's more, legs last. Everything else goes.'

In my chemise, I emptied the water I had used into the slop pail and wiped out the bowl so that it was clean for Aunt Susannah.

She herself had evolved an elaborate technique for washing herself without any part of her person being visible to an observer. She performed her toilette inside a tent made of hessian material with a drawstring round the neck. Under cover of this body bag everything went on – dressing, undressing, soaping, sponging, drying.

'Even Mr Huff,' she told me with an air of complacency, 'never once saw me naked. Never once. Gentlemen prefer a bit of mystery. Remember that, Charlotte.' Meanwhile the bag bulged and the bulges heaved.

Once we were both in our beds at night, the air in the room thick with Parma Violets, she talked to me, or at me, until one of us fell asleep.

I tried, unsuccessfully, not to surrender to Aunt Susannah by falling asleep before she did. I did not want her ever to see me asleep. Before, no one saw me sleeping except I suppose when I was a baby, and it makes me flinch even now when I remember, or is it that I just imagine, some big face looming over my cot, *looking*, pressing closer and closer. . . . As a child I trained myself to wake instantly at the sound made by the turning of my bedroom door-handle. When Mother or Jane came in first thing in the morning with the hot-water can and drew back my curtains I always met their glance with wide-open eyes. But I know that Aunt Susannah saw me sleeping.

Her bedtime conversation took the form of passing on her personal view of life. In her own way she was as much a born teacher as was Miss Paulina. What with Peter by day, and Aunt Susannah by night, I spent the months before my marriage mentally prostrate under the weight of instruction. Their blueprints for existence did not coincide at any point.

Peter and Aunt Susannah, between them, reinvented me,

passionately and at cross-purposes. But neither of them conquered my whole mind and my whole attention. I strove to hold them off, not altogether successfully, because I still hoped to invent myself.

Chapter Four

'A lady,' said Aunt Susannah, in the darkness of our bedroom, 'must be either pretty or elegant. You aren't bad-looking now, mind, up to a point, but it will not last. So you have to learn to be what they call elegant, for later. When your complexion begins to go, it will not improve matters to use paint. Or only for short public appearances.'

She approved of my eyes – not the colour, which was an ordinary grey-blue, but their size.

'Learn to use them. It's no good having eyes like that if you don't use them. Your mouth's not perfect. No one is ever going to call it a rosebud, are they? It's the mercy of God that you have good teeth.'

She passed on her worldly wisdom. 'Always buy your gloves from a proper glove shop, not from a department store. In a proper glove shop you have choice, quality, and personal attention from a trained man. These chits of girls they employ in the stores don't know their business and they've no idea about counting out the change. No idea at all.'

This was confusing since Aunt Susannah also said that most women were cleverer than most men. Her idea of the rights of women, however, did not tally with Miss Paulina's. I wrote carefully to Miss Paulina in my best writing – which was modelled on her own, right down to the back-flipped Greek 'd' – to tell her that I was engaged to be married.

She wrote a short note in reply, and called to see me, but not until June, and unannounced. She was looking very nice. It was mid-afternoon, and a hot day. Jane was in the kitchen, Father was reading the paper and snoozing in the parlour, Aunt Susannah was in the morning room, and Mother was moving around upstairs. There was nowhere we could talk in private. I went upstairs to fetch my hat while she waited beside 'The Light of the World', and we went for a walk.

We talked for a while about the school. The Misses Sweetnams' main anxiety was that Goodge Street itself, because of its street market, was now a danger to public health, a breeding ground for cholera. That short stretch of roadway was never, ever cleaned and, in the hot weather, what Miss P. called the 'mud salad' of horse-droppings, rotten vegetables and bad fish was poisoning the air of the schoolrooms even when the windows were shuttered and curtained. Apparently Goodge Street lay on the border between St Pancras and Marylebone, and neither authority accepted responsibility.

Miss Paulina described the lengths to which she and her sister had to go in order to protect their pupils from contagion. I disliked the idea of such darkened, stifling enclosure and felt perversely supportive of the disorderly life of the street.

I suspect the real purpose of Miss Paulina's visit was to persuade me to think again about marrying. She was as always exercised about the rights of women, and grew animated as we meandered in the sunshine up and down the residential roads, where roses were full out in the front gardens. She told me what I already knew from the newspaper, that the question of votes for women had come up in one of the endless debates on the Franchise Bill. The suggestion was to give the vote to eligible single women and perhaps widows, but not to married women.

I thought that the use of 'eligible' was funny. 'The eligible ones will all soon be married, and then they won't be eligible any more. And just who, while they are still single, is going to distinguish between the eligible and ineligible ones? And why do you think the proposal excluded married women?'

'Of course it is all absurd,' said Miss Paulina, 'especially as an acknowledged reason for giving the vote to women would be to procure for them equal rights with their husbands over custody of their children. The true reason for excluding wives is that even the most advanced man believes that a wife should agree with her husband, in which case one vote per household suffices. If she went her own way, the sanctity of marriage would be endangered. But did you know, Charlotte, that there is to be a new Divorce Act in France? Did you know that Oxford University is to follow Cambridge's example and let women sit for the degree examinations, and will classify their results, just the same as the men's?'

'Does that mean that the women who pass will graduate, and take degrees?'

'No. But it is an advance. We have to keep pushing, don't you see, Charlotte? A dear friend of mine, Miss Muller, is going to refuse to pay her taxes until women have the vote. She will say "No taxation without representation", just like the American colonies when they fought for independence.'

'What will happen to her?'

'If Miss Muller refuses to pay, her goods and furniture will be seized to the value of what she owes. She is very brave. I would not dare to do likewise.'

I did not want to line up with Miss Paulina's brave single women. Had Miss Paulina ever been kissed in the way that Peter kissed me? It seems to me that when conventional people go on and on about marriage being a woman's proper destiny, they are not referring to her sexual happiness, though they may, somewhere in the mud salad of their thoughts, be referring to her husband's sexual convenience. And why is it assumed that a woman loses all capacity and desire for independent thought and action when she marries? If I had the vote, I should not necessarily follow my husband's lead in my decision. I suppose that is precisely the kind of thing that our legislators fear.

Anyway, the subject of votes for women was dropped from the parliamentary debates that summer pretty sharply. I myself remained sceptical about the campaigners for women's suffrage, even though that June afternoon Miss Paulina quoted from a *Daily News* leading article: ' "There can be no question that sooner or later they will win." ' This was Miss Paulina's faith, her religion.

She herself had taught me that I, like any man or any woman, had a right to whatever I wanted – 'Knock, and it shall be opened unto you'. But because of my secret life with Peter, and because I envisaged my special destiny as my own and not as part of some general social movement, I saw Miss Paulina in a different and less golden light that afternoon.

Older people, when they assure you that you can have whatever you want, really mean that you can have whatever it is that they want for you. Step out of line, and the response is very different. I was too much in awe of Miss Paulina to try and explain to her how I saw marriage as a door on which I could knock – not a door shutting me up in an airless room, but a door opening into wide-open spaces and fresh air and freedom. Nothing, surely, could be more constricting than life as the daughter-at-home in Dunn Street, slipping out once a week to hear people like her dear friend Miss Muller lecturing in draughty halls about the rights of women.

But Miss Paulina will always be special to me.

Peter's work became more interesting, and more professional, during the months of our engagement. He joined the Society of Telegraph-Engineers and Electricians, and attended meetings in their offices beside Westminster Abbey. Mr de Ferranti, his young employer on the Holborn hotel installation, took him one night to a dining club, The Arc-Angels, where electrical engineers met lawyers and MPs to discuss legislation. Peter came back inflamed.

'Progress is so *slow*. It's all the fault of the Electric Lighting Act. Do you know, the maximum period for which a private electrical company may be licensed is only twenty-one years?'

'Why is that so bad?'

'Because serious investors will not put their money in something which may be forced by law to fold. The government is overcautious, and is protecting the gas interest, even though the competition is loaded already, because everyone believes electricity will be more expensive. The other problem is the lack of trained men.'

Peter was determined to be a trained man. Several nights a week he attended lectures and demonstrations at the City and Guilds of London Institute, which moved that summer from a cramped basement in the City to premises in South Kensington, calling itself the General Technical College. There was another branch in Finsbury, for boys between fourteen and seventeen. Peter was amazed how popular the classes were – dozens of men and young boys, he said, with no education, some of them employed in electric lamp factories, turned up regularly after their day's work.

The teacher who most inspired Peter was Professor Ayrton.

'He says that when I set up an experiment, even though I know what it is designed to prove, I must feel that I am the first person ever to investigate the matter – and I do. He is a very *stirring* teacher.'

Peter was sitting at the kitchen table, bending down to tie his bootlaces. He looked up at me suddenly:

'There's a lady who comes to Professor Ayrton's demonstrations.'

'A lady?'

'Miss Marks. She has studied at Girton College, at Cambridge, and passed the examinations for the mathematical tripos. She is very clever at drawing too. She has designed a device that makes it possible to divide any line into any number of equal parts.'

'Is that useful?'

'Of course.'

'If she is so clever and educated, why is she attending the classes?'

'She needs the applied physics. And she is assisting Professor Ayrton in his research on the electric arc.'

'What does she look like?'

'She is . . . she is very charming.' He actually blushed.

'How old is she?'

Peter considered for a moment.

'I suppose she must be about thirty.'

That's all right, then. But hearing about Miss Marks brought back Miss Paulina's hopes for me, and for the first time I experienced a flicker of longing. It did not last. Yet I was infected by Peter's romance with electricity. It was a crusade. There seemed to be new ideas and 'inventions' all the time, which were never even developed because someone else immediately came up with something even more promising.

My own notion of wedlock as a bid for freedom was confirmed too that summer. Because we were engaged, it was considered allowable for Peter and me to spend time together outside the house.

We travelled from High Street Kensington to Putney Bridge and back by the Metropolitan District Railway, because the carriages on that stretch were lit by electricity. I thought the lamps were horribly bright, they hurt my eyes. We went to the Savoy Theatre, not really to see *Princess Ida*, though we did, and I enjoyed it, but to see the stage lit by the new incandescent lamps. Twenty candle-power each, but run at eighteen, said Peter. 'The lamps last longer if they do not get too much current.'

'Fifty-five lights, and over seventeen miles of connecting wire!' said Peter. We were walking along the electrically lit stretch of the Thames Embankment. Waterloo Bridge was lit by powerful arc-lamps too; we stood on the bridge and looked down at the reflections in the water, and up at the night sky, which receded into smudgy not-quite-darkness because of the brilliance of the lamps and the yellow fog of the city.

We admired the new Law Courts in the Strand, bright and white as a wedding cake behind their arc-lamps; we stood on a platform at King's Cross Station and strained our necks scrutinising the double row of lights hanging thirty feet above our heads.

'Four thousand candle-power there!' breathed Peter. To him, it was poetry. I have never walked so long or so far in my life as I did with him in the streets of London that summer.

We went too, five or six times, to the Health Exhibition at South Kensington. That was the great public attraction during that torrid summer. It ran from May to October, and hundreds of thousands of people went to see it. Peter and I went on Saturdays, by Underground to the Gloucester Road station, and we went in the evenings, when I would travel into town by omnibus, bold as brass as Aunt Susannah said, and wait by the Albert Memorial for Peter to finish his class in Exhibition Road and come and find me. On Wednesday nights the exhibition, which was set up in the gardens on that huge space behind the Royal Albert Hall, was open until one o'clock in the morning.

Outside the exhibition there were stalls selling the usual rubbish – toys and ornaments, nothing to do with health at all. Inside the entrance was a massive statue of the Prince Consort on a horse – one cannot get away from him these days – and a board telling you what lectures were on that day. We looked in at a talk on digestion, which was mainly about saliva. There was reference to wastes, and a diagram of a stomach on the blackboard. We were assured that it was the stomach of a dog, which was intended to make it less disgusting. It made it even more disgusting. Most of the lectures were equally lowering. There was one on smoke, and one on the gross pollution of the Thames which put us off ever again drinking from the scullery tap at Dunn Street.

I was disillusioned by the whole exhibition in the end. It was more like a fair, and appallingly hot and crowded. The chief aim was to sell things. Every exhibit had an attendant passing out circulars and catalogues. There were advertisements on posters wherever you looked. The original intention may have been high-minded, but every exhibitor was out to part you from your money – in exchange for patent shower-baths, wedding cakes, kitchenware, sewing machines . . . I know a lot of the lectures and conferences were serious. Peter went to the one on Electricity and Health, and I peeped into the Library and Reading Room. But even there, a placard announced that the library furniture and decorations were by Liberty of Regent Street.

It should have been called the 'Things Exhibition', like all the other exhibitions that are mounted these days. It is a mania. The year after, it was the International Inventions Exhibition. The previous year, they had called it the Fisheries Exhibition. Well, there was an aquarium this year too, not to mention fish potted, tinned, dried, smoked and preserved. Nothing related to anything else. The girl in sixteenth-century costume in the model street of 'Old London' was selling photographs of today's society beauties.

Opposite 'Old London' were two other houses, real ones made of brick, labelled 'The Sanitary House' and 'The Insanitary House'. It was all to do with pipes, drains, cisterns, ventilation, poisonous paint and so on. We both thought the Insanitary House was the nicest, even though the Sanitary House had electric light both upstairs and downstairs. Some of the exhibits were pathetically bad. The Water Companies' Pavilion was empty apart from a half-hearted fountain, with hideous oil paintings of waterworks and reservoirs hung round the walls; it opened on to a court where a glass sculpture was illuminated by an ugly electrical lamp on a pole. The lamp emitted a frightful buzzing sound. Not even Peter could find anything good to say about it.

There was a lot of peculiar food and drink on show, much of it for sale, though you were given samples if you stared hungrily enough. There were long queues for the patent folding lavatories, which I always feared might patently fold at a crucial moment, and even longer queues for the restaurants. We never managed to secure places for the half-crown roast dinners in the salons off the South Gallery, and the 'shilling dinners' were even more disgusting than Jane's at home. We could not afford the Chinese dinners at 7/6, and did not fancy the frozen chops from Australia, nor the vegetarian dinners. In any case Peter was always anxious to be outside in the gardens at nine o'clock, to see the illuminated fountains turned on.

It really was pretty, the cascades of electric light in different colours playing on the water as darkness fell, like a magical sunset. The crowds sat down on the grass to enjoy it and girls who seemed to be dressed in little but pocket handkerchiefs brought round trays of tea. Two military bands played in two different bandstands, and if you sat between them you heard both at once, which was terrible. We were very happy. We watched the lights and we watched the women in risqué costumes and red veils who only appeared after nine. Peter said the red veils made them look as if they had measles.

We lay on the grass with our arms around one another like all the other young couples, and when the fountains and the lights were shut off we streamed out of the grounds with everyone else, and walked hand in hand across Hyde Park and back to north London in the small hours – by way of Norfolk Square, because Professor Ayrton lived there, though Peter did not know which house was his.

When the weather broke and autumn began, my mother and aunt fussed over arrangements for the wedding. Mother and I trailed all over town to choose my household linens, night-dresses, petticoats, drawers, camisoles, chemises, corsets, and ready-made dresses for everyday wear. Some dresses were to be made at home; we bought yards of ribbon and lace trimming, a length of very special watered silk for a formal dress (midnight-blue swirling into silver-blue eddies as it caught the light), printed cottons for blouses, white piqué for collars and cuffs, and dozens of tiny buttons; also tape, wadding, petersham, buckram and lengths of whalebone. The undertaking was a list-maker's paradise. But the list-making was the only part of it that I enjoyed.

Aunt Susannah did not come with us. Her legs were not up to her critical comments. She had wanted us to go to Whiteley's, the Universal Provider in Westbourne Grove, the only big store of which she approved. Probably it was the only one she had heard of, she did not know London at all, though she spoke as if she were an authority on everything. We could not go to Whiteley's because it had just burned down. That was the third fire at Whiteley's in eighteen months, the damage was said to be a quarter of a million pounds. There had been another one since, I don't know what it is with Whiteley's.

There were dreadful fires everywhere in the year I married, in factories, theatres, railway stations, public houses, offices. Big gas explosions, too, which made Peter cheer. I thought he was heartless, because people were hurt in that tenement in Bermondsey, but he saw everything as a contest between gas and electricity. For the first time in my life I saw the outside world as a dangerous place. I kept reading about railway accidents. There were more bombs on the Underground too, and explosions in St James's Square and actually in Scotland Yard itself. Cabs and cabhorses were blown up in the blast. The dynamiters were always Fenians. All I knew about Fenians was that they were something to do with Ireland.

At 49 Dunn Street the parlour was dedicated to dressmaking. The plant in its brass pot was removed from the table to make way for the sewing machine from the morning room. A screen between the piano and the curtained window made a changing cubicle for me. The sideboard and the high top of the piano were piled with half-made clothes and lengths of fabric.

Father obstinately read his newspaper at his usual hour in his usual chair, endangered by dropped pins, islanded in a geometry of fraying shreds, offcuts and the rustling paper shapes which to Mother and Aunt Susannah represented sleeves, or skirt panels, or overskirts, or sections of body. I saw how his eyes swivelled from his newspaper – though he did not turn his head – when the white crêpe de Chine was being sliced up to make my wedding undergarments, and how he stared when I emerged from behind the screen in a half-finished blouse. I wished he were not there.

I wished I were not there either. In Swan and Edgar, I was required to decide which of the spotted muslins I preferred. The salesman heaved down bale after bale from the shelves behind him, thumping them down athwart one another on the counter, each time allowing a foot or so of the airy stuff to float free. The white muslin was transparent, dotted with tiny tufts of solid colour. Did I prefer the pink spot, the yellow, the sky blue, the dark blue, the lilac – or the black?

Overwhelmed, I heard myself enquiring whether there was not a green? There surely must be a green, even though I would not have picked it anyway.

'We do not stock a green, miss. We find there is no demand.'

Immediately I wanted a green after all. I picked the lilac, and later was consumed by regret. Any one of the other colours would have been preferable. All this brooding and choosing was making me ill. I craved the violence of pure chance.

The blue watered silk was the most expensive stuff we bought. Aunt Susannah was paying for it. She would have done more, she said, but the mill-workers were on strike in Bradford and she feared for her dividends. The parlour table was cleared of its clutter. The sewing machine was deposited on the floor. My mother spread the silk over the table, supporting the remainder on a chair-back. She pinned on to the unbroken blue expanse two long, curving pieces of paper which represented the swathed parts of the overskirt, the bits we called 'hip bags' at school. Mother stood back, made an adjustment to her pinning, and picked up her scissors.

When she made the first crunchy cut, slicing through the blue, the flat of her left hand holding the slithery mass firm, I felt a sickly excitement. It seemed wanton, spoiling something that was so perfect. Something dangerous and destructive was happening.

But then, it was not. After two or three pieces had been cut out of the silk it became nothing more than a dwindling asset. The important new thing was the intricate dress being formed from the ruination of that river of blue. Mother fretted whether there would be enough for a proper fullness in the draped back part. Jane was tacking together the panels already cut. Soon the dress would be just a dress, to be folded away in my room with others already finished, not to be worn until 'after the wedding'.

I was treated as a privileged halfwit, expected to do little more than stand patiently to be fitted and, when not required for that, to use my acknowledged skills on details: tucks, lace inserts, drawn-thread work, braiding, padding, and the endless covering of small buttons with scraps of the stuffs from which the dresses were made.

We fell out over the subject of hem lengths. Skirts were being worn shorter, just showing the ankles. I liked the look, and I liked the coloured stockings that went with it. Mother and Aunt Susannah were very stuffy about this. After much argument I achieved the shorter hem length but they drew the line at coloured stockings; I had black ones and white ones and that was it.

There was a little trouble over dress-improvers too. I think all ladies, unless they are very saucy, get stuck in whatever phase of fashion prevails just before they become middle-aged, as my mother did. In my last year at school the girls with rich parents started wearing under their best frocks rolls of horsehair on a framework, which made their skirts protrude at the back just beneath the waist – over their bottoms, to be precise. Aunt Susannah called them bustles, which she pronounced to rhyme with bushels, but the genteel term is dress-improvers.

There were already the modern kinds in the shops, ready-made from linen and whalebone, topped with layers of starched lace flounces and tied round the waist with tapes. If, in addition, the top petticoat is reinforced with steel half-loops and ruching at the back, and the overskirt is nicely draped behind, the effect is delicious. Mother thought it ridiculously exaggerated. But the 'look' requires that the torso form an 'S' shape, and so it did not work for Mother, who was too flat in front even when she wore a bust-improver over her corset. I felt that the style suited me beautifully. I resisted Aunt Susannah's suggestion that I too needed a bust-improver. Her standards were formed according to her own mountainy contours.

I was set to embroidering my future initials on handkerchiefs, bed linen, and endless shoebags, brush-and-comb bags, bags for hair-combings, handkerchief sachets, nightdress cases, corset bags, soiled-linen bags, all run up by Jane from the offcuts.

'Why does everything always have to go in a bag?' I asked in irritation.

'For decency's sake,' said Mother. 'And to keep the smuts out.'

She was right about the smuts. We had to cover the goods on the sideboard and piano with newspaper every night. Once when we did not, there was a sprinkling of dirty specks over everything in the morning. If you tried to brush them off, they just smeared.

I ironed transfers of the letters 'c' and 'f' on to the handkerchiefs and linens. The symmetrical curves of the small 'f' were prettier than the broken-toothed appearance of the capital letter. Peter came to sit on the arm of my chair when I was filling in the tail of yet another 'f' – a tail long enough to touch, just, the open mouth of the completed 'c'.

'Do you know what 'cf' stands for?' he asked.

I was embarrassed. If he did not know, he was either very stupid or all these preparations were being made on the basis of a dreadful misunderstanding.

'You know what it stands for,' I replied.

'Yes, but it does not just mean "Charlotte Fisher". It is what they put in learned books, to refer the reader to another version of the argument in another place. They put "cf" as an abbreviation of "confer", which is Latin for "compare". I learnt that at the Institute.'

I was in truth subjected to an onslaught of conferring and comparing. I was frayed and fragmented. I longed for solitude as if solitude were my lover, but except in the privy, or when I took a bath, there was no solitude.

I spent longer and longer in the bathtub in the cool dark kitchen, filled by Jane before she went home in the late evening with cans of hot water from a pan on the range. If Father wanted to step outside to smell a rose he would have to wait, or use the article in the cupboard beside his bed upstairs.

Jane would leave an extra can of hot water beside the tub, and I liked to pour it over me slowly. The warm trickling gave me pleasure.

A greater pleasure was to be derived from lifting my body and pouring can after can of water between my legs. I know this is indelicate, perhaps indecent, to write down. I have never read about it in any book, nor in a ladies' magazine. But I should like to record the first time I knew that moment of almost, almost, almost . . . and then the shudder, the slippage, the hurtling over the edge into white water. Volcanic twists within, almost a pain. No, it cannot be put into words. In any case it did not happen every time, it does not happen every time.

Then I put on my nightdress and padded upstairs to climb into the little bed at the foot of Aunt Susannah's.

'No man will ever see you as clearly as I do, Charlotte,' said Aunt Susannah. 'No man will ever understand you. And that is the mercy of God. There is nothing so terrible as being thoroughly understood. Women can live with men because it is only with men that women can be alone. Up to a point. Living with women, you are never alone – even if you have a bedroom to yourself.'

Earlier in the evening I had walked with Peter in the water meadows behind the high wall of Ingleby's soap factory.

'An electric field is a store of energy.'

I looked at the field across which we were walking. 'A field? Any field? Is this an electric field?'

'It could be, if there were lodestone under the topsoil. But what do you understand by energy?'

'Energy is – how you feel, being well and able to do things without becoming exhausted. Mother doesn't have very much of it. I have a good deal of it.'

'You are on the right lines,' said Peter. 'Energy is the capacity for doing work. Energy is power, whether it is being exerted or not.'

'"They that hath power to hurt and will do none",' said I. 'Shakespeare.'

'That may well be. But it's not just people, but mechanical work – say, a coiled spring or a moving object, or light itself, which is independent of matter. Do you know what matter is? It means – everything. The substance of every physical object in the known universe. Animal, vegetable and mineral.'

'Some matter matters more than other matter matters.'

'Not in the eye of eternity. But to you or to me, yes. Your hair, your eyes – that is matter that matters.'

He turned me to face him in the middle of the meadow and his face had that inward, desperate look to which I was becoming accustomed when we were alone. He pulled me to him and he was shaking, his bony fingers pressing into my arms through the cotton of my sleeves. He hurt me.

'You have power, over me,' he said. 'Whether you choose to use it or not.'

Aunt Susannah, in her bed in the darkness, said:

'A woman's life is nothing without a man. A nice woman can be married to almost anybody. Up to a point. To anybody reasonable. No good waiting on for Prince Charming. He'd turn into a frog the moment you kissed him.'

Aunt Susannah laughed her grubby laugh, and her bed shook

and rattled. 'It's not that all men are the same. There's all sorts, like with dogs. Your Peter is all right, pet. He may look a bit weakly, but I've seen his thumbs. You can always tell the quality from the thumbs.'

I was aware of the size and nervous articulation of Peter's hands, but had not made a special study of his thumbs.

'Your Peter's got good thumbs. Big and spreading at the tip, and narrow just below the joint, like a waist. Thumbs with strong tendons, thumbs which bend back. Thumbs with will-power. Your own are not too bad either. You've inherited your Granny Henshaw's thumbs. Me too. Rose now, she has disastrous thumbs. Poor, peggy things. I always knew she would never come to much. And as for your poor father . . .'

Father had his moment when he gave me away at my wedding. We travelled to St Jude's in the last carriage. There was a bad passage when he and I stood alone in our finery in the hall beside 'The Light of the World' and I thought he was going to tear me limb from limb. But he turned aside to pick up his hat and gloves, and Jane came running up from the kitchen to hold the door open for us.

She and I looked long at one other – Jane in her apron, her cap crooked, preparations for the wedding breakfast not yet completed, and I the bride, with my hair in a high chignon topped by the gilt rose that secured my veil. I wanted to speak gratitude to her with my eyes but my veil was between us. I saw her through a white haze, and she saw – a bride. I took a deep breath and walked past Jane, out of the front door to the carriage. It was 13 December 1884. St Lucy's Day.

And so I was married, and fell off the edge of the known world.

Chapter Five

At precisely 5.45 in the evening, when the train carrying Peter and myself north was just puffing out of the station, there was a huge explosion under London Bridge. Some Fenians had gone out on the river in a hired boat and attached twenty pounds of dynamite to a grating at the base stone of one of the buttresses.

We read about this the next morning, in the newspaper. One of the Fenians lost his life in the explosion. I was afraid that it might be an ill omen for our marriage. Peter pointed out that although the wooden balks had been smashed, and bits of masonry had fallen off into the river, and people walking across the bridge were badly shaken, the bridge had held; therefore it was a good omen for us. I was touched by his optimistic fancy; which he spoiled somewhat by explaining to me, at length, how the dynamiters could have destroyed the bridge had they attached the infernal machine to the upper part, because dynamite explodes downwards, forming a crater.

The last night that I spent with Aunt Susannah in the middle bedroom had been ominous, too. The room, by the light of the single candle burning on my aunt's night-table, looked portentous, with various parts of my wedding gown hanging from the picture rail like cuts from a bride's carcass. The trimming of my aunt's new hat, squatting on top of its box in a corner, constituted a regular mausoleum – two stuffed doves and a robin. My aunt asked if my mother had 'spoken' to me about marriage. I knew what she meant and deflected the question.

'You don't want to be hoping for too much,' said Aunt Susannah, not to be put off. 'The Henshaws never get many babies. We're not strong in that department. Me and Rose, we just had miscarriages. All those miscarriages . . . Except then Rose got you. She never managed another one. You're the only thing I've ever envied off our Rose. It wasn't fair.'

'I'm just a miscarriage of justice then, am I?'

'You're so sharp you'll cut yourself one of these days.'

We lay in silence for a while. I thought about my mother, in the light of what my aunt had just said, and saw her anew. The Diseased Wife. All those weeks when she was poorly during my childhood, when she stayed in her room, and Father and I walked to church without her. And how many times before that, before I was born? One might have supposed that she would have idolised her only child. But for so long as I can remember she had been awkward with me. Perhaps she felt she had no right to me. It must have seemed outrageous that Mother got a baby and her big sister did not. Perhaps Mother felt she should be punished. Perhaps she preferred the might-have-beens to me, she was more comfortable with them.

Aunt Susannah heaved herself up in her bed and said, to my astonishment:

'I shall say a short prayer for you now, Charlotte. Sit up, then.'

I sat up in bed while Aunt Susannah prayed aloud:

'Lighten our darkness, we beseech thee, O Lord; and by thy great mercy defend us from all perils and dangers of this night. For the love of thy only Son, our Saviour, Jesus Christ. Amen.'

'Amen,' I said.

'And from the perils and dangers of the next night, and all the other nights of our Charlotte's life, in the name of God, Amen,' said Aunt Susannah, her voice shaking.

'Amen,' I said. I had to bring Aunt Susannah back to her everyday self or we might both fall into the crater and weep, or worse. 'What do you think God is like then, Aunt Susannah?'

She gave a snorty laugh. We were safe again.

'Something like your Granny Henshaw. She was God in our house. Ruled our dad with a rod of iron. Within doors, mind. When I get to the heavenly mansions and see God, I shall be expecting to see something very like our mam. She was God in our house all right. Behind closed doors.'

God the Father did not sound as if He had much of a chance with Aunt Susannah. Perhaps she had more time for His Son. I should not be indulging in blasphemous thoughts the night before my marriage. I brought the conversation back to earth, by way of my earthly father.

'What about the Mortimers, Aunt Susannah? Do Mortimers get babies more easily than Henshaws?'

'Pshah. Your father has a lot to contend with. I have a lot of time for your dad. He does what he can. But no one is that interested in the Mortimers, not even the Mortimers.' Aunt Susannah blew out the candle.

There were Mortimers, however, at the wedding – Uncle Digby Mortimer, Father's younger brother, with Aunt Marianne and five fat little girls, one still a tiny baby. My question about the Mortimers' fertility was made redundant by the sight of them all spilling out of the cab in their wedding finery. The Digby Mortimers lived at Kensal Green because it was convenient for the cemetery. Uncle Digby looked as Father might have looked had he, like his brother, been a prosperous undertaker: that is, cheerful.

Family gatherings make one feel insignificant, just a piece in the puzzle. I felt unoriginal, at my wedding. Peter bought me a kaleidoscope at the Health Exhibition. You shake it and hold it up to the light and every time the pattern is different. There cannot be an infinite number of patterns. The same one must recur, only no one notices. When I think about Darwin, and eugenics, and inheritance, and good blood and bad blood, I wonder if there were not someone identical to myself in every particular who lived one hundred years ago; and whether there might not also be someone just like myself in every particular who will not be born yet for another one hundred years.

The wedding itself and the party at Dunn Street afterwards are a blur now in my mind. But I made the acquaintance that day of people who made a great impression on me. The first was Mrs Fisher, Peter's mother, my mother-in-law. She was the smallest woman I had ever seen, no taller than the eldest of Uncle Digby's daughters and half the weight.

Aunt Susannah had chosen my wedding day to abandon her mourning apparel. No half-mourning for her. She was resplendent in magenta and sage green. Her overskirt was tied back into a train, falling from a jutting dress-improver upon which one might have balanced the teapot. Her bosom could have supported the cups and saucers. Mrs Fisher's figure was swathed in black with no perceptible saliencies fore or aft, and she wore the dimmest of bonnets. She and my aunt seemed creatures of different species. They could hardly look upon one another without wincing. But then, Mrs Fisher had eyes only for her son.

Peter, I could tell, was nervous about her. Mother had offered to secure for Mrs Fisher a room in an hotel, but Peter insisted that his mother would only come to London for the day, returning by the train that same evening. She had never eaten a meal away from home, let alone spent a night away, since she married Peter's father, and she was set in her ways, he explained. I was getting myself ready upstairs, there was so much to do, so I did not see very much of her, though I heard her coughing. Until it was time to go to the church, she sat in the parlour over a pot of tea, and Peter sat with her. At St Jude's, standing with Peter at the altar during the service, I heard her behind us coughing all the time.

She had brought us a present – a big, black, brand-new Bible. Peter carried it upstairs to me, passing it through the door with averted eyes as I was half-undressed and Jane was with me. I knew Peter's views on religion well, but he was tremulously eager for me to show gratitude. When he had gone downstairs again I sat on my bed in my chemise and opened the Bible. The tissue-thin flyleaf was covered with Mrs Fisher's handwriting:

> Do not drink wine nor strong drink, thou, not thy sons with thee, when ye go into the tabernacle of the congregation,

lest ye die: it shall be a statute for ever throughout your generations.

Leviticus 10.9.

And if ye shall despise my statutes, or if your soul abhor my judgments, so that ye will not do all my commandments, but that ye break my convenant:

I will also do this unto you; I will even appoint over you terror, consumption, and the burning ague, that shall consume the eyes, and cause sorrow of heart: and ye shall sow your seed in vain, for your enemies shall eat it.'

Leviticus 26. 14–16.

And underneath, in larger writing: 'Peter Fisher and Charlotte Fisher, 13 December 1884'.

I did not find this encouraging. Although wine and strong drink were not a regular feature of life at 49 Dunn Street, a case of Madeira had been ordered for the wedding party. Naturally I did not feel that I should partake, with Mrs Fisher's button-eyes on me, and Peter too took only lemonade.

My Uncle Digby Mortimer, however, partook of a great deal of Madeira, supplemented by nips from his hip flask. I found myself trapped in the crowded parlour between him and the piano. He made excessively agreeable remarks about my appearance and expressed his regret that our two families did not see more of each other.

'The Mortimers,' he said, 'are, as a family, not as one.'

'How is that, Uncle?'

'Our mother and father were not as one. Our grandmother and grandfather were not as one. The Mortimers are a very old family.'

'Surely all families are of the same age. Adam and Eve, you know, Uncle.'

He squinnied at me. 'For a bride, miss, you are pert. Our grandfather was a gentleman. Our grandmother was – not a lady. The Mortimers have come down in the world. There have been rifts. But in death – in death we are not divided.'

He produced a large white handkerchief and touched one eye

and then the other with it. I could see how he might be very effective in his profession, when sober.

I have read the whole of Leviticus in the black Bible now, and the second passage my mother-in-law copied out is just a small part of a long list of the absolutely frightful tortures that God will inflict on those who do not do everything He commands. The rules that are not about the blood sacrifices that He requires are mostly about washing. No wonder Peter was so concerned about his laundry, when he came to us. I may owe my marriage to Ingleby's Ingots of Hygiene.

Our cats, Jet and Amber, did not enjoy the wedding day. They disappeared early in the morning and I could not find them to say goodbye when my husband and I left. I thought we were going to leave without having said goodbye to Mother, either. She looked very sweet at my wedding, in silvery grey. But she was too pale. A wraith-mother. I found her at last in her bedroom, just sitting on the bed. I do not know whether it was exhaustion or emotion that had driven her upstairs. I never did say goodbye to Jane, for which I was very sorry.

Meeting Bullingdon Huff, Aunt Susannah's nephew by marriage, was the other outstanding event of the wedding for me. The moment I set eyes on him I said to myself, 'He is the Devil.' Not the devil, as in 'the very devil', but the Devil. He is very tall, over six feet, and bends slightly forward. He wears fashionably high collars, but his neck still looks too long. His hair is thick and yellow, combed back from his forehead, with the ruts made by the comb very apparent. He is clean-shaven and his features are all oversized – huge pale eyes with sleepy lids, long nose, fat lips.

The Book of Leviticus, by the way, is also the source for the Table of Kindred and Affinity. It does not say, 'A man may not marry . . .', but that he shall not 'uncover the nakedness' of, for example, thy father's brother's wife, for 'she is thine aunt'. The thought of Dr Bullingdon Huff being the one finally to uncover the nakedness of Aunt Susannah is enough to make a cat laugh.

Bullingdon's lady wife was not with him. She was at home awaiting an interesting event. He had come dressed very grandly in a morning coat cut wide from his shirtfront in a horseshoe shape. Father, a much shorter man, was wearing his best frock coat, buttoned high. As he stood beside Bullingdon on the parlour rug, Father looked downright seedy. At that moment, looking at the two of them, for two pins I would have offered to sit on Father's knee. As it was, I went over and kissed his whiskers.

Bullingdon flicked his coat-tails and leered at me. In the cultivated, overcivil tones that I later learned to dread, he said:

'I hope we shall have the pleasure of welcoming you and your husband to Diplock before too long. I feel sure that the new therapeutic applications of electricity could be of some interest to Mr Fisher.'

I did not know what to say. He saw my confusion.

'There would be nothing for you to fear, Cousin Charlotte. Lady Araminta – my wife, you know – and I have an ample private residence in the grounds, and there is no possibility of our guests experiencing anything . . . distressing, shall I say, as a result of an unexpected encounter with one of my unfortunate patients.'

His dear 'Minty', he assured me, was sorry not to have come to the wedding. She was quite ready to make our acquaintance, he assured me. Such condescension was clearly designed to be received as a gesture of sublime graciousness.

'She has charged me with many tender messages for you. As for myself – does the privilege of kissing the bride extend to cousins by marriage?'

'No,' I said, and knew as I spoke that I had made an enemy of this horrible person, although I had no idea then of how bad an enemy he was to be, nor of how truly horrible a person he was.

Miss Paulina Sweetnam came, with her elder sister, but they did not stay long at the house afterwards. They brought me presents, which I did not unwrap until Peter and I were unpacking our valises in our room at Blackpool that night. The elder Miss Sweetnam gave me Mrs Beeton's *Household Management*. Since I have never had a household that needed managing on the scale envisaged by Mrs Beeton, the book has been of no use to me. Miss Paulina gave me a long pen-holder of black wood painted with a scrolly design in gold, and a card of steel nibs. Thought I have had to buy more nibs, I am using that same pen-holder now, to write this. It is stained with Stephen's ink up a third of its length, and some of the gold pattern has worn away. The wood is all soft and splintery at the tip, where I have chewed it.

We went to Blackpool on our wedding tour ostensibly because Peter had been taken there once as a child, and had fond memories of the place. The real reason was that Blackpool had been the first town in the whole world to light its streets with electric arc lighting, and because the world's very first electric street tramway was presently under construction there between Cocker Street and the South Shore. We stayed in a lodging house off Cocker Street and Peter spent a good part of each morning lounging around watching the men at work and asking questions of the foreman.

It was bitterly cold. December is not the best time to visit a seaside resort in the north of England. Wrapped in my new pelisse and Peter's muffler, I walked alone up and down the promenade, and to the ends of the two piers, and looked out over the sands and the grey sea, and thought how mistaken I had been to believe that my real life began when Peter came to Dunn Street. My real life had begun now, with my marriage.

We remained in Blackpool for five days. By mid-afternoon it was growing dark, and we would return together to our lodging, not to leave it again till morning. Our landlady, who was very understanding, brought up our dinner at five o'clock and lit the fire in our small room, leaving a bucket of coal for us. The gas jets hissed, and when we opened the window for a moment for fresh air we could hear the sea.

We were very happy in that room. My chief anxiety had been about using the chamber pot in the night. But it did not signify, indeed it was just another part of our secret life. Every aspect of marriage delighted me. I shall not say more than that. I remember sitting in the bed and looking at Peter standing naked against the circle of firelight, facing me, arms spread high and wide and legs apart, as angular and springy as the frog.

'I am experiencing another power surge! I feel like God!'

It was I who was like God, because it was I who had made him come alive, but I did not say so. We were the objects of each other's desire and of our own. Yes, we were very happy in that room.

When we left Blackpool and became ordinary people in the world it was not so easy.

We returned to London via the West Riding of Yorkshire, visiting Bradford to see Peter's mother, on a day of icy rain. The outsides of the houses were black. Bradford is no dirtier than other industrial towns, according to Peter. Apparently the stone from the local quarries, used for building, is of a kind that just sucks up the smoke.

I was filled with pity for the conditions in which his mother lived, and ashamed of my ungenerous first response to her. 49 Dunn Street was a palace in comparison with her house. The front door opened straight from the street into the parlour, with no front garden and no hallway. She shared a privy and a wash house with four other houses in the terrace, and she fetched her water from a standpipe at the end of the street. Peter went out to fill her pails for her while I helped her to get our tea. She asked me if I had noticed the Temperance Hall on my way from the station. I said that I had.

When she opened the kitchen cupboard and took a loaf and some butter on a saucer and some boiled ham, I saw that she kept her coal on the floor at the bottom of the same cupboard. It was bad coal, too – a few great pieces of the kind that someone must break up with a hammer, and the rest just dusty slack.

Although the house had a peculiar smell it was spotless, from the scrubbed doorstep to the polished brass fender to the bricked floor. It seemed that my mother-in-law had just washed that floor, but thinking it over in the train afterwards I realised that the sheen of wetness had remained, and that it must be the result of the damp, or some other nastiness, seeping up between the bricks from beneath. Even the hearthrug was damp. No wonder she coughed. This was the house where my Peter had been brought up. No wonder he was so thin, no wonder he caught cold easily.

As we sat close over her parlour fire drinking strong black tea, Peter told her that we could not stop for the night, we had left our bags at the Midland station, and she did not press us.

'It'll be back to work then for you, my son,' she said. 'Praise the Lord, we weren't sent into this world for our own pleasure.'

It seemed to me, then, remembering Blackpool, that our own pleasure was precisely what we had been sent into this world for.

I did not touch Peter while we were with her, nor looked at him hardly, and she never addressed a word directly to me in his presence. It was not, I think, that she did not like me. I was an irrelevance. I bent to kiss her when we left, and she submitted to my kiss. On the doorstep she clasped her arms round Peter with passion.

She stood outside her door hatless, in the cotton overall that protected her dress, her arms crossed over her chest, watching us as we walked away down the street to the corner and the Bolton Road. There were people – old men and old women, and little children – sitting in the windows of all the front rooms of the houses, doing nothing, just looking out. The cobbled street was narrow, the faces seemed very near. Peter turned twice to wave to his mother, and raised his brand-new billycock hat to her, and I saw tears in his eyes. I put my hand in his once we were out of sight and on the main road. We did not speak until we got to the station.

We were back at 49 Dunn Street for Christmas 1884. Mrs Fisher was right in that pleasure was not what awaited us in London. There had been much discussion, before the wedding, about where Peter and I should live. We intended to move into rented rooms on our own, but the electrical work on the hotel in Holborn was all but completed, and until Peter had found his next employment it seemed rash to commit ourselves to the expense. The plan was for us to remain at 49 Dunn Street just for a few weeks, until the future became clearer. The weeks became months.

It was a disaster. The house, which had seemed to accommodate us all adequately before the wedding, seemed to reject Peter and me as a married couple. Aunt Susannah, in sole command of the middle bedroom, did not offer to make it over to us and no one dared to suggest that she should. We crammed ourselves and our possessions into Peter's old room. My small bed, removed from Aunt Susannah's room, had been pushed against Peter's, which left little space for anything else.

Peter was out all day, and at his studies in South Kensington some evenings. I could not find a place for myself in the household, even though I was in my own home. Now that I was a married woman, Mother and Aunt Susannah treated me differently. I was no longer at their beck and call, to be criticised and scolded and generally educated in the way that I should behave. Yet there seemed no other way of relating to me, to set in place of the old one.

They watched me, and Aunt Susannah in particular would have liked me to confide in her about the great subject of married life. When I passed the morning-room door she raised her eloquent eyebrows and paused in her knitting – but I never went in to her.

Mother had taken up knitting as well. I suspect she was getting into practice for becoming a grandmother. I gave her no hint that this was likely to happen in the immediate future, and had no reason to believe it was. So she began knitting me a shawl, out of curiously scratchy slate-blue wool.

Father was embarrassed, I believe, by having a married daughter in the house. He ceased making his silly jokes. He had used to look at me too much and too openly. Now he looked at me furtively. He seemed depressed.

The worst moments were after the evening tea, when Peter and I retired for the night. We tended to go up early, since our cluttered cell was the only place we had to talk in private. We tried going up separately, with ten minutes' gap in between, and we tried going up together. Either way, rising, saying our goodnights, and leaving the parlour was excruciating.

We found it hard to talk normally together in the company of our silent elders, who had nothing to say to one another. No one looked anyone else in the eye. They listened to us, while pretending not to. Quite soon we found it hard to talk normally even when we were alone in our room. We became all but chaste. Something had been extinguished. I used to lie awake at night listening to the dripping and trickling of the cistern in the roof space, not knowing whether Peter was awake too or not; not wanting to know.

If this was bad, it was ten times worse when the work on the Holborn hotel came to an end. Apparently only a quarter of the electric lamps came on when the work was officially finished. This seemed to me less than impressive, but Peter assured me it was only what was to be expected. After another week on the site they managed to have nearly all of them functioning.

Then Peter was laid off from the Hatton Garden workshop – temporarily, said Mr de Ferranti, but who knew for how long? Peter had nowhere to go by day. He lay on his bed and read, and sat on his bed and wrote letters – to his mother, to his old patron Colonel Crampton, to Professor Ayrton, and to the Society of Telegraph-Engineers and Electricians. He designed electrical circuits on scraps of paper and fiddled about with his bits of wire. He drew up a fantastical plan for installing electric light in 49 Dunn Street, just for something to do.

Peter received encouraging replies to his letters, but no definite offers of employment. One letter included some interesting personal news. He opened it at the breakfast table.

'Professor Ayrton is engaged to be married – to Miss Marks. Miss Hertha Marks. I never heard her first name before.'

We explained to my parents and aunt about the inspiring professor, whose first wife had died shortly before he began teaching at South Kensington, and his talented female pupil.

My father said:

'Poor wrong-headed creature, a woman in a classroom with all those men. I fear the professor is making a grave mistake. She cannot be a lady. And what kind of an outlandish name is Hertha?'

'Her grandfather came from Poland,' said Peter.

'You don't surprise me,' said my father. 'More greasy foreigners. Jews, I wouldn't wonder.'

Aunt Susannah added her pennyworth:

'If they are getting wed, that will be the end of her carry-on anyhow. A married woman has her husband and family to look after.'

'Professor Ayrton writes that she will continue with her research, as his wife,' said Peter. 'He is insistent on the point.'

There was respect and admiration in Peter's voice. Again, I felt that uneasy flicker of longing. Thinking back, I wonder in what ways my marriage to Peter would have been different, had I been more like Hertha Marks. I shall never know.

The house was too quiet. When just after lunchtime, one day in late January, the dynamiters set off two parcel bombs in the House of Commons, we heard the blasts in Dunn Street. The worst one was in the Chamber itself, tearing up Mr Gladstone's seat and sending debris flying right up into the Gallery. A brave policeman found the second bomb in the crypt and carried it up into Westminster Hall, where it exploded. The sightseers who are allowed into that part of the Palace of Westminster were hurt by flying glass and pieces of stone from the floor. It was a miracle that no one was killed. Because I had time on my hands I read the papers more carefully than had been my custom. The word 'Fenian' had got mixed up with the word 'fiend' in my mind. But I learned that they were Irish nationalists, who believed in Home Rule and a separate Parliament for Ireland.

I really cannot see why they should not have these things, if they want them so badly. Mr Gladstone, I am flattered to say, agrees with me. It would be more proper to say that it is I who agree with Mr Gladstone. I was impressed with him when he said that just because some Irishmen behaved detestably, there was no reason 'why justice should not be done to those behind them'.

Peter always argued that it was not so simple as I and Mr Gladstone made out. For one thing, he said, to grant Home Rule would give ruffians everywhere the idea that dynamite was the way to get what you wanted; for another, it was only a small proportion of the Irish people, many of them living far away in America, who supported the dynamiters' aims.

Because these bombings happened at a time when my own life was so uneasy, they reactivated my feelings of personal ill-omen. The only other person in the house who was not sunk in apathy, and who appeared to be suffering from an unease that exceeded my own, was Jane. Terrible bangings of pots and clatterings of cutlery came from the kitchen. Breakages were treated like bereavements at Dunn Street, and when Jane dropped the oval willow-pattern meat-plate on the hall floor, where it splintered into a hundred pieces, the tension in the house was unbearable. I had expected Father to rant and roar, but he said nothing. Mother looked grieved and turned her face away. It was left to Aunt Susannah to organise picking up the pieces. I helped Jane wipe up the mess on the linoleum, and the cats helped too by licking up the spilt gravy.

The next day Jane broke the sugar bowl belonging to the tea service. When I came upon her sobbing in her chair by the kitchen table, I presumed it was the breakages, and her disgrace, that were upsetting her.

'No, miss, it ain't that. It's – I can't tell you, miss. I can't tell no one.'

I comforted her as best I could, and lent her my handkerchief, and supposed it was some family trouble, or a quarrel with her young man if she had one. Jane was not a prattler, she hardly spoke at all in recent months unless one of us spoke to her, and I knew nothing about her home life except that she lived in Somers Town, behind King's Cross Station. I am ashamed, now, that I saw her every day at 49 Dunn Street, and let her do so many things for me, and yet since I grew up I never took any interest in her as a person. I might have been able to make a difference.

Jane's problems were wiped from my mind – temporarily – almost at once. Peter received another letter, which changed everything for us.

Chapter Six

Before the letter came, Peter was ready to give up hope. He had begun talking to me about returning to Bradford and finding mill work at Mitchell Bros., through the Huff connection. The thought of living in that low-lying black town, perhaps in a house like his mother's, perhaps living with his mother, perhaps becoming a mill-girl myself, made me feel sick. I said nothing at all. I was twenty years old, and drilling myself to accept the likelihood that the best of my life was over. I repeated to myself my marriage vows – for richer for poorer, for better for worse. I believe that I would have kept my vows in that grim instance, and endured a ruined life.

And yet I was play-acting. I know many people, not just myself, have a secret belief that something unforeseeable will transform their lives. Jane, in the kitchen, used to say to me, 'I'll have rings on me fingers and feathers in me 'at one of these days, miss, you wait and see. I'm just waiting on for my Prince Charming to turn up. He's taking his time, I'll grant you.' It was a joke, the shreds of her dreams, and it kept her going. My belief was not of that nature. It was a premonition.

The mention of Bradford was before the fire at Mitchell's in mid-May, which caused £150,000-worth of damage and left the firm in difficulties. They would not be taking on more hands for a while. Peter's despair was lightened, ironically, by news that the fire was caused by the explosion of a gas engine. These horrors were happening all the time.

'Electricity does not explode,' he said, sitting in his bed in his undershirt, unshaven, unwashed, coughing like his mother. It was a bad spring that year, 1885; there was snow on the ground into April. Peter caught a cold which would not go away.

'Electricity can give you shocks,' I replied. A shock of some kind was just what we needed then. If ever I become a teacher, I shall, like Miss Paulina, instil a vision of life's possibilities in my pupils. But I shall formulate it differently. Never give up hope, I shall tell them. Anything can happen at any moment. There is always a new chapter. Nothing is for ever. I shall also tell them this: there is something to be learned, and something gained, from even the most dreary and arid passages in your lives. Nothing is wasted.

But it hurt me to see the frustration of my poor Peter, who was so ready to work all the hours that God gave for what he believed in. He had been trained, he had gained experience, he had the power and he could not use it. The economic depression was biting. In America, the electrical industry was making great strides. Here no one was in a mood for experimental capital investment.

The day the letter came, towards the end of June, there was one for me as well. It was from Miss Paulina. I had not contacted her since the wedding, I had not the heart to do so. She had evidently not given up hope of me. She wrote in great excitement to let me know that the Camberwell Radical Club, having discovered that there was no law against female Members of Parliament – because the idea was so unthinkable, so unthought, that no law had been deemed necessary – was inviting Miss Helen Taylor to stand for Parliament. Miss Taylor had consented, on condition that by standing she did not destroy the chance of any working-man candidate. Miss P. wanted me to attend a public meeting with her, along with her dear friend Miss Muller, to show support for the first-ever female parliamentary candidate. It was, she said, an historic moment.

If I were to receive such a letter now, I believe I would respond with alacrity. I might even be interested – well, maybe – in meeting Miss P.'s dear friend Miss Muller. Not that anything came of it all; the returning officer refused to accept Miss Taylor's nomination papers. At the time, the contents of Peter's letter, and the opportunity offered to my own 'working-man candidate', put Miss P.'s appeal right out of my mind. I do not think that I even answered her letter – something else of which I am ashamed, something else that I should prefer not to think about.

The letter to Peter came in a thick cream-coloured envelope. It had been addressed to him at the Society of Telegraph-Engineers and Electricians at Westminster, and sent on from there. At the top of the letter-paper was a red coronet, and an address, also engraved in red: 'Morrow Park, Hertfordshire'. I still have it. The envelope is grubby now and the letter-paper worn and furry at the folds.

Dear Mr Fisher,

I have been thinking for some time of installing a system of electrical lighting here at Morrow. The explosion in April this year in London at Rotherhithe, which as you will remember destroyed several houses, was caused by a gas main catching fire. In the same month the fire at a paraffin and petroleum shop in Southwark caused terrible destruction and the loss of five lives. These events and many others like them seem to me to indicate that electricity is the safest method of illumination, although I realise risk is involved here as well, not to mention the expense.

I have been in touch with my acquaintance Col. Crampton, and have inspected his house in Porchester Gardens in London which was, I believe, the first private house to be electrically lighted in this country. I was much impressed. Not being sure about how to go about the matter on my own account, I asked for his advice. I am unwilling to go to a large firm. I prefer to work through personal contacts. Col. Crampton mentioned your name to me as a young person of talent, dedication and experience.

I shall need someone like yourself to be in complete charge of the whole operation. The house is large, and the problems will be considerable. You would have to remain in the neighbourhood for some months while the work was in progress. Accommodation could be made available on the estate, provided that your family is not numerous. If you were to feel that the work would be to your liking and within your capacity, I should be glad to see you here at Morrow, at your convenience, to discuss the matter in greater detail.

The letter was signed 'Godwin'. Just 'Godwin'. Huddled in our room, we read it over and over again. I did not want to embark on any discussion with my parents until we had come to a provisional decision. We took it downstairs and showed it to Aunt Susannah in the morning room. We thought she would know about the 'Godwin', and of course she did.

'It means he's a lord,' she said, 'Like that Disraeli, who is Lord Beaconsfield now. When a lord signs his name to a paper, he just writes Beaconsfield, not Benjamin Beaconsfield. Except to a friend, perhaps. So this one signs just Godwin. We don't know what his Christian name is, though. I expect it's George. Something like that.'

We all three read the letter over again, squashed together on the settee in a hot miasma of Parma Violets.

'Of course this one needn't necessarily be an earl,' said Aunt Susannah. 'He could be just an ordinary lord. A baron, they call it. Lovely handwriting. So *complicated*. You can tell he's an educated man. Well, you had better go and see his lordship. Both of you.'

Miss Paulina used to say at school – apropos of Wordsworth and 'emotion recollected in tranquillity' – that happiness is unself-conscious and unrecognised. She said that one only realises afterwards, looking back, that that on such-and-such an occasion one was happy. That is complete nonsense. I was happy on that first drive into Hertfordshire, and I knew that I was.

The railway station for Morrow is Hitchin, and the station is a little outside the town. As instructed, we took a cab – an old growler, with a horse who did not at first want to be parted from his nosebag. Our way took us down into the town and up out the other side. So it was that I had my first sight, through the treetops from the high ground, of Hitchin's ancient, spreading, comfortable church, with its tower and spike, and the little river beside it, and the huddled houses with their tiled roofs and tall brick chimneys. We rattled down into the marketplace, along Sun Street, up Tilehouse Street, and then off to the left out of the town on the road past Charlton Mill. The names meant nothing to me then. All I noticed was that there were a great many public houses in Hitchin, and many pungent, non-London smells.

But during the five-mile drive through the countryside I took in everything that now means 'Hertfordshire' to me. It was a hot July day. Just outside the town we passed between fields of lavender in bloom. I could not believe in the colour that met my eyes, nor absorb so much pure scented air, I thought I should weep with ecstasy.

The light was clearer and sharper than any I had known. The barley was ripe, and the wide fields curved in perfect sections of spheres against the sky. I saw windmills, black barns casting deep shadows, farmsteads sunk in wooded valleys; and so much sky.

The roads we followed were just cart tracks, with grass growing down the middle. We drove through high bright fields in which tight wedges of woodland were marooned like ships. Then we wound down, down, splashing through a ford, and on, turning at unmarked forks, clip-clopping through deep, dappled tunnels of arching trees between high banks of cow parsley. The lanes were so narrow that when we met a loaded farm wagon we had to turn off into a field entrance to let it go by. Looking down from the cab as we halted I saw, in the flinty earth, blue scabious and minuscule pink-striped convolvulus.

I did not know the names of the wild flowers, then. My only experience of the countryside was the dead fields of winter glimpsed through filthy train windows on our wedding tour. London – unless you count Blackpool and Bradford – was all I knew. I had thought of the country as something in poems; whereas to the man who drove us out to Morrow this was everyday reality, and London – only forty-odd miles away – just a word, and perhaps a whiff of wealth and wickedness.

We came into Morrow Green past the vicarage and through the scattering of thatched cottages round the church, known as Church End. In Morrow Green proper there is a big triangle of grass, with a duckpond, and a public house called the Bald-Faced Stag; its hanging sign shows a stag with a man's face. All round the pond there are cottages, one of which is the post office. The road bends to the right through Morrow End – another group of dwellings, and a farm – and then, on the right, the entrance lodge to Morrow Park and a long winding driveway. Peter and I clutched at each other's hands as we turned into the gates.

It was very quiet after the cab had gone. The house was huge. We were standing on the gravel sweep wondering whether we ought not to walk round to find the trademen's entrance when the high front door opened and a tall man of about thirty appeared and came bounding down the steps.

'I'm Godwin. You must be Fisher.' He and Peter shook hands. Peter introduced me:

'This is Mrs Fisher.' It sounded strange. I thought of my mother-in-law as Mrs Fisher, not myself.

'I am very happy to meet you, Mrs Fisher. I dare say we shall become well acquainted if this plan goes ahead as I hope.'

I trailed a few steps behind Peter and his new patron as they walked round to the stable block where the electrical machinery was perhaps to be installed. Lord Godwin was the taller by as much as eight inches. His narrow legs, in clean moleskin trousers, took one step to Peter's two. Peter was wearing the black suit he had bought for our wedding, even though the thick wool was overwarm for the day. The back of his thin neck looked greyish in the sunshine. He had a haircut for the occasion and the barber had not only lopped off his wild wiry locks but shaved up the back of his head. I was glad that his hat hid the way that his hair stuck up in spikes at the crown. In Dunn Street, Peter had seemed distinguished, intellectual.

Godwin's hair, glossy and crisp and bright brown under a

tweed cap set at an angle, fell in tendrils. His shoulders were broad. The back of his neck was sunburned.

I sat down to wait on a stone block in the stable yard while the two men inspected the available space inside. Two horses, the same colour as Godwin's hair, watched me over their half-doors. I could not hear everything that the men were saying but I listened to their voices – Peter's wary, but excited. He talked the most, explaining the processes and problems no doubt, sure of what he knew but unsure whether he knew enough. Godwin's voice, deeper and with amusement in it, was wary too. A great deal of money was at stake after all: about £1,500, Peter calculated, of which £650 was for the engine and dynamo. Peter's own fee was to be negotiated separately. Gas was already laid on at Morrow, so the engine was to be gas-driven – preferably an Otto, I heard Peter explaining. He wanted to combine this with a Siemens or a Ferranti dynamo.

I waited, endeavouring to keep my hem clear of the dirt of the yard. I foresaw an evening spent brushing the mud off, once it had dried. So much for country life. If we came to Morrow I would have to wear my skirts even shorter, like a servant, like Jane. I used to think that Jane revealed her ankles because she knew no better. Then when I was old enough to wear long skirts myself I realised, carrying a tray upstairs to Mother's bedroom, that unless a woman has at least one hand free to gather up the folds of material, she trips over the front hem of her skirt on every step. Jane was up and down the stairs for half of every morning – with trays of tea, hot-water cans, coal-scuttles, brushes and bucket, bedroom slop-pails and the chamber pots, which she scoured in the kitchen sink. I shall be doing all those things too, I thought, when we move out of Dunn Street. I shall have to boil up my own bloody rags too, when I am unwell. The rich girls at school had special towels of layered white piqué material, bought for the purpose in shops. That seemed as impossibly extravagant to me as Aunt Susannah's lace-trimmed lawn handkerchiefs seemed to someone like Jane, who wiped her nose on her sleeve, or blew it between her fingers or into a piece of newspaper. One result of becoming an independent married woman is that I shall become a sort of Jane, until we can afford to employ a Jane ourselves.

Lord Godwin emerged into the sunlight and stood over me, swishing a cane against his trouser leg. He really was immensely tall, and immensely handsome. Not knowing whether it was polite to sit while he stood, I made as if to rise from the stone seat.

'Please don't disturb yourself. I'll sit beside you if I may.'

His tone was friendly, his voice deep and supremely cultivated. I felt attracted to him, and at the same time hostile. We sat side by side in a silence which he was the first to break.

'I hope you will not consider it impertinent of me to mention it, but somehow I had not envisaged Fisher being quite so young, nor you so – so very pretty, Mrs Fisher.'

Why ever not? Why should not I be pretty? Because Peter was what he was, Peter's employer had expected me to be – ordinary. It was only because he was Peter's employer that Godwin felt free to make such a personal remark.

'Your husband is measuring up. Thinking it out. I am surprised how little space the machinery requires – an area of just sixteen feet by six, apparently. There should be no problem, but I left him to pace it out. Your husband is a clever man, Mrs Fisher.'

'He is very clever. His health has not been good, and he has not had many advantages in life. Until recently, he was entirely self-taught.'

'But if it were possible to strip away the advantages that someone like myself has had, Greek and Latin, and a family, you know, and leisure and health and foreign travel and books and all this' – he waved his hand vaguely at the archway of the stables which framed a view of his park, blotted with great trees – 'if you could strip all that away, and be left with the essence, Mrs Fisher, I suspect you might find that your husband was more able than myself.'

'I have no doubt that what you say may be true,' I replied. 'But those advantages cannot be stripped away from you, nor will they ever be available to my husband.'

'That too is true. But he may rise in the world, particularly since he has you at his side.'

The fuzzy surface of his jacket was brushing my arm. I felt it through my muslin sleeve. Infuriated by my involuntary response, and by his complacency masquerading as humility, and by his effortless excellence, I glanced at his hand, which lay on his knee rather near my own. Remembering Aunt Susannah, I looked at the thumb. It was delicate, straight, with a slim oval nail, but it looked strong. I could not interpret that thumb. Was Godwin all charm and drift, with no drive? Or what?

'My husband,' I said, 'believes that energy is the secret of the universe.'

'Energy? As in "vital energy"?'

'Energy is the capacity for doing work, and it is also the work done. Not just a person working hard, but what it is that powers the animate and the inanimate. Energy is power whether it is being used or not. The energy is sometimes unavailable, locked up. My husband says.'

'What makes it available?'

'All kinds of things, I believe. Danger, for example.' I turned my head and for a perilous moment met his eyes at close range. They were very blue. Turning away, I plunged on, parroting what I had learned.

'Electricity,' I said, 'is energy.'

'Of course. So you implied. Though there are, I believe, other sources of power and other kinds of power. Electricity is Fisher's passion, as I myself am drawn to geology and botany. The inexhaustibly lovely face of the earth.'

Later, we waited between the stone urns at the bottom of the front steps while Godwin went to find the key to the East Lodge. It was a big key on an iron ring, and when he reappeared he was swinging it from his forefinger. He had not looked into the lodge for some time, he explained, and had no idea of what state it might be in. The west drive was the way we had come in, and the Carneys lived in the West Lodge. The gates of the east drive were kept locked, and no one had occupied that lodge since his parents' time. But if it was any good to us, while Fisher was working on the electrical lighting, we were very welcome. Rent-free, that went without saying.

Casually he threw the big key to Peter, who lurched to catch it, missed it, and fell on one knee on the bottom step. He picked up the key and brushed stone dust from his trousers. 'Thank you, sir,' he said.

'Can you manage not to hate him?' I asked as we walked away from Godwin down the overgrown east avenue.

'Oh yes. It is of no concern to me what he is like. It is the work I am thinking of, not only the money but the challenge. And you?'

'I could hate him, but I shall not. I think he will be an amusing person to know.'

Out of sight of the house now, we joined hands. The trees, in seas of waist-high nettles, pressed in on the avenue. We saw the wrought-iron gates at the end long before we saw the lodge, set back to the left of the gates and half-hidden by tall weeds and thickets of brambles. Cows had churned up the ground all around. I despaired for my skirt again as Peter fitted the key in the door. The paint on it had weathered to peeling shreds of grey.

Inside, the cottage smelt damp, and seemed very dark. Ivy half-covered the downstairs windows on the outside, and on the inside they were clotted with cobwebs. Something scuttled away over the flagged floor. A ladder-like staircase took up one corner of the main room, which was also the kitchen. There was a table, two old wooden chairs of different designs, and a dubious-looking kitchen range. There was only one other room downstairs, very small but with a fireplace.

The staircase led to the bedroom, which was more like a large landing since there were no passages or interior doors anywhere. From this bedroom an archway and one step down gave access to another, smaller room, repeating the pattern beneath.

It was terrible, a rural hovel. Or so I thought, until I stood at the window of the bedroom. This window is the main feature of the house when seen from the outside – overlarge for the lodge, high and pointed, with curving interlaced glazing bars. It is like a window in a church. From within, the sill is almost on the floor and the pointed top touches the ceiling. In spite of the cobwebs and dead flies in the corners of the panes, the window was a glory even on that first visit, with its view over the east drive and the wood beyond to a high meadow, glittering in the sunlight, curving in a pure arc.

I turned to Peter. 'It will do. We will make it – picturesque. And it is not for ever, after all.'

Seeing the relief in his face I put my arms around him under his thick jacket and stroked him through the sateen back of his waistcoat. 'We shall have to buy a bed,' I said. 'Our first own bed.'

Everything happened very quickly. It was a shock, after the long weeks of inanition in Dunn Street. My unworn trousseau was packed up in Aunt Susannah's big trunk, with Peter's clothes, books, magazines and tools. A carter from Hitchin came to collect it. Godwin told us he would be cheaper than a London man. The carter was employed by Mr Odell, who hires out horses and vehicles from premises in Tilehouse Street. Godwin had rattled off names of shops and firms we should deal with, and which would be useful for Peter's work, while Peter took notes which seemed exotic when read over in Dunn Street: 'W. B. Moss provision merchant, Odell (another one, in Bridge Street) the best smithy, Foster in Park Street and Philip Allen in Bancroft for joinery, horse-bus station to marketplace 6d., ironworks at the Swan on marketplace owner John Gatward . . .'

We did not buy a bed after all. Godwin sent down to the lodge a quantity of furniture from the attics at the Hall. It was from his grandparents' time, plain and good if a little rickety. The bed was shaped like a gondola. We placed it so that we lay facing the window, which remained uncurtained. We could not immediately contrive how to fix curtains across its pointed frame, and soon the notion of curtains lapsed altogether. We learned that if you did not make alterations and improvements very quickly after you moved into a house, inconveniences that had seemed to be shouting for attention became less urgent by the day. There was a water tap outside the back door, which was more than might have been expected, but no privy anywhere. This was what Peter called 'something of a facer'. We had chamberpots upstairs, and by day we went in the woods – and after a week or two thought nothing of it.

The first night that we slept in the gondola bed, in mid-

August, a full moon shone in through our gothic window and at two o'clock in the morning, out of the deep silence, a blackbird sang. We were together again. Even better than in Blackpool.

I shortened my skirts by three inches, covered my dresses in coarse aprons, tied up my hair in a big handkerchief, and swept, scrubbed, swilled, scoured, washed, aired, and polished until my hands were cracked and red, the windows and furniture shone, and the house no longer smelt of damp and mouse-droppings but of Ingleby's Ingots of Hygiene, and of lavender. I bought lavender oil and lavender water at Perks and Llewellyn in Hitchin, and the scent of it soon spelled home to me. Goodbye, Parma Violets.

Carney was a great help to us. He was in charge of the outdoor servants and Mrs Carney was housekeeper at the Hall. He arrived on our second day, driving a cart piled high with timber for the fireplace and coal for the kitchen range. He stacked all this in the brick outhouse at the back of the lodge. The next day he stopped by and taught me how to tame the stove – how to adjust the damper and manage the flue, how the oven worked, how much fuel to feed in and when, and how to riddle and clean out the great black monster. I thought I should never master it, but I know all its little ways now, and can keep it in overnight for weeks on end.

Carney is a nice man. It was from him, sitting over cups of tea at the kitchen table in the late summer twilights, that we learned that Lord Godwin's parents had died within a month of one another three years before. Godwin had been travelling the world at the time, but returned to take over the place – after a fashion, as Carney put it. Godwin had a notion that he wished to live simply. He laid off half the indoor and the outdoor staff, and left the park and the old formal gardens to nature; the grass was cut, and the vegetable garden maintained, and the heated greenhouses for out-of-season fruit, and the home farm continued as before. But Morrow Park was not what it was. There were two sisters, married and living far away – one in Somerset, one in Leicestershire – and Godwin was much alone. He went sometimes to London, where there was another house belonging to the family, and sometimes he entertained his neighbours. But mostly he seemed content with his own company. Carney spoke of him with respect, and some concern.

'Mrs Carney and I, we wish he would marry a wife. While he is still young. He could become strange, all on his own up there.'

From what Carney did not say, it was evident that he considered the electrical project as a symptom of our employer's incipient strangeness. But he was kind to us. He sent one of the garden boys down with a load of useful tools: spades and a garden fork, a heavy long sickle which I could not handle and a short, half-moon-shaped one that I could, a trowel in its own leather sheath, a little bellows for squirting insect-killer, secateurs, something that he called a dibber, and a box of assorted packets of Toogood's seeds. But there was so much to do inside the house that it was a while before I got to grips with the outside.

Peter meanwhile spent every day up at the house measuring and surveying, and every evening working on a detailed plan of the building. He had to understand how the house was put together before he could make his provisional wiring diagrams. It became clear that the job was too big for one man to do on his own. Godwin came down to the lodge one evening for a conference. Peter told Godwin that he would like two men working under him.

'I need an older man with a sense of responsibility, someone I can rely on to follow instructions exactly. And then a young person, a boy, to whom I can teach the detailed work – making connections and joints, tasks that require dexterity.'

Godwin, his long legs stretched under our table, questioned whether any local boy would be capable of such technical and potentially dangerous work. Peter was adamant.

'An older person finds it harder to learn new things. His mind is set in certain ways, his hands are accustomed to their familiar skills. Whereas to a young person everything is equally new and unknown, and his mind is not prejudiced, so one thing is as quickly learned as another. At the City and Guilds in London, the boys were much quicker to learn the theory, and handier in the practice, than the men. A boy of about fourteen would be ideal.'

'Or a girl,' I said, remembering Hertha Marks.

Neither of them appeared to have heard me.

Godwin found it hard to think of anyone on the estate or in the village who might have the discipline and respect for accuracy that Peter required. Then he remembered the bell-ringers. So it was that a replacement was found for Martin Paternoster, the senior cowman at the home farm, and Martin and his young son Joe came to work with Peter. On Sundays the Paternosters rang the church bells as usual. There were three bells, and a third bell-ringer. But old Cardew was long past learning anything new, and when he was not pulling his bellrope he was generally to be found in the Bald-Faced Stag.

Peter and I began to go to church, arriving early for the pure pleasure of seeing old Cardew, with Martin and young Joe, eyes locked on one another's in concentration, pulling on the ropes in counterpoint and causing that wonderful jangling cadence to shake the village air. There is a little door beside the font that leads to the belfry – a plain whitewashed room with the bellropes disappearing through holes in the ceiling. We climbed the ladder in the corner and peered over the edge of the trap door to see the great bells hanging from their massive timber supports in the half-dark. I found their size and evident weight oppressive. My eye was drawn for relief to the sunlit treetops glimpsed through gaps in the stonework.

Martin Paternoster in his kind, slow way tried to explain how it all worked, but he used words which meant something in the ordinary world in such a specialised way – gudgeons, stays, soles, fillets, sliders, blocks, hunting and dodging, and goodness knows what else – that I could not make head or tail of it. Martin referred to his bell as 'she'. Godwin said bells are always spoken of as if they were women. I asked Peter whether he thought electricity was masculine or feminine. He had no answer. It was not his sort of conversation. There was already, I see now, a kind of conversation that I could hold with Godwin, whom I hardly knew, that I could not with my own husband.

I could tell that Godwin was still anxious about the electrical project. Walking back with us from the church, he confessed that it was not the expense that worried him, it was the danger. Yet it was the comparative safety of electricity, as against gas or oil, that had first spurred him.

'My neighbour Lord Salisbury,' he said, 'has electrical lighting at Hatfield. I was dining there recently when flames started coming out of wires that were hung across the ceiling. The family threw cushions up to put the flames out. They seemed to think it a great joke. But it can't be right.'

'Most certainly not,' said Peter. 'There must have been a faulty joint, or undue resistance, and poor insulation. No one knew how to do these things in the early days. You will not see any bare wires at Morrow, they will all run in conduits. I am afraid it means a great deal of joinery.'

'Something even worse happened,' Godwin went on. 'One of the gardeners at Hatfield took hold of the two wires that went into the dynamo. He was killed.'

'I heard all about that,' said Peter. (He had not told me.) 'They were high-tension wires carrying eight-hundred volts for arc lighting for the stables. It was an exceptional and avoidable accident. A normally healthy person whose body touches two terminals and therefore becomes part of the electric circuit will easily survive the shock given by a hundred volts, which is all we use for domestic lighting.'

'My husband is very careful,' I said, 'and he will teach the Paternosters to be very careful. You must not worry.'

It interested me how Godwin's anxieties centred on wiring faults and fatal shocks, and not on the gas engine that was to form part of the system, even though the danger of gas explosions had been one of his reasons for wanting electricity. A prejudice is quickly forgotten in the face of necessity or convenience, and one way of driving out an old fear is to conceive of a new one. Both he and Peter glided over the gas question, with some remarks about how cheap it was, and how Godwin would have to employ a full-time stoker if they used coal, or else redeploy the man who stoked the furnace for the heated greenhouses.

Godwin stopped in the roadway just outside the open west gates of the Hall and solemnly shook us both by the hand.

'We shall say no more about it. We shall go ahead. It is an

adventure, for the three of us. Now – to change the subject. What do you think of this road?'

We looked down at its flinty, dusty surface and did not know what to say.

'Pretty good, don't you think? Last year I had my ploughman turn over the whole stretch between here and the village. Then we relaid it. Carney put six men on the job – a foundation of faggots, then bricks, gravel, flints, a top layer of soil. About there, where the carts and carriages turn in, there was a pothole so big that we plugged it with a dead horse.'

I was taken aback. Country life was proving to be full of surprises. We walked over the bland surface of the horse's grave and turned into the drive, where Peter and I veered off through the trees to the East Lodge. My new life, like my new home, lay open to green woods and fields as far as the horizon. I had a sudden vision of the interior of 49 Dunn Street, with my parents and my aunt and Jane locked for ever into petty routines and rivalries, in a stuffiness of personal odours and unspoken discontents. I forgot Aunt Susannah's maxim that nothing is for ever.

Second Notebook

Chapter Seven

Peter was waiting for the heavy machinery to arrive. Meanwhile he set the Paternosters to digging a trench from the engine room in the stables to the house, for the main cables to run in, while he helped me make some sort of a garden round the East Lodge.

There was about thirty feet between our door and the driveway. With all the recent comings and goings, a path had already been beaten to the door, and another round the back of the lodge to the outhouse. We set to work clearing more ground, claiming a circle roughly thirty feet in radius all round the lodge. At the back, our cleared territory petered out into woodland. Wearing thick boots bought in Hitchin and leather gloves, we tore at nettles, docks, periwinkles and brambles, piling the rubbish in a great heap. Where the roots were ineradicable, we cut and sawed them off as far down as we could.

I kept imagining a deranged seamstress, working on a giant sewing machine with the tension gone; because the brambles and periwinkles spread by throwing up long flexible stems which, bending beneath their own weight, put down roots wherever the tips touched the earth. There were thickets of these great interlocked loops, like loose stitches. There were also two old apple trees, still bearing, the apples ripening. These we left.

Working with Peter, I understood how it was that his real work exhausted him so. He rushed at everything, as if it were a competition, as if all had to be done in a single morning. A spurt of energy is one thing; but he cut and slashed as if he expected to be able to maintain such pressure all day, and of course he could not. Gardening is like housework out of doors. I have seen women cleaning out rooms, I have done it myself. You have to establish a rhythm, and address each part of the task as if it were the only one, without your mind moving on to the next.

Mother and Aunt Susannah, being northern women, had set ideas about the way to 'turn out' a room, and they taught Jane and me their ways. They moved with deliberation, like cows. Start by cleaning the hearth and setting a new fire. This is the dirtiest job, spreading ash and coal dust, and if it were not done first all other work would be wasted. Carry out all loose rugs and small furniture, and wipe and clean the highest objects – pictures, picture rails, shelves – so that dust and smuts never fall on surfaces you have already cleaned. Large furniture is then pulled into the centre of the room and dusted, and curtains looped up or tied back, so that the window frames may be washed. Before you put the objects back in their proper places, you brush the carpet or wash the linoleum on which they stand. Then wash or wipe all the surround, whether stained floorboards or linoleum, and scour the carpet all over with a stiff brush, into a dustpan. Shake rugs outside the back door, or beat them on the washing line. Last of all, polish the furniture, dust all the ornaments and position them precisely.

It is supremely dull, slow work, and has always to be done again, and then again, but there is an uncanny satisfaction in it. I have seen my mother, when she and Jane have turned out the parlour, standing in the doorway, studying and scrutinising the effect of the 'done' room like a musician scanning an orchestral score. She would leave to do something else, and then two minutes later dart back for another long gaze, maybe stepping inside and adjusting the brass pot on the table by half an inch, and stepping back again. She could only 'see' the effect, in her intense way, by standing in the doorway. There is comfort in order, safely enclosed by walls and a door.

Housework can be more than itself, for the person who does it, just as clearing the garden was more than itself, for Peter and me. Because of my dogged, methodical ways, I was less tired at the end of the day than he was.

Then Carney sent a man down with a horse and plough, and he turned over the earth of our patch. I spent days raking over the soil, taking out basketfuls of roots, and the irregularly shaped black and white flints that surface in all the fields round here, new ones appearing however many are picked out by the farm women. The biggest flints look like the shoulder blades and knee joints of prehistoric animals. I arranged the best ones all around the outside of the house against the walls, and trod the smaller ones into our paths.

There was no point our growing anything to eat. We did not know whether we would be staying long enough to harvest, and in any case the vegetable garden at the Hall produced far more than Godwin and his staff could consume. Two or three times a week the garden boy brought us baskets of vegetables and fruit.

Some of the weeds grew back, but as much grass came up as weeds. It was wonderful waking up one morning after rain to see from our great window a patchy first fuzz of green on the bare soil.

Carney went into Hitchin every Tuesday, driving down in the cart to bring back seed, feed, ironmongery, twine, and sometimes wine ordered from London by Godwin, which came by rail and had to be picked up at the station. Tuesday is market day, and the town is always full of people from the villages round about. Farmers show samples of their grain in the Corn Exchange on the square, and the street called Bancroft, where the big Quaker families live, is crowded not only with people but with sheep, penned up and for sale. I often accompanied Carney in the open cart, to look around and do shopping of my own.

I bought a straw hat, made of the local straw plait, and lots of baskets. In and outside Bullard's shop beside the churchyard there are always hundreds of baskets, in all shapes and sizes: wicker trays and carpet-beaters, durable containers for storage, for laundry, for shopping, for bread, for cutlery, for firewood, little ones with lids for trinkets, picnic-baskets, bicycle baskets, dog baskets, baskets for babies and even basket birdcages. They are woven out of split, peeled withies cut from the willows that grow on the marshy ground at the bottom of Bancroft. I stood and watched a basket-weaver, and it looked quite easy. But when at his invitation I tried to do as he did, I could not. My fingers were neither agile enough nor strong enough.

I wanted to buy Peter a special basket to keep his tools in, but he said no, electricians always kept their tools in boxes. He ordered the Paternosters to make their own toolboxes just like his own, out of half-inch timber, the top opening up into two halves. That, said Peter, is what an electrician's box is always like.

Electricians also always provide their own tools. The poor Paternosters could manage hammers, hand-saws, crowbars – but Peter insisted that they also needed chisels, planes, files, wrenches, spanners, gimlets, augers, bradawls, drills, brace and bits, and goodness knows what else. The Paternosters appealed to Godwin. Godwin laughed, told Peter to give them the list, and put the cost from the suppliers in Hitchin on his own account.

Godwin was constantly down at our lodge to see the stuff that had been delivered. I looked forward to his visits, I found myself looking out for him. I felt comfortable with him, but Peter – presumably because Godwin was his employer – was never quite at ease. So neither of them could be quite at ease with one another. Godwin had a way of addressing me, when he really was speaking to Peter; and addressing Peter, when his words were really for me.

Meanwhile our outhouse was filling up with Peter's own equipment, most of which he must teach the Paternosters how to use. Stacks of softwood timber for making conduits and casings, some of it especially shaped already in sixteen-inch lengths with half-moon grooves. Two lengths were fitted together, the half-moons forming a circular passage, top and bottom, to accommodate the wires. Blowtorch, soldering iron, spirit level. Oil, chalk, resin, fish-glue, Chatterton's Compound. Boxes of round-headed brass screws, wiring clips, and cleats – which are the pieces of wood on to which the switches are fixed. The cleats, bought ready-made, have arched grooves carved in them, as the casings do, to hold the wires. Godwin, turning a cleat over in his hand, said it was made of sycamore wood.

I liked playing with the switches. The ones Godwin had chosen from the catalogue were brass domes, and the central pin on each had a small brass ball on top. Nestling in their paper wrappings in the cardboard boxes in which they came from the manufacturer, the switches looked like little round bosoms with movable nipples.

There were opal tulip shades too, for the bedroom lamps, and shield-shaped sconces for the hall, and silk shades for the library, and shades like cut-glass bowls to be hung on chains in the drawing room. We took these expensive and fragile things up to the house in their boxes, and Mrs Carney put them away in a safe place.

Every evening Paternoster and young Joe sat round our kitchen table with Peter, who was instructing them in the mysteries of electricity. He had to begin at the very beginning:

'You do not light it with a match, and you do not blow it out.'

That in itself took some time to sink in. They had to learn a whole new language – current, resistance, pressure, potential drop, insulation, earthing, volts, ohms . . . parallel circuits and series circuits, red wires positive, black wires negative.

Knowing Peter as I did, and having seen him studying his own old notes, I could tell that he was passing on what he had been taught, sometimes word for word. He was enacting his old teacher, and becoming in the process a teacher himself. There was something religious about it, and touching. He was so boyish and intent. I loved him very much, those autumn evenings. His hair had grown again, and was as wild and wiry as ever. He kept pushing his glasses back up his nose as he bent with the Paternosters over diagrams sketched on scraps of blue sugar-paper.

I fully intended to keep up with the Paternosters' lessons and become an unofficial electrician myself. But often my mind wandered and I just watched the three of them, and listened not to Peter's words but to the sound of his voice, as I had when I first knew him. He would have been amazed to know that I never did grasp the distinction between alternating and continuous current, nor did I know which system was being adopted at Morrow. Somehow it was too late to ask.

He gave the Paternosters practical lessons – such as how to connect the wires into a terminal block. He made them copy what he did, and pare away the insulation very carefully from the copper conductors. None of the hair-fine wires inside must be sheared off, and none must straggle out, or there could be a short circuit. He melted a stick of Chatterton's Compound in the candle-flames – making the kitchen smell for hours of tar and rubber – and they put blobs of it on the end of the insulation, to close off the ragged edges of the braiding, which was made of cotton thread wound over rubber. Then they had to twist the sheaf of wires and double it back on itself, push it through the terminal block and screw it down.

I think this was the first practical skill that they learned, and it was obvious, straight away, that Peter had been right about young people being easier to train. Joe was much handier and quicker than his father. But neither of them asked the sorts of questions, or brought up the sorts of arguments, that my family had when Peter first came to Dunn Street – not because their minds were less enquiring, but because they accepted a new thing as a new thing, having no position to defend. Oh, and they respected the Wireman. Joe in particular idolised the Wireman.

Peter was 'the Wireman' to everyone at Morrow after Joe appeared breathless at our open door one morning:

'The machines have come! They are asking for the Wireman. Who is the Wireman? Are you the Wireman?'

'I am the Wireman,' said Peter, rising from the table, knocking his chair backwards on to the floor.

The gas engine and the dynamo, which were tremendously heavy, had been brought on juggernauts – long open wagons, each drawn by eight dray-horses. For the rest of that day every man on the place, including Godwin, was occupied in heaving and pulling and levering the machinery into position in the stables. I kept well out of the way, only going to see the spectacle when the engines were being bolted to the floor. The dynamo was a construction of bobbins and barrel-shapes, with rather smart copper and brass fittings. They joined it to the gas engine with a thick leather driving belt: 'oak-tanned', as Peter said reverently. Do not ask me exactly how the gas makes the engine turn, because I really could not say. But, when the gas-company men had brought the gas pipe up to the engine, everything seemed to fit together. Peter was ecstatic about the dynamo.

'It's a hundred-lighter, sir,' he assured Godwin over and over again. He meant that it could make a hundred incandescent lamps come on all at once, each one giving the light of twenty candles. He had nailed diagrams on the engine-room wall showing the run of the main cables, and the connections for the main switchboard.

The switchboard itself, to be put up in the engine room, was going to be a work of art, framed in teak with a clock set into its pediment. Godwin had seen one like that in a house he had visited. The distribution board, with the various circuits mounted on it, was to go in the main house, in the stone-flagged passage behind the kitchens. This too was to be teak-framed, and glassed in, with a lock and key. All these fittings Peter had either to make, or have made. There seemed to be a great deal to do in wiring a house that had little to do with electricity.

The rolls of wire and cable were delivered in huge weighty coils, like giant cotton reels, each one with a hundred and ten yards of the stuff. The coils were tightly wrapped in canvas. Peter and I arrived in the stable yard to see Paternoster preparing to slit open the canvas with a blade. Peter leapt forward as though Paternoster were about to commit a murder.

'Stop! Leave that alone! For God's sake don't cut it, man!' When peace was restored Peter explained that the insulation of the expensive cable could be ruined by one nick of a knife. He and Paternoster rolled the canvas drums under cover, and unwrapped them tenderly. He imbued in us all the importance of treating cable gently. Never let the unrolled cable have kinks or twists in it. Never step on it, never let it become damaged or damp. Peter treated cable as though it were sacred snakes.

The arrangement with Godwin was that Peter was to be paid a

third of his fee at the beginning of the installation, a third half way through, and a third on completion. After the dynamo was installed, he received his first payment. It went to our heads. We bought bicycles.

We had become very velocipede-conscious, because of the remoteness of our temporary home, and because the headquarters of the London Cycling Club were in Hitchin at the Temperance Hotel, of all places. My mother-in-law would have appreciated that. Every weekend the narrow, peaceful lanes around Morrow became hazardous, as strings of bicyclists streamed round the corners, ringing their bells. There were as many women as men. That is what fired me to learn to ride – and to ride a real modern safety bicycle with solid rubber tyres, not an ordinary bicycle with a huge front wheel, or the big, safe three-wheeler that both Peter and Godwin thought that I should have. Professor Ayrton, said Peter, had even designed and developed an electric tricycle. That was the transport of the future. The world is not ready for it, I told him, and insisted on two wheels only.

The bicycles were the most expensive things that we had ever bought. Mine cost £12 and Peter's £15, even though they were second-hand. Carney brought them up from Hitchin on the cart. Mine was a black, heavy machine. It had been a butcherboy's delivery bicycle, and had a usefully large basket on the front. It also had an oblong metal plate hanging from the central bar. The butcher's name had been erased, but the words 'FRESH MEAT', in white paint, were still there, on both sides. Peter's was newer and was called 'the Ariel'. He became infatuated with the machine. It was, he said, the most efficient means ever devised to convert human energy into propulsion. He oiled and polished it, murmuring to it about cranks, crank axles, crank brackets, sprockets, endless chains, chain-stays and, Lord help us, threaded nipples. The Ariel was Peter's baby.

The Bicycle Club girls wore 'rational dress', which meant some kind of trouser arrangement. Having established that one could not ride a safety bicycle side-saddle, as I had first supposed, I had to decide what to wear myself. I cut up an old skirt and stitched it together again so as to make two very full leg-sections.

We taught ourselves to ride the bicycles on the drive outside the lodge.

I mounted, I fell off. I mounted, I fell off. Over and over again. Until one day, after about a week, we both stayed on – and pedalled wildly towards the Hall, speeded across its front façade, zigzagged down the west drive, out of the gates, and bumped and flew down the hill into the village, autumn leaves swirling around us all the way and the low autumn sun blinding us in flashes. That was one of the great days of my life.

We ended up in two tangled heaps on the village green. The women who were standing in their doorways gossiping and doing their straw plait came rushing forward to pick us up. Peter went into the Bald-Faced Stag to have a drink with old Cardew, and I sat on a bench on the green with Joe Paternoster's mother Sarah. She went on with her straw plait. All the women do straw plait round here. They buy the bundles of prepared straws, nine or ten inches long, at the Hitchin market. The finished plait goes to the hat factories in Luton, to be stitched together and shaped on the blocks.

Or it did – business is not so good for the plaiters nowadays, because of cheap imports of straw from I think China. Sarah said that sometimes, when the women take their rolls of plait to the market on Tuesdays, to their special spot beside the Corn Exchange, no hatters' agents come to buy. But they go on taking their work to the market, hoping for better times and for the sake of the chat. They go on making the plait too. Their fingers are uneasy without their habitual occupation, it is what they know how to do. Sarah Paternoster went to what she calls 'plait school' when she was four; that's the only real kind of school so far as she is concerned, she calls the other kind of school 'reading school', and doesn't see the use of it for the likes of her. Her Joe went to reading school for a few years. Joe can read and write and add up and subtract. Joe can do straw plait, as well. That is another reason why he is so handy with fiddly electrical fittings.

Sarah Paternoster sat beside me on the bench with the straws tucked under her left arm, weaving them together into a single, seamless strip, deftly introducing a new straw every few minutes. She hardly seemed to look. Her fingers had a life of their own. It was like watching Aunt Susannah knitting but better.

'Will you let me try?'

But I could not do it. It was not like plaiting my hair, when I was a schoolgirl. I had been quick and neat, I thought, with my hair, and I had done it without looking – but that was just three thick strands, over and over. Sarah's straw plait was of seven strands, the straws slipped in my fingers, and I could not grasp the principle of the pattern – each village has its own, with a name. The Morrow pattern is called 'bird's-foot', don't ask me why.

I sat with Sarah until it began to grow cold, and wavering lights were coming on in the windows of the cottages. Then I took myself and my bicycle home – uphill all the way, a very different matter. I pushed it, from halfway up, and was tired when I got back.

I already knew that I was most probably going to become a mother, and that I should be more careful. I had not yet told Peter this news, partly because I was not sure myself. Peter stayed in the Bald-Faced Stag for hours and was the worse for drink when he and the Ariel got home, well after dark. I was already in bed. For the first time ever, I pushed him away from me.

The bicycle gave me freedom, and a speed four times faster than walking – on the flat, that is. Downhill, I went like the wind. I was no longer dependent on Carney for journeys into Hitchin. The only unfortunate element was FRESH MEAT. Trying to read the words half-concealed by my trouser-skirts concentrated the attention of bystanders on my pumping legs to a degree that was embarrassing. The rough men and women from the courts and alleys off Dead Street who hung around the marketplace started to shout the words out at me as I went by, laughing with horrible innuendo. In the end Peter blotted FRESH MEAT out with black paint.

At Morrow, routines became established informally. Often Godwin and I would be standing together watching work in progress, whether in the engine room or in the stable yard, where Peter measured out and cut cable and Paternoster was working on the joinery.

'I declare that the Wireman is a Manichaean,' said Godwin.

'What is a Manichaean?'

'A Manichaean strives to banish the world of darkness from the world of light. In the human soul, I mean. When next you meet a handsome, clever young parson, ask him to tell you about the Manichaean heresy.'

Godwin and I took to drifting off, separately or together, in the late afternoons. I could not deny myself the pleasure of his company. Through the stable-yard arch, on the other side of the gravel driveway, lay the park. He and I walked together across the long meadow grass, under the great trees with their leaves turning to gold. The first time, he said:

'Well, Mrs Fisher, what shall we talk about?'

'Anything, but not electricity.'

He told me the names of all the trees, pulling down a leaf from each to show me its form: beech, oak, ash, alder, elder, hazel, hawthorn, wild cherry. The next time, he tested me to see what I remembered. He told me the names of the plants and wild flowers in the grass and hedgerows. He pulled apart the flowers into my cupped hand, and I learned his vocabulary of petal, sepal, stamen, pistil, anther, calyx, bract. Those flowers that I picked and took home I drew, by candlelight in the evenings, and later showed him the drawings. He said I was very accurate, and gifted. He made me label the flower drawings with their common and botanical names, and the date on which I had picked them. I drew diagrams for Peter too, and made line drawings of tools and machines, and details of joints and splicings. I drew in all my spare time, that summer.

Godwin told me about the land we were walking on. It was chalk, he said. Chalk with flints. Chalk absorbs moisture, which is why the air of Hertfordshire is so dry and bracing. Chalk is a soft limestone rock, he said, made up of millions of fragments of seashells. He knew where to find fossils of sea urchins and sponges in the chalk, one day he would show me.

'But we are nowhere near the sea.'

'Thousands of years ago, this part of Hertfordshire was the bed of an ocean.'

In bed in the East Lodge, with the moon hanging outside our

gothic window, I lay fathoms deep beneath that ancient ocean, the hull of my gondola rocking on crushed white seashells. I said nothing about my walks with Godwin to Peter, even though at that time we were doing nothing wrong. Godwin no longer called me Mrs Fisher. Because Peter was the Wireman, he called me Wirewoman.

He led me one day through the woods that bordered the park, on a damp day when the ground underfoot was spongy with new wet leaves over layers of leaf mould.

'Today we are looking for mushrooms – mushrooms, toadstools and puffballs. Keep your eyes on the ground.'

I walked these woods nearly every day. Dutifully, without optimism, I trudged along beside him, my eyes down. Incredibly, within three minutes, I saw them:

'Look – oh look!'

A small army of mushrooms on delicate stems, rising as if by magic from the deep leafy mulch. Nothing so strange in that. But these were of a bright, deep, lilac colour – stems, gills and cap. They were like something from a fanciful illustration to the Grimms' fairy tales.

Godwin crouched down and picked one.

'Remarkable. This is *Laccaria amethystea*. I have not seen it here since I was a boy.'

He was silent, while we gazed on the coloured thing in the palm of his hand.

'Fool's luck,' he said abruptly.

'What do you mean?'

'Beginner's luck, if you prefer. You will never make such an extraordinary find again, so quickly and casually.'

He was not really pleased by my discovery, I could tell. He would rather have found the lilac miracles himself, and shown them to me with proprietorial triumph. He was the expert.

'The common name is Amethyst Deceiver,' he said, casting the lilac mushroom down and wiping his fingers on his handkerchief.

He led me another day beyond the home farm and across a meadow that sloped steeply down to a stream. We followed the stream to the corner of the meadow, where we pushed past a hawthorn tree and come upon a clean, shallow pool on a bed of gravel. Here, it seemed to me, the stream stopped.

'No,' said Godwin, 'here the stream begins.'

He trailed his long brown hand in the centre of the pool and displaced the gravel, releasing a small spout of clear water jumping up from underneath. It was a spring. It was – adorable. That is the only word for it. All around the pool, and in it, sprawled the dark-green leaves of watercress. Godwin broke off two sprigs and gave me some to eat – crisp, peppery, violent. At the top of the field, on our way home in the fading light, I looked back and saw the white ribbon from my hair caught in the hawthorn, fluttering. I was happy to leave it there, like an offering.

Once, he was late back from riding. I went walking in the park and over the fields by myself. Standing with my hat in my hand on a high, windy headland beside new-ploughed land, I saw him from far off. He looked quite small. He was walking along a ridge over the grassy dip that lay between us. I stood stock-still and watched him begin to descend the ridge at an angle. There was no one in the landscape except himself and me, and no house in sight. It was the end of the day; the last of the brightness was behind him. He made no sign that he had seen me, and I did not call or wave. If it had not been Godwin, I should have been afraid. When there are only two creatures in a wide and empty landscape, an invisible wire tightens between them. One must become the hunter and the other the hunted. There is no alternative. I dare say there is a critical moment at which you choose which to be. Up to a point, as Aunt Susannah would say.

I walked along the top edge of the flinty ploughed field, my boots growing heavy with mud, and down the side against the hedge. The angle of our trajectories narrowed as we moved downhill. We finally came face to face at the field gate in the hollow. He leaned his elbows on the top rail of the gate, and so from the other side did I.

'The mare went lame,' he said. 'She has lost a shoe, and she is in foal. I left her at the farrier's in Baldock until tomorrow.'

He leant over the gate and picked up a lock of my hair, and looked at it and rubbed it between his fingers.

'For a naturalist such as myself, you are a wonderful object of study, Wirewoman.'

I suppose that I was very naive.

Peter was teaching the Paternosters how to make joins in the conductors. At least, he was teaching Joe. His father, after a while, laid down the two wires and his knife, rested his chin on his great fist, and watched. I watched too. Peter had made them wash their hands at the tap outside before beginning. Everything had to be scrupulously clean – even the strands of wire that were to be joined had to be wiped with a rag. Joe imitated everything Peter did, taking in everything he said:

'Cut the insulation on a slant, like this, as if you were paring a pencil.'

These were coarser wires, inside the insulation, than the fine brass threads they had been playing with before. I suppose they served a different purpose. Peter and Joe spread all the stiff strands out like dead spider's legs, first from one cable-end and then from the other, and began to join the two up by twining the strands together in an elaborately twisting pattern, one by one, tightening each into its place with pliers. Peter's join, when he had finished, was a neat spiral-shape, like a coiled spring. Joe's was irregular and lumpy. But he tried again, and the second time his join was indistinguishable from Peter's. Then they went to the outhouse to seal the process with solder – equal parts of tin and lead, that I do remember. And resin. And then the join was bound with rubber tape.

I made Paternoster and myself a pot of tea and we sat companionably by the range and waited for them to come back. I do not imagine that Paternoster was dismayed by his limitations. He was a confident wookworker, and would come into his own when they started building and fixing the conduits under the floors and up the walls of the Hall. Paternoster was a solid, quiet, sandy person. We never talked very much, he and I, when we were alone. So I drank my tea and drew patterns, and thought about the private intricacies of straw-plaiting, and of basket-weaving, and of wire-joining. I thought about Peter, Godwin and myself. I imagined them as two electrified rods, and myself as a filament between them, binding them together and holding them apart.

But of course Peter and I, as a married couple, were an entity completely separate from Godwin. Also I knew, after another significant date had passed uneventfully, and from other signs, that I was most certainly expecting a child.

Chapter Eight

I lost the baby. Was that when my real life began, with the loss of a child's? Afterwards, I was different.

Godwin sent down a melon from his greenhouses, with a message that it was ripe. Neither Peter nor I had ever tasted a melon before. It had a hard, grey-green outside, broken in patterns like the bark of a tree.

I cut it in half, bisecting the globe across its equator, and found pinkish-orange flesh, with a pond of juice and seeds in the centre of each half. A strong aroma was released into the kitchen – warm fruit, or warm animal. It proved impossible for me to remove the seeds and leave the juice, which was syrupy, and clung to the seeds, and clung too to the fleshy wall of the melon by means of a ragged membrane. I broke the membrane with the edge of a spoon and scooped the seeds and the sticky liquid into a saucer. Then I scraped with the spoon around the wet hollow, digging out irregular slices of flesh, which I put in a glass bowl for our supper.

The melon is not connected with what happened, or so Dr Hibbs later assured me. Yet it is, in my mind. At about five the next morning I woke with terrible stomach cramps. I felt sick, I was shivering. I crept downstairs and opened the door to the chilly dawn. Barefoot, I walked bent over in pain round the house and across the mud and new grass to the woods. There I crouched, my feet like ice, twigs sticking into me, my nightdress growing wet and heavy with blood and dew, while the makings of my child came away from me in clots like heavy fish, and then in thin sharp blood. Out in the open the light was grey. Where I was under the trees it was still dark. When I crawled to one side and looked back to where I had been, there was no red colour on the ground, just a deeper darkness swamping that patch of undergrowth. Trained by Godwin, I knew the plants that I had befouled: bugle, dog's mercury, wood sage, dock.

The cramps had diminished, though I felt a dragging ache in my abdomen, and I was bleeding heavily. I took off my nightdress, staunched myself with that, and walked naked back into the lodge.

I lay in the gondola bed for a week, as weak as a kitten and low in spirits. I thought, I am a Henshaw, I am like my mother and Aunt Susannah, there is something wrong with me inside and I shall lose child after child.

Peter said perhaps it was all for the best. It was not the ideal time, nor the ideal place, for us to become parents. I knew he was right, but that did not stop me accusing him of being unfeeling. He had gone out to the wood on that first morning with a spade and dug over the patch, turning the earth and the sullied green stuff until all the horror was buried and one saw just bare soil. So he told me. It must have been terrible for him. He bore this alone, without my sympathy or gratitude. I had not the strength to double my pain by sharing his.

Mrs Carney came to see me every day, bringing delicate things to eat from the Hall kitchens. When after the first week I was no stronger, she spoke to Peter down in our kitchen. They both came back upstairs together and put the plan to me. Lord Godwin, said Mrs C., was suggesting that I should convalesce up at the Hall, where it would be easier for her to care for me, and where there would be help on hand all day; for Peter, naturally, had to get on with the electrical work. My heart leapt at the idea, and I feared at once that Peter would not allow it. But he looked enormously hopeful, and was watching for my reaction as nervously as I was watching for his. When we realised this, we smiled at each other with love and relief.

So, for the first but not the last time, I moved into what I still think of as 'my' room at Morrow Hall. It is called the Grey Room, and it looks westwards, over the park. The windows are long, and curve in a great bow. Even the glass panes of the side windows are curved. Within the bow is a writing-table and chair. The big bed faces the window from the other end of the room, which must be at least thirty feet long. There are faded Persian rugs on the boards, and a white marble fireplace in which a fire was lit for me daily, with an easy chair and a low table beside it. On the walls hang a set of prints of Niagara Falls, though I did not examine those for some time. The faded wallpapers and hangings are not exactly grey; they are of a blue that is almost grey, or a grey that is almost blue, and when the evening sun slants into the room, the angles in shadow become lilac-coloured.

There I lay, lapped in peace, cleanliness, comfort and grace, cosseted by Mrs Carney and the silent housemaids. Mrs Carney brought me endless clean towels for the bleeding. At first it all seemed a dream, an extension of my illness. Then, it seemed like paradise on earth. Later still, I began to take it all for granted, and fretted like a born lady when the maid was late with my hot chocolate. And of course, I began to get better.

Peter came in early every morning to see me, before he started work. He and the Paternosters were in the house every day by then, wiring up the downstairs circuits. There is a water closet next door to my room, with a big polished wooden seat, a white china bowl painted with orange flowers, and a brass handle. When you pull the handle, a gush of water from a cistern above sweeps all away. I thought it was wonderful. I had never seen anything like it in my life; at the Health Exhibition, before Peter and I were married, we had passed by the displays of sanitary arrangements without a glance, by mutual consent, to avoid embarrassment.

To my surprise, the water closet at Morrow Hall shocked Peter. He was deeply upset by it. He thought that it was all wrong, and completely unnatural and disgusting, to have such an arrangement inside a house. He did not think it was hygienic. He would not use it. Looking at him over the top of my sheet, I reminded him of our bedroom articles, which we used with no such delicate scruples.

'That is quite different. One knows it is to be carried outside, and disposed of outside, where it belongs, at the earliest opportunity.'

'But it is carried outside here, too, down the pipes. I don't know where it goes, but it certainly goes out of the house, it passes on, it goes on its way.'

Every person, however radical and progressive, draws the boundary line somewhere. Peter looked sweet and strange in my room, very black-and-white with his dark work-clothes, his black mane of hair, his pale face. He sat beside my bed for half an hour at a time and held my hands in his big knuckly ones. We did not always talk very much. I did not have to worry about his physical well being, because he ate his dinner with the Carneys in the West Lodge, and occasionally with the Paternosters in the village, speeding back and forth everywhere on the Ariel. But I felt a pang as he left me at the end of each morning visit – a pang for the lost intimacy of our daily, nightly life together, and perhaps a pang of betrayal, too.

And then I would sleep and dream, and eat what was brought to me, until the second visit of each day. Godwin came in to see me straight after his afternoon ride, before he changed out of his riding clothes. He brought me flowers and grasses, which he arranged himself and placed on the table in the window where I could see them. He sat on the bed and stroked my arms, and we talked. He brought me a book, I must have it still, among the belongings that I left in London: *The Sagacity and Morality of Plants* by J. E. Taylor, published by Chatto and Windus. It announces itself as treating plants as sentient beings, with a system of ethics. This is something of a tease. The author describes plant behaviour in a conventional way, only playfully attributing their characteristics and adaptive behaviour to conscious decision-making. He does not, for example, suggest that plants know right from wrong. Nevertheless, I have observed Carney talking quite sharply to his tomato plants at the West Lodge, so maybe there is something in it all.

The book was a gift. Godwin had originally bought it for himself. His signature is on the flyleaf, as I saw when he left me that day. 'George Godwin, Morrow 1884'. *George.* Aunt Susannah had been right. But I went on thinking of him as Godwin. Talking with him, I never used any name at all, and I did not say 'sir' as Peter did. Underneath his own name, Godwin had written: 'For the Wirewoman. Morrow, October 1885'.

He gave me the three beautiful manuscript books too. They have stiff covers with a pattern of peacock feathers, marbled endpapers and, in between, all these blank pages of thick cream paper. They had belonged to his mother, he said, she had bought them in Florence for writing cookery receipts in, though she never did.

Perhaps she too was overawed by the beautiful books. I told Godwin that I feared I should never dare to use them.

'Write about yourself, begin with something you remember and continue from there,' he said, and strode out of the room in his riding boots, leaving the books on my bed. I wrote nothing then. It was not the right time. There the books lay, splayed on the blue-grey coverlet. Later I piled them on the writing-table in the window, where they remained until I went back to the lodge. There, I put them in the dresser drawer, where they stayed until I took them out on my return from London just recently, and began this writing.

I did not see Godwin for quite a while after I left the Hall. I thought about him all the time and wondered whether he thought of me. Something stopped me from going up to the engine room in the afternoons in the hope of encountering him. Our relation had changed, and we could not go back to how we were before. The autumn was drawing in. In any case, I was not yet strong enough for those long muddy walks over the park and fields.

I was only just picking up the threads of my life at the lodge when the letter came from Aunt Susannah:

My Dear Niece,

I think you should know that poor Rose is gravely ill and Dr Hibbs is very worried about her. He visits her every day. He says that there is very little that he can do for her now. She is taking a lot of chloral to ease the pain and make her sleep. If you want to see your mother again you should make arrangements to come soon. Your Father is bearing up wonderfully and I do what I can for him. The house is not kept as nice as I should like since that fool Jane has got herself into trouble and is no good for anything. She is a disgrace. She is always crying in the kitchen, whether for Rose or for her own trouble I do not know. She will have to go of course before the expected event but I do not like to engage a strange girl with your Mother so poorly. Altogether I do not know what to do for the best and if your situation permits it your Father and I think you should come. We will understand if Peter is too busy to make the journey.

It was most unlike Aunt Susannah not to know what to do for the best. She must be severely shaken. Like Jane I too cried in the kitchen, after reading the letter. I had thought very little about 49 Dunn Street in the past few months. Now the rooms and everything in them arose vividly before my mind's eye, as if I had been transported back by magic.

My agitation was as much on Jane's behalf as on my mother's. It seemed so stupid, that I should lose a baby that I could have cared for with everyone's approval, because I was married – while she was going to carry her baby to term, and become an outcast, thrown on to the streets because she was unmarried.

I was shocked by Jane, nevertheless. I had not thought she would be so bold as to take such risks. I myself would have had neither the opportunity nor the courage. She was such a thin, mouse-like little thing. I wondered what I, or anyone, could do for her. All I knew about her family was that her parents were dead, or gone, and that she lived in a room somewhere in Somers Town with two younger sisters whom she supported on the wages that my mother paid her.

My agitation about Jane screened my fear that my mother

would die. That fear lay in wait, and only pounced on me, making me tremble and sweat, once I was on the train to London. I did not leave Morrow straight away. I dreaded going home. I had a selfish reason for wanting to go, however, which had nothing to do with the sad situation at Dunn Street. I wanted to consult Dr Hibbs about my miscarriage and my future prospects.

A week after the letter came, Carney took me to the station at Hitchin in the trap. Peter came too to see me off. There was no question of his coming with me. The installation was at a critical stage. He fretted to me on the way to the station that the Paternosters were insufficiently careful about the way they drew the wires through the wooden conduits and casings. The wires must not lie athwart one another, and they must be smeared with soap so that they do not jam. They must run straight and parallel. Untrusting, he had before we left set them to petty tasks. Paternoster was whittling plugs by which to fix screws in the plaster walls, out of spare bits of timber. Neat-fingered Joe was twisting coloured silk-covered wires to make flexible 'drops', from which lamps would be suspended from the ceiling rose in the drawing room. They were working at our kitchen table. I felt a tug at the heart as we left them, as though they were my real family.

I was wrong not to have gone to London sooner, and right to have dreaded the visit. Half an hour after Peter got back to Morrow from the station, a telegram came for us telling of my mother's death. There was nothing that he could do about it, he had no means of letting me know before I arrived.

At 49 Dunn Street, Jane opened the front door to me. The unfortunate event that she was expecting was obviously imminent. She burst into tears when she saw me and I put my arms round her. But Father and Aunt Susannah were looming in the narrow hallway behind her, already talking to me, pulling at me, taking me over. Aunt Susannah looked huge, in the black that she had worn when she first came to us, minus the jet encrustations. 'Jet after six weeks' was a tenet of her religion. She had put on flesh. My father had shrunk; I was taller than he was now. I went with them into the parlour, and they told me how my mother had died. Then I went upstairs, alone.

My dead mother lay in the big bed in the front room looking like a small girl asleep. Sweet and safe. I was no longer afraid for myself, losing her. I was no longer afraid of her, losing herself, because I saw that she had found herself. I put my face beside hers and whispered over and over: 'Rose Henshaw, Howden Farm. Rose Henshaw, Howden Farm.'

The house was now neat and scrupulously clean. My father was sleeping in Peter's old room. I slept in the small bed in Aunt Susannah's room. That first night, I felt I was back where I had begun and that my life with Peter, and my life at Morrow, were hallucinations. Aunt Susannah talked in bed, as in the old days. She talked about Jane.

'It's always the plain ones that get into trouble. I've always noticed that. A good-looking girl knows early on that she can have her pick. She's fighting them off from the age of twelve. She's well used to saying no. A plain girl now, that no one's ever laid a finger on before, she'll be the one that falls. She'll get a taste for it, too. Make herself a nuisance to some gentleman that was only after having a bit of fun. I can say this to you, Charlotte, now that you're a married woman.'

I longed to ask Aunt Susannah which kind of girl she herself had been, and whether Uncle Samuel Huff had been a gentleman who liked having a bit of fun, but I did not dare. This seemed a strange conversation to be having with my mother dead on the other side of the partition wall.

'I feel that I led a very protected life, before I married,' I said. 'I had no opportunity to discover which kind of girl I was.'

'You're like me, our Charlotte,' said Aunt Susannah. 'A slow burner. A late starter, and always something new around the corner. You'll never be without, don't you worry. If that's what you want.'

I thought of my walks and talks with Godwin, and my longing for his company, and dismissed the thoughts.

I am dishonest with myself. What I was longing for was his touch.

I returned to the sad subject of Jane.

'What about the father?' I asked.

'Your father,' said Aunt Susannah, 'has done nothing he need be ashamed of.'

Had Aunt Susannah misheard me? I think that she had, and that she had not. She kept on talking.

'He's a man that needs to be made comfortable,' she said. 'Poor Rose was not great in that department. But she died happy. She was spared. Give that Jane her due if I must, she isn't altogether a bad girl. Not vindictive. And she was ever so fond of Rose.'

Did I then put two and two together? I did and I did not. At any rate, not until after the funeral.

Peter came down by train, just for the day. I was tremendously pleased to see him. He was in truth my other self. He brought me a letter of condolence from Godwin. I opened it in the privy, since that was the only place I could count on being alone.

My Dearest Wirewoman,

I am so very sorry. I know how hard it is to lose a Mother, even as a grown person, and even though a Mother's death is a natural and necessary event. The life cycle of men and women, as of plants, presupposes death – and also eternal renewal. We have spoken of these things already, my Wirewoman. I know there will be much to do and arrangements to make, but please return to us as soon as you can, and know that there is always a place for you at Morrow and in the heart of

Yrs Afftly.,
G.G.

I felt warmed by this, although what he wrote about eternal renewal would have meant more to me had I not lost my baby. Fortunately Peter did not ask to see the letter. We hardly had two words in private before he was off again. He did not come back to Dunn Street after the ceremony, but went away in a hansom to catch a train back to Hitchin.

Uncle Digby Mortimer, naturally enough, did the honours at the funeral. As I had suspected at my wedding party, he was very good at his job. He looked happier at the funeral than he had at the wedding. His coaches were well turned out, as were his hired men. Not many people came, just the family and the neighbours.

There were prayers over Mother's coffin in the chapel at Kensal Green cemetery. Then the clerygman, Father, Peter, and the neighbour husbands followed Uncle Digby and his helpers out into the cold air to put my mother in her grave. Father was crying as he walked out behind the coffin. He was crying for himself, I could tell. Maybe every older person who cries at funerals is crying for himself, and for all lost loved ones. The loved one whose passing is being mourned is perhaps just the contact point for an accumulation of grief.

I, Aunt Susannah, the neighbour wives and Uncle Digby's wife Aunt Marianne waited in the chapel. We sat there in our blacks, looking at our fingernails, turning the rings on our fingers. I fingered Godwin's note in the black velvet bag that I carried. Aunt Susannah could not tolerate the silence. She wittered on and on and I did not listen, until she said to me:

'I'll be staying on, you know, with your father. He cannot be on his own.'

So that was how it was going to be. I still did not answer. I was too exalted. The clergyman from St Jude's was unwell, and our old sweet-voiced vicar from St Luke's conducted the funeral. I think Mother would have been pleased. One of the prayers he had read made my heart leap. I responded as though it were written for me. I asked him, as we walked back to the carriages at the cemetery gates, where it came from. He said it was written by John Donne. I found it later, with Godwin's help, in the library at Morrow, and copied it out:

> Bring us, O Lord God, at our last awakening into the house and gate of heaven, to enter into that gate and dwell in that house, where there shall be no darkness nor dazzling, but one equal light; no noise nor silence, but one equal music; no fears nor hopes, but one equal possession; no ends nor beginnings, but one equal eternity: in the habitations of thy majesty and glory, world without end. Amen.

The words united everything for me – real things, nothing to do with the vicar's God. The prayer held within it Peter's vision of electrical power, Godwin's trust in the cycle of nature, my own belief in the doors that would be opened to me, and – this was childish – the three houses in my life: 49 Dunn Street, the East Lodge, Morrow Hall, all so different and so intimately known. There was at that moment no reason why Peter, Godwin and I should not for ever be sustained in harmony, in 'one equal possession'. I floated in this sweet, alluring entropy.

Not for long. I travelled back in the first carriage, with my father and my aunt. As we approached Dunn Street I saw that the front door was wide open. Jane must have left it open to welcome us.

The hat stand lay on its side across the hallway. We called out for Jane, but there was no answer. Stepping over the hat stand we went into the parlour. It was worse than disordered. It was wrecked. The statue of Garibaldi and the Venetian vases were smashed on the hearth. The red bobble-fringed runner was half in the fire, and smouldering. The brass plant-pot lay on the floor spilling out its earth. The table and chairs had been thrown over on their sides. There was stinking nastiness on the carpet, and smeared over the piano keys. We saw all this in a few seconds which lasted for ever. I was the first to speak.

'A poltergeist?' I said.

'No. Jane,' said my father, his face the colour of sour milk.

'It's the same difference,' said Aunt Susannah. Then she barked at me:

'Stop them coming in.'

I hurried back to the front door, stepping over the hat stand, and stopped Uncle Digby and Aunt Marianne in their tracks. I ran to the next carriage, which had brought the vicar and two sets of neighbours. They stood round me in consternation as I stammered out that unfortunately we could not invite them in after all, there had been a terrible robbery. Everyone wanted to help, or at least to obtain a sight of the disaster. I ran back into the house and slammed the door firmly, leaving them standing on the pavement.

In the kitchen, the willow-pattern plates from the dresser were in smithereens on the floor. The kitchen chairs had their legs and backs broken. The murder weapon – the poker – was lying beside them on the floor. The contents of the dustbin from the yard – bones, heels of loaves, tea leaves, vegetable peelings, rags, dust – had been upended over the wreckage on the floor.

The back door was open. Pots and pans were thrown all over the yard, with the Brussels carpet from the morning room. The privy door hung wide. Father's hats from the hat stand, those that were not trampled on the privy floor, were shoved down the hole.

Back to the house. In the morning room the books from the bookshelves littered the bare linoleum, their spines broken and pages torn out. The contents of the coal scuttle had been emptied out on top of the bits and pieces of books. In the coal scuttle Aunt Susannah's Indian shawl was screwed up into a dirty ball.

We picked our way among the ruins in our mourning clothes like wraiths. Everything was spoiled, but nothing seemed to be missing – except Amber and Jet. The cats never did come back. But then, neither did Jane.

I tiptoed upstairs, terrified of what I might find, but there was no one in any of the bedrooms and nothing there had been disturbed. Aunt Susannah called me back downstairs. She was in the parlour. She pointed to the chimneypiece.

'Look – it's for you.'

A folded paper, with 'Miss Charlotte' scrawled upon it with a pencil, was propped against the honeymoon photograph of my parents at Bridport, on the bare mantel shelf. The photograph was the only object in the room that had not been moved or harmed. There were very few words on the paper when I opened it. I cannot record exactly what they were, because within seconds Aunt Susannah, reading over my shoulder, thrust out her mittened hand, tore the note from my fingers and cast it on the fire. But I had read it. It was a crazed, misspelt message of despair and revenge, and it named my father.

We never spoke of Jane again, nor referred to her letter. I fully intended, at first, to go secretly and look for her, to talk to her. But I did not even know her surname, nor where she lived in Somers Town. My good intentions petered out. I am deeply ashamed about this. When I read a few days later a report of the body of a young woman being taken from the Thames at Blackfriars I wondered whether it was Jane. But bodies of young women are constantly taken from the Thames. I dare say the words are left permanently set up in type by the printers.

There was so much to do. Aunt Susannah had been only waiting for the funeral to be over to dismiss Jane, and she had already engaged another servant in readiness. Mrs Rabbitt, who is middle-aged and squat, was sent for immediately. The fiction of the terrible robbery – my aunt would speak sorrowfully of her 'jewels' and of the nonexistent 'family silver' – was sustained so doggedly that after twenty-four hours my aunt and my father believed it implicitly.

Starting that evening, when we changed out of our blacks into work-dresses, Aunt Susannah, Mrs Rabbitt and I worked behind closed doors to restore order and cleanliness. It was such terrible work that I do not wish to write about it. Oceans of water and mountains of Ingleby's soap were used up. We sent my speechless father, who like some gremlin figure was always in the way, to stay with his brother Digby and Aunt Marianne. His bereavement, we told them, necessitated a spell away from the scene of his sorrow. The Digby Mortimers received him with professional aplomb.

We slept like the dead, only to rise again and continue the task. After three days, when all was clean and polished and set to rights, Aunt Susannah and I went shopping for new kitchen chairs, more willow-pattern crockery, another crimson bobble-fringed runner. The house looked the same as before, but not. The furniture was not rooted, the smaller objects had not settled, the air still shook. Father came home, and sat down with the newspaper in his usual chair in the parlour. Strangely, normality returned with him.

I remained in Dunn Street for a whole week after that in case I was needed, which really I was not. I went to consult Dr Hibbs at his house. He is a decent man, I have known him ever since I can remember. I told him about Jane and what she had done. He said:

'You do not altogether surprise me. There is an epidemic of female insanity at the moment. The asylums are overflowing. It's the speed of modern life that is to blame. Telegrams, railway trains, that kind of thing. Female organisation is labile at the best of times, and canot adapt.'

There had been some despatching of telegrams from Dunn Street, but I do not think that Jane ever travelled on a train. Dr Hibbs and I talked a little about Mother. We did not speak of Father.

It was a growth in her womb that had killed my mother.

Dr Hibbs felt my pulse and looked at my tongue, and asked about my bowels, and whether I had any pain, or vomiting, or fits, or choking sensations, and whether my monthlies were regular again. He could find nothing amiss; but even had there been, I cannot see how he would have found it out.

By the time I left, the house had taken up its secret life again. It was I who was the unrooted thing, out of place. I am always nervous before a journey. The afternoon that I left Dunn Street, waiting for the fly that had been ordered to fetch me, I sat in the parlour on a straight-backed chair at the table, with my travelling bag on the floor beside me. Mrs Rabbitt sang as she clattered about in the kitchen,

'Champagne Charlie is me name, Champagne drinkin' is me game . . .'

and then broke off abruptly, no doubt recalling that she was in a house of mourning. I remembered that other afternoon, two years back, when Father and I had waited in the dusk in the same room for young Mr Fisher to arrive.

Now, it was Aunt Susannah and Father who sat in the easy chairs on either side of the fire. I do not quite know how to say this, but I became aware, looking at the pair of them, of a shared sensuality peculiar to their advanced stage in life. They were waiting, without much regret, for me to go. They knew a great deal about one another, and if there was also much about one another that they did not know, they did not strain after it. There was ease between them in spite of their ageing limbs, their bad teeth, their odours. Even though she talked all the time and he hardly spoke, there was, between them, 'no noise, nor silence, but one equal music'. I could leave them to their untranscendental harmonies with a clear conscience.

I thought of the bedroom directly above where we sat. Would they think it worth doing what the greedy young do? Would they need to do that? I have never known, I shall never know. I did not love my father. But I felt then that Aunt Susannah would save him, and restore his better self to him. Aunt Susannah, the deceased wife's sister, would make him comfortable. Discreetly, she would make an old man happy.

I was as foolish in this optimism as in my hour of exaltation at my mother's funeral. Within months, my father was dead. I did not go to his funeral.

I have written that I did not love my father. It was more than that. I hated my father, as a child hates. I hated him with all my love.

And whatever went on between the two of them after I left, I think his bones would have snapped, had Aunt Susannah agreed to sit upon his knee.

Chapter Nine

I scrubbed and polished the lodge like a madwoman on my return to Morrow. At least one small corner of the universe should be made safe, and my very own. I became fussy about the exact arrangement of cups and mugs on the dresser hooks. I felt agitated if the chairs were not aligned with perfect symmetry around the kitchen table. Every night, before I went to bed, I tidied away everything from every surface, and repeatedly checked the kitchen and our small sitting room, twitching at imperfections and irregularities.

When Peter came in one rainy evening from his work, tracking dirt and wet leaves across the kitchen floor, I went for him as though he had attacked me personally and on purpose. After that, he always took his boots off before he entered, and moved circumspectly, and sometimes I caught him watching me covertly, as one watches a dog that cannot be trusted.

It rained endlessly that autumn. We picked the wet apples from the two trees on our plot. As instructed by Carney, we stored the kitchen apples in a bin, and the little russets on shelves, in the outhouse. Indoors, there was a leak from the roof. We had to move our bed a foot to the right, and keep a saucepan on the floor to catch the drips. Soon there was a cluster of saucepans beside our bed, and still some of the drips evaded containment. Peter spoke to Godwin about the leak, and Carney came round to inspect. It was strange seeing a man other than Peter in our bedroom. I was all anxiety and expectation, but Carney was unperturbed by the leak.

'It's only what you would expect,' he said, 'in an old house like this. You should see our place. You should see the attics up at the Hall. The trouble with water is that it travels. It has a mind of its own. It gets in through a crack somewhere and creeps along until it finds a weak spot that it can get through. You wouldn't know where it would be starting from. There's not a lot you can do about it.'

'Maybe there is a tile fallen off, or slipped?' I suggested.

'The tiles look all right to me. Could be the flashing. We'll get the ladders up and check when the weather's better.'

He never did, of course. After he left I sat down on the bed and the drips went on chinking into the pans in their syncopated sequence, each on a different note. I was defeated.

'I suppose,' I said to myself, 'that it's too much to hope that any house could be made entirely waterproof, with all that wetness out there.'

I looked out of the great window at the grey, steady downpour. My little house was not an ark, impermeable and afloat upon the waters. It was just a meaningless clumping of material among all the other material in the universe. It was easily penetrated, and could be easily reduced to undifferentiated matter. There was no sensible reason why mud and wet leaves should be considered acceptable out of doors, and intolerable indoors.

Yet I continued to scour and wipe and straighten, I continued to arrange my household objects in the order that I had determined was the right one.

The rain stopped. The sun came out. Since my return from London I had hardly left the house. Now, I could not stay indoors.

On an afternoon when the sky was a hard cold blue and the trees were showing their tracery through the few remaining leaves, I went across the park and into the paddock where

Godwin's bay mare was grazing with her foal beside her. The mare looked up and began to follow me, and the foal on its awkward legs followed the mare. The three of us reached the further gate together, and when I had opened it and closed it behind me, the mare remained looking at me over the rails. The ground was still crisp with frost. We had made wavering dark tracks in the grass of the paddock.

My destination, merely for the sake of having a destination, was the barn on the far side of the second field. I love the look of that barn, which like all the barns around here has a pitched roof, and wooden weatherboarded sides all painted black, and high plank doors with heavy iron hinges. In the hard, brilliant light the barn cast a shadow blacker than itself. One half of the double door was ajar. I suppose that was why I pushed it a little further open.

From where I stood on the threshold, I saw Godwin lying on his back on a pile of hay at the foot of a stack that reached to the rafters. One knee was drawn up, and his left arm, nearest to me, lay slackly, stretched outwards. Beneath his spread hand was an open book, upside down. He was fast asleep. He was snoring a little. He lay there all unconscious, long and loose and lax. Sensations flooded me, when I saw him sleeping. Then it happened inside me, a convulsion like an explosion, seeming to have nothing to do with me. It was frightening. I was left gasping for breath, clutching myself in an ugly manner, feeling like one of those foreign flowers in the greenhouses at Morrow which open up their gross carnivorous lips the moment they are touched. Only this had happened to me without a touch, without a word or a look from him. I should not have thought that it were possible.

Perhaps I made some small sound. Perhaps the brighter light from the open door woke him. He opened his eyes and saw me, and seemed not at all surprised.

'The Wirewoman has come.'

He raised his left hand towards me. I should have stayed where I was. But I went into the barn, took off my hat, placed it on the upturned cart in the corner, and sank down on my knees in the hay beside him, my skirts billowing. He had touched me before, when I was in bed at the Hall. His hands were not strange to me. But they were purposeful now. Had I been innocent, I should not have properly understood his hands' purpose. I was not innocent, I was a married woman, I knew what led on to what, and how, and I was as soft as butter on a hot day. My knowledge made absorption in pleasure more sweetly easy for both of us, there was no awkwardness.

I cannot say that I was seduced. But I should like to place on record that I did make an attempt to stop before it was too late. It was a provisional protest. I said, my mouth against his:

'No, not here, not now.'

'If not here, where? If not now, when?'

I have constantly been troubled, while writing this, to know what to include and what to omit. Clearly one cannot set down everything that happens. If I recorded a single day at Morrow in its entirety, it would take more than a day to read the account, since it takes longer to describe looking out of the window and seeing a hare running round in a circle and then disappearing into the edge of the dark wood than it does actually to look out of the window and see a hare running round in a circle and then disappearing into the edge of the dark wood. Which is what I saw just now, when I laid down my pen for a moment.

This is a somewhat fanciful problem. I am hardly more innocent in story-telling terms than I am in sexual terms – less, since I have only known two men intimately and I have read more than two novels. The real problem is the barrier between what is actually in my mind, or what actually took place, and what I can write down in words.

It is curious to consider the thoughts which have perhaps never been written down, but which must pass through the minds of all ordinary women. I know that there are indecent books written by men (who know nothing about how women think), but that is not what I mean. Comparing man with man, for example. If I wanted to say how it was with Peter, I should want to say that he was frantic, and slippy and whippy, and that he was a quite different Peter, in our bed, from the Peter of our daylight hours. If I wanted to explain how it was with Godwin, I should say that he was a lazy, confident oak-branch; and that the Godwin who pinned me down in the barn was the same Godwin who lent me books and taught me about plants. That would be only the beginning of what I could say, because it reveals nothing about myself, and how or who I was with Peter, and with Godwin. It is as though, were I describing 49 Dunn Street to a friend, I were to tell her only about the exterior.

Maybe some women confide these most private matters to a sister, but not, I think, commonly. Even my clients, after I left Morrow, did not in their jagged, whispered confidences take me far beyond the bedroom door. Thus the most important and interesting observations about ourselves, and about the connection between men and women, are never passed on. We talk a great deal about love, but as an emotion. In the flesh, every woman has to start again alone, from the beginning, like Eve with Adam. She does not know whether her experiences and her responses are unique, or not. I used to imagine, when Peter and I kissed in the kitchen at 49 Dunn Street before our marriage, that it was the same for everyone. I felt as if we were joining some worldwide secret society of lovers. Now, I am not so sure.

Women who have borne children discuss the details of their confinements, behind closed doors, without holding anything back. But the little that women do say to one another about the sexual act itself is unspecific, impersonal, and generally depressing. The most intimate communication is made in the form of a sigh, or a sly joke. There are indeed jokes to be made on this subject, but the real ones are not shared.

The most personal conversations I have ever had in my life so far were with Aunt Susannah, and she was more given to pronouncements than to joking. As I lay in the barn with my skirt and petticoats still up around my waist, I recalled one of her nocturnal utterances:

'When there is something going on what shouldn't be, between a man and a woman, it is always the woman's fault.'

I looked up at the motes of dust and hay swirling in a low shaft of sunlight from the door. Godwin was picking particles of hay from my hair and out of the open top of my camisole.

When we stood up he did up my buttons, turned me around

and brushed the hay off my back. I did the same for him. I picked up my hat and put it on. He put his book in his pocket, and took a halter from a hook on the wall. He was going to take the mare and foal back to the stables for the night. He accompanied me to the door and stood leaning against the barn wall, swinging the rope halter at his side, as I walked away across the field. We did not speak of when, or if, we might meet there again. There was no need. The sun had gone down, the day was over, but there would be other days. At the five-barred gate the mare and the foal still waited. They accompanied me as I crossed their paddock, one on each side of me this time. We made new sets of tracks, crisscrossing the old ones. In the middle of the field I turned, and so did they, and standing between them I waved at Godwin, who raised a hand in answer.

I did not look back again. Walking home through the park I did not feel shame, nor guilt, nor ecstasy, nor anxiety about the future. I felt calm and prosaic. When I came to the lodge Peter was bent over the running tap outside the kitchen door, his sleeves rolled up, having a wash. He asked me if I had seen his big hammer, which he thought he had left on the dresser. I said I had not. I picked up a pail, went to the outhouse and took some potatoes out of the sack, put them in the pail, waited for Peter to make way for me at the tap, covered the potatoes with water, and went into the kitchen to scrub them. The evening passed normally. He found his hammer the next day, in the stable yard.

Most of what I know about the dark, sinful edge of life I learned from my clients, after I left Morrow.

That is a grossly hypocritical statement. Most of what I know about the dark, sinful edge of life I learned all by myself. What I did learn from those unhappy women was that there are two kinds of infidelity. Some adulterers – why avoid the word? – wish to be discovered, whether they know it or not. It is they who sigh, and appear distracted, and fail to respond to a spouse's loving touch; it is they who confide in one or two dear friends, and who have the misfortune to drop letters accidentally, to be discovered by the one person who must not see them. Whether they know it or not, their every action is directed towards precipitating a crisis. They want to be discoverd, usually because they want to be rescued, to be stopped – but only after having punished the spouse sufficiently for his or her shortcomings. Just sometimes, they want to be discovered because the marriage has become intolerable, and they prefer to face the scandal and difficulty involved in separation.

Some adulters do not wish to be discovered. They run, temporarily, for connubial cover at the slightest whiff of danger. They hide their tracks. They perfect their untruths. They confide in no one. They never write compromising letters, and destroy any that they receive immediately after reading them. They are unfeignedly happy at home, and are neither more nor less loving towards the spouse than in the days of innocence. These are sunny, ardent adulterers, who have no intention of mending their deceitful ways; yet they would leave the illicit beloved to be crushed beneath the wheels of a passing cart rather than risk endangering their own domestic harmony.

I fell, roughly, into this second category, although I do believe that I should have risked my reputation to save Godwin's life, had it been necessary. I behaved no differently towards Peter after my visits to the barn, and I felt no differently towards him either. I performed my domestic duties no less energetically than before. In all this I was sincere. I was not play-acting. A partition wall had been erected in the chamber of my mind. In one half was my union with Peter, in the other my liaison with Godwin. There was no door in the partition. It did not enter my head to stop seeing Godwin. He found a way of letting me know when I should go the barn; I need not go into our ways and means. In the fifteen minutes that it took me to pass between my two worlds – crossing the park and two fields on the way there, and the same in reverse on the way back – I moved purposefully enough, but I thought neither of Peter nor of Godwin. I simply observed the changes in the trees and hedges, the growing chill in the air, the wind direction, the insects and small creatures in my path, the rapid growth of the foal.

It had been decided that the electric lights would be turned on at Morrow Hall for the very first time on New Year's Eve, and

Godwin was planning a great party to celebrate the event. At the touch of a single switch, the whole house would be a blaze of light.

Not only did all the wiring, the lamps, the shades and so on all have to be in place, but the house itself had to be cleaned and done up for the party. Mrs Carney was very excited. She said it was like the old days. The place was full of upholsterers, French-polishers, distemperers, sewing women, piano-tuners, clock-winders, and delivery men coming and going, getting in the way of Peter and the Paternosters.

I asked Godwin if there were anything that I could do to help. We were in the billiard room, which became our refuge when the weather made the barn too cold for comfort. It was chilly in the billiard room too – ordering the fire to be lit would have attracted attention – but Godwin had brought down some blankets and we were cosy enough on the big sofa. It grew dark so early that it was easy for me to slip out of a side door into the garden, unseen, when it was time to go home.

Unseen? What can I be saying? More people than I dare to think about must have known what was going on. But if you have a secret life you have to believe that it is a secret. If nothing is put into words, nothing is happening.

One afternoon, Godwin asked me to beat him with a billiard cue. I complied, feeling very silly. I do not know what he hoped for from the experience, but it was not a great success and I was relieved that he did not ask again, subsequently. I think he was disappointed. Something was required of me, more than just wielding the cue, something that I did not know by instinct – particular words, perhaps, or an attitude. I have heard about such desires and their fulfilment from my clients, since then. At the time I was puzzled, and inadequate.

If Godwin were to appear before me at this moment I think that I might beat him within an inch of his life, from frustration – mental, not physical frustration. I realise that I am quite unable to give a coherent account of him. I know that he is not a *bad* man, because so much that is useful and valuable to me came through him. But I do not know what he is really like, nor what powers him. I cannot even describe his face. The thought of him still dazzles me. He has so many views on the world from so many windows. I see everything from Dunn Street.

When I offered to help in the house, before the party, he at first demurred, saying that he would not wish his sweetheart to become his servant. He warmed to the idea when he remembered the library. It was to be repainted before the night of the illumination; it must be cleared and cleaned first, and was full of precious things that he would not wish servants or decorators to handle.

So it was that we emerged from the billiard room together, all decorous formality, on our way to inspect the library. Almost at once we encountered Mrs Carney and a girl, a new maid as I supposed, in the gas-lit passage, carrying over their arms laundry of some sort. In his usual amiable way Godwin said:

'Good evening, Mrs Carney. Good evening, Mary.'

They pressed themselves against the wall as we passed by. I glanced at the girl and saw that she was startlingly pretty, with black curls falling on her shoulders and a tall, slim figure. She looked me straight in the eye. I tried to catch Mrs Carney's glance, in normal friendliness, but her eyes were cast down.

'That's Mary Carney,' Godwin told me in a low voice as their footsteps receded. 'She has a very pretty singing voice – really quite remarkable.'

'I didn't know they had a daughter.'

'She returned when you were ill, and now she's started working here with her mother. She'd been stopping with cousins in Ireland.'

'I didn't know that the Carneys were Irish.'

'He is, or his father was. His father came over as a boy to work on the railways. Mrs Carney is local, from Gosmore.'

We did not discuss the Carney family any more that day. I had never been in the library at Morrow before. Godwin moved away into the darkness to my right and lit three candles in a silver sconce, and then three more, and three more. A beautiful, shadowy, rectangular room was gradually revealed, all wood and leather and gilding, with crammed mahogany bookshelves everywhere. There were books around and above the door through which we entered; books from floor to ceiling all over the long wall on the left; books fitted round the stone fireplace on the shorter wall opposite where I stood; books in narrow columns of shelving between the three high sash windows on the right. The windows reached to the ceiling, their sills were almost on the floor.

In front of each window was a chair and writing table, and on each writing table was a three-candle sconce. His parents had never had gas lighting in the library, Godwin said, because of the damage that the fumes would cause to the precious books. The candle-flames were reflected in the polished tables, and in the small panes of the high windows; it was pitch black outside by now. The books insulated the room from the rest of the house. The atmosphere was thick, musky, peaceful. The only discordant notes were three twisted-silk cords dangling from new plaques on the ceiling, casting snaky shadows. There were brownish smears of plaster round the plaques. The cords had not yet had the lamp fitments, lamps and silk shades affixed to them, and the bare copper wires glinted in the candlelight at the ends of the flexes.

Down the middle of the room were three glass-topped display cases, such as one sees in museums, their contents concealed by dark velvet covers. Godwin took my wrist to draw me close, then released me, throwing back the cover of the nearest case, and holding his candelabra low over the glass.

'Are you interested in precious stones? Gems? Crystals? Quartz?'

When, afterwards, I handled all these pieces from the glass cases, Godwin taught me something about them. He understood how much they moved and interested me, and he wrote their names, with descriptive notes, on a piece of paper. Godwin's handwriting looks elegantly clear – until you attempt to read it. Then it becomes a confusion of strokes and curves – *complicated*, as Aunt Susannah had said. I may have deciphered some of the geological names wrongly.

The collection at Morrow does not consist of jewels in the common meaning of the word. Godwin's parents, and afterwards he himself, collected raw materials hacked from the earth and the rocks. The rich women who wear expensive necklaces and earrings set with shaped and polished chips and splinters know absolutely nothing. They think that rubies are red, sapphires are blue, jade is green. Rubies and sapphires are the same thing. Both are varieties of corundum. At Morrow there is a piece of white jade, a sapphire from Ceylon that is a clear golden-yellow, a garnet that is green, and a topaz that is light blue as well as others in all the expected tones of brown and yellow. Topaz is aluminium fluosilicate. Aquamarines and emeralds are both beryls: beryllium aluminium silicate. Godwin has what he calls 'tumbled emeralds', which look like pebbles that have been sucked.

Diamonds are nature's chance choices. Or choice chances. Diamonds are formed from pure carbon, exactly the same as poor drab commodities such as soot and graphite. The play of colour in an opal is a diffraction of light waves. The line of light caught inside a tourmaline is called 'chatoyant', after the gleam in a cat's eye. At Morrow there is a tourmaline of the richest, mossiest, clearest green imaginable.

In the centre of the second display case is a crystal ball of flawless quartz, which Godwin's parents brought back from China. The crystal ball is as clear as water and very, very heavy. When half-looking at the crystal, I saw it filled with shapes and colours. But when I gazed into it directly, trying to see my future, I saw only a bright mystery. On one side of the crystal ball there are pink crystals, rhodochrosite from Colorado in America. On the other side are yellow-green sulphur crystals in weird shapes. One could look at those crystals for ever, seeing in their forms all manner of ferns, leaves, stars, petals, diseased growths, wormcasts, teeth, flaky pastry.

'These are my true loves,' whispered Godwin, as he raised the cover of the third case. There was a blaze of purple glitter, every shade from pale lilac to black violet, beneath the wavering candlelight. That case, the one nearest the fireplace, contains nothing but amethyst. He had been in Brazil, collecting more amethyst, when his parents died. He bought some in Canada too. He is right to love it. Amethyst is the most beautiful and powerful quartz of them all.

Godwin set down the candelabra, felt for a ring of keys from a small drawer in one of the writing-tables and passed them through his fingers until he found the one he wanted. He opened the amethyst case so that we could touch and feel. There were half-globes like fruits – I thought of the melon – with a rind of rough greenish-black rock on the outside. Next to the rock was a stratum of splintery white crystal, like iced pith, and then the flesh of the fruit – silky shining sharp peaks of purple, like Alps in miniature. I thought that the brilliant facets and points must be man-made, but Godwin said no, they were natural concretions. The globes of amethyst are called geodes. Before they are split open to reveal the astonishing interior, they look as dull as cannonballs.

Godwin removed two chunks of amethyst and set them on the nearest writing-table. He carried all three sconces to the table, and in the dazzle of nine candles he invited me to sit down and hold the pieces in my hands.

'First one, then the other. Tell me about them.'

The larger piece was cut out of what must have been a massive geode. It was rectangular, and lay almost flat on my palm. It was as long as my hand and must have weighed at least two pounds. The purple mountain peaks were high and sharp.

'It is beautiful, but hostile,' I said. 'It is not something to love. It looks dangerous.'

'An Amethyst Deceiver, perhaps. Try the little one.'

The other piece he had brought out was half the size, and cut or broken from a much smaller geode. The shining purple peaks were modest, and there was an indentation in the middle, where the concretions were not mountains at all but prickly hillocks. When I held it in my hand, my palm fitted its curve naturally, and my thumb, lying neatly along the central valley, held it secure.

'It is less perfect, but I like it better.'

'It is yours, Wirewoman. Yours to keep.'

He dropped the amethyst into a green velvet bag, folded over the top, and presented it to me with a bow. It was the best present I had ever had. It goes everywhere with me, although it has lost its virtue. It is lying before me now, in its bag. I can slip my hand into the bag and hold the hot-cold quartz without removing it from its shelter.

★

Mrs Carney and I cleared the library together. There is a study, or book room as Godwin calls it, opening out of the main library, on the left of the fireplace. The door is invisible until opened, concealed by the continuous regiments of books. I climbed the high wrought-iron steps, which move on wheels, and passed armfuls of volumes down to Mrs Carney. We stacked them all in teetering piles in the book room, filling it entirely.

My special responsibility was the precious stones. I removed each piece from its place, wrapped every one separately in soft black cloth, and piled them carefully in rush baskets. Mrs Carney took the silver sconces, cleaned them, wrapped them in black paper and locked them in the pantry cupboard. The decorators from Hitchin carried the rush baskets away to be stored. They also moved out the display cases, the three writing-tables and the three chairs.

On my own, one sunless morning in early December, I swept out the empty library. There was no colour remaining in the room. In the cold light from the three windows, the wide oak floorboards were ashen. I began sweeping in the left-hand corner, bringing the curls of dust and fluff beneath the broom towards the centre of the room. There were no sounds apart from the scratchy swish of the twigs on the boards, and my own footfalls. I swept and swept, and when I had covered every inch of the floor I gathered up the soft pile of dust and tipped it into a bucket. Then I began again, starting in the same place, sweeping the room a second time in exactly the same sequence of actions, as if mesmerised. I have a recurring dream in which I am still and always sweeping out the empty library at Morrow as if mesmerised, always starting in the left-hand corner, constantly returning to that same corner to twist my broom into the angle again and again. In the dream, I never finish the sweeping.

I suppressed the impulse to sweep the room for a third time, and walked out leaving the library to the loud-voiced decorators with their planks and trestles, their brushes and their buckets of paint. I left the Hall by the front door that day, passing the open doors of the big drawing room where Mrs Carney and the maids were working, and the dining room which had already been cleaned and painted. I saw that Carney was putting back together the great mahogany table with its many leaves.

We hardly made any preparations for Christmas that year, everyone was so busy. Peter was ill with the strain. I see that now. The whole celebration depended on him and on the success of his electric lights. His reputation, both professional and personal, was at stake. He had become dangerously pale and thin, and he was sleeping badly. He coughed too much. He drank too much in the Bald-Faced Stag on Saturdays. His temper was short. I felt then that the only person who understood Peter and gave him any real support was young Joe Paternoster, who never left his side and obeyed all his commands like a little soldier.

I was taking insufficient trouble with Peter's meals. I never knew when he was coming back to the lodge for his dinner until I heard the metallic crash of the Ariel as he flung it against the wall outside. It seemed after a while hardly worth troubling to cook meals that would only spoil. But I should have persisted, and insisted. He wolfed bread and cheese standing up, and was off again.

If I am to be honest, I must record that in some sealed compartment of his strained mind he must by then have known, if that is the word, that I was no longer wholly his. Not that I ever contemplated separating from him. He was my husband. The thought that I might not continue to be his wife never entered my mind. The option did not exist. But I was much away from the house, up at the Hall, and sometimes I was not there waiting for him when he did return for rest and food.

The head man from Gatward's in Hitchin, who had provided the clock for the pediment of the main switchboard in the engine room, also had his men check and synchronise every clock around the place. The one over the archway of the stable block, its hands regilded and its face repainted sky blue, has a chime. Peter and Godwin agreed on a plan. Before the electricity was let loose, Joe was to run around turning every switch in every room in the Hall, upstairs and downstairs, to the 'on' position. Shortly before midnight on New Year's Eve, when the Hall was full of guests, all candles and other lamps were to be extinguished.

When the stable clock, and the gilt French clock in the drawing room, and the grandfather clock in the hall, and all the other clocks began to chime for midnight, the main switch in the engine room was to be thrown and the whole place would suddenly be a palace of lights. The first moment of 1886 was to be the first day of creation: 'Let there be light'. No wonder Peter was all nerves. He was not only an electrician now, he was to be God, or at the very least a theatrical impresario. He must not fail.

In the evening of Christmas Day, Godwin turned up at the lodge. I had roasted a chicken and some potatoes, and boiled a cabbage. I had made an apple tart, from our own apples. Peter, well warmed and with his stomach full for once, had relaxed. He was nearly asleep at the table, tilting back his chair, his legs and stockinged feet stretched out before him. When we heard the knock on the door he roused himself feverishly, scraping the legs of his chair on the floor, and was bent over hauling on his boots as I let Godwin in.

Godwin and I, without ever discussing the matter, had perfected our public manner. I had no fear that he would betray me. I offered him a slice of tart, which he charmingly declined. Nor did he sit down with us. He had brought us, on a flat basket, a bunch of ripe grapes from his hothouse – purple grapes, tightly clustered, lying upon a bed of green leaves from the vine. He placed the basket in my hands. I thought of my amethyst, safe in its green bag. We thanked him, and I arranged the grapes on a green plate and put it on the table.

Godwin's visit had another purpose. It would be outrageous, he said, leaning with his casual grace against the dresser, if we did not have some pleasure at the culmination of so much hard labour. He was inviting us to be his guests at the Hall for the New Year party. Peter looked at him as if he were crazy, and bluntly said that was quite impossible. He, Peter, must be in the engine room, to see that the gas engine was up and running; it must be he himself, he said, who threw the main switch at the right moment; and after that he must go around checking that there were no short circuits, no burned-out lamps, no faulty connections, no failures.

I knew that Peter was right, and thought the invitation showed how inadequately Godwin understood the complexity of the undertaking. It is most unusual for a new installation to work one hundred per cent the first time it is switched on. Customarily there is a test period, with time allowed for corrections and modifications. Turning everything on at once would mean putting maximum stress on an untested system. All this I had heard from Peter repeatedly, in a nervous monotone, in the darkness of our bedroom.

In reality Godwin understood all this perfectly well.

'I appreciate your responsibilities, and your dedication,' Godwin said to Peter. 'It was stupid of me to think that it might be otherwise.'

He paused. And then, without looking at me, he said to Peter:

'Would the Wireman perhaps allow Mrs Fisher to attend, to represent the family firm and receive congratulations on your behalf?'

There was a pause. Then Peter said, not looking at him:

'If she has a mind to.'

Peter and I glanced at one another briefly. I looked down at my hands in my lap.

'I should like it very much,' I said. 'I shall go for both of us. Thank you, Lord Godwin.'

Chapter Ten

'If you stay on at the party for a while after midnight,' Godwin whispered in my ear, in the billiard room, 'you can attend the seance. I have invited a medium from London. She is said to obtain quite startling results.'

'Why are they called mediums? It makes them sound so very *middling*.'

'She is the magnetic link between the sitters and the spirit world. She is a medium of communication.'

That was how Peter defined electricity.

'Do you believe in spiritualism, then?'

I was lying in the curve of his arm. He stretched his legs as best he could on our narrow sofa bed and twined his fingers in my hair.

'Frankly, it's all the rage at the moment. Our local MP is very caught up in it. But that is not why it interests me. It is ignorant to insist that such phenomena cannot be, just because there is no scientific explanation for them. I do believe that our individuality can make contact with some universal power, so that one cannot tell where one begins or the other ends. I have experienced it – in wild places, and at sea, and beneath the Niagara Falls, and in . . . in lovemaking. Have you not?'

I did not deny it.

Later, I asked him who else would be at the seance.

'The medium is bringing two cronies with her, Mr and Mrs Moss. They all belong to the London Spiritualist Alliance. That is an only moderately respectable organisation. The serious, scientific one is the Society for Psychical Research. The Alliance is more amusing. Mr Moss is a clergyman, but he does not have a parish. Then there will be myself, and you, and two other friends of mine – and Mrs Carney.'

'Mrs Carney? I did not know you were so democratic.'

'Mrs Carney is essential. She is a sensitive. Many home circles centre round one of the maids in the household. The uneducated mind is not prejudiced. It is only recently that professors and public figures have interested themselves in spiritualism. What they and the Psychical Research people seek is scientific proof of the spirit world.'

'Have they found it?'

'They probably never will. We may not have the right language any longer to express what everyone once knew. Occult phenomena operate according to a different logic. Philosophers pick up certain ideas, and drop or forget others. People long to identify one final explanation of life. It would be so nice and tidy. When you think how crystals and plants grow without fuss, it does not seem impossible that there should be some ordering principle behind man also.'

Spiritualism had the same effect upon Peter as did indoor water closets. When I informed him that I should like to go to the seance, he was contemptuous.

'I have told you often enough. All events, whether physical or mental, are phenomena of matter. Terms like "telepathy" and "clairvoyance" are like "resurrection", they are just words, they explain no process.'

'They could be names for facts. If it were true that we could communicate with spirits—'

'If it were true that we could communicate with the dead it would be a scientific revolution as important as Copernicus or Darwin. But it is not true.'

'You are stupid to say that. Even you do not know enough about, oh, electrons and atoms, to be quite certain. So many people find something in it. Simple people like servants, and highly educated people, even perhaps Godwin. . . .'

'Your precious Godwin is just amusing himself. Table-tilting and automatic writing and all that is a game for dissipated toffs. They are not concerned about the immortality of the soul. They have continuity from the past, from their dungheaps of ancestor worship and wealth and what they call their heritage.'

'What about the simple people?'

'The poor are deceived by vulgar commercialism and fraud, just as they are by canting clergy. They have no past worth remembering and precious little in the present. All they might still have is a future – pie in the sky. Intellectually, most people in this country are on the level of savages who believe that the lightning signifies the anger of some god. Nobody would long for life after death unless it was happy. It is eternal happiness that men seek. Bliss and poetry. They call that the religious temperament.'

I did not dare to bring up the subject of his mother and her religious temperament, in which bliss and poetry were not to the fore.

'What about the unconscious mind? Has it nothing to teach us?'

'The unconscious mind is a cesspit. It is chaos. It is filth. It is darkness and disorder. It is to be controlled. That is the task of civilisation.'

'But might not the darkness and disorder in the unconscious mind be the compost for ordered structures in the conscious? I remember you telling me about undifferentiated matter and – oh, I can't remember now. But seeds germinate in the dark, and babies too.'

'And maggots. You are talking garbled nonsense, like all half-educated females. Listen to me. Faraday did some experiments thirty years ago which showed conclusively that table-tilting is produced by involuntary muscular action by the sitters. You can call that animal magnetism *if* you like.'

This was the longest conversation Peter and I had had in

weeks, and it was a quarrel. I tried to bring it to a close on a conciliating note.

'There is no harm in it, surely, even if it is not true, if it makes people happy.'

'Happy? Happy? Have you ever known anyone who was happy? Only a halfwit is happy.'

He was his mother's son after all.

'We were happy, Peter, before. Or at least, I was happy. I think you were too. And in spite of what you say, I think I should like to go to the seance.'

'Then you are a fool.'

My blue watered-silk evening dress had never been worn. It was still lying folded in the long, flat cardboard box in which it had travelled from London to Morrow. I lifted the box from the bottom drawer and laid it on the gondola bed. To raise the lid and take the body even halfway out was to be back in Dunn Street, standing in the parlour while Jane pinned the silk to my figure and Mother and Aunt Susannah squabbled about hem lengths and bustles. Tears pricked my eyes.

I had never felt nostalgic about my old home before. I remembered watching Mother folding the overskirt, the underskirt, and lastly the body of the dress, and carefully placing them in the box, patting them flat. Hers had been the last hands to touch the silvery-blue material, and now she was buried under the earth. If she knew I was going to the party at the Hall, without Peter, would she say, 'Charlotte, this time you are going too far'? But she and Aunt Susannah must have had some unformed notion of an occasion when I should need such a dress, or they would not have taken such trouble.

The day before the party, I felt a great need to spend some time with Peter. I did not intend us to grow any further apart. I wanted to give him strength for his ordeal. I also wanted to feel secure in our partnership, so as to forget about it, before embarking upon the next phase of my adventure. At five o'clock I had a meal ready, but he did not come home. I waited until ten, and then I went to bed. I lay waiting for the whirr and crunch of the Ariel's wheels until two o'clock in the morning. Fear for his welfare was mixed with resentment that I was losing sleep, and so would not look my best the next day. How selfish I was. But then so was he.

When he came upstairs I lit the candle. He sat on the other side of the bed with his back to me, peeling off his clothes.

'Where were you all this time?'

'Out.'

'Have you eaten?'

'I took a bite with the Carneys.'

No more was said. No more was done either, apart from a perfunctory exchange of goodnight kisses. I blew out the candle. After the great illumination, after the party, I promised myself, we would start again, as married lovers. We would repair the damage. I touched the amethyst in its bag, under my pillow. I should stop meeting Godwin. But not yet. I was learning so much from him. That was my justification.

In those luxurious weeks, it seemed to me that my association with Godwin was some special nourishment, which was extremely agreeable, but which I could easily forgo, when I chose. I did not recognise that I was an addict, just as much so as any degraded woman who is dependent on laudanum or strong drink and will not confront her weakness. I was, in short, in love; but because seeing Godwin was so easy, and so regular, and I never experienced the pain of thwarted passion, I did not acknowledge my condition.

I achieved no marital reconciliation. On New Year's Eve I hardly saw Peter. He was preoccupied with great electrical matters and I with trivial personal ones. The weather was rough and damp. I could not dress at the lodge, and make my way on foot in the dark to the Hall. My shoes, my dress, my hair would be ruined. Even Cinderella had a coach to ride in to the ball. I could hardly hoist my blue silken flounces up around my knees and careen up to the door on my bicycle.

That is what I did, however. There was no alternative. I cycled up the drive past a row of stationary carriages, in the shafts of which the horses stirred and stamped. I waved wildly at poor Mr Paternoster, who was to remain in charge of them during the party; the drivers were sent round to the kitchen quarters to sit in the warm.

I left the bicycle at the garden door and, clutching a bag in which were my lightest shoes, the amethyst, a paper of hairpins, my brush and comb, and a bottle of lavender water, I slipped up the small staircase to the Grey Room which, as Mrs Carney kindly informed me, had been set aside for the lady visitors to leave their wraps and adjust their toilettes.

As I approached along the dim landing I heard female chattering, and a group of ladies emerged from the Grey Room and made for the main staircase. I stood in the shadows beside a pier table, on which was an arrangement of jonquils in an urn. I broke off the heads of three of the creamy, scented flowers from the back of the arrangement.

In the Grey Room Mrs Carney was in attendance. She looked just the same as usual, with her dark hair sleeked back into a knot from a middle parting, in her practical black silk dress with no puffs or drapery, high at the neck and with long, tight sleeves. Her round, plain face was a comfort and quieted my nerves. She helped me to straighten my side panniers and put up my hair. I splashed myself liberally with lavender water. I tightened the tapes under my dress-improver so that it stood out as high and as salient as possible. The heavy silk folds of my overskirt fell away from it behind me like a waterfall. Mrs Carney secured the jonquils in my piled-up hair on the crown of my head, close together so that they looked like a single bloom.

'You have lovely hair,' she said, 'and so does my Mary. Most of these grand ladies, what's at the back of their heads is not their own. Nor their rosy cheeks neither, nor their figures. Their husbands must get a rare shock on the wedding night.'

A long looking-glass had been brought into the room for the occasion. I saw myself from head to foot for the first time in my life. It was most interesting to see how well all the parts of me fitted together. The only thing that displeased me was the bare expanse of my throat above the low square neck of the dress. Mrs Carney said it did not matter and that I had a beautiful skin.

'A real princess does not need diamonds. But you cannot go into company without an evening bag and gloves. Wait now for a minute.'

She glided out of the room and returned with a white satin bag and a pair of long, narrow white kid gloves, with pearls for buttons at the wrist.

'They were my lady's. The very best, from Paris.'

It was terrible forcing them on over my hands, which are small but square. The tops of Godwin's late mama's gloves touched the lace trimming of my sleeves, leaving no bare skin showing.

'That's better. Now down you go and enjoy yourself.'

'Lord Godwin has invited me to the seance, afterwards.'

'So I understand.'

Mrs Carney turned away and began arranging the velvet wraps and furs that had been thrown on the bed.

'Pride goes before a fall. You want to watch out for yourself, with Master George. They are all the same. And I have known Master George since he were a little lad. Not that it is any of my business.'

I refused to take offence on such a night. I put a handkerchief and my amethyst into the satin bag and said nothing.

When I opened the door of the Grey Room, the noise of the party rose up to meet me. I left the room and began the descent of the wide curling staircase, taking the shallow steps slowly, holding up the front of my dress for fear of tripping.

Down in the hall stood a knot of gentlemen in evening dress with glasses in their hands. They felt silent, their faces upturned, watching me. They ceased talking. Godwin stepped forward and held out his hand. I took the last steps down into the hall and put my hand in his.

'I should like to present you all to Mrs Fisher,' he said to his companions. 'As the consort of our heroic electrical engineer, she is the presiding goddess of the evening.'

That was the best moment, for me. There were bowings and flattering murmurs, and Godwin led me on his arm through the group and into the overwhelming crush of people in the hot, flower-scented drawing room. Then there was a less good moment. As we passed, I heard one man say to another something about George and his 'new girl'. His companion gave a short barking laugh. These two elegant gentlemen were every bit as crude as the boys from the back streets of Hitchin.

The room was a blur of faces, colours, and glittering points of light. A maid came up to us with a tray of filled glasses, but Godwin waved her away.

'Champagne is too coarse for you, Wirewoman. I shall give you something finer.'

He drew me aside to a table on which were dark-green bottles packed in ice. He poured wine from one of the bottles into two glasses with long, barley-sugar stems. One for me, and one for him. The wine was very pale, almost green.

'This is the best of the best,' he said. 'I import it through my man of business in Paris. Now let me introduce you to someone.'

The first someone was a large, bearded man, so bow-fronted that he seemed all white waistcoat and watch chain.

'Lord Dimsdale, our new member,' said Godwin, and, to my alarm, drifted away.

'Of what are you a new member?' I asked.

'What an extraordinary question! Of Parliament, of course,' said Lord Dimsdale, rocking on his feet.

'In what interest?' I asked.

'I am proud to describe myself as a Conservative of the old school,' said Lord Dimsdale, stroking his beard, 'as is our host George Godwin, as also my neighbour in the county and my leader in the House, the Marquess of Salisbury. It is incumbent on all men of good will to stand together and stem the rising tide of democracy. And incumbent, indeed, on all ladies of good will too, my dear . . . my pretty dear.'

He was looking down the front of my dress. Close up, he smelled of peppermint. He threw back the remains of his champagne and, with an agility astonishing in so pompous a man, swivelled to subtract a fresh glass from a passing tray.

'I fear,' I said, 'that I myself may be part of that rising tide. My husband I think would call himself a Radical.'

'Then you, my dear, are the fairy foam on the crest of the tide. And as such, most acceptable. More than acceptable.'

'Acceptable to whom, sir?'

I fended him off for another few minutes. I was impertinent, and he was overstimulated. Lord Dimsdale is a toad. I could not assert myself against him. I see now that I should not have tried.

When I confessed my social incompetence to Godwin later, in

the dark in the library, he said that it was a question of practice. Because of my inexperience, he said, I was not attuned to the small continuous diplomacies and evasions of social intercourse, and was therefore too direct in my responses. A room full of society people, said Godwin, is a room full of wobbling cyclists all steering round one another, colliding only glancingly and for strategic reasons.

'Your demeanour does not matter a damn, because you are sufficiently young and pretty to deflect any challenge and any criticism. But you might *prefer* to be more like other people – I mean, more like other ladies.'

Godwin had rescued me from Lord Dimsdale, and Lord Dimsdale from me, and led me over to a sofa on which were sitting a gentleman and a lady. The gentleman had a white sheep's face, a clerical collar, and a long, thin body which he unfolded in order to rise politely when Godwin made the introductions:

'The Reverend Percy Moss and Mrs Moss. I shall leave you in their good care.'

The Mosses made room for me on the sofa between them. Mrs Moss, having ascertained that it would be 'my first time', at once began talking urgently into my right ear about the forthcoming seance.

'The spiritual rewards to you will be incalculable, my dear. Our psychical work is not a religion, nor a substitute for religion, you need have no fears on that count. It is a supplement to our holy religion. It enlarges the place in which the mind and spirit may range. It opens a special door into Heaven.'

From my comfortable vantage point, wedged between the Mosses, I was busy scrutinising all the ladies' dresses. They were not quite like mine which, for all its fashionable drapery, seemed plain in comparison. The dresses worn by Godwin's guests were all very bright, and none of them – apart from the black silk gowns of the elderly ladies – were of one colour only. There were green hip-bags and trains over golden-brown skirts, red over dark blue, and combinations such as pink and yellow which seemed to me quite horrible, like pastries bought in shops.

'Christianity has its origins in psychic phenomena.' Mrs Moss was persistent. I longed to inspect what she herself was wearing, but could not peer sideways at her without seeming to inspect her bulging bodice. 'The annunciation, the miracles, appearances of angels, the resurrection, the Holy Spirit, the speaking in tongues. It all makes such perfect sense. You must subscribe to our weekly periodical, *Light*. I know you will find it most illuminating.'

'Is the medium present?'

'She is in the house, dear, but sitting apart, with Mrs Carney. She must rest before her ordeal. She gives so much. A great deal of psychic energy is required.'

Like me, Mr Moss was eyeing the ladies. He began speaking breathily into my other ear.

'I do not know what your own position is, Mrs Fisher, but Mrs Moss and I are so privileged to be here, so infinitely obliged to Lord Godwin. Of course, were it not for our psychical work we should not be invited to Morrow Hall. I realise that. I do. Our very special work has enlarged our social range. It opens a door into the most desirable milieux. Fortunately, we are adaptable.'

Straight in front of us, about ten feet away, a very tall, brilliant figure held the attention of a cluster of laughing cavaliers. She was a young woman of about my own age, with the kind of prissy little mouth which Aunt Susannah would call a 'rosebud', and a turned-up nose. Her costume was brighter than anyone's – gleaming satin, in contrasting shades of emerald green and deep cerise. She appeared to be teasing Godwin. He appeared to be enjoying it. She too had a barley-sugar glass of the pale wine.

'That is Lady Cynthia Loring,' breathed Mr Moss. 'The only daughter, the only child I should say, of Lord Cumberlow. I understand Lord Cumberlow's estate marches alongside Lord Godwin's. Lady Cynthia, as I am sure you are aware, is constantly mentioned in the social columns. It is so very, very rewarding to see her in the flesh.'

His hushed reverence for the flesh of Lady Cynthia was really quite spiritual. I myself did not find the contemplation of her in the least rewarding.

I remained glued to the Mosses, and did not know how to extricate myself. As a result, Mr Moss escorted both Mrs Moss and myself into the supper room. In the throng, I felt a tap on my shoulder. It was Lord Dimsdale again. He was now disgustingly intoxicated.

'Not only a member of Parliament, my dear, but a member of White's, Boodle's, and the Carlton as well. What's more, I am a male member . . .' and he began to mutter such filth into my ear that I tipped my dish of ice cream over his white waistcoat. That certainly created a diversion. Lord Dimsdale lurched backwards and collided with the sideboard. Regiments of silverware crashed off its shiny surface, and a tall pyramid of little red and white apples teetered and collapsed, the apples bumping and bouncing all over the place and rolling away under everyone's feet.

Later, after the disasters of the supper, I went upstairs to the Grey Room to check my appearance. Who should be in there, on her own, but Lady Cynthia Loring. She was standing in front of the long mirror, her knees slightly bent because of her great height, her body gracefully inclined. She was dipping her long neck, and with her gloved hands twisting up escaped tendrils of hair by the light of half a dozen candles. I sat down well out of the light, on the edge of the bed.

'I hope that I am not disturbing you.'

'Of course you are not. I shall not be many minutes, and then the looking-glass shall be yours.'

I could see her reflection in the mirror. Her hair was of an uninteresting dun colour but it was, so far as I could tell, all her own. Where I wore the jonquils, she wore a half-moon of diamonds and emeralds. More emeralds glittered in her ears, on her wrists, round her neck. But it was the accent of her voice, not her jewels, that humbled me. It was like the icy wine being poured from the green bottle – smooth, lilting, perfect of its kind, which was not my kind. Lady Cynthia made me feel common.

I said something about how much I admired the contrasting shades of her dress.

'You will understand the beauty of it better when the lights go on. Electric light bleaches out pale shades and all-over colours. It makes them insipid. Everyone in London is wearing mixed bright colours now, for evening, on account of the brilliant lights.'

She caught my eye in the glass and halted in her titivating.

'Not that you look insipid, not in the least. Your dress is quite charming. I have heard so much about you and about Mr Fisher from George. The romance . . . of electricity!'

As she spoke she turned from the glass and struck an attitude, as if in a tableau. She laughed, I smiled, and she turned back to her reflection.

'What I cannot decide is . . . oh, what I just cannot decide is whether I should marry George Godwin or not. It would be so convenient, so pleasant. This is a nice house, don't you think? And after all, I must marry someone. Come now, Mrs Fisher, you are a married woman, what do you advise?'

It was out before I could check myself:

'Has he asked you to marry him?'

'Has he asked me? Has he asked me? What an extraordinary question! This is 1885, not 1785. No, it's nearly 1886. We must hurry down or we shall miss the great moment. Please excuse me, I should never have troubled you with my personal affairs.'

She was gone, with a swirl of green and cerise satin, leaving a miasma of musky scent which was neither Parma Violets nor Perks & Llewellyn's lavender but something infinitely more expensive. Probably imported from Paris.

'I do not believe for one moment that he has proposed to that horrible woman, nor does he intend to,' I whispered to my ill-bred, insipid self in the mirror, pressing my face against the glass, clouding my reflection.

When I went back into the drawing room I saw that Carney was moving slowly around the edges of the room between the guests, extinguishing the hundreds of candles one by one with a silver snuffer on a long handle. There was space on a sofa, beside Mr Moss again. Mrs Moss had taken an independent course. I saw her speaking earnestly to a group of older ladies, and took the opportunity to make up my mind about her gown. I think it was what is called 'artistic dress' – a shapeless high-necked tent of gold and green brocade with, very evidently, rather little beneath. There was some kind of medieval girdle in front, over which her bosoms dangled like two long, fat teardrops. One teardrop hung down further than the other. I think, in her place, I should not choose to dispense with a substructure of corsetry.

On the sofa, Mr Moss was turned away from me, speaking to someone behind us, so I was relieved of the necessity of attending to his conversation. Godwin was standing by the fire, one arm on the chimneypiece, talking to Lady Cynthia and the male member. To be accurate, it was Lady Cynthia who was talking to Godwin. The member looked to be beyond speech.

Gradually the room grew dimmer. Through the open door I saw soft-footed figures pass across the shadowy hall with snuffers. All over the house the lights were being put out. In the drawing room Carney had left just a few candles alight. In the glimmering half-dark the colours looked richer, the shapes more dramatic. The great room was a cavern, with brightness glancing off porcelain, silver, crystal, polished wood, satin, brocade. The paintings were gilt-framed mysteries, the walls receded infinitely. The hearth was the brightest thing in the room, and drew one's eyes. Above the fire, in the middle of the chimneypiece, was the ornate French clock.

Servants flitted among the guests with trays, offering fresh glasses of champagne. Gentlemen took out their gold watches and peered at them, inclining the dials to the firelight. Godwin, his eyes on the clock, raised his hand as if to start a race, and the room grew hushed. Beside me, Mr Moss stopped talking. Even Lady Cynthia stopped talking. Two minutes to go.

I thought hard in those two minutes of Peter, outside somewhere all this time with Joe Paternoster in the cold dark, by now in the engine room watching the clock, waiting for the first chimes of midnight, his heart beating, his hand poised over the switches.

A Fenian must feel much the same, preparing to detonate his infernal machine.

I should have been with him. I nearly fled from the house to find him, or at least I nearly rose from the sofa.

The clock above the hearth began to chime. All eyes were

fixed upon the row of inverted cut-glass bowls hanging by chains from the ceiling. A dim yellow glow appeared in each one, and in the shaded lamps upon the side tables. The glow increased in intensity. It grew brighter and brighter. A long, rising exclamation of 'Aah!' arose from sixty or seventy open mouths.

The brightness increased excessively, dazzling the eyes, and then suddenly died. As the room was plunged into what now seemed total darkness, another 'Aah!' this time descending the scale, broke from our throats. My heart was pounding, my armpits were pricking.

Again the bowls were suffused with a dim glow, again the light increased in brightness, but not to such a garish extreme – and it held steady.

'Hurrah!' shouted Godwin.

'Fiat lux!' cried Mr Moss.

Lady Cynthia threw her arms around Lord Dimsdale. Perhaps she could marry *him*.

I escaped from the mêlée and ran through the bright hall to the front door, which stood open. I read the notice that Peter had nailed on the panelling just inside the door. He had intended it half-humorously; he was so tired of being asked the same ignorant questions over and over:

> THIS HOUSE IS EQUIPPED WITH EDISON ELECTRIC LIGHT. DO NOT ATTEMPT TO LIGHT WITH MATCH. SIMPLY PRESS SWITCH ON WALL BY DOOR IN EACH ROOM. THE USE OF ELECTRICITY FOR LIGHTING IS IN NO WAY HARMFUL TO HEALTH, NOR DOES IT AFFECT THE SOUNDNESS OF SLEEP.

I strained my eyes to see if I could see Peter somewhere out there in the dark, and I called his name. No answer. I heard a horse stamp and blow far away down the drive, and called out for Paternoster. He too seemed to have vanished. I went back inside and wandered away into the library. The electric light was on there as well. Then it went out. That was because Godwin had followed me in, and depressed the nipple switch at the door. He felt for me in the dark and found me.

We did not stay long. The guests were beginning to go; we heard their carriages being moved up the drive to the front door, and Carney calling out names. Godwin turned the light on again. He left me, to bid farewell to his guests.

There is a looking-glass over one of the writing-tables in the library. I smoothed my dress and tidied my hair, feeling suddenly exhausted. My reflection alarmed me. I noticed how pale I was and how dark the shadows under my eyes. There was a hair-fine red vein in the skin over my right cheekbone. Was this new, or had it always been there?

I think that electric light is not flattering. Electricity does not suit the library at Morrow, either. The flat, uniform brightness broke its spirit, which survives only in my dream.

Chapter Eleven

'The spirits cannot abide electric light,' said Mrs Moss as we filed into Mrs Carney's sitting room. 'Too much illumination weakens the power.'

The small, cosy room beside the now-abandoned servants' hall had been the resident housekeeper's sanctum in the old days. Mrs Carney used it as the place for giving housemaids a piece of her mind, and for drinking private cups of tea, a practice in which I had sometimes joined her.

The room was lit, if that is the word, by a single candle on the chimneypiece and another on a whatnot by the curtained window. Mrs Carney and a lady in black were already seated at the round table, far apart, both of them so motionless, so composed, that between them they consumed all the available serenity. Just looking at them, I became febrile and nervous.

I glanced behind to check who was coming in apart from myself, Mr and Mrs Moss, and Godwin – and saw to my disgust that the last two participants were Lady Cynthia Loring and Lord Dimsdale. We stood around awkwardly in the constricted space. Mrs Carney and the other lady remained seated, their eyes cast down.

Mrs Moss took charge. She closed the door, and then placed us one by one as if for a dinner party. We sat like this:

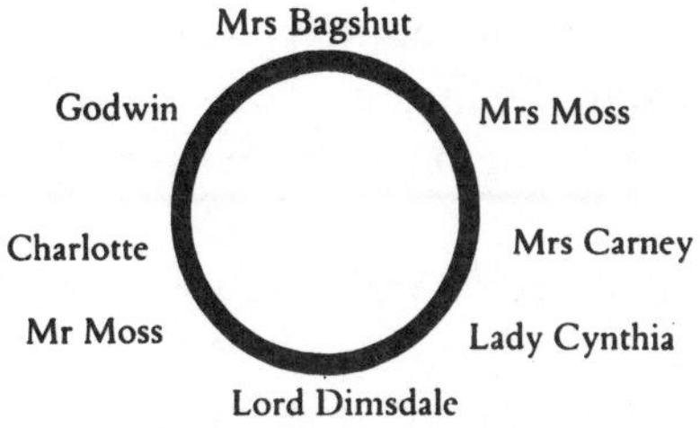

As we seated ourselves, I quickly peeped under the table, half-expecting to see some machinery which would persuade me of the medium's fraudulence. I saw only the thick central support of the table, and its splayed tripod foot. I dared to take a look at the medium. She was a bulky woman with an ugly dog's face and eyes like black pebbles. Her hair too was black, crimped in a fringe over her forehead and gathered up behind in a wispy knot.

The medium closed her eyes. Mrs Moss alone remained standing. She stood in her place, leaning forward, her unequal bosoms swaying over the polished table, and addressed us in a hushed voice:

'Welcome, ladies and gentlemen. I am very happy to present to you our medium, Mrs Bagshot—'

'Bagshut,' said that lady, snapping her eyes open for a moment.

'Mrs Bagshut. Our sitting will last for one hour. The conditions are ideal – a private circle of friends. Four would be sufficient. Any more than eight – our quorum tonight – would be too many. It is desirable that at least two be negative, passive persons, preferably female, and that so far as possible male and female should sit alternately, and negative-passives should alternate with positive-actives.'

'How do we know which we are?' asked Lady Cynthia, giggling.

'If you do not know whether you are male or female, my dear,' said Lord Dimsdale, 'I for one should be delighted to investigate the mystery.'

'No more levity, if you please,' said Mrs Moss. 'Any levity,' and any feelings of hostility towards one another or towards our undertaking, will result in a failed seance. Either the spirits will not communicate at all, or they will cause disturbances and perhaps do harm to the medium, Mrs Bagshot.'

'Bagshut. The name may be written Bagshot, but it is Bagshut.'

I was aware that, like myself, Godwin was having trouble in quelling his levity.

'Bagshut. I know which of you are passive-negatives, having taken the precaution of making the acquaintance of each one of our circle during the course of this evening. You are seated accordingly. Mrs Bagshut, Mrs Carney, Lord Dimsdale and Mrs Fisher are our passive-negatives. It is they who make the best conductors for spirit messages. Now may I invite you to banish all antagonism and triviality from your minds, and to relax. I should like you to place the palms of your hands on the table.'

We did so – eight pairs of hands of varying sizes and colourings. Lord Dimsdale's were veined and blotchy. Mr Moss's were long and pale. But his thumbs were expressive. I thought of Aunt Susannah, and of how much she would have enjoyed all this.

Mrs Moss sat down and spread her own hands on the table.

'You may touch one another's fingers and form a linked circle if you like, but it is not obligatory.'

I shifted the little finger of my left hand an inch and touched Godwin's. For appearance's sake, I did the same with my right hand, and made contact with Mr Moss. Glancing around, I saw that the only gap in the circle was between the little fingers of Mrs Carney and Lady Cynthia. Perhaps it was a question of social class? Or maybe Mrs Carney was fastidious. For the sake of the spirits, I strove to suppress my loathing for Lady Cynthia and Lord Dimsdale.

'Now,' said Mrs Moss, 'perhaps you would just talk gently among yourselves for a few moments, to release the residual tensions.'

I said quietly to Mr Moss:

'I think your wife must have made a mistake. I am neither passive nor negative, I assure you.'

'My wife does not make errors of that nature. Your confusion only confirms her judgement. Our greatest illusion is to believe that we are what we think ourselves to be.'

'Are you and she positive or negative?'

'We are, unfortunately, both positive. In our home circle, we have to rely upon our maid as the channel for the spirit messages from lost loved ones. Happily she is a very superior type.'

'How did you become interested in the spirit world?'

'Mrs Moss and I are not unacquainted with grief, Mrs Fisher. We have lost three of our little ones. I am a man of the cloth, and I know that the good Lord created us with an unquenchable desire to penetrate the veil, and that it was not intended that this desire should be disappointed.'

I did not know how to reply. In any case, the conversation around us was dying away. In the expectant silence that followed I recalled Peter's description of science as 'a search for causes'. Spiritualism seemed its mirror image: a search for effects. I tried hard to make my mind vacant, but could not help speculating about the marriage of the Reverend Percy Moss and Mrs Moss. In the language of electricity, two positives repel one another.

The silence became total, and oppressive. Mrs Bagshut had opened her eyes and was staring glassily into the space between Mrs Moss and Mrs Carney. The only sound was of her heavy breathing. After having felt too hot all evening, I was suddenly chilly. There was another sound – the creaking of the table. It began to tilt, I felt it rising under my hands. I experienced a strange sensation in my head, as if there were a feather tickling my forehead from within.

Mr Moss addressed the medium in a low voice:

'Is there somebody on the other side who is trying to get through?'

There were three loud raps on the underside of the table. I checked the pairs of hands on its surface; all in place. But then there seemed to be some kind of deadlock. The table ceased to tilt and vibrate.

'She cannot come through,' said Mrs Bagshut in a staccato voice unlike her own. 'She is here. But she cannot speak directly. She must speak through another. . . . There is someone present who impedes the spirit. Someone who is not sufficiently collected.'

She raised her head and looked across the table at Lord Dimsdale. He was sitting crookedly in his chair and looked as if he might fall off it.

'Perhaps, my lord,' said Mrs Moss, 'if you were to leave us . . . I am so sorry. I think you are not quite well.'

'Please,' said Lord D., suddenly pathetic, like a child. 'Please permit me to remain. I have been so unhappy. I was so hoping . . .'

The last words came out as 'I was sho-o-o-ping'. There was a horrid silence. Abruptly he rose, breaking the circle, and blundered from the room. Mrs Carney rose with him and closed the door, then returned to her place. Mr Moss moved his chair closer to Lady Cynthia's, re-forming the circle, with a gratified air. Lord Dimsdale's lurching footsteps receded down the stone passage. I thought I heard him groaning. At that moment I almost pitied him.

The silence closed in again. It was stronger now. The tickling sensation behind my forehead spread until my whole head was an empty geode being caressed from inside by feathers. I felt faint. I removed my right hand from the table and placed it on the amethyst in my bag. Mrs Moss was staring at me.

'Mrs Fisher is affected,' she said softly. 'Have you a message for us from beyond, dear?'

To this day I do not know why I said what I said:

'It is a little baby. . . .'

There was a slow sigh from all around the table, and from someone a snob. Even though I was, shall we say, beyond myself, I was aware of a stab of gratification. I was someone dreaming who knows that she is dreaming.

I woke up, I lost the thread, because Mrs Bagshut had begun keening and moaning, rocking her body to and fro. In retrospect, I suspect that she determined to regain control of the seance – she was after all the professional. For the next twenty minutes she was in full flow. She did in truth seem possessed – first by lost babies and then by different people talking in different voices and accent, never her own – which was common-or-garden London, like Jane's.

I regret that I can remember few of the messages from beyond. They were not memorable. The Mosses repeatedly asked the spirits whether they were happy, and they replied that they were, utterly happy. A female spirit with a cultivated voice, speaking through Mrs Bagshut, asked where the white dress was. This was for Lady Cynthia. Someone else, who seemed to be a man, addressed Godwin: 'Pride goes before a fall.' I glanced at Mrs Carney, but she was rapt. Then the man's voice spoke gruffly in a foreign language and Godwin replied, haltingly, in the same language. Finally Mrs Bagshut spluttered her way into silence, dropped her head upon her breast and seemed to sleep. Mrs Moss signalled to us to remove our hands from the table. It was over.

Godwin rose and switched on the electric light. That was terrible. Everyone's faces looked drawn and exhausted. It was nearly two o'clock in the morning. Godwin walked round the table and spoke a word to Lady Cynthia, leaning over her. I tried not to look. I turned to Mr Moss and said, without having planned to:

'What Mrs Bagshut does . . . I could do that.'

'I believe you could, I believe you could. You have many natural advantages. Come and call on me at the Rooms.'

He took a card from an inner pocket and gave it to me.

Godwin returned to my side.

'You must be anxious to get home. I will see you out.'

We stood together for a moment at the garden door.

'What language were you speaking with Mrs Bagshut?'

'It was Portuguese, something about climbing a ladder. The ladder of life, was it? I learned a little Portuguese in Brazil. Mrs Bagshut has never learned it. Her conscious self could not have spoken it.'

'But how can that be?'

He shrugged. 'Unseen forces? The power of the unconscious mind? It was amusing, anyway. An entertainment for you.'

He kissed me lightly and pushed something round and cool into my hand. Not a crystal. A nectarine.

'I must see Cynthia to her carriage, and pay Mrs Bagshut her fee.'

I wobbled away down the dark drive on FRESH MEAT.

★

I shared the nectarine with Peter. Nectarines are the most delicious eatables in all the world. When Peter, in a clean white shirt, went up to the Hall for a formal discussion with Godwin about the routine operation and maintenance of the electrical system, he returned with a whole basket of nectarines, left over from the party. I drew them, before we began to eat them.

There was a sense of anticlimax. There was no question but that the electric lighting was a success. Peter still had a few tasks to complete. Many of the electric lamps had burned out that first evening. They had to be replaced and the fuses and connections checked. There was unfinished business in the kitchen passages. Here the wires were not boxed in, as they were in the main house, but still hung in festoons on the walls. This is bad practice. Peter had several days' work to do aligning the wires neatly, and securing them to the walls with little leather tabs nailed down on either side.

The only serious problem was with the arc lighting in the stable yard. It failed intermittently, it kept 'bobbing out' as the Paternosters put it.

'When I have seen to all that, and received my pay,' said Peter at supper, a week into the New Year, 'we shall have to be making arrangements to go from here.'

I peeled another nectarine as I took in what he had said. Of course I knew that we were only at Morrow so that Peter could do the installation. I knew that our life here was only temporary. But I had not faced up to what I knew. How could I leave the East Lodge, my first own home? How could I leave Godwin?

'We cannot go back to Dunn Street,' I said. 'Remember how it was before we came here. I do not think I could bear it, and nor could you.'

'We shall find furnished rooms, somewhere where we can get our washing done in the house. I can afford it, with what I have earned from Godwin.'

'I wish we did not have to leave.'

'Do you imagine that I am anxious to go from here? You think only of yourself these days. But then, when did you ever take an interest in my doings?'

'Peter, that is cruel nonsense. Our lives have revolved round you and your – your romance with electricity, from the very first day I knew you.'

We must not quarrel again. I dragged myself back from the edge, and asked, in a normal voice:

'Will you look for another job like this one, in a big house in the country.

He said that he would not; but that the experience he had gained at Morrow, and the way Joe Paternoster had taken to the work, gave him confidence to think he might take on apprentices. He intended to write a report on Morrow for the Society of Telegraph-Engineers and Electricians, and perhaps to publish the layouts and technical details in *The Electrician*.

The coming thing, he said, was not individual installations but schemes involving whole streets, whole areas of cities, all supplied with electricity from one central power station. That was the field in which he wanted to work.

'High-tension feeders, high-voltage systems, long-distance transmission. Power stations are the cathedrals of the future.'

Then he went out – to the Bald-Faced Stag, he said. I sat in the kitchen and thought about him, aimlessly removing the glass chimney from the oil lamp on the table and teasing the cotton wick with my finger, making it flare and smoke. A dangerous game. I knocked the chimney with my elbow. It rolled off the table and broke into smithereens on the floor. I swept up the pieces and went outside to wash my hands, which were dirty with soot-flakes from the lamp, and bleeding from a tiny cut. It was snowing. Neither Peter and I were quite in control, I thought. He was still edgy, living on his nerves, coughing too much, fretting about the faulty arc lamps and about his ambitious future plans.

In the last weeks before the lights were turned on at the Hall, he had helped me not at all around the house. I had accepted in the short term the necessity of bringing in the firewood and coal, riddling the range, disposing of the clinker and ashes, carrying water and so on, all by myself. I needed help now because all the split logs had been used up, and those that remained were the heavy, awkward ones. I did not believe I had the strength to use either the big saw or the axe, and so I told him.

'I'll chop you some wood first thing, before I go up to the engine room,' he promised late that night, when he came in.

But when in the morning I had cleared the range, and went to the outhouse to fetch fuel, I found that he had not done it.

It was an icy day. There was ice in my heart as well. The snow had settled. I knotted the scratchy blue shawl – the one that my mother had knitted – firmly round my shoulders, and resigned myself to the inevitable. I contemplated the saw and the axe, hanging on nails inside the shed. I chose the axe, in the belief that it would do the work more quickly, and with less effort on my part.

I dragged a section of tree trunk from the pile to a clear space on the shed floor. I put all my weight on the back foot, my left one, and raised the axe over my right shoulder. I brought it down as hard as I could. The axe blade slipped on the ridged bark and came down on my right foot.

I saw it happening. The blade sliced through the leather of my boot, through my stocking and my skin, through my bones and tendons. Part of the boot, and part of my foot, fell away and lay at an angle.

I felt nothing.

It can only have been seconds, but it felt like minutes, before I toppled over. I vomited over the thick layer of sawdust and bark fragments that littered the floor. An earwig, three inches from my watering eyes, was a prehistoric monster. Then the hot bleeding began, and the pain.

I hauled myself into a sitting position, I pulled at the knot of the shawl to remove it. I could not at first bind my mutilated foot at all, because the sole of the boot was not wholly cut through. A shred of tough leather still held. I tore at the sole until the complete end of the boot, with my toes in it, came away. I was shivering and my hands were unsteady, but I wrapped the shawl as tightly as I could around what remained of my foot. I had the sense to prop my leg up on the log, before I passed out.

When I woke up I was in the big bed in the Grey Room at the Hall. The curtains were drawn, a fire was burning in the grate, everything was clean and neat. A vase of bronze chrysanthemums stood on the table in the window. It was as if I were back in the time after the miscarriage.

My right foot was throbbing. The toes on that foot were hurting unbearably, something between an ache and an itch but worse than either. I bent up my knee and placed my hand, under the sheet, on my foot – or rather on a bandaged stump. No toes. It was the spirit of my toes which was hurting, one might say. A ghost pain.

I learned about what had happened, and what was happening, from other people. Each in turn came to sit upon my bed.

Godwin told me how he had called in his own medical man, Dr Chapman, who would come again. This doctor had injected me with morphia to kill the pain and keep me sleeping while he examined the damage. He had told Godwin that I lost consciousness not only because of the shock, and the loss of blood – it was fortunate that I had propped my foot up – but on account of the consequent fall in blood pressure. The doctor had told Godwin that it was fortunate, too, that I lost only the toes, and hardly anything from some important bones called the metatarsals. As it was, I should be able to walk again – but with a limp, since only one set of toes remained to do their work of projecting me forward.

This last gave me a small shock. It had not entered my head that I might not be able to walk normally again. Godwin was very tender with me.

Mrs Carney, in her turn, told me how she had broken the bad news of my accident to the Paternosters, father and son, down in the kitchen. They had been very upset indeed. Young Joe had begun to cry – and then his crying turned to laughing, and suddenly they were all three roaring and shouting with laughter at a joke that was not quite there but which was utterly necessary. Mrs C. was afraid that I might be upset by this story, but I was not. But my emotions ran in reverse to theirs – I began to laugh at Mrs Carney's abashed account, and my laughing turned to tears of weakness. Mrs Carney was kind. She brought me a pile of Godwin's big linen handkerchiefs.

'These will be more use than my lady's little lace scraps. You'll need to do a bit of crying, I'd say. It's the shock.'

And Peter . . . Peter's story came out gradually, over several visits to the Grey Room. The first time he came, he simply cradled me in his arms, and stroked my hair, and kissed all the parts of me that he could reach. I clung to him in gratitude, realising how our love for one another had been there all the time – blocked, unavailable.

His story was this. The iron rim had come off the Ariel's front wheel. As he wanted to ride into Hitchin for some more of the tiny nails which secure the leather tabs (the ones that hold the wires firm against walls), he returned to the lodge at mid-morning to borrow FRESH MEAT. He looked for me – and found me lying in the outhouse. He raced off to raise the alarm on FRESH MEAT, and Carney drove a cart down to carry me up to the Hall.

There was something on my mind, but it was hard to put it into words. It seemed shameful.

'My piece of foot . . . it must be still there.'

Peter told me how of his own accord and with a quaking heart he had looked for it the next day. It was a few moments before he saw what he was seeking. There is not much light in that outhouse. The severed half-foot had come apart from the half-boot.

I wondered if an animal had been at it in the night but did not want to ask.

Peter had tried to squash the half-foot back into the half-boot, but could not make it fit.

He had burned the bit of boot in the range, and buried my toes. First he fetched a plate from the kitchen to carry the toes upstairs to the bedroom. He found my jewel box with the picture of Osborne House on the lid, and tipped my trinkets out. He laid the toes on the magenta satin and closed the lid. He took the spade and dug a hole in the wood at the back of the lodge. He buried the box. Then, feeling strange, he lay down on the cold ground in the wood until he was himself again.

'It was like – it was like with the poor baby that never was,' I said.

'No,' he said, 'it was not like that at all.'

One must love a man who can perform such actions alone, without melodrama but with ceremony and respect, and I did love him. I could not stop crying then, for his ordeal, and for the part of me that was already dead and buried.

For his sake I pulled myself together. I hugged him, and said:

'Now I shall begin to get better. I'll soon be on my feet again – or, I should say, on my foot again.'

I thought of a better joke:

'You know what Mother would have said if she had seen my half-foot on the plate? She would have said that the only thing to do with it was to curry it.'

We really laughed, then, and cried too. He told me he was going to begin fixing the arc lamps in the stable yard the following morning, and he kissed me goodnight.

The next afternoon I was stronger, and Godwin carried me from the bed to a chair at the table in the window. Mrs Carney put a shawl around my shoulders and a blanket across my knees. My bandaged stump was supported on a footstool. A jug of Mrs Carney's lemonade and a bowl of nectarines were placed within reach. There they left me. I did not want to read, or talk. It was a great pleasure to look out over the bare trees and long snowy vistas of the park.

I saw two figures in the far distance, near the park's boundary with the fields. They must have been walking slowly, for it was a long time before they were near enough for me to make out that one was a man and the other a woman. They were of much the same height, and they were walking close together, their arms apparently touching, their heads bowed. They seemed deep in conversation, and intimate with one another. When walking and talking with a mere friend or acquaintance, one is more animated.

The man was Peter. All at once I knew him by his shape and his walk, from afar.

I continued to watch the lovers, as I had already designated them. I could do no other. They stopped for a moment, and veered off to the right, behind a thicket. Moments passed. When they emerged, the woman was bare-headed, swinging her hat at her side. Peter's hands were in his pockets. He began to run ahead of her, kicking something – a snowball, a stone? – like a schoolboy.

They were almost on the gravel sweep beneath my window before I realised that the young woman was Mary Carney. I shifted my chair back from the window, lest they should look up and see me.

'Sitting in the dark?' said Mrs Carney, when she brought in my supper tray. 'You don't need to do that, not now.'

She snapped on the electric light. She helped me back to bed.

What I do not care for about electric light is that it is either on, or it is off. Where now are those hours of half-light before the lamps were lit, those long, quiet passages between day and night? When, now, do we have time to think, and to not think? In the dusk, we used to sit with our hands in our laps, no longer able to sew or read, waiting while the earth turned. Then the lamps were lit one by one, the brightness increasing gradually, leading us over the threshold into the evening.

I asked Mrs Carney to bring me two candles and to turn off the electric light. When Peter came for his evening visit the candles were burning on either side of my bed. I had been thinking back to all the times when he had been out until the small hours, all the times he had 'eaten with the Carneys', or visited the Bald-Faced Stag. I knew in my bones, too, that Mary had been with him out in the dark on New Year's Eve. I did not challenge him about Mary. I could hardly do so without confessing about myself and Godwin. Positions would have to be taken up. Right or wrong, yes or no, black or white, love or hate.

What I do not care for about electricity is that it conceals as much as it reveals. Everything is made significant, so nothing is. Small, important truths are swamped by gross, unimportant ones.

We were quite together, in my dusky bedroom, and not, I think, unhappy. We talked about our families. We had heard from Aunt Susannah how my father was deteriorating. Peter told me that he had written to his mother about the accident to my foot. We were not positive, not negative, but neutral, natural. A time would come, I believed, to look at our marriage in a new light.

It was not the right time. But if not then, when? I never saw Peter again.

What I do not care for about electricity is that up to the very last minute it seems stable, predictable, even benign. But one false move and it runs amok without warning, releasing its lethal energy. Then it is evil. The plunge into darkness is absolute. And there is no candle left burning in the hall, no oil-lamp turned low on the kitchen table. No wonder the children are afraid to be born.

I knew something was wrong, from the voices and running feet downstairs. Godwin and Joe Paternoster came up to my room together. Godwin sat on my bed, Joe stood, white-faced, twisting his cap in his hands. Poor little Joe.

Peter had been up a ladder inspecting the faulty arc-lamp over the stable arch. He had dismantled most of it, and in the process the fitting became detached from the brick wall. He wanted to bang the nails in again. He called down to Joe to throw him up his big hammer. Joe, ever helpful, threw the hammer and Peter caught it by the head with his right hand. His left hand was on the lamp, holding it steady. Instantaneously there was a flash, like a bolt of lightning Joe said, leaping between the lamp and the hammer. Peter cried out and fell, bringing the ladder down on top of him. His head was broken by the fall. But it was the power of the high-voltage electricity that killed him.

What I shall never understand is why Peter had not switched off the power in the engine room before he began his work. Perhaps he could not tell what was wrong unless the power was coming through?

Joe had raced into Hitchin on the Ariel to fetch Dr Chapman, and returned with the doctor in his gig, the bicycle strapped on behind. They carried Peter into the engine room. There was nothing that Dr Chapman could do for him. Dr Chapman came upstairs to the Grey Room after Godwin and Joe had left me. He renewed the dressing on my foot, gave me morphia again, and talked to me.

He told me that nervous exhaustion, ill-health, emotional stress or psychic disturbance reduces the resistance of the human body to electric shock by as much as five times. I said that Peter had been under pressure, that he was never strong and had not been really well for some time.

Dr Chapman said he was certain that Peter felt no pain:

'He went out like a light.'

*

Martin Paternoster tolled the mourning bell for Peter at the church down in Morrow Green. Mrs Carney, who sat with me, opened the window, and we heard it sounding on and on and on, a single repeated note in the thin winter air.

The day after Peter's funeral I received a letter from his mother, written in response to the news of my accident. It was not a real letter. It was not even signed. On a sheet of thin paper, in the tight black handwriting that I knew from her inscription in the Bible she had given to us, was another passage from Leviticus, her favourite book of the Old Testament:

> And the LORD spake unto Moses, saying,
>
> Speak unto Aaron, saying, Whosoever he be of thy seed in their generations that hath any blemish, he shall not approach: a blind man, or a lame, or he that hath a flat nose, or any thing superfluous,
>
> Or a man that is broken-footed, or broken-handed . . .

There is more, but I cannot endure transcribing it. The general drift of the passage seems to be that a person who has the misfortune to sustain any physical defect or disability is guilty of a personal affront to his Maker.

I must own that I laughed. Had Peter been with me, I should have felt obliged to pretend to a modicum of respect. I did not feel sufficiently composed to write to Peter's mother and inform her that her son, my husband, was dead. Lord knows what paroxysm of biblical abomination I might have called forth upon my head.

Godwin wrote to break the news to her, and received no reply. I never saw Peter's mother again.

I wept uncontrollably for Peter. Where *was* he? Was he crying for me, as I cried for him? Where was his spirit?

I believe, now, that he is in the hands of the Power that people glimpse, and then diminish and distort into rival notions of God. The Power cannot but sustain him better than I did, because it is consistent and unwavering. He is in that unplaceable place 'where there shall be no darkness nor dazzling, but one equal light'.

But many months were to pass before I found this degree of comfort.

Third Notebook

Chapter Twelve

Peter and I once discussed the nature of melancholy. I said:

'Melancholy is watching tulips die slowly, day by day, watching the water level fall in the vase and not refilling it, seeing the petals change colour and fall one by one and not sweeping them away.'

Peter said:

'Melancholy is not replacing burned-out Edison lamps, not because they cost five shillings apiece but because you no longer care.'

There are worse states than melancholy.

They brought me Peter's spectacles. One lens was missing, the other was shattered in a star-shape.

I saw distorted things, whether sleeping or waking I cannot tell. I saw my dead baby, a curved gobbet, turning over and over in a red stream to the ocean. I saw it under the earth, pulled about by snouted creatures.

Peter forced a copper skewer through my half-foot, and my electrified toes danced off down the drive with the two ends of the skewer sticking out of them.

Peter said terrible things to someone whom I could not discern:

'She is a puddle on a paving stone, reflecting the sky. She makes reference to all things pure and lovely, but she is cold, shallow, unclean.'

He said: 'She wheedles the unwilling heart from your breast, and when you have handed it over to her she tramples upon it, not from malice but from carelessness.'

He was speaking of me. This was not language that he would have used in life.

I saw the horse buried under the road by the gates of Morrow Hall. I saw it alive, with shining flanks and rolling eyes, not wishing at all to lie down in the hole. I saw it decayed, its flanks fallen in, its eyes eaten away, the rubble half-covering it. Surely no pothole could be big enough to contain a whole horse? Did they use the different parts for filling different holes? Where was its head?

I asked Godwin:

'Did you bury the horse under the road all in one piece? Or did they cut it up first?'

My father died around this time. Aunt Susannah sent a telegram. Godwin asked me if I should like to see the clergyman who had read Peter's funeral service. No. Clergymen have their own language of blood sacrifice and I did not wish to hear it.

I lay there, and Mrs Carney and Godwin came and went, and the weeks of winter passed. Where *was* Peter? I set my piece of amethyst beside me on the pillow and gazed at the shining purple peaks from close range, looking for something hidden in the central hollow.

I thought at one time that I was running away down a wide curling staircase, only to be faced with a closed door. I said to Godwin:

'Am I at death's door?'

'Certainly not,' said he. 'You are at life's door.'

He told me what his father had told him, when he was a small boy and unable to fall asleep. His father had instructed him to imagine opening a door and discovering on the other side a green valley with a clear river running through it over pebbles. On the bank were three horses, grazing. He told his little son to walk into the valley and see something beautiful, and to smell, hear, touch and taste something beautiful, and then to lie on the grass by the river and enjoy his five pleasures.

'Telling you this is like sending a message from my father, through me, to you.'

'A spirit message?'

'Perhaps the only kind there is. Certainly, the best kind.'

So I passed through the door into Godwin's father's valley, and saw lavender fields in bloom in the misty distance. I smelt the lavender on the breeze, and touched the green velvet grass. I lay down in the sunshine beside the river and ate a nectarine.

The three horses were closing in, rolling their eyes at me as they tore rhythmically at the grass with their yellow teeth. I was afraid of them.

Godwin put his head round the door of the Grey Room once more.

'I omitted to tell you,' he said, 'that the horses are on the other side of the river.'

One must love such a man, and I did love him, from the bottom of my damaged heart.

My stump had healed. It was time to walk. Carney made me a triangular crutch out of two ash poles bound together at the base. He padded the crossbar at the top with horsehair and leather, secured with rows of brass-headed upholstery pins. I thumped around the room on the crutch, and sometimes I abandoned it, learning to limp and lurch in an ugly fashion on my own. This was reality, and it was depressing. The efforts I made exhausted me, and I would crawl back into bed.

Confined to my room, and bored, and too restless to read all day, I hobbled and bumped around, studying every item in sight, as if the pictures, fabrics and furniture might teach me something. For the first time, I looked properly at the two old prints of Niagara Falls and, as was my wont, read the small print. They were published by Ackerman in the 1850s, and engraved by C. Hunt from drawings by a Lieutenant-Colonel Cockburn.

The one over the bed is called 'The Falls of Niagara from the Upper Bank, English Side'. Lieutenant-Colonel Cockburn seems to have been more interested in drawing the sheep in the meadow in the foreground. The distant Falls look distinctly unimpressive, though there is a rainbow. The other, which hangs over the fireplace, is called 'General View of Niagara from the English Ferry' and is scarcely more striking than the first.

Godwin had been to Niagara. I asked him about the Falls.

'These engravings are of no use except as an *aide-mémoire*. The artist did not confront what he saw. I have seen the world, but standing close to the Niagara Falls, and then standing down below, in the caves of the rock with the roaring curtain of water filling one's view, was like no other experience of my life. A greater volume of white water crashing down from such a height cannot well be imagined. On and on, for ever and since always. It makes a man insignificant, impotent – a leaf. It reduces one to awed silence. It is the wordless power of Nature made visible.'

'A benign power or an evil power?'

Godwin drowned me in numbers. Eighteen million cubic feet of water fall over the precipice every minute of every day. That is the equivalent, every minute of every day, of the power of nine million horses. Two men had just recently risked their lives by going over the precipice in a barrel – and survived. But many did not, and there were suicides.

'But is it a benign power or an evil power?'

'You persist in asking a meaningless question. Power is neutral. It knows no values. When we dread the power which transcends us, we call it evil. When we desire union with it, we call it divine. Niagara cannot differentiate between a falling cork and a falling human. It cannot be deflected. It just continues to do what it does, it goes on its way.'

'The power is stupid. No, it is stupidity itself. Single-minded stupidity.'

'That is to say that God is stupidity.'

'Christ said that His Father cared for every sparrow that falls.'

'Do you believe that?'

'No.'

'Well, then.'

Niagara made me quarrelsome. It was not the only subject on which we fell out. We were speaking of the Carneys, and Godwin referred idly to the fact that Carney's father had emigrated from the Godwin property in County Cork at the time of the potato famine, to work in England on the railways. I had no idea that Godwin had a place in Ireland.

'I have the land, but I no longer have a house there. It was burned down – oh, seven years ago now.'

'How? By whom? The Fenians?'

'It was the rascals they call the Land Leaguers. The tenants refused to pay rent. A landlord must be very rich indeed in order to survive that. We had to evict. There was bad feeling. It was a bad time. That was why my parents travelled so much.'

'And now?'

'The rents are paid again. But I shall never go back now. I have a good agent, another of the Carney family, who has had the sense to make something of himself. It was the Irish rents that paid for the electrical installation, and the redecorations.'

It did not seem quite right to me that a landlord should buy luxuries with money paid by poor people whom he did not know for the use of land in another country which he never visited. I could understand how the agitators felt, and I said so.

'But it is my family's land, Charlotte. Our property. Without the Irish rents I might not be able to keep this place up at all. I have already made economies. Morrow does not pay for itself. All farmers are losing money. You would not wish, no one would wish, to see the country houses of Ireland and England, their libraries and art collections, their parks and gardens, all broken up and destroyed, or built upon.'

I could not see much of a case for the labour of many contributing so much to the life of ease of an intelligent, able-bodied man such as Godwin. I was used to the notion that a man earned his living by some kind of work. Nor could I see why one man, or one family, needed so much house or so much land.

'My heart is in the right place,' he said.

'Where is the right place to be, for a heart?'

'On the side of the angels.'

'Whose side are the angels on?'

'Oh Charlotte, do not be difficult.'

Godwin preferred to take my arguments as a joke. He said one of the things that made me 'difficult' was that he could not tell when I was joking and when I was not. Sometimes I made him laugh. I generally felt gratified by this. But now he wanted to know whether I was intentionally 'amusing', or not.

I thought about this. I could not, at the time, express my thoughts. What I in fact believe is that there is no definite line between a joke and not a joke. Men, I have found, like to be sure one way or another. If I tell a story and my hearer finds it funny, then it is funny. If he does not, then it is not. I myself do not greatly care either way. I tell a story because it interests me, for itself. What I find amusing, another might find tragic. I do not have a tragic sense of life. Life is neutral, like Niagara Falls. Knock, and it shall be opened unto you. Life is what happens to you on the other side of the door. Life is *who* happens to you.

So Godwin and I wrangled in the late afternoons in the Grey Room, and I must confess that I wept a good deal, and he sulked a good deal, and then he would return to kiss and stroke me, so that when he said again that I was 'difficult', it became the most tender of endearments.

It was not only my difficultness that drove Godwin to seek help. I had a relapse. The nightmares returned. Waking, I had no control over my emotions, thrown back and forth like a twig in a torrent. Godwin was still tender with me, but impatience underlay the tenderness.

'How long is this going to go on, darling? Can you not pull yourself together?'

I had no answer. Afterwards, when he came to see me, he was brisker.

'I have done something without asking your permission,' said he, holding my hand. 'I have called in a new doctor. A nerve specialist. You have had to bear more than any person can bear without breaking.'

I was suspicious at once. He knew it.

'It is a man whom I have known for a long time, we were at Oxford together. His name is Dr Bullingdon Huff, and from what I have read he is the leader in his field.'

I sat bolt upright in the bed and tried to explain to Godwin why it was quite out of the question, telling him much too fast about Aunt Susannah and Uncle Samuel Huff and how I had always felt that Bullingdon was the Devil. Godwin did not understand my agitation. He appeared to think that my connection with his friend the mad-doctor was all to the good. It seemed to raise me in his esteem.

'Just fancy your being related to Bully Huff. It will be all right, you will see. Give him a chance.'

Bullingdon was coming by train and Carney was to meet him with the trap.

'He will be here in time for dinner. I shall bring him to see you in the morning. Try to have a little sleep now.'

I heard the trap arrive from the station, and Godwin's voice greeting his old college friend at the front door.

'Hey, Bully! Welcome to Morrow. I am only sorry it is not a happier occasion. Come in, come in.'

It was a warm spring evening and, later, my bedroom window was left open to the dusk. So was the dining-room window below. I could hear Godwin and Bullingdon Huff talking in a rumbly, desultory way, with gaps in their conversation, and sudden low laughs. It was about nine o'clock. They must be sitting over their port.

Perhaps they were talking about me. I got out of bed and, barefooted, limped as quietly as I could out of my room and across the landing. I stopped at the head of the stairs. I heard their voices more clearly, but I still could not make out what they were saying.

I descended beyond the turn in the dark staircase, from where I could see the open dining-room door and part of the room. I saw the sideboard with two silver candlesticks and lighted candles, and Bullingdon Huff, in profile, sitting at one end of the table. Godwin would be in his usual place at the other end, his back to the open French windows. I could hear everything they said now.

I retreated and crouched down against the banisters on the lowest step of the upper flight of the stairs, out of sight, so that if Bullingdon turned his head his eye might not be caught by my white nightgown. I could not see him but I could still hear. It took me a few minutes to realise that he was talking about his patients at Diplock Hall.

'Those little mad girls, all slack-bodied and soft, great eyes, perfect skin. Examining them . . . you can imagine. Sometimes they scream. There was this little one with long dark hair, bright eyes, she would not speak, never made a sound, never let anyone touch her, so they brought her to me. She let me touch her. But she was rigid. She knew I wanted to rip her open to fuck her warm little guts.'

An abrupt question that I could not quite make out from Godwin, and the harsh noise of his chair scraping on the floor. The sound of wine being poured.

'Well, naturally I wouldn't do that, Godwin. I brought her around though. I felt her with my fingers, and I used to shove my tongue into that tiny mouth and churn it around, pushing against the little white teeth and her clean little gums, her little pink tongue, my God it was the grandest sensation of my life. It gives me a cockstand now just to think about it.'

'Good Lord, Bully, that is unspeakable. Do doctors really do that kind of thing? However did the girl take it?'

'Girl? She was a baby. Five years old. She grew to like it, Godwin. She liked it all right. I had her put in a private room. She lolled her head around for it when I came in to see her. She'd look at me out of the corner of those eyes and open her mouth and mew for it. I'd been having a little difficulty with Minty – my wife, you know. Not any more. I only have to think of my big tongue in that baby's mouth and I am an engine, Godwin, an engine, a cast-iron mechanical hammer.'

'What happened to that wretched child?'

'She died. Children die so damned easily. I never tried it with another one, because I have never again had one at Diplock that did not speak. You wouldn't know what they might say. I think I might have got her talking, mind, had she lived. She said something one time, she said, "Mama, Mama." It could have important therapeutic implications. For hysteria, you know.'

'Bully, you are atrocious.' Godwin said something else that I could not catch. I was peeling the too-long nail off my remaining big toe, my chin on my knees.

'Well, you're right, of course, even though the modern theory is that it's affection cures these children, rather than discipline. But ignorant persons might misconstrue. It was somewhat unorthodox. Or was it? I wonder. As you suggested. I wonder . . . . It's not a typical case-study, of the kind that a medical man would ordinarily write up for a learned journal.'

'I really do not think that you are suitable person to treat Mrs Fisher. I regret saying this to a guest in my own house, but I must ask you—'

Bullingdon interrupted. 'Good God, man, you don't imagine— I was merely indicating to you, man to man, the subtleties of the profession. Scientific interest. It is not as if you were a plaster saint yourself.'

'But not with *children*.'

'Who knows who might not do what, in certain circumstances. The secrets of the human heart are not pretty, George. Besides, I have come a long way at great inconvenience at your request. I could choose to insist on seeing Mrs Fisher, if that became necessary. She is a member of my own family.'

Godwin's chair grated again against the floorboards, it sounded this time as if he were getting up from the table. I slipped back to my room, softly closed the door, pulled the curtains across the window, and climbed back into bed. I chewed my peeled-off crescent of toenail, and in my mind I went over what I had heard.

I was nauseated but not amazed. There was something in what Bullingdon said that I already knew about, or almost, but I did not know what, it was a fish that I could not catch. Later, I heard the two of them moving around in the dark garden, still talking. I suppose they had gone out to smell a rose.

Listening to him had cleared my head. Whatever became of me, I was not going to let myself fall into the hands of Bullingdon Huff even if Godwin could or would not protect me.

Godwin brought him up to the Grey Room in the morning. Bullingdon dragged a chair closer to my bedside and sat down. Godwin sat far off, at the table in the window, reading or pretending to read. At least he was not going to leave me alone with the enemy.

'Well, Cousin,' said Bullingdon, 'so you have not been well.'

He asked me questions about the accident to my foot, about my mother's death, my father's death, the loss of the baby, and 'the recent terrible tragedy': Peter. Some of his questions, about my most private functions and responses, were indecent. He kept on and on and I answered him not a single word. I just stared at him, my eyes wide open, seeing that his too-thick yellow hair with the comb marks in it was like old stable straw, it looked all right on top but underneath it could be full of rot and slime. When I would not answer him, he was put out.

'Why then, miss,' he said. 'I see that you are badly out of order, but I have much experience in the successful treatment of young females like yourself. You are in a condition that we in the profession call "Borderland". One way in which I might help you is by the use of electricity.'

I could not believe my ears. This man had the sensitivity of a steam engine.

'Electric baths, perhaps, or the Wimshurst machine. I expect that you have heard of the Wimshurst machine. The patient stands between two circular plates which generate static electricity – self-exciting, under any conditions.'

I happen to have met James Wimshurst. He is a rather eccentric marine engineer with an experimental interest in electric-light machines and other electrical novelties, which he puts together in the workshop at his home in Clapham. His wife is a jolly cockney lady, formerly a Miss Tubb. Peter took me to meet them, when we were living at Dunn Street. Probably, I know more about Mr Wimshurst and his machines than Bullingdon does, but I was not going to let any vanity of that kind persuade me to break my silence.

'I know that Cynthia Loring has had treatment from the Wimshurst machine,' remarked Godwin, sounding relieved, from the other side of the room. 'I really cannot say why, since she is invariably perfectly well. But I believe the treatment to be harmless.'

'Indeed. Many ladies find it very efficacious for toning up the system, after a hectic London season. Also, for my Cousin Charlotte, we could try live current, passed through the – er – intimate parts of the female organism. Or the Galvanic belt, or Faradisation. All painless, or virtually so, and most stimulating. Your late husband, I feel sure, would have been most interested in the medical applications of his own speciality.'

I raised my head and spat in his face.

He pushed back his chair violently and retreated to the window, wiping his face with a handkerchief. I snapped my eyes tight shut and listened to him talking in a quiet, too-controlled voice to Godwin, by the window.

Another set of power-words, another language, and all of it evil. The healer is the destroyer, God is the Devil. Better to die in a ditch.

'I have come across cases of this kind before. I should like to take her back to Diplock with me this afternoon and make a start with a course of vaginal shocks. Or ice, or leeches, applied internally. I suspect a systemic exhaustion of the sexual parts. We are quite used to this kind of problem, ninety per cent of our patients are disordered young females.'

'Why in the world should that be?'

'Defective organisation, and the deleterious speed of the modern world, combined with a harmful amount of mental exertion for which women are poorly adapted. Unsuitable notions – Radicalism, the Rights of Women, that kind of thing – can precipitate severe nervous disorders. I believe that may have been my own wife's trouble. But in this particular case . . .'

He lowered his voice so that I could only pick out words and phrases:

'No blood relation of mine, but . . . morbid heredity, I know the family of course, the grandmothers on both sides were . . . possibility of moral insanity . . . symptomatic of degeneracy, bad blood there . . .'

Then, in a slightly louder voice, which I was still not, however, intended to hear:

'What do you say, then, Godwin? Shall I take her back with me today? Take the fair young widow off your hands? Of course that may not be what you would wish. Your own business, of course, though I should have thought that a neurasthenic cripple of her class was hardly the ideal – er – not my affair, well, no. Although perhaps you could give me some guidance as to whom I should present my account.'

'You may send it to me. But as for her going with you to Diplock – certainly not, Bully, it is out of the question. In most matters I am content to defer to professional opinion. But I am not happy about it, and I am certain that Mrs Fisher agrees with me.'

'Perhaps my cousin is ready to make her own decision now.'

Bullingdon Huff is not my cousin, except by marriage. No drop of my blood, thank God, no cell of my body, is akin to his. He came back to my bed and sat down upon it. He leaned over me. I felt his breath on my face. I longed to open my eyes, knowing that he might harm me if he believed that I were sleeping. Yet against all sense I kept my eyes tightly closed because I could not bear to see his face.

He spoke over his shoulder to Godwin, who remained standing stiffly at the window:

'I suspect that my final diagnosis will be sexual neurasthenia, a depression of the vital powers. It is known that women's limited funds of energy are channelled into the reproductive process, which accounts for their somewhat inferior intellectual development. If reproduction is blocked or faulty, as in this case, they are apt to run out of control in unfortunate ways. The lower nature, you know. My wife has been a different woman since the little one came. . . . With my cousin, it may merely be a question of moral management. If I might just examine her?'

I felt his hand plucking the edge of the sheet. I felt his hand inside the bedclothes, then his finger and thumb inside the front of my nightgown, on my left nipple, tweaking.

I began to scream, and I continued to scream.

I cannot say that I decided to scream. Yet even when we are most lost, we still have a choice. Even the lost puppy running up and down determines his trajectory. The final choice is between submission and resistance. Then, even that choice becomes irrelevant. It makes no difference to Niagara Falls whether a woman crashing to certain death in its flood submits or resists. I do not know whether or not it makes any difference to the woman herself, in her final seconds.

Perhaps I did choose to scream. Perhaps I just like to think that I did, in order to give myself the illusion of having control over events.

I screamed so loudly and steadily that I cannot tell quite how Godwin got Bullingdon Huff out of the room, but I heard the door banging shut and then Godwin was beside me, holding my hands, stroking my arms, saying comforting nothings. I opened my eyes and looked into the face that I loved.

'Say I shall not go to Diplock. I shall die if I go to Diplock, I know I shall.'

'I made a terrible mistake. He is a monster. I had not known. You shall not go to Diplock, darling.'

'Swear it.'

I reached out to my night-table and found the green velvet bag. I took out the amethyst, placed it in the flat of his palm and folded his long brown thumb down over the central valley. I laid my own hand over the top.

'Now swear.'

He swore that he would not send me to Diplock. He said more, holding the amethyst, looking into my eyes:

'I swear that I shall do you no harm, and that I shall always be there to help you when you need me.'

I slept then, and when I woke up it was afternoon, and Godwin was back again, sitting where Bullingdon had sat, watching me.

'Charlotte,' he said, 'what would make you well?'

'I am well now,' I said, and it was true. I was bruised and shocked by events, grieving for Peter and for what might have been, and horribly fearful for the future. I should have been a madwoman were I not bruised, and shocked, and grieving, and fearful. But I knew now that I would get well.

From that evening we were happy again. I should not write this down, because being so recently widowed I should never have allowed it, but Godwin took off his coat and boots and breeches and slipped into bed with me to test, as he said, and then to celebrate, my certain recovery. We turned my sick-bed into a pleasure garden. It seemed far more thrillingly wicked than when I was a married woman.

Mrs Carney made a bag out of butter muslin to fit the empty half of my right shoe, and filled it with sand. We had to empty out some sand, and then replace some sand, and change the shape of the bag a little, but in the end we achieved our aim – which was to weight the end of the shoe in order to minimise my disability. I shall always have a limp, and stairs are difficult, but with my shoe or boot padded in this way the limp is not serious unless I am tired. Godwin bought me some velvet slippers which, with the sandbag in place, made me feel like a pretty woman again. He was light-hearted, and I followed his mood. He issued an invitation:

'Tonight we will have a special dinner. Downstairs. Just you and myself. No one shall wait upon us.'

I thought I knew what was about to happen. Of course, we should have to wait until a full year had passed. I had given the matter some thought, I must own. I planned to insist on no substantial changes at Morrow, knowing how much store he set on tradition and continuity. But I should like to have plate glass put in the drawing-room windows, to make the most of the view.

I wore the lilac-spotted muslin dress which had been part of my trousseau. It was not an evening dress, but it was fresh and pretty. In the dining room, candles were lit. Candlelight, the illumination of the poor, had returned to Morrow to mark celebration and ceremony. So much for the romance of electricity.

Godwin sat at the head of the table and I sat on his right, in a pool of unstable light. The polished surface of the table flowed into the shadows. Cold food was arranged on the sideboard: quails' eggs, a salmon, mayonnaise sauce, glass bowls of radishes, lettuce leaves, small potatoes; and a silver platter of raspberries on a bed of leaves. Godwin was attentive. He served me. He touched my shoulder as he passed by my chair, he touched my hand as he placed my plate in front of me.

'Tonight we must talk seriously.'

After we had eaten the fish, and the salads, he cleared the table.

He half-filled a stemmed glass with white wine and dropped into it, one by one, the largest, reddest, most perfect raspberries from the silver platter, until the glass was brimming. He held it up close to my eyes. The glass magnified the raspberries. They lay piled up upon one another in the liquid, each fruit a concretion of globules, each globule a fruit in miniature. Bright bubbles rested on them. Where the hulls of the raspberries had been pulled away, their mouths pressed against the glass.

I was waiting.

With our heads close together, we fed one another with raspberries, taking them one by one from the glass in turns, scattering drops of wine over the table. His fingers lingered on my mouth, and mine on his. I was waiting for the moment when he would speak.

I was waiting for him to ask me to marry him.

He kept his eyes on my face as he spoke.

'You must think of your future, darling. You cannot stop here for very much longer. It does not do. Have you – have you a plan?'

'I thought that we . . .'

'Nothing is for ever.'

My expression, and the rush of tears which I could not prevent, must have told him everything. Most probably he knew everything already. I must record in his favour that he did not look away, as would have most men. He kept his blue gaze firmly upon me.

'We have had great happiness. I shall always be grateful. But it cannot be. This is very difficult for me.'

That is such cant. It infuriates me even to write it down.

He had some genuine difficulty in saying the next words, but he said them nevertheless:

'I cannot marry you.'

Then his gaze wandered, as he talked his tortuous way out of my life. The family, the place, his position in the county, our different backgrounds, his responsibilities, his way of life, his sense of the order of things. It was all nonsense to me. Equally, it all made perfect sense. The explanations hardly hurt, in themselves. They were merely ways of signifying that he did not care for me enough.

He spoke of raising a family, of the children he hoped to have, and that hurt. He implied, in the most indelicate manner, that since I had lost one baby and failed to conceive again, I was not a 'good bet' – those were his words – as the provider of an heir.

I needed to understand him fully, and found the boldness to ask:

'Would it make any difference if I told you that I was carrying your child?'

'You are not.'

'But if I were?'

Again, that steady blue gaze:

'I should have provided for you and the child, if you had chosen to keep it. But no, it would not have made any difference. I could not make you my wife.'

How can anyone who is so kind be so cruel?

Only someone who is so kind can be so cruel – and I do not mean 'cruel to be kind'. Extremes meet.

We remained in the dining room another two hours, he in his place at the head of the table, smoking a cigar, constantly refilling his glass. He was drinking claret now and was on to the second bottle. I was pacing with my arms crossed on my chest, cold not only from despair but because the fire had burned low and he did not think to stir it. We talked and we were silent. Sometimes I threw myself down on one of the chairs at the far end of the table, in the near-darkness; then stood up to pace and face him again. I remember asking:

'Why were you so good to me? You looked after me, you saved me, you taught me, you reinvented me. How can I go back now to what I was?'

'You do not have to go back to what you were. You can become whoever and whatever you want. You are not penniless.'

He was referring to the money still owed to Peter, which had been paid to me. Godwin wanted to give me comfort as well as money:

'Nothing is for ever, but nothing is ever over. The loving we shared remains, in the eye of eternity.'

'It must be agreeable to take such a long view. In the shorter term – will you marry Lady Cynthia Loring?'

That surprised him. My bluntness was not in the best of taste. Desperation makes one sarcastic, and I had nothing to lose.

'Possibly. Possibly not.'

He looked down the length of the room at me. I was standing near the door, as far away from him as I well could be. The candles were guttering. He said:

'I am not afraid of dining alone.'

Feeling for the door handle, my hand encountered the light switch. I depressed the nipple button and, in the immediate glare, saw food-encrusted plates, dirty cutlery all awry, smudged glasses, crumpled napkins, smeared mahogany, empty bottles, chairs askew. The room smelled of fish. My romantic hero, sprawled in his high-backed chair at the top of the table, looked bleary. Streaks of stubble darkened his chops.

'Goodnight, Lord Godwin.'

Chapter Thirteen

That is not true. 'Goodnight, Lord Godwin' is what I wish I had said. There would have been dignity in that. In reality, I said nothing at all. Finding myself near the dining-room door, and then with my hand on the knob, I simply switched on the electric light, saw what I saw, and left the room.

I spent what remained of that night in the Grey Room. I did not sleep. When the sun came up I crept downstairs and found Mrs Carney already busying herself in the kitchens. I told her that I was leaving.

'I dare say it's all for the best,' she said.

She found me a big wicker basket with a leather-hinged lid and a strap. I packed my belongings into it and dragged the basket down the drive to the lodge.

I had arranged with Mrs Carney that her husband would come with the trap and take me to the station at midday. I tidied the lodge as if I were just going out for an excursion, leaving everything clean and nicely arranged. I stowed FRESH MEAT in the outhouse.

I began to bleed. It was the wrong time of the month, too early. Yet there was something correct about that occurrence – a relief, a release. The sight of the blood put a stop to any lingering fancy that I might, after all, be carrying Godwin's child.

I thought, as I rummaged for old towelling to tear into strips, how much I was losing now that I was no longer the uncrowned queen of Morrow Hall. No more crisp, creamy bed-linen, regularly changed by other hands. No more discreet supplies of spotless cotton wadding for my private needs, no more silent removal of soiled goods. No more marble-floored, mahogany-seated indoor WC.

If only blood were not red, or not so shockingly red. Miss Paulina said that the red was nature's way of alerting us to danger, so that we should know that we were hurt. That is claptrap. Women's blood is not a danger sign. It is a sign that all within is in order, even though when we are bleeding they say that we are 'out of order'.

When I cut off half my foot I did not need to see the pumping scarlet in order to know that something terrible had happened. Spanish bulls are said to attack the toreadors when they see their red capes. Red is the colour of anger. One speaks of men being inflamed with rage, and of blood lust. Men wish to see the red blood of their enemy in order to know that they have wounded him. If blood were not red there would be no war.

If blood were not red there would be no war. That is the kind of general statement that would provoke Peter, or Godwin, or Ralphie Doggett, to scornful rebuttal. There is one great advantage to living alone. No one can contradict. One is infallible, like the Pope of Rome, behind closed doors.

It was still early. I felt calm, and as unfeeling as a log of wood. There were three tasks that I had to perform. The first was to ride down to the village on the Ariel (in some discomfort) with Peter's heavy toolbox jammed into the basket on the front. Sarah Paternoster was flustered to see me; she was still in her flannel wrap, with her hair in curlpapers. Paternoster himself was away already on a job. Joe was not yet up. I was not sorry, I could not have borne to say goodbye to him. I told Sarah Paternoster that I was going back home to London, and that I was leaving Peter's bicycle and Peter's tools for Joe to have as his own. I impressed upon her how gifted Joe was at the electrical work. I found in the toolbox a scrap of paper with calculations in Peter's hand, and a blunt pencil. On the back, I wrote down the address of the City and Guilds College in South Kensington. Joe should get a proper training. If he did not want to go to London, I told his mother, he should go to classes at the Mechanics Institute in Hitchin.

I added to what I had written: 'GOOD LUCK, DEAR JOE'.

Sarah Paternoster, her roll of straw plait under her arm and her hands already busy, stood at the cottage door to watch me go. I walked all the way back up the hill, and once I was in the grounds of Morrow Park I struck off through the wood to the West Lodge. I had to see Mary Carney.

The door of the Carneys' house stood open. Mary was on her hands and knees washing the stone flags of the kitchen floor. Her back was presented to me. I saw how well made she was – how delightfully rounded her haunches under the gathers of her grey-striped work-dress, how trim her waist, how graceful her bare arm as she pushed her floorcloth as hard and far as she could, in widening black semicircles of wetness. When she heard me, she knelt upright, twisted round, and pushed the tendrils of dark hair out of her eyes.

'Miss Carney. I am going away. Please may I have a word with you? I am sorry to disturb your work.'

When I had spoken to her, once or twice, at the Hall, I had called her 'Mary', as Godwin did. She, working with her mother, was one of those unobtrusive people who made life there run so smoothly. But now we were equals. I was perhaps less than her equal. So I said 'Miss Carney'.

I sat and waited for her on the bench outside the kitchen door. She carried out a hard chair and set it down so that we sat at right angles to one another.

'I am going away,' I said again. To my surprise and dismay my eyes filled with tears.

'He's no good, you know. Not for the likes of us. I could have told you. He's like a child. Has to have what he wants.'

I had intended to speak to her, I knew not quite how, about Peter. Now I stared at her, a new truth dawning.

'I wasn't in Ireland like they said, when you first came. I was in London. In a Mother and Baby Home. With the nuns. That's what he and Mother decided. They called us Magdalens, we worked in the Good Shepherd Laundry. It was all in cellars. It was horrible.'

'Did you – did you have the baby? Where is your baby now?'

She shrugged. 'Fostered. Adopted. How should I know. Gone, they took it away. Then I came back.'

'But he is so kind . . . he taught me . . . he gave me . . .'

'He does that. He likes to do that. He is very generous. He taught me to read music, he gave us the parlour piano, didn't he? It doesn't make no difference in the long run. There's many a girl round here that's been down in the woods and fields with your Lord Godwin. Summer and winter, in all that damp grass and thistles.'

'The Amethyst Deceiver . . . Oh, it doesn't matter.' Mary looked baffled, but continued speaking. I had imagined that I had much to say to her, but she had more to say to me.

'Everyone loves him, they can't help it. He's not a *bad* man. My mother says he's just spoiled. He's never had a day's sickness, or a day's dullness, in his life. He's never felt thwarted. Provided he has this place, and his old friends from school and college and that, there's nothing can really touch him.'

'I did touch him. In his heart. I know I did.'

'You thought you were different. Well, so you were, we are all different. He likes that. That's what he likes.'

I could not stop the tears from falling. She did not try to comfort me. My grief and confusion fused and became fury, directed against her.

'And what about my husband then? Hadn't you had enough?'

Mary looked me full in the face. She has lovely brown eyes, quiet eyes. I was ashamed.

'Mr Fisher was worried and overworked and you were – you know. He needed company. He needed his bit of comfort. He wanted someone to talk to. Now, he really was different.'

'Don't you tell me what my own husband was like.'

But I was on shaky ground. I put out my hand to her, and she took it, and looked at it, and gave it back to me. I think that Mary Carney is a strange person, soft and hard at the same time. We sat in silence for a while. I asked her:

'What will you do?'

'There's Jim Cardew wants to marry me. That's the grandson of old Cardew that rings the bells. He works at the Sun in

Hitchin, driving the horse-bus. I might just do that. I might marry Jim. He says we could take Mullen Cottage, down at Church End.'

I knew that 'he' meant Godwin. I suppose practical assistance, such as Mary's Mullen Cottage, was what Godwin meant when he swore on the amethyst always to help me when I needed it. Mary did not ask me what I would do now. I did not ask her whether she loved Jim Cardew. It did not seem a question that could hold any definite meaning. But when I think about Mary, I do not see her as 'ruined', or as a castaway. Not like Jane. I wanted to ask her whether her baby had been a girl or a boy, but I did not dare. Did Godwin ever ask her? I do not suppose so. I recall the time when he and I passed Mrs Carney and Mary in the passage when we came from the billiard room, and the unperturbed smoothness of his greeting.

'Please take my bicycle from the outhouse, if it is of any use to you.'

I said goodbye to her, and we stood and shook hands. When I looked back, she had already carried the chair back indoors and was emptying her bucket out into the garden with a fierce, vigorous movement. The water rose and fell in a shining arc.

It was nearly eleven o'clock. There was one more thing to do. I returned to the East Lodge and took the amethyst out of its bag. With the amethyst in my hand, I walked as if under instruction to the spot to which Godwin had once led me – the field where the spring bumps up from the gravel in the stream bed, where the watercress grows. I pulled away a leaf and ate it, to know again the peppery taste.

The sun on the water dazzled my eyes as I crouched by the stream. I submerged the amethyst, laying it down on the gravel in the clear shallows where the spring water bubbled. The sun caught the amethyst in its rays. I lifted the amethyst out, and immersed it a second time, and picked it out again. I was about to rise and go when I was compelled to cleanse the amethyst a third time. After that, whatever I had been doing had been properly done.

I did not go straight back into the lodge, but walked past it out of the Hall gates and turned right, away from the village, up the steep lane to the chalk dell. The beech trees cast long shadows over the pit. The chalk, where the sun's rays penetrated, shone white. I touched the slanting boles of the trees with the amethyst, walking all the way round the hollow. I placed the amethyst on a ledge of chalk fringed with moss, and left it alone there while I turned away and walked up and down in the dell. Then I collected the amethyst, bent my head, and touched the spot where it had lain with my forehead. The chalk was cool.

I do not know why I did all that. I have no language for telling. A part of me was looking on, mocking. Another part of me believed that I was connecting myself to unseen forces that would give me strength. I still keep the amethyst always with me.

I was tearful again, from exhaustion, as I walked back to Morrow, and when I was back in the lodge I was overtaken by such a storm of weeping and shivering that I subsided on to the gondola bed and surrendered to my sadness.

Not for long. There was no time. I repacked the wicker basket with what I would take to London. I had one black outfit, which I wore for my mother's funeral. After Peter's death, Mrs Carney had dyed most of my other clothes black. Until the night when I wore the spotted muslin, I had rarely dressed fully; I sat around in my room in a wrapper. The black garments, which are of a very dim, uncertain kind of black, looked unappetising. But I chose from among them a plain skirt, a blouse, a shawl, and a black straw hat. I looked at myself in the mirror: pale, drawn, extinguished. Only my hair was alive.

I already knew what I intended to do. Because of my foot, I am unfitted for active work. I had almost no experience of the world. Whatever I did to earn my living must be done behind closed doors, alone, or rather alone with a client, but in such a way that I could remain in control. I was not proud of my decision then, and still less am I proud of it now. There was no alternative, other than an even more shameful one. It seemed inevitable, too, in order to preserve my connection with Peter. He had manipulated an invisible force for profit, and I intended to harness a rival force for the same purposes.

As I waited for Carney to collect me, I held in my hand the card that Mr Moss had given to me at the New Year party. It is bigger than a gentleman's calling card; it is more like an advertisement. I have it still. On the front is printed:

> The Rev. Percy Moss.
> Deputy Editor, *Light*, a Weekly Journal of Psychical, Occult and Mystical Research.

The London Spiritualist Alliance, 16 Craven St, Charing Cross.

On the reverse side there is a whole paragraph:

> Regular Talks and Meetings in the Rooms at 16 Craven Street: Mesmerism, Trance, Clairvoyance, Thought-Reading, Apparitions, The Human 'Double', Presence at a Distance, Haunted Houses, Communion with the Departed, Materialised Spirit Forms, The Spirit Rap, The Spirit Voice, Spirit-Writing, Automatic Writing, Movement of Physical Objects without Physical Contact, Theosophic Doctrines, etc. etc.

It reads like a school curriculum. I knew that I should not be able to manage all, or even many, of these accomplishments. But I felt sure that there must be a place for me among the 'etc. etc.'.

When I heard the sounds of the trap coming down the drive, I left the lodge, locked the door behind me, and put the key where Peter and I had always kept it – beneath an upturned flower pot under the tap.

So the widow returned to London.

I left the wicker basket at the station, and went first to 49 Dunn Street. I did not know where else to go. I sat with Aunt Susannah in the parlour and drank tea: two bereaved women in black, one thin and one fat.

I understood after five minutes that I could not move back into that house. My aunt was now paying the rent, and she left no place in it for me. She filled every cranny with her presence and her scent of Parma Violets. She kept the rooms very hot, with fires lit in both the parlour and the morning room. She had bought large blue and white vases from Liberty for the parlour mantelpiece, and filled them with ostrich feathers dyed purple and red. The photograph of my parents, and the photograph of Samuel Huff, stood between them. There were a great many new table-runners, antimacassars, crocheted mats and little tables covered with lace doilies. One could hardly breathe without dislodging something. At six o'clock Mrs Rabbitt came in, piled more coal on the fire, set the table, and served the evening meal. We had thick brown soup, steak and kidney pie, and a rice pudding with strawberry conserve in a glass dish.

It was all so changed that those things which remained the same cried out to me – the willow-pattern crockery, the old velour curtains, the brass pot in the centre of the table, 'The Light of the World' in the hall, the black kettle on the range in the kitchen, which I saw when I passed through to the privy.

'I buried him beside our Rose. It was what she would have wanted. I was very fond of your father,' said Aunt Susannah, dabbing her mouth with her napkin, peering at me from under her eyebrows. 'I looked after him all right. He did not outstay his welcome in this world, and he went peaceful, when he went.'

'You made an old man happy, then,' I said.

'I did. And he was not an old man.'

After we had eaten, she fetched from the top of the piano a silver-plated tray and a cut-glass decanter (neither of which I had seen before) and poured some Madeira into each of two tiny matching glasses. The drink did not immediately ease the situation. Aunt Susannah only relaxed when I made it clear that I was not intending to move in with her. We agreed that I should sleep in the house that night, and find lodgings in the morning.

We spoke then, at last, of Peter, and of his terrible death. Godwin had known him only as an employee, a clever member of the lower orders. With the Carneys, although they had been kindness itself, there were complications that I now understood. Until that evening with my aunt, there had been nobody to whom I had been able to talk freely about the Peter whom I knew, the Peter whom she too knew. I asked about his mother;

Aunt Susannah had heard that she was very ill. I imagine that she must by now be dead, and in her own dry heaven.

I slept in Peter's old room, the back bedroom. The supply of Ingelby's Ingots must have at last run out. Even the soap in the soap dish on the washstand was violet-scented. The fierce jade-green of the ewer made the cold water even colder. Aunt Susannah was using my parents' old room, which I presume she had shared with my father. To sleep in the middle bedroom would have been, for me, too close to her and to the past for comfort.

But talking about Peter had melted a chip of ice within me. Lying in his narrow bed, I remembered with absolute clarity a certain sunny Sunday morning at Morrow. I had woken early, and stepped outside the lodge on to the wet grass in my bare feet, wearing only my nightgown. The birds were singing their hearts out, the sun – still low in the sky – shone behind and through the trees, so that the leaves were a thousand thousand green lamps lighting up my world. I thought I should overflow with happiness, and called Peter down to see. He came and he looked, and he put an arm around my bare shoulders, but I could not tell whether he saw it all quite as I did. I thought, when he took me by the hand and led me back upstairs, that when we were old I would remind him of the magic morning when his great work and the promise of our love were new with the dew under our feet.

I clawed at the pillow on which Peter's head had lain and wept for him, and for myself, and for the loss of the living fire of him. He was a good person. He might, had he lived, have become a great person. I was too immature when I married him to know what a jewel he was.

Was I already seeing Godwin secretly then, in the time of that magic morning? I cannot remember. It is possible. How can a woman be so two-faced? All I can say is, she can. Two-faced, and both faces true faces.

Up to a point, as Aunt Susannah would say. She gave me a key to 49 Dunn Street when I left in the morning.

'You'll be needing this, maybe, one of these days.'

I recognised it as the spare key that had always hung from a nail in the cupboard under the stairs. It has a red silk tassel attached to it.

I found a first-floor back room in an old flat-faced house in Southampton Street, between Covent Garden and the Strand. I paid a month's rent in advance out of the money Godwin had given to me, which had been owed to Peter. The landlady, Mrs Cross, had swollen and bandaged legs. She did not come upstairs with me to see the room. She told me that there was only one other lodger, a young gentleman named Mr Doggett, who had the room directly above mine. There was also her daughter Amy and Mr Cross, her husband, whom I glimpsed slumped in a chair at the parlour table as I stood at the foot of the stairs. In all the weeks that I lived in that house, I never heard him utter. Mrs Cross said that he suffered from a 'medical condition'.

There was, after all, an inside WC, partitioned off the half-landing with matchboarding. It was used by everyone in the house. It was not clean. A smeared handwritten notice was pasted up on the cistern: 'If tank empty pleas use buckitt.' It was the task of Mrs Cross's fat daughter to fill up the tank every morning by means of the hand-pump in the back kitchen. Sometimes she failed to do this, and sometimes the tank was emptied before the end of the day. It was also Miss Cross's responsibility to see that the 'buckitt' beside the throne was kept filled from the downstairs tap. This too she neglected to do. I discovered in myself a belated sympathy for Peter's aversion, and thought with nostalgia of the old outside privy at Dunn Street – the excursions into the cold air, the scent of sooty earth and leaves, the light filtering through the cracks in the plank door, the privacy.

In my room, there were flimsy curtains drooping from a string across the dirty sash-window. The material, which had once been floral, had faded to grey and yellow smudges. There was an iron bedstead with sagging wire mesh beneath the mattress, a wardrobe whose door had to be wedged to stay shut, and a chest of drawers with some of the knobs missing. The paper on the walls was decorated with yellow and mauve roses. Whoever designed it had not looked closely at a rose. The floor was covered in brown linoleum with a geometric pattern which in places had worn through to the rough weave of the backing. Half a candle in a yellow china candle-holder stood on the bedside cupboard. Over the minuscule fireplace, which looked as if no fire had been lit in it for a hundred years so caked was it in soot, there was a framed picture cut from an 1872 annual, entitled 'The Grief of the Good Mother'. I shall not waste the space remaining in this book by describing it.

Nor do I wish to waste too much space on Mr Moss. When I presented myself at 16 Craven Street – only a short walk from my lodgings, on the other side of the Strand – I was shown into his office without difficulty. He remembered me, however, with considerable difficulty, eyeing me with suspicion until my embarrassed invocation of the magic names 'Lord Godwin . . . Morrow Hall . . . Lady Cynthia . . . Lord Dimsdale' set him to smirking and rubbing his long hands in the way that I remembered. I told him that I was now a widow, and that I wished to train as a psychic.

'So that you yourself may make contact with your lost loved one, no doubt?'

I had not thought of that. Even if I had, Peter's aloof ghost would surely have no truck with such indoor frowstiness. I had a sudden picture of Peter in his Heaven, winging through space and time with a toolbox in his hand, contracted to wire up the Throne of God for electric lighting. St John Chapter xiv: 'In my Father's house are many mansions.' There was work there for him for all eternity. I wanted to laugh, but with Peter, or with someone who loved Peter. It was not a fancy that I could share with Mr Moss. So I said:

'No, no, not really. So that I may earn a living. I believe that I have the capacity, the gift, to be a psychic. To help other people to make contact with their – er – their lost loved ones.'

The cant phrase stuck in my throat. But if I was going to do this, I must learn to speak the language.

'You will have to make your own way, my dear,' said Mr Moss. 'You have looks and a figure – somewhat unusual in our profession if I may say so, and not necessarily desirable, Mrs Moss excepted of course – but it remains to be seen whether you have the gift. We observed at Morrow Hall that you were what we call "affected", but that is not sufficient. There is little that I can do to help you. You must understand that I am a very, very busy man.'

He proceeded to waste ten minutes of his time in telling me all the ways in which he was very busy. There was the current issue of *Light* to be delivered to the printer and then proofread. There was work still to be done on the forthcoming talk on 'Success in the Home Circle', to be given in the Rooms – here he cast his eyes heavenward, so I presumed the Rooms were on the floor above. He was also preparing an account of the automatic writings achieved in his own home circle at Ealing – messages from his and Mrs Moss's infant lost loved ones – to be published in book form. And there were many country-house visits to be made. He was in great demand. It was deeply gratifying both to himself and to Mrs Moss that their spiritual gifts brought them into such intimate contact with ladies and gentlemen in the very highest reaches of society.

I sat on a hard chair, gripping my gloved fingers, while on the far side of his writing-table Mr Moss soared in the spirit. He returned to earth, gathered together some past issues of *Light* from the confusion on the table, stacked them neatly, and pushed them towards me.

'So you see, my dear, that I have no time to deal personally with novices. Study these. My best advice to you is to visit Mrs Bagshot . . .'

'Bagshut.'

'Mrs Bagshut . . . Yes. I myself do not do initiations. I believe Mrs Bagshut does do initiations. For a fee. She will take you on if she believes that you have the gift. If she is not convinced, she may pass you on to her friend Madame Mercure, who is more – er – shall we say showy, and less reliable, and will charge you more.'

Mrs Bagshut took me on. She lives in lodgings further down Craven Street, in a house close to the river. The ground floor, or what I have seen of it, is horribly damp, with furry black mould rising from the floors and spreading like a disease up the walls, which were once painted a dark pink. Flakes of this pink lie all along the angles where the floors and walls meet.

Her own room – upstairs, first-floor front – is stuffy and snug, with a coal fire, gas lighting, and green plush curtains drawn over the windows even in the mid-afternoon. Old carpets hang on the walls, and another is spread over the round table at which we sat. In the middle of the table is her crystal ball, which she uses, she told me, for consultations with personal friends only.

She was even uglier than I had remembered, like a fat frog, and more common, and kinder. Some people dislike sharing their special knowledge. They hug it to themselves. Mrs Bagshut delights in sharing what she knows.

'I want to be a medium,' I said. 'A medium of communication.'

'Ah . . .' She looked at me for a long time, and I did not find her gaze threatening. It was as if she were listening to what her eyes told her.

'You'll do,' she said, 'but you're a deal too pretty. Your looks will win you clients quick enough, but you will have to be careful, or gentlemen will get the wrong idea about the services you are offering. You must never, ever flirt.'

I swore that I would not. She named her initiation fee, and, looking aside, daintily requested payment in advance. It seemed to me to be an inordinate sum. Lord knows what Madame Mercure would have charged. I counted the money out exactly on to the carpeted table. She squirreled the coins away at once.

Then she made me comfortable. For the initiation, I lay on her sofa, with my feet up, covered by a rug. She turned the gas down low, so that we were in the deepest twilight, and she herself sat where I could not see her.

'What I tell you, now it's going to trickle slowly into your mind, and then into what's below your mind, just like honey dripping through the sections of a honeycomb when you stick a spoon in it. Never mind now just what's below your mind. I'm not one for the big words. We'll leave that to the likes of Mrs Moss. Today I shall just take you over the threshold into what we call Borderland.'

Borderland. That was the word that Bullingdon Huff had

used, in another context. For a moment, I stiffened in panic. Mrs Bagshut sensed it.

'There's nothing to be afraid of. I'm only going to be telling you what everyone knows only they don't know they know it.'

I went to see Mrs Bagshut three times, for visits of about two hours each, and her words did indeed sink into and through me like honey through the sections of a honeycomb, so that it was not so much like learning as like opening doors into rooms that were already there. When I think about what one might call my 'technique', I cannot say how much of it was laid down by Mrs Bagshut and how much of it was evolved by myself. But I should never have opened those doors without hearing her insidious, thin, vulgar voice, winding on and on in that hot little room at the damp end of Craven Street. She was without charm, yet she was spellbinding.

I shall never, now, work as a psychic again. But like all professional expertise, psychic skills have their uses in everyday life, which is where they truly belong, only most people have no contact with the power. Mrs Bagshut did not like the word 'unconscious'. She said that it was a negative word for a positive phenomenon. She did not use the word 'phenomenon'. She did not use the term 'subconscious mind' either, or 'divination'. But what she conveyed to me was that the divinatory faculty can most easily be released by giving the conscious mind a complicated pattern on which to work.

Women who sit at kitchen tables reading the tea leaves at the bottom of each other's cups know this by instinct. The 'rules' by which a certain formation of tea leaves signifies, say, a dark stranger, are accretions. They bear the same relation to true divination as church practices do to the truly divine. Tea leaves will serve their purpose – as will playing cards, or beans spilled over a plate, or lines on the palm, or animal's entrails as in the days of the Romans, or, I dare say, iron filings and a magnet.

Alternatively, and this procedure is more advanced, the unconscious mind can make contact with the mind of another if the sensitive completely starves her conscious mind of stimulation, rendering her consciousness as transparent as glass, through which one can see to the deeper levels. This is where the crystal ball comes in. I told Mrs Bagshut about my amethyst, and she approved of it as a professional tool. 'Highly original,' she said brightly, as if I had been describing the trimming on a bonnet.

She is such an extraordinary mixture of the spiritual, almost of the holy, and of the everyday and earthy. She told me that sometimes she composes her shopping list, over the top as it were, while deep in trance and transmitting spirit messages. So does she really believe in what she is doing, when she is the medium at a seance?

She does and she does not, and from my own experience that is all that one can say. She knows what she is doing, though it may not be quite what her sitters believe that she is doing. She has great personal magnetism and intuition. She describes being in trance as like being in a dream when you know you are dreaming, or as like acting in a play in which the lines, unlearned, come to one automatically.

She has a strong disinclination for putting anything into more precise terms. The learned professors who insist on seeking scientific proof of the spirit world will never, she said, find it. She reminded me how one only sees a shooting star by not looking directly at it, but by catching it in the corner of one's vision. She took trouble explaining to me how, when one feels some new knowledge rising up from the depths, one must never drag it up into the light too fast. It must shape itself in the darkness, unwatched. One must be psychically open and receptive to what comes – from others' minds, from one's own, from the spirit world – in much the same way as a woman's body opens to a man in the night. She said, or implied, this much only after ascertaining that I was not a woman of no experience.

After the final session she rang for tea, which her landlady brought up on a tray. As we sat with the crystal ball and the teapot between us, I felt sufficiently confident to ask her about what had been troubling me.

'Why is the content of much spiritualistic activity so utterly silly? Why the moving tables, why the raps? Why such trivial questions and answers? Why do mediums so often get the most basic things wrong, such as the names of lost loved ones?'

Her black eyes snapped. Of course, she said, any dialogue with spirits must be trivial. The sitters' craving is to believe; they will only be convinced by the citation of specific events or petty preferences personal to the lost loved one. The sitters are trapped in the materialistic world; only gross physical manifestations such as loud noises and moving furniture can awaken them to the truth. As for proper names, they are simply hard to transmit. A case of ethereal mishearing, or faulty connection, like a bad telephone line. She confessed that she had never seen or used a telephone, and neither had I for that matter.

Sometimes, Mrs Bagshut said, an irrelevance comes through, the medium receiving an image of something adjacent to the significant object, but which the sitter fails to recall. Rather, I suggested, as though a spirit were trying to convey the Niagara Falls, but the medium only received an image of the trees and sheep in the foreground. Something like that, she said.

We agreed that I should test my powers not in a seance, but by taking individual clients, trying my hand at clairvoyance, with the amethyst. Mrs Bagshut said that I should put an advertisement in the back pages of *Light*. She composed it for me there and then, scribbling on the back of an envelope:

> Young Lady Psychic, educated and refined, newly arrived in London from foreign tour, now available for private Consultations. Clairvoyance and Spiritual Guidence Offered. Discretion Assured. Mrs Fischer, 12 Southampton Street.

'It's not altogether true,' I said, and laughed.

'It's the same difference,' said Mrs Bagshut. 'You say educated and refined because you want a nice class of person, no roughs. Real ladies and gentlemen get uncomfortable saying too much to the servant class, unless it's their own servants. I could never get away with it, but you can, at a pinch. Putting Discretion Assured means you'll get all the love troubles. And you want to charge a lot. That way they'll know they're getting something special.'

'I am afraid you have spelled my name wrongly.'

She had also spelled 'Guidance' wrongly, but it would have been unkind to mention it.

'I've spelled you in the foreign way, on purpose. Continental. One must appear distinguished. Now you run across to Mr Moss and see that he puts it in this week's issue.'

The advertisement appeared at the foot of a column, just below Madame Mercure's. She was offering Thought-Reading, the Spirit Rap, and Thrilling Renewal of the Vital Powers. My own access to the unseen forces seemed pathetic in comparison. But I was in business.

Chapter Fourteen

My career as a medium was brief. I could cast the blame for my downfall upon Ralphie Doggett. At first, I did so. But that was not just. I must take the consequences of my own actions.

I became acquainted with Ralphie at the breakfast-table. Breakfast at the Southampton Street house, served in the gaslit basement, was a grim business. I, Ralphie Doggett and the speechless Mr Cross would be seated around the table by half-past seven in the morning. Places were laid on the oilcloth for Mrs Cross and for Miss Amy Cross, but they never came to sit with us. Mrs Cross waddled in breathing heavily under the weight of her big brown teapot, deposited it, and waddled aout again. Her daughter slapped down a plateful of sliced shop-bread, which we ate with smears of bright-red factory-jam. I thought of the preserves – blackcurrant, gooseberry, plum, and the celestial raspberry preserve made with uncooked fruit – which we had eaten on fresh pieces of Mrs Carney's home-made bread at Morrow. Amy gazed dolefully at Ralphie, and then stumped off, under orders to fill up the tank by cranking the pump. Occasionally, and one could measure the probability from the variations in kitchen smells, we were presented with an enamel platter of hairy bacon-rashers.

My first morning, I assumed that Ralphie was a son of the house. I heard the male sound of boots being dropped on the floor in the room above mine the night before, and attributed them, correctly, to Mr Doggett. But the youth sitting next to me at the breakfast table, enlarging the slashes in the oilcloth with the point of his knife, did not look like a Mr Doggett. He was puny and pale, shorter than myself, and seemed pitifully young to be out in the world on his own account. He was older than he looked; his stunted growth made him childlike. He wore on all occasions, indoors and out, a striped woollen muffler wound several times around his neck. Leaving the house, he pulled an outsize tweed cap from his pocket and slapped it on his carroty head. I do not believe that he possessed an overcoat.

He came from Liverpool. He had no mother. He reminded me, just a little, of Peter. But Ralphie is Peter without the grace, without the passion, without the intellect, without the integrity. If Ralphie Doggett were a puppy, he is not the one that I should select from the litter to take home as a pet. Life has taught him to be sly. He has avid, unreliable thumbs with square ends and bitten nails.

I noticed the nails, because his hand hovered so purposefully and so frequently over the plate of bread. Mr Doggett was always hungry. In another kind of house, he would have been hailed as 'a growing lad', and pressed to take more. But the plate was empty too soon. Pitying him one morning, and amused by his dedication to nourishing himself, I picked up a half-slice of bread from my own plate and slipped it on to his. We looked sideways at one another. His sharp dark eyes were summing me up.

After that, we were friends. Normally no one spoke at breakfast. But we set up a habit of muttering to one another, our words masked by the harsh hee-hawing of the pump in the back kitchen.

'You can call me Ralphie.'

'I am Mrs Fisher.'

'Oh, yes? So I have heard. I knew a Fisher, once. A rum sort of chap, he was. Clever as they come. Too clever for his own good.'

*

I never ascertained where the Cross family slept. They did not come upstairs to bed. I suspect that they slumbered in an insanitary proximity in some windowless back room in the basement, just in case a potential lodger should call to enquire after the upstairs rooms.

No one did, during my time there. Thus Ralphie and I had the top of the house to ourselves. Not only did I hear him drop his boots – one, two – every night, but I heard the creaks of his bed. He was a restless sleeper, or else he was not sleeping. I think he washed only rarely. There were no splashings from above, no chink of water jug against bowl. I thought about him before I myself fell asleep, if only because it was hard to forget his nearness. I dare say that he thought about me, too. My sheets were always slightly damp, and smelled musty. I dare say that his were the same.

Ralphie attracted me and disgusted me. Compared with Peter and Godwin, he was nothing. My mental dialogues with Peter and with Godwin – and, to a lesser extent, with Miss Paulina and with Aunt Susannah – continued unendingly. I talked and argued and pleaded with them in my dreams, and in my head as I sat at the breakfast-table, as I walked in the streets, as I took my dismal dinners in the Aerated Bread Company teashop in the Strand – I did not brave the chop-houses – and as I undressed and washed myself in that poky little bedroom below Ralphie's.

The evenings were closing in, and the nights seemed long. There was another exhibition on at South Kensington, the Colonial and Indian, but I did not have the heart to go on my own. They say it has made a loss. There is much unemployment, and the streets are unsafe. The mass meetings scare me. The police are just as rough as the roughs. Even the weather in the streets is rough. There was a terrible gale in the middle of October, with carts and market stalls blown over and horses running beserk.

Ralphie was a distraction. I was desperately lonely in London, even lonelier than I have been here, all by myself. Had there been a puppy in the house, I should have formed a not dissimilar attachment to it, and would have received more physical comfort therefrom. There was never any impropriety between myself and Ralphie. His grubby hands wandered once, and only once. We were never on what the police reports in the newspapers call 'terms of intimacy' with one another.

Yet the very fact that I formulate that possibility, withal negatively, betrays the fact that it *was* a possibility, for me as well as for him. The evenings when I had no clients were so dull, the nights so cold, the sheets so clammy. Did anything that one could call morality prevent me from encouraging him, or just fastidiousness and fear of disease? I would rather not think about it any more. I wish that I had not even written it. Yet I should never, now, condemn another woman for loose behaviour. I understand how these things may happen.

Amy Cross was infatuated with Ralphie. She had a pet name for him, which she employed with a terrible archness. She called him 'Mr Doggy'. She was a pathetic creature, as lonely as I was, though in the bosom of her family. I could not make a friend of her. There was not much in her head. Jane was a genius in comparison. Ralphie spoke most disobligingly to me about her in those first days. It is deeply humiliating to realise that Ralphie was in exactly the same relation to Amy as Peter had once been to me – the landlady's susceptible and inexperienced daughter.

The genuine bond between Ralphie and myself was that he had known Peter, from afar. Ralphie had been one of the promising young boys about whom Peter had spoken warmly when he was studying at the City and Guilds – not that Peter had mentioned him by name. Ralphie now had a regular job at the Grosvenor Gallery in New Bond Street.

'But they have had electricity there for at least three years,' I said, remembering.

'It was a terrible system – just a portable plant in the back yard. They were always having breakdowns and overloading problems. Now the power is coming from a proper generating system with overhead cables.'

'And are you the wireman? Are you in charge?'

Ralphie flushed. 'No. They've just brought in this Ferranti chap. He's only young but thinks he knows it all. He aims to get a power station built over Deptford way, to light the whole of London.'

The name 'Ferranti' was a little stab-wound. It was with Ferranti that Peter had worked in Hatton Garden, when he first came to lodge at Dunn Street. All these names, all these associations, a world, now slipping away from me.

'So what do you do for Mr de Ferranti?'

'Maintenance. There's ten thousand lamps working off that generator.'

Ralphie had vitality, and I am persuaded that he knew his job. Yet there was something unstable about him. He was a live wire; he was not earthed. He was interested in everyone else's business. He was outrageously interested in mine, especially since I received my clients in my room in Southampton Street. I had to divulge my new profession to Mrs Cross. I could see that she was sceptical.

'I cannot say whether Mr Cross will allow it. This is a respectable house. I have to think of my daughter.'

All she meant was that she would double the rent if her suspicions were justified. She insisted on answering the door – not a propitious beginning for my clients – and was only mollified, though cheated of her rent increase, when she discovered that the callers were ladies. Then she lost interest. Ralphie was inquisitive:

'What do you do exactly? Do you see coloured auras?'

'No.'

'Do you make spooks materialise?'

'No.'

'Do you have fits and talk in funny voices?'

'Not exactly.'

'Do you do automatic writing?'

'No.'

'Why is it always quiet in there? I thought I should hear rappings and hear your table falling over, and screams and sobs. Can I come and hide under the bed and listen, when they come in the evenings when I'm home from work?'

'No. Ralphie, that's enough. It's not a joke. It's bad enough hearing you upstairs in the evenings, thumping around in your room. You disturb the spirit influences. You deflect the power from its proper channels. It could be dangerous for me.'

He did not know whether or not to take what I said seriously. I myself did not know whether to take what I said seriously.

So what was I doing? Before anyone answered my advertisement, I had to part with a frightening amount of my money. No person of any quality would return for a second sitting unless I made my room appear less squalid. I did what Aunt Susannah would have done. I went to Liberty in Regent Street.

I had determined on a colour scheme of blue and green before I remembered, with a sinking of the heart, the yellow and mauve wallpaper. I opted therefore for purple and gold.

I bought two yards of purplish ribbed silk for a bedcover, and another yard to hang over the string across the window. I bought two cushions covered in yellow satin with gold fringing, to make the draped bed look like a sofa. I bought a round table, and a purple plush table-cover. I bought oriental ebony candlesticks, and wax candles. I bought two ornate upright chairs with seats uphostered in purple. I bought a black shawl edged with a deep fringe of jet beads, for myself. When Liberty's van, drawn by a smart black horse, drew up outside 12 Southampton Street to deliver these goods, there was a furore.

'Where's the money come from for all of this, that's what I'd like to know,' said Mrs Cross.

'From the legacy left to me by my late husband,' I replied.

'Go on! Tell me another. No better than she ought to be, that one,' said Mrs C. under her oniony breath, lurching off downstairs to the kitchen, no doubt regretting that she had not after all put up the rent. I began to hate that woman.

My room still looked horrible when I had arranged all my new possessions. It was horrible in a different way. Apologetically, I placed the amethyst – the source, I hoped, of my power – on a square of black velvet (cut from my best bag) in the centre of the purple plush table-cover. Then I stood in the doorway to assess the effect.

I recalled the old-fashioned restrained colours, the graceful, sparse furniture, the fresh flowers, the quiet air of the rooms at Morrow Hall. My room was not the room of a lady. Of course it was not, it was the room of a medium. In my last interview with Mrs Bagshut, I had asked:

'But is not one just telling the sitters what they hope to hear, giving them what they want, what they expect?'

'I should certainly hope so,' she replied. 'What good are we to them otherwise? Why should they come back, otherwise? We are the comforters.'

The room which I had composed, and the woman whom I was in that room, were what my sitters would want and expect.

My first visit was from Amy Cross. She came upstairs to look at my newly arranged room. She was overwhelmed. She thought it was beautiful. I showed her my advertisement in *Light*.

'Would you do the clairvoyance for me, miss? And the spirit guidance, like it says you do in that paper? Would you tell my fortune, miss? Would you?'

'You will have to cross my palm with silver, Amy, or the spirits won't come.'

This was not strictly true. Many psychics give seances for no money. I had a living to earn.

I tied the black Liberty shawl round my head, allowing the jet fringing to dangle on my forehead. I covered the window, and lit the two candles, one on each side of the amethyst. I seated myself in one of the new chairs, leaving the other invitingly angled on the other side of the table. This was my dress rehearsal.

Amy returned with a sixpence tightly clutched in her hand.

'It's from my savings, miss. I'm saving for my wedding.'

Taking a leaf from Mrs Bagshut's book, I spirited the warm little coin away at once. I gazed into the glinting mountain ranges of the amethyst, and indicated that she should do the same. Silence fell. I heard Amy's heavy breathing, and waves of her personal odour wafted across to me. I concentrated upon the amethyst, and upon Amy. I wanted to do the best that I could for her.

Concentration, candlelight, sympathy and silence: they have a power of their own. I asked her what she most hoped for. I asked her what she most feared. I think it would be wicked to commit to paper the confidences given to me in my professional capacity.

But it was all, poor girl, to do with herself and Mr Doggy. I found, then and later, that I had to say very little, but the little I said must be precisely right, like a fish cleanly caught in the drifting half-light under the surface of the sitter's mind and mine, in Borderland.

I had always spent more time in that condition than I realised. In the half-light, before the lamps were lit at Dunn Street, Mother and Jane and I moved around gently, continuing our tasks, our sense of touch and our familiarity with every object under our hands gradually taking over from our sight. Textures of stuffs, the skins of vegetables, the handles of knives, came alive in the twilight. We were quiet, caught in a collective trance. If one of us dropped a spoon, or a cotton-reel, or clattered a pan lid, the sound jarred. When Mother said, 'The lamps, Jane. And the gas in the parlour, please,' there was regret in her voice, and with the coming of the artificial lights the echoing blue outside the windows became flat black, the frontiers were established, we were no longer part of the dusk. At Morrow, in the Grey Room, Mrs Carney startled me by snapping on the electric light. I remember Godwin too coming to the Grey Room at twilight, when the trees in the park were tangles of seaweed rocking upon an ocean, and I a creature without a name in a sea cave.

'What, sitting in the dark?'

And he turned on the electric light at the door. It always seemed easier, between Godwin and myself, when he and I did not see one another too clearly. It always seemed easier, between me and myself, when I was not too clear about what I was doing. I am sure for example that there is a difference, in the profession, between a medium and a psychic – the same as between alternating and continuous current, perhaps – but I never asked Mrs Bagshut to explain it.

So I talked softly with Amy in the candlelight, and the words that she needed to hear spoken came to me. The concentration, and the current of feeling between us, made me light-headed. I had again the misty, feather-feeling behind my forehead, like the first effects of a soporific drug, which I had experienced during the seance at Morrow Hall.

I did attempt, with the first ladies who came in answer to my advertisement, to be a clairvoyante according to the procedures that Mrs Bagshut had suggested to me. I emulated her acute, rapid observation: the cut and colour and material of the sitter's clothes, her hair, her hands, her rings, her complexion, her figure, her shoes, her gloves, the trimming of her hat, the inflexion and accent of her voice, her mood, her temperament . . . . When a lady had been with me for just five minutes, I could have told an enquirer more about her than I would have guessed after five hours in her company, before.

I discovered that no one came to me who did not have some pressing anxiety, guilt, or grief. I discovered that there was something that they needed rather more than they needed messages from the spirit world. That was what they had been expecting, of course, for their comfort; and mediums are most happy to perform, and to demonstrate their powers.

What the women really wanted was not to listen but to talk. The amethyst released them. They did not want messages – or was it that I, the stranger, opened to their secrets and closed off from their ordinary lives, was message enough?

'What do you most fear?' I asked them, and 'What do you most hope for? Do not look at me, look at the amethyst.'

I listened, in those dark autumn afternoons, to rich women with veiled faces, to poor women with darned cotton gloves, to young girls with no gloves at all, to widows, wives, mothers, daughters, spinsters, to bitter, life-soured women, to beaten, abused, unloved women, to selfish women, lustful women, deceived women, diseased women, disappointed women, exhausted women, stubborn women, proud women, unreasonable women, and one or two silly, silly women. . . . Sometimes I wanted to laugh, with the unstoppable, exorbitant laughter that used to overcome Jane and me over nothing at all when I was a schoolgirl. Mostly I did not want to laugh. So many whispered stories, nightmares, terrors, so many tales of what happened twenty years ago and of what happened last week, tales of hardship, sacrifice, desire, incomprehension, disappointment, sickness, sorrow, betrayal and, against all the odds, a defiant sort of hope. It was hope, not despair, that brought them out of their houses. Despair crouches behind closed doors.

At night, as I lay in bed in that same room, their voices still whispered. The echoes were not oppressive. If I and the amethyst sent them away with new fight in them, they did the same for me. In the half-light of the sittings, pain belonged to no one person. Pain floated – not away, but out, out from the overloaded heart. Those weeks were my spiritual convalescence, and a spiritual investment.

But in the material world, my expenditure exceeded my income. I had to pay my rent, and to buy my food, some warmer clothes, boots, gloves, stockings, coal for my minuscule fire, and my laundry. Mrs Cross did not attend to her lodgers' washing. Amy did Ralphie's, surreptitiously, but I had to send mine out. The furnishing of my room had made a huge hole in the money I had from Godwin. I lent Ralphie some money to go to his father's funeral in Liverpool, knowing as I did so that I should never see it again. My clients stayed a long time at each sitting, and I did not evolve a technique for sending them away. I should have been seeing double the number, to make a good profit. Nor did I have the heart to charge the young girls or the poor mothers of large families. Mrs Bagshut I knew would have condemned my behaviour as unprofessional.

One day in late October I had a male client. Fortunately Mrs Cross and Amy were out. I admitted him to the house myself. He was a large fair man in his thirties. He handed me a card: Mr Thaddeus Thompson. We went upstairs.

He was embarrassed and so was I. We did not sit at the table straight away. He made a great business of putting down his hat and stick and hanging his coat on the hook on the door. He had a leather bag with him, which he seemed loath to let go. He was carrying a newspaper, and showed me a photograph of a massive female figure that had just been erected at the entrance to the harbour of New York. She represents Liberty. She is one hundred and fifty-one feet high, on a pedestal that is even higher. The sculptor's name is Bertholdi.

'It is hard to imagine something of the same kind being erected here,' I said. 'In this country they only put up statues of queens.'

'Not so,' he said. 'Just a fortnight ago, in Walsall, they

unveiled a statue of Sister Dora, who worked among the poor all her life. It was the poor who paid for the statue, too.'

He had an appetite for facts, like myself. I liked Mr Thompson. He seemed familiar, although I had never met him before.

When I had finally guided him to his place at the table, and directed his attention to the amethyst, I took a close professional look at him. He is burly. In later life he may become portly. He wore a black city suit – not, I felt, his usual clothes. His boots were brown and workmanlike, like the ones Peter and I had bought in Hitchin, more fitted for lanes and fields than for city streets. His face and neck are ruddy in the manner of a man who is out in all weathers. Carney at Morrow had the same deep, bright colouring, all the year round.

I did not break the silence for some minutes. I let it grow thick and sweet around us. Then I asked him:

'Why are you here?'

He remained silent. I prayed to the amethyst for inspiration. My eyes positively stung with staring into its jagged depths. Then he began to speak fast, gaspingly, as if under frightful pressure.

'I lost all my Beauty of Bath. It was that bad. I didn't have the heart to see to the harvesting, I sent the pickers away. You have to pick Beauty of Bath by second week in August, and get her into the markets right away. She doesn't keep, and she drops. I hadn't had the straw put round the trees, either.'

I have said that I made it an absolute rule not to commit to paper the personal stories of my sitters. I shall make an exception in the case of Thaddeus Thompson. He is an apple farmer, with twenty acres of apple trees at Chittenden on south-sloping land, he said, near Maidstone, in Kent. Two months before he came to me, he had lost his wife. She had been expecting a child. They had been married for a year. Her name was Clemency. Since her death, he had fallen to pieces. He was disconnected, he had lost his energy, he was lonely, the newly furnished house was a mockery, the whining of Clemency's pet dog a torture. His days had no purpose, his work was neglected.

'Same with the Hunt's Early. I wasted that crop too, not that it's so important, only for the local markets. There's not much call for Hunt's Early at Spitalfields. I brought some up to the house, at home, they're only little apples, and very sweet, but she couldn't . . .'

The big man wept, and talked for two hours. I summoned up my courage, and the residue of Mrs Bagshut's influence, and asked him:

'Do you hope to make contact with your lost loved one in the spirit world? Is that why you are here?'

He raised his eyes from the amethyst and looked straight at me with overflowing eyes.

'Is such a thing really possible?'

To gain time I passed him a large white handkerchief from the stock I had bought for this purpose. My clients frequently wept. The laundering and ironing of these handkerchiefs added to my weekly bills.

Mr Thaddeus Thompson is a man to whom one must tell the truth. I dropped my eyes and my fingers pleated the stuff of my skirt into folds.

'I cannot tell. I believe that the past and the future can – overlay one another. It is not we who cause it to happen. But we can however enter a space, or a pause, a moment, in which all is contained and also flowing. . . .'

I expressed myself badly. For one does not arrive in that pausing place directly, but down corridors, in the way that electricity runs in conductors, in the way – as Godwin showed me – that plants seed themselves, and small animals run, along hedgerows, culverts, ditches, strips of cover.

'I believe that we can help one another, if we have the mind,' I said, raising my eyes to his.

'Thank you,' he said.

He had seen my advertisment in the current issue of *Light* that he had bought on impulse at W. H. Smith's bookstall at Charing Cross. He was in London, he told me, with a bag of samples, mostly culinary apples, soliciting orders from the station hotels, the gentlemen's clubs, and Simpson's in the Strand. It was a step towards rebuilding his life. Visiting me was another, although if I had not been living so near the station he would not have made the effort.

'They all want Bramley's Seedlings now, since it won the Certificate. But Grenadier and Lord Derby,' he said, 'are best for dumplings. And Wellington for making mincemeat.'

'At home, when I was a child,' I told him, 'we always had Annie Elizabeth. Cooked to a mush.'

'Well, that's a reasonable apple,' he said. 'Pick it in December and it will keep until June. Named for the two daughters of the Leicester man who raised it, did you know that?'

He was slow to go. He was standing in the doorway of my room with his hat and his bag in his hands, his head bowed, as if forgetting what he must do next, or as if awaiting judgement.

'One of the little girls died, Annie or Elizabeth, or both, I don't know. . . .'

It was only after he left that I realised why he seemed familiar. He looks like myself, or rather he looks as I should if I had whiskers, and were fatter. We have the same strong and wiry fair hair, the same large light eyes, strong nose, serviceable white teeth. He could be my elder brother.

He left behind the newspaper and his stick. I cut out the picture of the statue of Liberty and stuck it into the frame of 'The Grief of the Good Mother'. There was more encouragement in it. His stick is slender, varnished an orangey-brown. The handle is of ivory – not a knob, but set at a right angle, and shaped on the upper side to fit the palm of a hand. I placed my hand where his customarily rested. The ivory felt warm. At the bottom of the stick, all around the ferrule, the wood was chewed and gnawed, like the top of my pen. Clemency's pup must be the culprit.

He returned the following evening, for his stick. He seemed to be feeling better. I saw his smile for the first time. I was uncertain whether he wished for another sitting with the amethyst, and hesitated. My black shawl was not in place over my head, and my hair was pinned back all anyhow. Awkwardly, he asked me to light the candles, and without further ado we placed ourselves at the table.

'Do you believe that your amethyst has special powers?'

'For me, it most certainly has. For the purpose of the sitting, it serves as a focus, to banish fleeting perceptions and release the unconscious mind.'

He asked me to remove the amethyst. I did so, unwillingly. I rose, and placed it upon the chimneypiece. He opened his leather bag, and took out something wrapped in paper.

'Sit down and close your eyes, Mrs Fisher,' he said.

When I opened them, there on the square of black velvet, gleaming in the candlelight, was an apple, a perfectly round, regular apple with a flat top where the bit of stalk was. The apple was speckly orange on one side and yellow-green on the other, with stripes and streaks of crimson. We both gazed upon the shimmering thing.

'It is a dessert apple, a Blenheim Orange. A king apple. That means it comes from the middle blossom of the truss. It's a shy bearer when young, the Blenheim Orange.'

Mr Thomspon took a small knife from his pocket, picked up the apple, and cut a slice from the coloured side. He looked across at me.

'The mature wood of Blenheim Orange trees is very hard, we can sell off the old ones to the railway company for making cog wheels.'

He spoke as if the interest to me of this information was beyond question. And indeed I do believe that it is important to know about things, as well as to *know things*, which is different.

He ate the slice of apple from the blade of his knife, and nodded to himself.

'Not too dry. They can be dry.'

He cut a second slice, and passed it to me on the blade of the knife, holding my gaze. I hesitated.

'Will you not take it?'

I stretched out my hand and took it, in the knowledge that I risked taking Mr Thompson as well, like Eve in the Garden of Eden, only it was the wrong way round, and what about the serpent? The flesh of the apple glowed yellow in the candlelight. It tasted cool and nutty.

'I can only stop one more day in London,' he said. 'This is the busiest time of the year, we are harvesting the main crop. What's left of it, after that gale. Tomorrow, shall we go for a walk?'

That night, in bed with my eyes closed, I saw the apple suspended as it were behind my forehead, like a lamp. But in the morning, I threw the browned remains of the Blenheim Orange away. It was just an apple, like a thousand others. Prosaic.

Twenty acres of apple trees in blossom in the spring sunshine must be a wonderful sight.

Chapter Fifteen

'You'd have to go up to Lancashire to find a Royal George. You'd have to go to Surrey for a Scarlet Crofton. You'd have to be in Sussex for a Colonel Vaughan or a Skinger.'

Thaddeus Thompson's map of England is an apple map. His lists are apple lists. We were walking on the grass in the Regent's Park, skirting the railings around the back of the Zoo, with the last of the autumn leaves falling all around us.

'You won't often see a Tyler's Kernel or a Crimson Queening outside of Herefordshire, or a real Webb's Russet outside of Norfolk.'

The language of apples is a tough kind of poetry. I wish that I had a language of my own. An outside language. Mostly, women do not. Women have the languages of the bed, the kitchen and the nursery. These are indoor, inside languages. Aunt Susannah, for all her fluency, was monoglot. Miss Paulina has, or had, the language of Women's Rights, which has a narrow lexicon, but perhaps I should have studied it as a first step. Women are grounded birds. We have wings, but do not learn any of the languages necessary for flight.

Some of Thaddeus Thompson's apple language was familiar to me from my time with Godwin, words which are used to describe all vegetal life – pistil, stamen, sepal, carpel, stigma. But Thaddeus Thompson's special knowledge was rooted in process and practice. He was speaking his native language when he talked to me about shy bearers and poor furnishers, about spurs, whips, and maidens.

He told me about the tragic deceptiveness of 'seedling vigour': wonderfully heavy cropping in early years on trees which had been propagated sexually, and then, disappointingly, fewer and fewer apples every year as the tree matured.

Like first love – or love for the wrong person?

He told me that he had to keep the mid-season apples well separated from the late maturers in the store, or the late maturers would contract premature ripeness from the earlier ones. Like little children picking up precocious knowledge from older children.

There was a melancholy five minutes when he told me about pests and diseases – a litany of woolly aphis, capsid bug, scab, canker, bitter pit. To change the subject I told him about Morrow, and the high pyramid of apples that came crashing down off the buffet at the party. He made me describe them. I did my best: they were small, pretty, flat-topped apples, red on one side, almost white on the other.

'That would be Api. Pomme d'Api. We call it the Lady Apple. French. But they import them from New York now. They are not much to eat, more for decoration. If you look in the markets around Christmas time, you will see boxes of them, wrapped in different-coloured tissue papers.'

I told him about the exotic fruit in the greenhouses at Morrow, and the two apple trees outside the front of the East Lodge. I described for him the lopsided sweet russets, and the big, round, green and yellow kitchen apples which Peter and I had picked and stored in a bin in the outhouse a year ago. I had made a tart from them, at Christmas. This year, had anyone picked them? I told him the bare facts about my marriage, and why we were at Morrow, and about Peter's death.

'We are two of a kind, then, you and I,' he said.

'We are.'

We walked a way in silence. I supposed that he was thinking

about our mutually widowed condition. I myself was thinking how companionable and likeable he was. He may just possibly have been thinking something similar about me, but clearly, for his own satisfaction, he also needed to identify the apple trees at the lodge.

'There's something called a Hitchin Pippin, but I never saw it. Most likely the sweet ones were Brownlees' Russet. That's a good Hertfordshire apple. Likewise Lane's Prince Albert, that'll be your kitchen apple. Lane's Prince Albert will keep until March if you store it well – somewhere dark and cool and damp.'

He spoke of apples, naming them, describing their qualities, rather as I had heard Godwin and his friends speaking of wines and vintages. He was an apple pedant.

'Those fancy fruits – pineapples and nectarines and so on – they were just a rich man's fad while they were a rarity. Anyone can have them now, imported, you see them in the markets.'

The trouble was, he said, that flour barrels of apples were being imported as well, from America and the Colonies, in the cooled chambers of ships. Not just the pretty Christmas apples, and no kitchen apples, but quantities of cheap dessert apples from October onwards. These imported apples were large and evenly shaped, not like our knobbly, irregular country apples. But they didn't have the flavour, he said stoutly, nor the variety.

He told me about the small, purplish, winy Devonshire Quarrendon – 'they call it "Quarantine" at Spitalfields' – which he liked to grow to pollinate his Beauty of Bath.

'It's no good at all commercially. It gets soft when you pack it. It'll go, it'll disappear. Like my Mabbot's Pearmain, that's a decent, solid little apple. And Maid of Kent, that's a big red kitchen apple with a lemon flavour. No future. I don't know. . . .'

'What do you do with all the apples you cannot send to the markets?'

'I sell them off to the jam factories. That mixed-fruit jam they make for working people in towns has a good deal of apple in it. There's a demand. My father was getting two shillings a half-sieve from the factory in his day. I can get twice that now.'

'The jam is not very nice, however,' I said, thinking of the falsely red sweet stuff we were given in Southampton Street at breakfast.

'But I can sell any amount of top-quality Bramley's Seedling for cooking, and any amount of Cox's Orange Pippin, for eating. That's all anyone wants really. When I went up to the Apple Congress at Chiswick in 'eighty-three there were fifteen hundred varieties on show. Cox's Orange was voted Best Apple at the Congress. That's what has done it. Bramley's Seedling won its First-Class Certificate at the RHS show that year too. Bunyard's in Maidstone, where we get our stock from, keep all of eight hundred varieties. But it cannot continue like that. I don't know. . . .'

He looked so worried. I felt sorry, and a little bewildered by this total immersion into an apple universe. Yet I was warmed by him. He was a good person to walk and talk with. Then we sat on a bench.

He rested his gloved hands on the ivory top of his stick, between his knees.

'Would you care to come and see the orchards? In the spring? In blossom time?'

'Oh, I should like it very much.'

'We grow gooseberries between the rows, and damsons and wildings for windbreaks.'

I wanted to ask whether Clemency had made jam. But she had had so little time.

'The house – the house, well, it's a good house. My grandfather built it. My brother and his wife live alongside. He's never settled, my brother. He is going in for hops now. It's mostly hops or apples, down our way.'

'Does your house have electric light?'

'Goodness me, no. We don't have town gas, either. We have paraffin lamps, and candles. Same as everyone else in Chittenden. The electricity won't come to the villages in my time, I don't suppose. Not that I shouldn't welcome it. It's only common sense.'

I was taken aback. I had heard electricity described as the force of creation, and as the force of destruction, but never just as a 'common sense' commodity. Some people make a mystification of everything. Others make a mystification of nothing. Who is right? I thought about his house. I imagined a cool slate-shelved larder, and rows of jars of damson and gooseberry jam and crab-apple jelly, labelled.

'You would take the train, and I should meet you at the station at Maidstone.'

'Yes. Yes.'

'If you are not used to trains, you would want to be careful not to miss it. Railway time is not ordinary folk's time. And you would want to travel in the Ladies Only carriage, else I should be worried about something happening to you. There's nasty things happen in railway compartments.'

Was this just 'seedling vigour' between us, or something better? What would the passion of such a man as Thaddeus Thompson be like? I cannot say that I have not thought about that.

He walked with me all the way home to Southampton Street. My half-foot was hurting, and I began to limp. Halfway down the Tottenham Court Road, he passed me his stick, without comment or question. It was dark when we reached the Crosses' door.

'May I write to you? I don't know. . . .'

'Yes. Please.'

'And you will come in the spring?'

'Yes.'

'My name is Thaddeus.'

'Yes, I know. . . . Thaddeus. My name is Charlotte.'

'Charlotte.'

He looked at me sideways. His mouth spread in a great shy smile.

'You will be my Apple Charlotte.'

Oh. Mr Thompson had made a joke. It could have been worse. He could have said that I would be his Apple Dumpling – though I dare say that might come too, in time. I returned his stick to him. He propped it against the area railings while he rummaged in the leather satchel in which he kept his samples. He brought out an apple wrapped in newspaper. Well, I suppose it could have been a tennis ball, but that was hardly likely.

'This is for you to eat on the last day of this month, All Hallows' Eve. It's best to have one about you at Halloween. Apples keep the spirits away.'

'But if the spirits keep away, I shall lose my livelihood.'

That is exactly what happened. I lost my livelihood, and my reputation.

Thaddeus left his stick behind again. Amy found it in the area in the morning. It had fallen down between the railings.

'I can take care of it. It belongs to an acquaintance of mine,' I said at breakfast. Ralphie raised his eyebrows.

I ate Thaddeus Thompson's apple at Halloween, thinking of him, sitting up in bed in my room. I do not know what variety it was. It was crisp and tart, and the juice spurted out and trickled down inside my nightgown. It was, in its own way, every bit as delicious as a nectarine.

I had serious money worries. I gave up lighting my little fire. I saved some money by stopping my advertisement in *Light*, which was a false economy. My clients fell away, and no new ones came. I thought of going for advice to Mrs Bagshut, or even making the acquaintance of Madame Mercure, but did not have the energy to do so. I was so cold, so tired. When Ralphie again knocked on my door asking for a loan, I confessed my predicament.

That was when he came up with his 'good idea', which he outlined to me as we sat in the evening at my seance table, with paper and pencil between us and the gas jet turned up high.

I was shocked.

'But it's cheating,' I said.

'You were cheating anyway, weren't you?'

Was I? I cannot say.

'We need the money, don't we? Both of us? With your so-called special powers and my professional knowledge, we cannot fail. We'll harness the invisible forces as never before. Just a little investment in equipment – and I can lift most of what I want from the workshop – and the right kind of publicity. Advertisements in the newspapers, flysheets, posters . . .'

'We can't do it here, though.'

'You must hire the Rooms at Craven Street, once a week for a month. We must advertise. We must charge the earth, to show that this is something special. You to pay costs of setting up, and of our clothes, since the idea is mine. All profits to be split fifty-fifty between us, afterwards.'

He grabbed the pencil and paper and began scribbling:

> The Beauteous and Gifted Madame Fischer, the Season's Sensation, Presents a series of Select Seances for those who Move in the Highest Circles of Society and the Scientific and Artistic professions. Unprecedented Proof of Spirit Manifestations. Invisible Forces. The Spirit Rap. The Spirit Shock. Personal Magnetism. An Experience to astonish the Many, available to the Privileged Few. Book now and avoid Disappointment later.

'Then at the bottom we shall have printed the dates and times, and the ticket price. I think we could ask as much as one guinea.'

I went along with it. The only hard part was convincing Mr Moss that I should need access to the Rooms for one hour before and one hour after each sitting.

It was essential, I said to Mr Moss in his office on the ground floor of 16 Craven Street, that I compose myself beforehand, to ensure that I was receptive to the spirits. It was equally essential, I said, that I rest undisturbed afterwards, to allow the unseen forces to dissipate naturally. Otherwise, I seriously feared for my health. I passed the back of my hand across my forehead, and sighed, and opened my eyes wide at Mr Moss.

'It has been almost too much for me, the discovery of how much I am capable in this line,' I said, loosening, as if absentmindedly, a long lock of my hair from beneath a new hat. 'It is a strain, though also a great privilege.'

'I shall speak to Mrs Moss, my dear, and let you know.'

Mrs Moss's curiosity was greater than her prudence, and we received the required permission from her husband. She even, graciously, offered to preside and to introduce me.

The only other problem was how Ralphie was to bring his equipment into 16 Craven Street without anybody seeing it. He solved this by going in early on the morning of 'the day', when no one was yet there except the servants, sweeping and dusting.

The Rooms are not as grand as they sound; they comprise the first-floor back and front drawing rooms of the house, divided by double doors. In the front room, there is a round rosewood table and a great many upright chairs. In the back room, which is an 'overflow' room for social functions, there is an armchair, a Chinese screen, and a large glass-fronted book cupboard used for storing back numbers of *Light*. It was in this room that Ralphie concealed what he had brought, behind the screen. Fortunately for his purposes, the centres of the parquet floors in both rooms are covered by big squares of turkey carpet.

From my dwindling resources, I paid for the advertising and printing, for the hire of the Rooms, and for a black suit for Ralphie. I myself made do with the blue watered silk dress I had worn for the party at Morrow, with the black Liberty shawl over it, and the little black hat which I had bought in order to charm Mr Moss. It is trimmed with shiny blue cherries.

I brushed out my hair and let it fall in waves upon my shoulders. Ralphie said that I must look truly 'beauteous', and as young and innocent as possible. We were at the Rooms by four o'clock. The seance was announced to begin at five. Ralphie had to work fast.

I am still not completely sure how the whole arrangement was contrived. The first thing he did was to wire up and secure a long, flat tin box under the edge of the table top, where I was to be sitting. He placed another tin box – a fancy gold and black one pinched from Mrs Cross, it had once held tea leaves – in the centre of the table. That too was wired from beneath.

He rehearsed me in the part that I was to play. I was to tap the box under the edge of the table, and he, controlling the proceedings from behind the folding doors, would cause the sound to come from the box on the table.

He also slid two pieces of sheet-iron beneath the turkey carpet, one under my chair, and one under the chair on my right. He connected these to a battery and an induction coil on the other side of the double doors. Ralphie said that if I stood on one of the sheet-iron plates, and my neighbour on the right stood on the other, the circuit would be completed when we both held the fancy tin box at the same time, and we should receive electric shocks. I, of course, as the source or conductor of the power, must pretend that I felt nothing.

Where the wires emerged from under the carpet, we rammed them down into the cracks between the floorboards, which fortunately ran from front to back of the house. We kept reassuring one another that the light would be very dim; a single candle on the mantel shelf, another on a narrow pier table opposite. The back parlour, where Ralphie must lurk, would have no illumination at all.

It was while we were down on our knees, concealing the wires, that Ralphie took a liberty. I had the sense to give him a good slap. He still had the red mark of my hand on his cheek when he stationed himself at the top of the stairs, to issue tickets and take the money. I retired into the dark back parlour and sat in the armchair, the amethyst in my hand. Just before we left Southampton Street, I had been trembling with fear and shame. Now I felt nothing at all. The die was cast. I had to go through with it.

That very afternoon, I had received a letter from Thaddeus. I only had the time to read it once, and quickly. Somehow, in the rush and confusion of that day, I mislaid it. This was bothering me more than anything else, as I listened to footsteps and the swish of silk skirts in the adjoining room, and the growing murmur of voices.

Ralphie was suddenly beside me in the gloom.

'They're all here – lords, ladies, professors, Members of Parliament – I made them sign their names in a book they have. We've done it! I've taken fifty guineas. All you have to do is remember what I've told you.'

I stood up, straightened my shawl, perfected my posture, and walked through the doors into the other room. I pulled the doors almost closed behind me, leaving just a crack. I heard a long-drawn-out 'Ahhh!' as I entered and took my seat in the chair nearest the double doors. I set the amethyst down in front of me.

The door to the landing and stairs had been closed and locked. Mrs Moss was sitting directly opposite me, her back to the heavily curtained window. She stood up and began to speak. I hardly took in what she said. I was realising just how crowded the dimly lit room was; all the close-packed chairs at the small table were occupied, and behind them more ladies and gentlemen were standing, crammed one behind the other against the walls. It was too dark for me to recognise anyone except the Mosses, although I did notice how many well-dressed, serious-looking gentlemen were there. To judge from the smell in the close air of the room, or rather the absence of a bad smell, no poor people were present.

Aunt Susannah used to complain that Jane smelled bad, especially when she was unwell – 'like all that class of girl'. I remember biting back the opinion that Aunt Susannah would smell bad too, however lavishly she splashed on the Parma Violets, if she lived as Jane and her family lived, with no privacy, no piped water in the house, no money or time to spend on herself. I know now from my experience of life in Southampton Street that a fragrant cleanliness is indeed an expensive luxury.

Yet there was a smell from one of these well-heeled folk, and in my vicinity too – the smell of peppermint. I recognised, to my horror, my immediate neighbour to the right as Lord Dimsdale, the Member for Hertfordshire, who had done nothing at all to make my life easier or more pleasant at the New Year party at Morrow. As Mrs Moss sat down, and there was a general murmur and a settling, he wheezed something odious in my ear. But at least he was sober.

I put Lord Dimsdale out of my mind. I did all the right things. Quietly, I called for quietness. I had the sitters place their hands upon the table. I allowed the concentrated silence and stillness to thicken. I drew power from my amethyst, upon which I fixed my gaze. I became a medium of communication. I opened myself up, inwardly, like a rose, to everyone present. None of this was feigning. There was a power in that hushed, crowded room. I would swear to that, before God.

Outside, the carts and cabs and cries of the Strand sounded faintly.

Wait, wait. A little longer. Whatever comes when I break the silence can only be—

—but a woman was weeping, the silence was already broken, and so I began, for twenty minutes identifying and answering the yearnings for lost babies, fathers, mothers, lovers, in a voice that was not always my own, in words which were not always my own.

Then my other self became impatient – the self that was not away in Borderland, the self that in Mrs Bagshut's case made shopping lists while she uttered mysteries in a trance.

This other self became aware of Ralphie behind the double doors, and remembered the plan. I made sure that my hands were hidden in my lap, and then interrupted myself:

'There is someone attempting to come through. With some urgency. This spirit cannot speak through me, the spirit cannot use words. Will you all be very still please. . . .'

I closed my eyes and let my head fall sideways. I sustained my gaze upon the amethyst, but allowed my eyes to lose their focus. I was putting on an act now, thoroughly in control of everything, and the realisation was like a power surge. Taking care not to move my hands, I began to tap rhythmically with the fingernail of my right index finger on the tin beneath the table top. The sound, greatly magnified, came out from the gold and black tin on the table. The effect was electrifying. (For once, imagery is precise.) The whole room crackled and throbbed with the audience's rapt attention. Not entirely rapt – on my right, Lord Dimsdale shifted in his chair and breathed heavily.

It became like a game. One rap for No, three raps for Yes.

A man standing in the dark beside the main door called out in a strangled voice:

'Ask the spirit, does my Lavinia remember? Does she remember? Does she?'

Like a miracle the raps came, one, two, three.

An old lady sitting somewhere near Mr Moss quavered out her question:

'Ask the spirit – ask the spirit to find out from my Benjamin whether I should sell the lease. The children are tormenting me over it. How am I to tell whether or not I should sell the lease?'

Dear me. I gave the spirit ample time to locate her Benjamin while I pondered what his answer should be. I must not be irresponsible. To be on the safe side, I gave her a single strong rap.

Thus we proceeded. This could have gone on for ever, but the seance must last only an hour and there was the second game to play. I made the raps feebler, and then let several questions pass unanswered in order to demonstrate that the spirit had retired. Then I roused myself delicately from my trance.

I told the people, in a voice barely above a whisper, that since the seance was so successful, and my sitters so unusually receptive, I could perhaps communicate the vital power from the spirit world in a new and unmistakable manner, through personal magnetism. The potency would pass through me, to another. This process was so draining of the energies of the medium, I said, that it should only be attempted once in a sitting.

I cast around with my eyes, as if selecting my subject, until I reached Lord Dimsdale. He was the last person I should have picked, but I had no choice. It was his chair that stood over the second metal plate. I asked him to rise and push back his chair, and I did likewise. He looked excited, and pathetically hopeful. I leaned over, and placed my hand on the gold tin box in the centre of the table.

I requested Lord Dimsdale to face me. I held the box up a few inches with my right hand.

'I should like you to place your left hand on this box, sir,' I said, 'and if, as I hope, you should feel the life force from Beyond surging through your being, perhaps you will communicate your experience to our assembled friends.'

Ralphie had overdone the voltage. I felt a very considerable electric shock the instant Lord Dimsdale's pudgy fingers touched the box. I was expecting it, but he was not.

Lord Dimsdale let out a bellow. He turned purple. He and I were still clutching the box. The continuous shocks were severe. I let go and he staggered, half-turned, and grasped at the rim of the table as he fell. He clutched at what he found beneath, which came away in his hand. He crashed down on to the floor with the other tin box, the one upon which I had tapped, held high. Wires, pulled from their concealed trajectory, trailed from the boxes towards the double doors.

Mr Moss was out of his seat and into the back parlour in an instant. I heard Mrs Moss calling for a match, a taper. As Mr Moss emerged from the darkness dragging Ralphie by the collar of his jacket, the gas jets over the chimney piece flared. There was hubbub, chairs were overturned. Lord Dimsdale remained rolling around on the floor, stomach upwards, groaning loudly. Learned-looking gentlemen threw the furniture around, searching for further devices. Ladies were shrieking and falling. 'Give them air!' shouted someone. The door was unlocked and thrown open. There was an immediate surge towards the stairs.

Ralphie eluded Mr Moss's grip and was off like a flash, twisting through the throng, too small and thin to be noticed, out of the door, down the stairs and away.

When I saw that he had escaped, I took refuge in the back room. I sat in the armchair and buried my face in my hands. Mrs Moss came and stood over me like a jailer until her husband had cleared the other room, hauled poor Lord Dimsdale to his feet, helped him down the stairs and, I presume, put him into a cab.

One is not obliged to chronicle every last humiliation. I should rather forget the next half-hour. It is worth, however, recording that Mr and Mrs Moss, that refined and superior couple, possess a range of insult and invective that would do credit to a stevedore. There is a whole lexicon of words in English with which to execrate undesirable females, and they know them all.

'A lost soul. Rotten at the core!' Mrs Moss was still abusing me while I crawled about on the carpet in the front room searching for the amethyst, which had been knocked off the table in the confusion. I found it. I went out into the November night alone. It was pitch dark and foggy. The gas-lamps were dirty yellow blurs. I ran in my lopsided fashion all the way back to Southampton Street, almost getting myself run over by the traffic as I crossed the Strand. A drunken man lunged at me, men on the pavement jeered at me. Once inside the house I ran upstairs and locked myself in my room.

If I heard any spirit voice that night, it was Peter's – a voice of reproach, disgust, disassociation. I had dishonoured him again, in a different, but no less appalling way. I had gone too far.

*

I was wakened at five the next morning by sounds of dismay and outrage from downstairs. I opened the door in my nightgown and wrap. Mrs Cross, in the hallway, heard me, and stumped quarterway up the stairs, which for her was like climbing the foothills of the Himalayas. She shouted up hoarsely:

'My Amy's gone!'

Amy had not slept in her bed. She was nowhere to be found, and what is more she had taken her savings with her.

Without a word, I ran up the stairs to Ralphie's room, above mine, and knocked at the door. No answer. I looked inside. It is usual to say, 'His bed had not been slept in.' Ralphie's had not, but it needed an expert on Ralphie's habits, such as myself, to determine the fact. Ralphie's bed was never made, it always looked like a dog's basket. But his new suit was not anywhere in there; nor were his cap, his muffler, nor his electrician's toolbox. This last seemed conclusive.

Slowly I went downstairs to break the news to Mrs Cross. We sat in the kitchen drinking tea. We had both lost something. She had lost Amy, I had lost my profession and my share of the fifty guineas earned – is that the right word? – the night before. I wondered why Ralphie had decided to take Amy with him. Maybe he had fancied her all along. Maybe he fancied her savings. Maybe she had surprised him on his way out of the house, and made an emotional scene, or threatened to alert her mother – to whom Ralphie owed three months' rent – unless he took her with him. Amy at least had what she wanted. She was with Mr Doggy.

'After all I did for that young man. Treated him like my own son. He was a snake in the grass. I just hope he will be good to her, and make an honest woman of her,' said Mrs Cross, wiping her tear-bleared eyes on her sleeve, looking more like a mud-stained turnip than ever in the dawn light. Yet for the first time I found her likeable, or potentially so. She did not attempt to evoke Mr Cross's Olympian paternal fury for my benefit. Convenient fictions cannot survive inconvenient disasters.

'A snake in the grass,' she repeated over and over. The formula seemed to satisfy her need for any further explanation.

'I am sure that he will be good to her,' I said. I am not sure of it at all. As for myself, I discovered when I went back upstairs, I had precisely five shillings left to my name in the whole world.

I was ill, after that. I stayed in my room for two weeks, limping downstairs for cups of tea and jam sandwiches, which I carried back upstairs to my lair. Mrs Cross and I treated one another carefully, like invalids. I owed her for the rent, but she did not mention it.

I do not know whether she heard gossip about my disgrace. The Mosses had told me they would keep the affair out of the newspapers, but only so as not to smirch the honour of the Spiritualist Alliance, or to damage their own standing with their influential friends. Mr Moss would feel impelled, he told me during that bad half-hour, to write personal letters to everyone who had signed the book, disassociating the Society from the shameful episode. 'An impious female charlatan has abused our trust,' and so on.

Perhaps Mrs Cross heard something in the local shops. Her demeanour towards me changed. She remained kind, but lofty. I envisaged a future in which I never found the strength or means to leave that house, but remained there for ever, becoming by default Mrs Cross's servant, becoming Jane.

There was no word for Mrs Cross from Amy. A picture postcard came for me from Thaddeus. The picture was of Maidstone railway station. He asked whether I had received his letter, and trusted that all was well. He would, he said, be very happy to hear from me.

I wrote to him. I told him how upset I was that I had lost his letter. I told him that I had been in bad trouble, that I had been ill, and did not know what to do. I told him that I remembered our walk in the Regent's Park as the last happy day that I had known. I wrote five pages.

Then I tore my letter up. I wrote again, very briefly, saying that I was taking good care of his stick and would restore it to him when I visited Chittenden in the spring. I signed the letter, 'Your friend, Charlotte Fisher.'

I addressed the envelope. I tidied my foul bedroom, opened the window, washed myself, dressed, put on my boots with the stuffed right toe, and walked out into the day to buy a stamp and post my letter.

Chapter Sixteen

I have never talked to anyone about the death of Aunt Susannah, except, later, to the coroner. There has been no one whom I wanted to tell.

I cannot say what impelled me to go out to Dunn Street. Perhaps it was the Lady Apples. I took my walks northwards, into Covent Garden, since I risked meeting the Mosses or some other censorious figure from the Spiritualist Alliance if I ventured into the Strand. I saw in the market tiers of boxes containing the alluring little red and white fruits, lying in rows in their coloured papers, just as Thaddeus had described to me. They signalled the approach of Christmas, and Christmas made me remember my family, or what remained of it.

I woke up one of those raw, grey mornings with a compelling need to visit Aunt Susannah. In case she should be away from the house, I placed in my pocket the key with the tassel which she had given to me on my last visit. I hailed a cab at the junction of Southampton Street and the Strand, and was driven all the way to Dunn Street – a hideous extravagance, given my circumstances.

When we reached the door of number 49 I asked the driver to wait. Maybe I had a premonition.

The curtains were drawn across the front parlour windows, but that was not unusual. I knocked, and waited, but no one came. I let myself in with my key and called out. There was no answer. All the doors downstairs were closed except the kitchen door at the bottom of the hall passage.

So, peeling off my gloves, I went into the kitchen. It was clean and quiet, and icy. The fire was not lit, the range was cold to the touch. The sink in the scullery was clean, and in the sink the enamel bowl was upturned, a dish-rag spread over it. I touched the rag; it was stiff, bone-dry, as were the bristles of the scrubbing brush on the draining board. The wood of the board was sweet and clean, with no slime in its grooves. I turned the tap, but no water flowed.

Everything that came into the house from outside, including as I discovered the gas, had been shut off. The table and chairs were neatly in place, the familiar willow-pattern crockery was on the dresser tidily arranged, the floor was spotless.

I went back down the passage to the front of the house. There was an odour – sweetish, and unpleasant. It is customary to describe the hallways of such houses as smelling of cabbage. In my experience they do not. To say a house smells of cabbage is a euphemism for saying that a house is common and vulgar; or perhaps, for suggesting unmentionable fumes from drains and inside privies, Peter's old obsession. The smell in the Dunn Street house that day was of Aunt Susannah's Parma Violets, with something else.

I opened the door of the little room that she had usurped from my mother. Here too everything was in perfect order, with an air of settled permanence. Jane's acts of destruction and defilement seemed, in retrospect, unbelievable. The fireplace had been cleaned out and the hearthstone washed. There was not a speck on the Brussels carpet nor on the linoleum surround. The barrel-like cover was clipped over the sewing machine. There was no wrinkle in the Indian scarf spread over the back of the settee and the cushions were plumped up.

The same in the front parlour. I drew back the old velvet curtains. As in the other rooms, the windows were closed and the catches fastened across the sashes. The piano top and the mahogany table were polished to a high shine, as was the brass plant holder. Father's old armchair and the other one were set symmetrically aslant on either side of the empty grate.

The house was a tomb, enclosing a frozen orderliness. I dreaded going upstairs.

All three bedroom doors were shut. I peeped quickly into Peter's old room at the back, and saw the jade-green toilet set, a clean white counterpane on the narrow bed, nothing untoward. All traces of our joint occupation had been removed. In the room I once shared with Aunt Susannah the big bed had a dustsheet over it. There was a new toilet set, I noticed, to replace the odd jug and basin I remembered. It was of white china with a sprawling pattern of orange flowers. Not very pretty. I opened the wardrobe and saw an old brown dress of my own, a tatty grey pelisse that had been my mother's, and on the floor of the wardrobe some scuffed boots which could have belonged to either of us, I didn't remember. Horrible.

Then I opened the door of the front bedroom.

Aunt Susannah was lying on her back in the middle of the double bed, her head on a mound of fresh pillows. Her hands were folded over a clean, ironed linen sheet. She was wearing a white nightdress. I knew that she was absolutely dead. One cannot be just a little bit dead, it is all or nothing. Her face was all smoothed out, her skin a pure dark ivory. Her hair was neatly arranged under a starched cap. Under the aberrant eyebrows her eyes were half-open.

I stood beside the bed. I touched her cold hand. I said aloud:

'Aunt Susannah . . .'

I did not kiss her, I did not think of it or perhaps I should have done so. I sat down on the chair furthest from the bed, quite suddenly trembling all over, and cold. I was afraid that I was going to faint, or be sick. I put my hands over my face and rocked back and forth.

The nausea passed. I rose from the chair and opened the window as wide as I could, not only to let the Parma Violets and the other odour out and to air the room, but to let her spirit fly free. It would be terrible for her soul, any soul, to be locked up in

49 Dunn Street for all eternity. Why does one say 'all eternity'? There is no such thing as a portion of eternity.

Until I opened the window I had, like the house, seemed in suspension. I looked out into the street and saw my cab waiting. The outside world existed.

Turning back into the room I looked around. It was completely neat and tidy, like the rest of the house, no clothes on the chairs. But there were two sealed envelopes on the dressing-table. One was stamped, and addressed in Aunt Susannah's handwriting to Dr Bullingdon Huff at Diplock Hall. The other was for me: Mrs Fisher. No stamp, no address.

I sat on the edge of the bed beside my dead aunt and opened the envelope.

Dear Niece,

I had intended to write you a letter but I have fairly worn myself out tidying and cleaning up and there is little to say now I come to do it. I have paid Mrs Rabbitt what she is owed, and written her a good character, and let her go. I have left everything in order in the house. Do not try to grieve, there is no call for it. My Will is in the Bank, I have told Bullingdon all that he will need to know, in my letter to him. He has my money and my goods and chattels, for Samuel Huff's sake. The rent is paid until the end of March, so you must think if you want to keep the house on, the lease is still in your Father's name. I should like to have done more for you. Take any small things of mine that you want. Take the Heart pincushion. There is something inside it and I should not want that Minty to have it.

Your aff$^{\underline{tc}}$ Aunt,
S. Huff.

I looked sideways at Aunt Susannah's yellow face, and imagined her writing the two notes after spending a day, two days, three days, putting the house to rights once and for all. She must have been planning her death for weeks, all on her own, telling no one, not insane as doctors would imagine but in control to the end. She made up the bed with the best linen as her deathbed. I did not weep, I stroked her feet through the sheet and the rose-patterned quilt. I wondered whether she was in the presence of God, or of Granny Henshaw. 'She was God in our house.'

I do not know how my aunt had taken her life but I can imagine. She would have known what to take, and how much, from her powerful array of powders, draughts, pills and tinctures.

It was only later that I understood that she had been dead for about three days and that she had, so far as is possible, laid herself out, plugging her back passage with a piece of towelling. No loss of control for Aunt Susannah. Self-respect, she would have said. Consideration for others.

And why had she done it? There was no one to stay for, I suppose. 'A woman's life is nothing without a man.'

I opened a drawer and was faced with her collection of black wraps and tippets – arranged neatly in piles, not all in a confusion as they had been when I was sharing a room with her. I did not want any of her clothes. I closed the drawer. On top of the chest her black lace mittens lay in a crumpled ball. I could not touch them. Dead spiders.

I took a half-full bottle of Parma Violets as a memento. The velvet pincushion hung as always from its twisted cord on the pinnacle of her mirror. I unhooked the cord and pressed the soft fat heart between my fingers. Yes, there was something inside it.

I closed and secured the window again, picked up the letter for horrible Bullingdon Huff from the dressing-table, and looked a last goodbye to my aunt. There was a curling black hair growing out of her chin. I took the nail scissors from the top of her chest and snipped it off. I think that is what she would have wanted. I came back down the stairs. I took the Bridport photograph of my parents from the parlour mantel shelf, but nothing else.

It was a waste of Aunt Susannah's time really, all that cleaning and ordering. Perfection cannot hold. Already the house had lost its meaning. Those who would soon come, sent by Bullingdon to pack her ornaments, linen and silverware into crates, and her mahogany chest and Brussels carpet into a van, would have no idea how intimately these objects had been known by her, as I know those Mortimer things that have always been together as if parts of the same body – the brass plant-holder and the dining-table, the bobble-fringe hanging from the mantel. Clumpings of matter, unclumped and dispersed. It's the same with people. Already there was no trace of my father in the house. It was as if he had never lived there. Aunt Susannah too would be packed in a box, taken away and buried in the earth.

In the kitchen, I slit a seam in the pincushion with a pointed knife. Whatever it was fell out on to the floor. I picked it up.

It was a gold ring set with a jewel – a rectangular faceted diamond with a point in the centre. I learned later, when I sold the ring, that a diamond cut in that way is called a baguette, and the pointed centre is called the pavilion. The diamond was cold and faintly greasy to the touch.

Godwin – or was it Peter? – told me once that a diamond will burn, if heated high enough. It must be surely be the strangest thing, to see a diamond burst into flames.

Mine was only reflecting the available light, but in that dim kitchen it seemed the source of all light. I made out some letters around the inside of the ring, at the back, engraved in copper-plate: 'S.H. to S.H. For Ever'. Samuel Huff to Susannah Huff. Nothing is for ever.

I put the ring on the middle finger of my left hand. I found pen and ink in the dresser and wrote a note to Dr Hibbs on the back of a receipted coal bill from the same drawer. I recommended my uncle Digby Mortimer for the funeral arrangements. At least Aunt Susannah should be handled by one of the family. In death we are not divided, as Uncle Digby said to me at my wedding. Oh, but we are.

With difficulty I dragged my glove on over the diamond, took a last look round, and on impulse ran upstairs again to my old room and took from the wardrobe the grey pelisse that had belonged to my mother. Aunt Susannah made quite sure that I should remember her. In economic terms she had saved my life. She had given me her heart. But it was my poor forgotten mother who gave me my life.

I never thought I would have been glad of that pelisse, but my goodness I have. It is round my shoulders now.

I found a dark-red oilcloth shopping bag on a hook in the

scullery, into which I put the photograph, the heart pincushion, the folded-up pelisse, and the Parma Violets. As I left the house I paused and took a last look at 'The Light of the World' in the hallway.

There He was, still standing on the threshold, His right hand still on the latch of the door, His halo and His pretty lantern still shining. I said to Him aloud, in an Aunt Susannah voice:

'Well, are you going out or coming in? Make up your mind.'

The words rang out in the dead house. I was perspiring. I felt chilled to the bone. I stood for a moment in the doorway and then stepped out on to the path, into the fresh air, shutting the front door firmly behind me.

I directed the cabby to drive me round to Dr Hibbs's house, two streets away. There I handed in my note to the maid who answered the door. I did not want to speak to Dr Hibbs. I returned in the cab to the West End, rid myself of the letter to Bullingdon Huff in a pillar box in St James's Street, dragged myself back to Southampton Street, fell on my bed and slept for I cannot tell how long. I was never so exhausted in my life.

I went to Hatton Garden to sell the diamond. Hatton Garden is not a garden, but a wide street running between the Clerkenwell Road and Holborn. I approached it crabwise, through alleys leading from Leather Lane, where there is a street market far more interesting and various than the one outside my old school in Goodge Street. Almost at once, I spotted 57 Hatton Garden – it is on the corner with the narrow street called Hatton Wall – and looked up at the grimy windows of the attic storey, where Peter had worked with Sebastian de Ferranti. I knew Ferranti was no longer there; he moved to a better workshop in Charterhouse Square soon afterwards. I should like to have met him. Now, I never shall.

Peter used to tell me how the houses along Hatton Garden were occupied by pawnbrokers and diamond merchants, mostly Jews fleeing from troubles in foreign parts. Entering that street is indeed like walking into another country. The Jewish diamond men stand on the pavements in two and threes, with their big black hats and long black coats and thick black beards, peering at what one of them holds in a curved palm, something in a screw of paper.

I did not dare to approach these traders, but chose at random one of the shops a few doors down from number 57. It was an old house with a bow window, and the hanging sign said: 'Edward Barnard. Est. 1680', so I reckoned they must know their business.

I had to knock on the door. It was opened unto me by a very old man. I never penetrated further than his hallway. He took the ring, squinted at it for just a few seconds, and said:

'One hundred pounds.'

This was too abrupt for me. I could not part with the ring with so little discussion. I said:

'Thank you, I must think about it.'

I continued down the same side of the street towards Holborn, past the charity school, and went at random into another shop, which had the name 'Landsberg' painted over the door.

There was a young man in a skullcap at the front counter, which was of plain polished wood. There were no jewels in sight. I showed him the ring and asked him what it was worth.

He took trouble. He brought out a square of black cloth and laid the ring upon it. He looked at it. He fixed a glass in his eye, picked up the ring and examined it. He gave me a keen glance, and then disappeared with the ring through a door at the back – to speak to his brother, he said. I felt guilty, fearing that I should be suspected of having stolen the ring. While I waited, I rehearsed my true story as though it were a lie.

In the event, I was not interrogated. The young merchant was more interested in talking than in listening. He spoke softly in his private language of baguette, pavilion and carat (four: good). He regretted that the setting was out of fashion. He offered me – one hundred pounds.

I accepted the offer. One hundred pounds must be the ring's true worth, in Hatton Garden. The complacency with which he concluded the transaction, paying me with used £5 notes which he counted out in front of me, and placed in a cloth bag, suggested that the stone was worth more, to someone, somewhere.

A diamond is pure carbon, the element which makes coal, coke, soot, black lead and lampblack what they are. An element is an ultimate component, a fundamental principle. To me, one hundred pounds is a fortune. A fundamental principal is, that people must eat. On my way home, I bought two hot mutton pies – one for me, one for Mrs Cross – and a pound of the pretty Christmas apples. In the olden days, they used to believe that diamonds averted insanity. It might be more true to say that the wealth which diamonds represent averts starvation, preceded by insanity.

Ask, and it shall be given unto you. Having money again, I made an attempt to acquire yet more, in the only way that I knew. Going up in the world, as I imagined, I hired a room above the closed-up music hall in Leicester Square, the building in which Madame Mercure holds her sittings. The warren of apartments behind and above the hall are let out to surgeons specialising in female complaints, attorneys, moneylenders, actresses, French teachers, and so on. Their cards are pinned up on a board just inside the doorway. I wrote out one of my own. I brought the purple table cover, the amethyst, and my black shawl from Southampton Street, and waited, looking out of the window.

The foyer of the Alhambra, on the opposite side of the square, is a place where professional females meet their clients. Ralphie used to loiter there on Saturday evenings. Looking back, I can see that the room in Leicester Square was a mistake.

I was fascinated by the women and young girls whom I watched going into the Alhambra under the fizzing gaslights, and coming out again on the arms of gentlemen. I felt that the statue of Sir Isaac Newton, he of the clockwork universe – in the left-hand corner of the gardens on my side of the square – was apt, and a link with my former life. With Peter's life, I should say. I still had, still have, my own. Diamonds, as it happens, are very poor conductors of electricity. And it was Sir Isaac Newton, as it happens, who discovered the combustibility of diamonds. I wish I could remember how hot a diamond must be before it becomes a fireball. Something over eight hundred degrees, I believe. Hotter than Hell.

I suspect that the first client that I had in the Leicester Square room was a streetwalker. She simply wanted to know if and how she should find a kind husband. I took her money.

When I spoke to her, from out of the deep place which I entered whenever I stared long enough at the amethyst, I spoke with the voice of Aunt Susannah. I do not know whether my aunt was repeating what she had said to me in our bedroom, or whether she was saying what had not been said by her before.

'There's tricks, you know, to getting a man attached.'

Hearing the voice that was coming out of me, I glanced at the girl. She was looking surprised.

'Don't you take your eyes off that amethyst,' said Aunt Susannah. 'Pay heed now. When you are introduced to a nice-looking gentleman, and shake his hand, give him a good long look but do not smile at him. Then, when he's just thinking to himself that you don't like the look of him, you want to give him a great big smile, sudden-like, using your eyes, as if you have just realised that he is one of the wonders of the world. That always hooks them.'

I struggled with Aunt Susannah but I could not silence her.

'Remember, in moments of intimacy, never call your shift a shift. Shift is dead common. Refer always to your "chemise".'

It was even worse with the second woman that came to me. She was a poor thing, young and shabby, engaged to be married to a man who had elaborately good manners, she said, but who frightened her desperately for some reason. I took her money.

I could not control what I said with Aunt Susannah's voice, and I could not speak with any other.

'You will have to share a bed with him, you know. And then he'll do what it is that he has to do.'

'Does it hurt the . . . the woman?'

'Don't you fret, it fits like a foot into a shoe.'

The upper part of my mind, hearing the words that came out of me, thought of a big hairy foot forcing itself into a small shoe. My little client, her eyes never leaving the amethyst, looked paler than when she came in.

'Does it hurt the . . . the man, then?'

'No, it doesn't hurt the man. It's what he wants, it's what he is thinking about most of the time, when he is making polite conversation to you over his cup of tea. Passion, my girl, we are talking about passion. That'll last for four years maximum, then you'll be able to manage him. Nothing is for ever.'

'Is that all?'

'And don't you be taken in by those lovely manners of his. There's gentlemen who will rush to take the tea tray from you as you open the parlour door and all your aunties will envy you such a considerate husband. But pass him in the morning on the stairs when you're carrying heavy slop-pails and he'll be looking the other way. He's the kind that will open the carriage door for you and hand you down as if you were a princess, when there's folk watching. But if there's no one by, he won't even carry your shopping.'

'Do you think perhaps I should not . . .'

Aunt Susannah could not be stopped. She interrupted the poor woman.

'That's the sort will stand back for you to enter before him through the gates of Hell.'

After that day, I never went back to the room over the music hall. Aunt Susannah short-circuited me. The contact was broken. The current did not flow. Energy drained from me daily, I could feel it ebbing. My amethyst was just a sharp lump of coloured matter.

I explained to Mrs Cross, over our endless cups of tea, how life could be understood as nothing more than irrational rearranging of matter, whether dust, printed words, ingredients of meals, cups on shelves, ourselves from place to place, thereby manufacturing an elaborate illusion of meaning, fitness, purpose – when all the time, in eternity's eye, all matter is mere matter and it matters not at all how the dust lies, how the vegetables are chopped, how the cups are arranged, how we ourselves dispose of our clothes and our dirt and ourselves. The lunacy of humanity is in believing that matter matters. Without that sustaining lunacy we are considered insane.

I imagined that Mrs Cross, a natural slattern, would be mildly diverted by this line of reasoning. But she was not listening.

Pushing her tea cup and saucer towards me over the cracked oilcloth, she said:

'Read my tea leaves, then, dear. And find something better in them for me than you managed last time. Find where my Amy is.'

I walked and walked. Walking is as good as a drug. When I set out each day, it seemed as if I were too tired to go far. Then the rhythm of my walking established itself, my mind slowed, my thoughts drifted, the pain in my foot thrummed like an accompaniment. I leaned a good deal on Thaddeus's stick.

I was near the Angel at Islington, my mother's pelisse heavy on my shoulders, the amethyst lying dead in its velvet bag in my pocket, when I met a carrier's cart going the other way. For no reason, I turned to see it pass – and read on its tailgate the painted words 'Odell, Hitchin'.

I ran after the cart, stopped the driver, and asked him to let me ride with him to Hitchin. The cart was piled with empty sacks. He had been delivering barley to a brewer in the Mile End Road. After imparting this information he trundled in near silence up the Great North Road. We reached Hitchin in the middle of the afternoon.

He dropped me outside Mr Odell's in Tilehouse Street and I bought some bread and cheese and walked all the way back here to Morrow. My foot was paining me, in spite of the stick. I was hobbling like an old woman by the time I arrived. The key to the lodge was where I had left it, under the flowerpot by the outside tap.

Nothing has been changed inside. It felt like coming home. I swept the floor and brushed cobwebs from the rafters. I ate my bread and cheese and slept soundly under damp blankets in the gondola bed.

Since then I have done little but write. I have been here for three weeks and have only left the lodge briefly, for essential purposes. There was firewood in the outhouse, and a half-sack of potatoes, which I dragged indoors. Someone has picked the apples, and left them too in the outhouse. The russets have shrivelled a bit.

and I have been eating the kitchen apples raw, relishing the acid. There is stale tea in the caddy, and some porridge oats. That is what I have been living on, contentedly enough.

I have not ventured up the drive to look at the Hall, even after dark. I invented for myself a story that Carney and his daughter developed Fenian tendencies and burned the great house to the ground to avenge their family in Ireland. Mary dances in the ruins, sparks in her flying hair.

But I know that Godwin is at home because in the quiet of the evening I hear the gas engine and the electrical machinery starting up in the stable block. Thud, thud, thud, and a roar like the sea.

Peter used to say that soon we should be running our entire lives by electricity. We shall be writing by electricity, and eating by electricity, saving ourselves the trouble of raising knives and forks to our mouths. Waves of light can be transmitted by electricity, by means of an electroscope. Combine that with the telephone, Peter said, and two friends talking to one another from a hundred miles apart will be able to see one another, and take photographs of one another. Some people of my grandparents' generation used to think that photographs were sacrilegious, abusing the image of God in which man is made.

It strikes me that the new electric age will be made unbearably noisy by disembodied voices and by the thuds, whirrs, clicks, roars, growls, bells and constant hummings of all these machines.

Where will the silence go? Silence will still flow, silence will be the unseen force. Silence will frighten people. They will feel it leaking from the night air into their houses. They will fear the darkness, too. Where will the darkness go, driven out of the night sky by the glitter of the city? When Peter and I stood on Waterloo Bridge, before we were married, we could not see the stars. Here at Morrow, I see them. Diamonds scattered on black velvet.

The only book here is the Bible that Peter's mother gave to us when we married. The Bible is very sure that the light is in the right. Yesterday I was reading St Matthew's Gospel:

> The light of the body is the eye; if therefore thine eye be single, thy whole body shall be full of light.
>
> But if thine eye be evil, thy whole body shall be full of darkness. If therefore the light that is in thee be darkness, how great is that darkness!

That was something which Jesus said. This Bible has marginal references, directing one to similar passages elsewhere. So, obediently, having nothing better to do, I turned to St Luke Chapter xi, where Jesus said the same thing, almost word for word. As with the two diamond merchants offering me the same sum for the ring, replication implies correctness. But St Luke includes a rider:

> If thy whole body therefore be full of light, having no part dark, the whole shall be full of light, as when the bright shining of a candle doth give thee light.

That conjures up the picture of the body as a lantern – translucent, lit from within, like an Edison lamp bulb. But if there were no surrounding darkness, the incandescence would be invisible.

I am becoming quite the theologian. If in these days I should meet a handsome, clever young parson, I dare say I should be undone. Up to a point.

Today I began on St John's Gospel. 'In the beginning was the Word.'

If there were just one word, I could bear it. There are a billion words in a thousand languages being spoken aloud in every minute, and some of them conveyed silently for thousands of miles through the deep-sea cables – and none of them the Word. When the Word was spoken, before the first day of Creation, there was no one to hear it. So no one knows what the Word is, except that, according to St John, the Word is God. If the Word were to be uttered a second time, no one would recognise it. To all intents and purposes the Word is a Silence.

Peter believed that God was electricity and that he was electricity's master. He was electricity's servant. I remember Mr

Moss, at the seance at the Hall on New Year's Eve, saying to me that our greatest illusion is the belief that we are what we think ourselves to be.

I have made a list of what I honestly believe myself to be. I should die of mortification if anyone were to read these words. This is what I wrote: self-determining, independent, superior (in some indefinable way), instinctual, ignorant (of facts), lovable.

If Mr Moss is right, what I really am is passive, easily influenced, undistinguished, calculating, receptive of knowledge, unlovable.

This could be true. Miss Paulina, Aunt Susannah, Peter, Godwin, Mr Moss, Mrs Bagshut, even Ralphie – they all left their scorch marks on me.

I do have a drive of my own. There is a me who has a plan when I do not. Mr Moss calls it the secondary self. I should call it rather the primary self. It plugs in to the certainties of others, takes something from each one's power source, and goes on its way. 'Charlotte, you go too far!' I went too far. 'Ask and it shall be given unto you.' I asked for the wrong things.

But I am proud of my resistance to the power of Bullingdon Huff. And I do not think that I am unlovable, because I have loved and been loved.

When I was sitting on the sacks in that bumpy cart, I suspected that I should end my life when I reached my former home; I should just pass on, go on my way. There is a tin of rat poison up on the beam in the outhouse. I thought, as we passed through Stevenage, that what might stop me would not be fear of the unknown, which is no worse that fear of the known. Nor would it be fear of pain, or of damnation.

Part of me would have to stay behind. I did not like the idea that somebody would have to see me – not sleeping, but dead.

It was not for that person's sensibility that I cared. What I could not bear was that I should be seen inanimate, pitiful – out of control, finally. I could control my dying. But after that, I should be prey to others' hands and eyes.

Control. That is what everything has been about, all along. Control cannot be sustained. How much vital energy is lost in the attempt!

*

I had not been back here for an hour before all thoughts of extinction were forgotten. I came upon the peacock-patterned books in the dresser drawer and immediately began writing. It has been an emptying-out. I remember less and less, if I now lost these books I should be able to recall scarcely a quarter of what I have written. A twig broom is sweeping out the inside of my head with long, slow strokes.

Today is Saturday. Tomorrow, I shall make a new beginning. My real life begins now. I have disabilities. I am an unsupported female with no useful connections, no qualifications, and I am lame. I am also young, strong, good-looking, intelligent and free. Yes, Mr Moss, I really am.

I could become educated and trained, like Hertha Marks – Mrs Ayrton as I presume she is now. I could do drawings and diagrams for technical textbooks and manuals, with no further training. I could learn to do automatic writing – not the Mosses' kind, but with a typewriting machine. If I had paid employment, I could keep up the rent of 49 Dunn Street, and live there sparsely with my ghosts. I do not share Aunt Susannah's belief that a woman is nothing without a man. I might rename myself Charlotte Henshaw.

But then, I should like to marry again. I might marry some handsome, clever young parson whom I have not yet met.

Or I could marry Thaddeus Thompson. Peter used to say that the simplest solution of a problem was frequently the best. I should like to have children. Two daughters, Annie and Elizabeth. And two cats. Thaddeus already has the puppy.

This is the last page of the third and last notebook. There is one more event which I must record, although I shall have to write close to fit it in. Yesterday, while I was drinking my milkless tea, there was a sound outside and a letter was pushed under the door. I sat staring at it for several minutes before I crept across the room and picked it up. 'Mrs Fisher' was written on the envelope, in Godwin's unmistakable hand. Inside was a short note:

Wirewoman – I know you are there. I have seen the smoke

from your chimney. Come up to the Hall at three o'clock on Sunday afternoon, to the garden door. I shall be waiting for you. If you do not, I shall come down to find you. Yours as ever, G.G.

I do not know his intentions. I do not know whether he is engaged to Lady Cynthia, or not. I do not know whether he is good or bad – or neither, like the Niagara Falls. Shall I go to meet him?

Shall I wait for him to come to me?

Sunday afternoon, waiting for the stranger.

Twenty acres of apple trees in blossom in the spring sunshine must be a wonderful sight.

Shall I leave here at dawn, take the train to London, and make my own way.

I shall go to bed, and when I wake my mind will be made up.